Contents

Maps and Tables

Maps

Tables

The Politics of Jerusalem
Since 1967

Introduction

Writing this book has sometimes felt like using a telescope and microscope simultaneously to focus upon the city. There are so many lenses through which to analyze Jerusalem that to examine it with one level of magnification is meaningless unless reference immediately is made to other levels. It is, for example, a small city, located at the eastern edge of a semi-enclosed sea, yet during some epochs it was regarded as the center of the world. It is a city seated on a barren highland ridge, away from the main trade routes and bereft of a wealthy agricultural hinterland or other significant resources, yet it has been a valuable prize for successive invading armies. It is one of the most ancient cities of the world, with ruins stretching back to the early Biblical periods, yet is also an ultra-modern city with a high-technology economic sector and plays a central role in the politics of the region. It is a city whose problems have been consigned to the end of the agenda of the current peace negotiations, yet the failure to resolve them may jeopardize the whole of the negotiations. The interplay of these opposites, of these different levels which have created lasting conflict, runs through the history and politics of Jerusalem.

The chief reason why Jerusalem is no stranger to conflict is its unique position in the world as a place sacred to three monotheistic faiths—Judaism, Christianity, and Islam. As a result, the city was much coveted by kings, emperors, sultans, and presidents, since it provided a divine legitimation of secular power when legitimation was and is lacking under regimes without a popular mandate. In the contemporary period, despite its absence of economic or military value, Jerusalem continues to serve its traditional symbolic role and presents the peace negotiators in the Arab-Israeli conflict the ultimate test of ingenuity and political will.

Israel's insistence today on maintaining control over the entire city and its immediate hinterland is based upon many imperatives. Jerusalem is at the very heart of the history of Judaism and the struggle for a Jewish homeland; many Israelis are convinced that the city is theirs by divine right. Difficulties of access to the Jewish Holy Places during periods of Muslim and British rule are considered blights upon its history. Furthermore, the right of conquest is also strongly felt, with many Israelis convinced that Jordan's participation in the 1967 War justifies their retention of the city. Finally, strategic factors play a crucial role: permanent Israeli control over the city and its hinterland would divide the West Bank in two, thereby weakening the embryonic Palestinian state by fragmenting it into smaller components—the Gaza Strip, the northern West Bank, and the southern West Bank. Israeli control also has the prospect of creating a direct link from Israel to the Jordanian border, bypassing the Palestinian state and thereby avoiding any economic leverage a Palestinian government may have over Israel in that direction.

In addition to these important considerations, there is a domestic one: Jerusalem provides the mortar for national unity in an otherwise politically divided country. Insistence on Israeli Jewish control of Jerusalem unites the orthodox Jews with their more secular counterparts, the Ashkenazi elite with the growing Sephardi and Oriental Jewish majority, the Jews of Israel with the Jews of the diaspora, and even to some extent the Jews of "Greater Israel" with the Jews of "Israel within the Green Line."[1] As the blurred contours of a peace settlement become more distinct, the weakening of the perceived external threat from other Arab states could make the deep divisions within Israeli society, postponed for decades, come to the fore. It is thus that Jerusalem's role as a focus of national unity in Israeli and Jewish politics can be expected to dominate the various proposals suggested in resolving the contest over the city's sovereignty.

But the Palestinians, too, have religious and historical claims to the city. These are partly but not entirely subsumed under their Christian,

Muslim, and Arab historical identities. Because the Arab and Islamic character of Jerusalem was not in doubt until the arrival of Zionist immigrants at the turn of the century, but has become seriously so since the mid-1970s, the bitterness of their resistance against Israeli domination of the city has increased. The Palestinians are being asked to acquiesce in, not only a change of the city's regime but also a total change in its culture. Centuries of Arab and Islamic cultural hegemony are being overturned and reduced to a quixotic Biblical backdrop for western tourism. And aside from the historical and religious claims, the question increasingly posed by Palestinians is why does Israel's definition of "Jerusalem" have to include villages and areas that historically never formed part of the city, and why does Israel's "Jerusalem" seem to keep expanding? After decades of struggle for some form of national independence, the Palestinians are faced with the prospect of a Palestinian state that is not only bereft of Jerusalem—a central component of Palestinian identity—as its capital but also geographically split by the wedge of an ever-expanding entity called "Jerusalem." Yet another aspect of such a development is that as much as a third of the Palestinian population of the West Bank would be located in areas around Jerusalem under Israeli sovereignty. Such a prospect, if it materializes, would seriously undermine not only the viability of a Palestinian entity but also the credibility of the political elite that would accept such a formula.

It is difficult to see how an Israeli-imposed formula along these lines could create a stable future for either a Palestinian state comprising the West Bank and Gaza Strip, or an Israeli state whose capital city would contain a significant minority that does not accept its sovereignty. One of the underlying premises of this book is that a durable peace and the security and prosperity of both peoples—Israeli and Palestinian—depend not only on the creation of a viable Palestinian state but also on a formula assuring a shared Jerusalem in which both can have their capital.

A complicating factor in any bilateral agreement on Jerusalem between Palestinians and Israelis is the high degree of international interest in the future of the city—one not confined simply to an interest in how a resolution to the conflict can lead to greater regional stability, thus securing trade and access to the Middle Eastern oilfields. It is an intrusive interest, based on long historical links with the city, that can reach right down to the municipal and street level and embrace the administration of services, the collection of taxes, the presence of which ethnic and religious groups live in which residential areas.

Historically, this international interest has been expressed in the concern over the administration of the Holy Places, with different Christian, Muslim, and Jewish sects soliciting the assistance of different powers to further their influence. While there is no doubt that the foreign policies of the U.S., Russia, and the European Union are the key factors in the current international interest in Jerusalem, it is also clear that religious influences continue to play an important part even today. The Vatican and the Greek and Armenian Orthodox Patriarchates are still important players in the equation through their extensive landholdings in Jerusalem and the external alliances with Western powers. Similarly, the worldwide Islamic Conference Organization and its al-Quds (Jerusalem) Committee keep the issue of Israeli domination of the third holiest city in Islam alive in the foreign and domestic policies of the Islamic world. The rivalry between Iran and Saudi Arabia, between Jordan and Saudi Arabia, and between Morocco and the others over preeminence in the Arab and Islamic world is often played out in the support of different political and religious factions in Jerusalem. The intense involvement of Jewish groups of the diaspora in the construction and expansion of Israeli Jewish Jerusalem is another aspect of this para- and non-state interest in Jerusalem which impinges upon a bilateral negotiation.

Whether these forms of interest are legitimate or helpful is to some extent beside the point. They *are* a factor and they underline the point that Jerusalem is not just a city contested by two parties. It is also a city holy to many more people throughout the world than the Israelis or Palestinians combined. In this sense, Jerusalem is also an international city and a solution to its problems will also need to accommodate the international interest in the city.

This book, begun in 1992 during the intifada and completed just after the introduction of Palestinian autonomy in Gaza and Jericho, attempts to draw together all these themes. While focusing primarily upon the post-1967 period it tries to show the historical context of contemporary developments and the emergence of trends that can be traced back over decades and centuries. It also examines policies and developments that impinge upon the negotiations between Israeli and Palestinians and have to be taken into account. Written during a period of great political flux and transition, this book cannot hope to produce a formula for the resolution of the Jerusalem issue. So many variables are already in play, with so many others about to come into play, that any such attempt would merely add to the list of interesting ideas already put forward. Nevertheless, the book does attempt to highlight those features which will either assist or hamper a negotiated settlement and these are brought out where relevant in the different chapters.

The material is presented in straightforward fashion according to themes, each comprising a chapter with a basic chronological structure. The first chapter sets the scene, illustrating with broad sweeps the rich and varied history of the city and placing the latest episode of the post-1967 period into context. The second chapter looks at the administration of the city and the various legal and jurisdictional developments which have led to the city's current structure. Anomalies, such as the role of the semiautonomous Muslim endowment system, and significant trends such as the expansion of the Municipality borders westward rather than eastward, are examined. The critical issue of the uneven demographic growth of the Palestinian and Israelis is the subject of the third chapter. Particular attention is given to the geographic spread of this growth and implications for the future administration of the city.

Chapter 4 is devoted to issues of urban planning and the provision of housing. This is a necessary complement to the Israeli government's policies of increasing Jewish residence in the city and has a direct impact upon the space available for Palestinian housing and development. The fifth chapter examines the utility infrastructure of the city and the provision of water, electricity, and sewage disposal are taken as case studies. The attempt to integrate utility networks, which had been separated between 1949 and 1967, has political implications for the possible future division of the city and these are also discussed. Chapter 6 is a detailed look at the three religious communities living in the city, their institutional structures, their internal problems, and their relations to the Israeli state. Issues such as land ownership, the respective demographic growth of the communities, and external political and financial support are also included in this examination.

The Achilles Heel of Jerusalem as an urban settlement has been the lack of a viable economic base (a problem largely dependent on the lack of sufficient quantities of water). Chapter 7 traces the Israeli government's ongoing efforts to diversify Jerusalem's economy away from its dependence upon tourism and government service. It examines how this has an impact not only on the Palestinian community but also its own regional planning. Chapter 8 discusses the role of the international community in the Jerusalem issue, focussing in particu-

lar upon that of the United States. A briefer examination is also made
of the role of Great Britain, the European Union, and the positions
taken by the Palestinian Liberation Organization and the Arab states.
The final chapter tries to draw together the main themes of the book
and in the light of these refers to the various proposals put forward for
the resolution of the issue. No specific alternatives are suggested but
the prerequisite components of any solution are spelt out.

Data for this book have come from a wide variety of sources. As a
general introduction to the politics of the city, much use has been
made of secondary sources. However, because of the paucity of material on utility networks, on housing issues, on the institutional development of the religious communities, on economic trends, and on foreign policies of external powers with regard to Jerusalem, a considerable amount of primary research was also required. Indeed, it was
surprising to discover that there were literally no other books in
English covering the same ground even if finishing at an earlier
period. There are many short studies in Hebrew by Israeli scholars,
particularly on demographic and economic issues and these are widely
cited in this book. The publications of the Jerusalem Institute for Israel
Studies are especially noteworthy. In Arabic there is almost a complete
dearth of serious academic material on contemporary Jerusalem,
although toward the end of the research for this book the Palestinian
Academic Society began to publish books of relevance. To this extent,
it is hoped that this book can contribute to filling a serious gap in the
study of Jerusalem at this historical conjuncture.

The research and writing of this book was funded by the Ford
Foundation through the Institute for Palestine Studies, Washington,
D.C. My warmest thanks to Salim Nasr and David Nygaard of the
Ford Foundation in Cairo for supporting this project. Similarly, I am
very grateful to Professor Walid Khalidi and Dr. Philip Mattar of the
Institute for Palestine Studies for overseeing the implementation of
the project. I am particularly indebted to Linda Butler of the Institute
for her critical comments, which sharpened my analysis and taught me
a great deal about structure and clarity in the presentation of data.

Many other people have helped me in the compilation of this
book—politicians, academics, students, officials and friends—that any
brief mention such as follows cannot do justice to them all. Despite
running the risk omitting some names, I would most gratefully like to
thank the following people: Josie Glausiusz, my research assistant for a
year, for her energetic and intelligent collection of relevant data in

Hebrew. Russell Harris, for his prompt synopses and translations. Kevork Hintlian, Ibrahim Daqqaq, Fiona McKay, Dr. Yitzhaq Reiter, Sheikh Hassan Tahbub, Father Timotheus, and the staff and researchers of the Jerusalem Institute for Israel Studies, especially Israel Kimhi, Professor Menachem Friedman, Dr. Yossi Shilhav, and Professor Michael Romann, for their time and patience with my rather basic questions. Professor Antony Coon, for his comments and criticisms of chapter 4. Dr. Glenn Bowman, for his comments on chapter 6. Raja Shehadeh and Sidney Bailey for their comments on an early draft of chapter 2. Haifa Khalidi, Dr. Chris Smith, and Tina Schmallenbach for their hospitality during my research trips. Finally I would like to thank all at Beech Hill, Devon, for accepting my moods, frequent absences, and preoccupation with this subject without rancor.

Finally, a note on diacritical marks: For ease and consistency, transliteration from the Arabic of the ayns (') and the hamzas (') will be replaced by a single vertical mark '.

Michael Dumper
July 1996

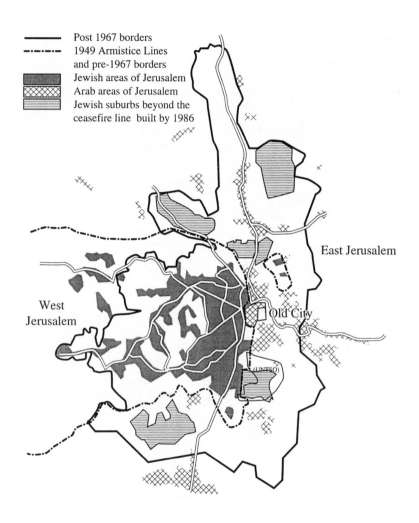

Post 1967 borders
1949 Armistice Lines
and pre-1967 borders
Jewish areas of Jerusalem
Arab areas of Jerusalem
Jewish suburbs beyond the
ceasefire line built by 1986

East Jerusalem

West
Jerusalem

Old City

(UNTSO)

MAP 1.1. Jerusalem: Political Divisions

1 | The Significance of Jerusalem

"I shall rejoice in Jerusalem,
and be glad in my people:
no more shall be heard the sound of weeping
and the cry of distress.
—Isaiah, 65:19.

A sin committed in Jerusalem
is like a thousand sins,
and a good work there
is equal to a thousand good works.
—Hadith

At 5 p.m. on Sunday, August 13, 1967, members of the Israeli Municipal Council of Jerusalem filed into the Council Chamber in the Municipality building off Jaffa Road. It was a historic occasion and the first Council meeting devoted to the future of Jerusalem as a result of the 1967 War. The Jordanian army had been defeated and Israel now controlled all of Arab East Jerusalem and the West Bank. The Israeli government had already announced that East Jerusalem and adjacent parts of the West Bank were now part of Israel and would be absorbed into the Israeli Municipality of West Jerusalem.

The opening address of the meeting was given by the popular and efficient Mayor of West Jerusalem, Teddy Kollek. It was neither eloquent nor inspired. Delivered in the usual phlegmatic manner associated with Israeli Jews of Middle or East European origin, it concentrated on down-to-earth problems and challenges:

> It seems to me that before we can achieve a city which we all want to see, we must first establish a city with a comparatively decent standard of living, for only then will we be able to guarantee those matters which we want. We must think carefully about the population growth, by immigration, by attracting professional and intellectual forces to Jerusalem. In order to guarantee this, we must think care-

fully about suitable employment, which for its part, in any case, produces a relatively high income, for only then will it be possible to provide services at the required level.

In the same style, Kollek proceeded to examine the need for industry and the role of national institutions in the city, the need to acquire land, the urgency of restoring the Jewish quarter of the Old City and of introducing new roads and bus routes and, finally, the need for careful planning.

Other council members, more aware of the historic nature of the occasion, tried to instill a sense of drama with their contributions. The previous mayor of West Jerusalem, Mordechai Ish-shalom, injected color when he declared:

> Our job, the job of the city council today, is to prevent the Jerusalem of gold being turned into worthless base metal. And there is a danger of that, and here time will tell. And if we, all of us—the city, the state—do not make use of the understanding and responsibility of seeing what has happened in these days, of seeing the great hour, the hour of will, the great revolution which has taken place around Jerusalem, if we continue to live our lives at the same old pace, we will miss this great opportunity. If this council session has any job to do, it is that of reading, of declaring to everyone to approach the affairs of Jerusalem with a completely different criteria, with criteria that these days call for.

A deputy mayor, Rabbi Cohen, continued in a similar vein, weaving Biblical references and religious injunctions appropriate to his calling into his speech:

> If our sages of blessed memory emphasized the uniqueness of Jerusalem as the city from which the Bible went out to the world, as the city suitable for wisdom, whose sons are wiser than the sons of other cities—this was out of deep vision of the singular character of Jerusalem as the city over which the spirit of God dwells, as the city suitable for spiritual creation as a capital, to which the whole world will go for its light. This is what our sages of blessed memory said— and I want us to remember these things: Jerusalem can become a beacon for all the nations of the world, and they will walk about in its light. It is our duty to construct this beacon. It is our duty to set a light in it. This is a great and difficult historical responsibility.

The discussion continued, alternating between the wide-ranging and specific, the visionary and parochial, the magnanimous and triumphant. Topics such as the need for government ministries and other national bodies to complete their relocation to the city, or the need for the development of sporting and cultural activities, youth centers and new economic enterprises were all proposed and discussed.

Apart from a few digs at orthodox Jewry by secular council members, there was very little disagreement over the future of Israeli control over all Jerusalem. What was emphasized, however, in one speech after the other, is the fear that the projected growth of the Palestinian Arab population may rob, in time, the Israelis of their victory in 1967. How could Jerusalem be truly Jewish and Israeli if a third of the population was to remain Palestinian and Arab? Already in these early discussions one can see how Israeli efforts in all spheres—immigration, economic development, government assistance, planning restrictions, and Palestinian family reunification schemes—were to be directed toward increasing the numbers of Israeli Jews and restricting those of Palestinian Arabs in the new borders of unified Jerusalem.

Lying behind this concern for the demographics of the new situation was the Israeli council members' awareness of a huge unpalatable fact: despite the centrality of Jerusalem in Jewish history, ritual, and liturgy, the Jewish presence in the city has for long been extremely tenuous. Many centuries had passed since it had been under Jewish control and sovereignty. The intervening years have seen the rise and fall of numerous dynasties and administrations, the boom and slump of economic growth and construction, and the flowering and decline of the city's prestige and role. These successive epochs had come and gone with little reference to Judaism and Jewish culture. In crude terms, the simple addition of all the years that Jerusalem was under Jewish control since the earliest archaeological evidence of settlement in 1800 B.C.E., reveal that Jerusalem was under some form of Jewish control for little more than 10 percent of that time.[1] Thus in the context of the vast history of Jerusalem, the Israeli occupation and control over the whole of the city in 1967 is possibly as ephemeral and finite as the previous presence of Jews in the city. The precedents of history and the logic of demography threaten to overwhelm any ambitions for a lasting Israeli Jewish control over the city which may have been harbored during the historic council meeting of August 13, 1967.

Clearly the events of 1967 are rooted in history. The competing claims of the respective ethnic, religious, and national groupings have had an impact upon the developments that led to the 1967 War and the political events that have taken place since. Jerusalem remains at the heart of the Arab-Israeli conflict and its significance did not suddenly emerge when the guns fell silent in June 1967. History was there before, waxing and waning over the course of centuries, providing simultaneously the inspiration and the obstacle to peace. It continues that role today.

The earliest archaeological evidence for human settlement on the site that became Jerusalem was during the Jebusite period around 1800 B.C.E..These include a walled settlement, foundations of houses, water-supply installations, and some tombs and caves.[2] Following the conquest of Jerusalem by Israelite tribes under King David, Jerusalem acquired strategic value as being midway between the two tribal areas of Judah and Benjamin. It acted as the capital of a united kingdom.[3] Under his successor, Solomon, there was greater construction and expansion.The Jewish Temple was built on a grand scale on a specially engineered plateau above the traditional site of the city. The fortifications were enlarged and Jerusalem became also a commercial center with major trading routes of that time passing through its walls.[4]

The next period of Jerusalem's history, the Babylonian invasion of 587 B.C.E., heralded the end of the longest period of unbroken Israelite rule in the city. Ruling members of the population were executed and the elite were deported to Babylonia.The Babylonians, in turn, were succeeded by the Persians in 539 B.C.E. While allowing the exiles to return and rebuild the Temple, they did not allow the Israelites, or Hebrews as they were then called, to regain independent political control over the city. During the Hellenic period between 332 B.C.E. and 168 B.C.E. the renewed flowering of Jewish ritual and law in Jerusalem took place only to be crushed under Antiochus Epihanes who destroyed the city and Temple and made Torah observance punishable by death.[5] A succession of revolts against the Seluecid Greeks led to the reestablishment of Jewish control over the city under the Maccabeans in 141 B.C.E.

The Roman period succeeded the Hellenic. Lasting some 700 years, from 63 B.C.E. until the Muslim invasion in 638 C.E., it can be divided into two parts. The first encompassed the period when the Empire was ruled from Rome and followed pagan gods, the second when it became Christian and the eastern part was ruled from Byzantium. The first period of Roman rule saw an initial regime of religious autonomy for the Jews in Jerusalem. Attempts, however, at political independence from Rome were severely crushed, culminating in the destruction once again of the Temple in 69–70 C.E..[6] Finally, impatient with the constant dissension by the Jewish population, Emperor Hadrian exiled two-thirds of the city's population and made it a Roman colony, Aeolia Capitolina. It was also during this early part of the Roman period that the first Christian community was established following the execution of the Christian leader, Jesus of Nazareth. His death in the city and alleged return to life led to the beginnings of the Christian pilgrimage trade which was to remain a fundamental element in the city's economy. It was also destined to entangle the city with political rivalries of the region.[7]

The second half of the Roman period, from the beginning of its control by Byzantium to the Muslim invasion, was of great importance for Jerusalem. The most significant event was the conversion of Emperor Constantine to Christianity. As the British historian of the period, John Wilkinson, writes: "Jerusalem was thus turned from a Roman city with very little interest to the Empire into a city of great importance."[8] While Jews were only allowed an annual pilgrimage to Jerusalem, Christian churches, infirmaries, hospices, and hostels were built on an extensive scale. A further boost to the Christian presence was given by the visit of Emperor Constantine's mother, Queen Helena, in 336 C.E. She claimed to have found the "True Cross" and encouraged the construction of the Holy Sepulcher on the supposed site of Jesus' crucifixion. For the next three hundred years the role of Christian pilgrimage to the city became central to the economic and cultural life of the city.

The conquest of Jerusalem by 'Umar ibn Khattab, the successor to the Prophet Muhammed and the First Caliph in Islam, in 638 C.E. opened a new era of Muslim rule in the city which, save for the interruption of the Crusades, was to last until 1967. Jerusalem was of little military and strategic significance at that time and its conquest was mainly for religious purposes.[9] The sanctity and religious significance of Jerusalem had already been well-established by Christians and Jews, but for the Muslims too it had great significance. Jerusalem had been the first *qibla*, or direction of prayer, which Muslims were obliged to carry out five times a day; it was also the destination of Muhammed's "night journey" and the site where it is believed he ascended briefly to heaven, both events being recorded in the Qur'an.[10] Caliph 'Umar came to an agreement with the city's existing Christian population that in exchange for the payment of a poll tax their property, churches, and personal safety would be assured.[11] Jews were allowed to return only as pilgrims, but over time more and more began to settle in the city.

The political significance of Jerusalem grew in measure with the growth of its religious significance. Between 685 and 709 C.E. the Dome of the Rock and the al-Aqsa mosque were built in an enclosure that became known as al-Haram al-Sharif, or the Noble Sanctuary. It became the third holiest site in Islam after Mecca and Medina. Michael Burgoyne, a leading architectural historian, has described their construction as "a symbol of the political supremacy and moral prestige of Islam" over its competitors that added to the consolidation of the sanctity of Jerusalem in Islam.[12] It is also interesting to note that one effect of these actions by the Umayyads was to draw pilgrims away from Mecca where their political rivals held sway. By enhancing the prestige of Jerusalem they were also enhancing their political stature.[13] The flowering of a corpus of literature known as the *fada'il al-quds*, or the "merits of Jerusalem," was part of this sanctification and prestige-enhancing process. Right up to the eleventh century the praises of Jerusalem were sung and it became known as the *bayt al-maqdis*, the house of Holiness, from which the Arabic name for the city, "Al-Quds," is derived. Jerusalem also became a focus of the long-standing rivalry between Sunni orthodoxy and the popular mystical movement of Sufism. Religious colleges and hostels were built to promote the appeal of these competing groups who sought to benefit from the reflected glory of the city.

The rise of the Abassids in 750 C.E. and the transfer of the seat of the Caliphate from Damascus to Baghdad led to a relative decline in the fortunes of Jerusalem. Nevertheless Caliphal visits took place and repairs on the Holy Places were carried out. There is evidence that the Christian presence continued to thrive. Harun al-Rashid's diplomatic relations with the Emperor Charlemagne led to the construction of many new buildings that catered to Christian pilgrims. During the Fatimid dynasty's rule over Jerusalem, Cairo became more important to Islam and the number of Muslim pilgrims to Jerusalem declined.[14] The Christian and Jewish role in the city increased as more became involved in the government and administration of the city.[15] Indeed, writing in approximately 985 C.E., the celebrated Muslim geographer al-Muqaddasi observed that the Christian holy days also regulated the rhythm of the year for the Muslim population.[16]

The increasing Christian pilgrimage continued to have a considerable impact upon the city and to cause disaffection amongst the Muslims. In 1065 C.E., nearly 12,000 pilgrims arrived in the city. In those days such a mass arrival was akin to an invasion. Thus by the late tenth century and throughout the eleventh century, the Muslim domination of Jerusalem weakened. In 1099 c.e. Crusader armies had laid siege to its gates and entered the city.

The Crusader period in Jerusalem was inaugurated by the slaughter and expulsion of its existing inhabitants.[17] This was followed by a massive program of church building. The remains of some sixty-one churches have been found dating from this period.[18] Interestingly enough no significant damage or changes were made to the Dome of the Rock, although in 1142 c.e. it was consecrated as a Christian church.[19] Despite making it the capital of the Crusader Kingdom and an important center for Christian pilgrimage, the Frankish forces did not stay and populate the city. Instead Christian minority groups from Syria, Lebanon, and throughout the Middle East settled, establishing the heterodox nature of the Christian community in Jerusalem that survives until today.

Another lasting legacy of the Crusader period was its impact on Muslim perceptions. Its occupation by European forces sharpened Muslim and Arab interest in the city and its status in Islam was re-enhanced. Salah-ed Din (Saladin), the commander of the Caliph's armies, was constantly reminded by poets and religious scholars of his religious duty to liberate Jerusalem and al-Haram al-Sharif from the Franks.[20] To a large extent the Crusader period also provided the impetus for the great energy invested in Jerusalem in the succeeding Ayubid and Mamluk dynasties.

The Ayyubid period following Salah-edDin's capture of Jerusalem in 1187 c.e. was marked by a huge investment in the construction of houses, markets, public baths, and pilgrim hostels. Large *waqfs*, or Muslim religious endowments, were set up, bringing income into the city and providing funds for the refurbishment of al-Haram al-Sharif.[21] However, for the greater part of the thirteenth century, Jerusalem lacked any strategic or military value for the Ayubid leaders beset by their internecine struggles. It declined to virtually the status of a village, coming to life only for the visiting pilgrimage group or passing caravan.

Soon after the establishment of Mamluk rule came a flowering of Islamic culture in the city. While it remained unimportant administratively, politically, and militarily, its importance as a Muslim sacred place returned. As a home for exiled and retired Mamluk princes and dignitaries, and as a recipient of funds from large and wealthy endowments, its building work attained a level of rare architectural magnificence.[22]

Indeed, such was the attention lavished upon Jerusalem by the wealthy that a bureaucracy was set up in order to introduce some coherence into all the endowments that were being made. Muslim pilgrimages to Jerusalem also increased and became an important feature in its economy.[23] Jerusalem's sanctity to Islam was also reinforced during this period through writings of poets and religious scholars. At least thirty *fada'il* can be traced back to this period.[24] It should also be noted that the small Jewish community in the city attained what was known as *dhimmi* status under the Mamluks, meaning they were a recognized and protected religious minority. Subsequently, they were allowed to own property and set up enterprises.

A period of decline, during which Bedouins in the hinterland hampered access to the city, heralded the twilight of the Mamluk era and the dawn of the Ottoman, which would last until the twentieth century. Originally Turks from Central Asia, the Ottomans occupied Jerusalem in 1517 C.E., with Sultan Selim receiving the keys of the Dome of the Rock and the al-Aqsa mosque. While they never built on such a grand scale or over such an extended period as the Mamluks, the Ottomans were, nevertheless, responsible for the construction of the city walls standing today. Waqfs continued to flourish, and in 1551 the Khasski Sultan Waqf, the largest in Palestine, was set up. Indeed, much of Ottoman economic life in Jerusalem centered on the role of religion in the city. Revenue from the pilgrim industry, endowments, and bequests to the Christian and Jewish communities sustained a city that was some distance from ports and the trade routes of the coastal plain and lacking in natural resources or a manufacturing base. A religious and political hierarchy evolved which administered the Holy Places of the three religions and these were dependent upon waqfs, endowments, and donations from abroad.[25]

The Ottoman period also saw the introduction of what was probably the most significant development in the modern history of Jerusalem: the gradual emergence of European influence in the city. As we have already noted, Jerusalem has always been a center for Christian pilgrimage but this was a transient population and pilgrims rarely settled in the city. The indigenous Christian community were Ottoman subjects and lived there also under the relatively protected status of *dhimmi*. From the signing of the first "capitulation" treaty in 1535 C.E. with France, to the arrival of General Allenby at Jaffa Gate in 1917, European involvement and interference in the affairs of Jerusalem began a slow but seemingly inexorable advance. The successive capitulation treaties gave different European countries various powers over the administration of the Christian Holy Places which they exercised either through the churches under their tutelage or through their consuls. By the late nineteenth century, the French and British consuls had considerable influence over political developments in Jerusalem.

The hegemony of the Greek Orthodox church over Christian religious life in Jerusalem was severely curtailed by this European involvement. Roman Catholic, Armenian, Russian Orthodox, and latterly Protestant hierarchies struggled for control over the various Christian Holy Places and for the prestige such control would render their interpretation of the faith and their European backers. Violence and bloody clashes periodically erupted to the extent that, at different points during the Ottoman era, the Sultan in Istanbul was obliged to intervene. These interventions were finally codified into an edict issued by Sultan Uthman III in 1757 C.E.[26] The edict laid down procedures and questions of precedents regarding the conduct of ritual and the maintenance of the Holy Places and became known as the "Status Quo."[27] The Status Quo established a crude "pecking order" which, since it reflected the balance of European and Ottoman power of the day, was a cause of much friction and dispute when that balance of power subsequently altered.

In the nineteenth century Jerusalem became a major administrative center in the region while subject to growing European involvement. Following a ten-year period of Egyptian rule from 1830–1840, during which time minority religious groups and foreigners were allowed relatively greater freedom, the Ottomans made Jerusalem the administrative capital of the *sanjak*, or province, of Jerusalem. This was both a recognition of the greater religious and political importance of Jerusalem and an attempt to exert closer control over its affairs. Rather than monitoring the situation through governors based in Damascus or Beirut, Jerusalem was now directly accountable to the Ottoman central government in Istanbul.[28]

At the same time the growing weakness of the central state had three main effects. First it was unable to resist strong pressures for greater regional autonomy on the part of local notables and dignitaries. In 1863, for example, Jerusalem was given an administrative council, or *majlis*, which had responsibility over the civic affairs of the city and was controlled by leading Jerusalemite families.[29] Second, it allowed European influence in the city to increase dramatically, both in terms of the powers of the consuls and demographically, as a European-style "New City" began to appear outside the city walls to the east.

The third effect is closely connected to the second. As Ottoman state power in the city weakened, greater opportunities were created for the playing out of European rivalries. Britain, for example, took on the protection of Jews in the city as a means of furthering its influence. As the noted German historian Alexander Schölch has written:

> The European powers did not strive for territorial control in Palestine, but for "influence." The easiest way to establish "influence" was the policy of the "protection" of religious minorities. The Russians already had the Orthodox Christians and the French had the Catholics to "protect." To draw even, England and Prussia (later Germany) had to find or to create their own minorities to be "protected." From 1839 the British took the Jews under their wing, and a small Protestant community was created by way of conversion. The policy of religious-cultural penetration and of "religious protectorates" thus made Jerusalem an arena of European rivalries.[30]

The waxing power of the British Empire meant that increased Jewish immigration to Jerusalem received British protection. By the seventies Jewish building societies had been established and the Mea Shearim quarter built to the north west of the walls.[31] By the nineties, these developments had proceeded to such an extent that leading Jerusalem Muslim families were protesting against Jewish immigration and land acquisition.[32]

By the beginning of the 1914–1918 War, Jerusalem had become the biggest city in Palestine. While still under Turkish and Muslim rule, the arrival of General Allenby in 1917 and the British takeover of the city merely signified, in military terms, the political and demographic changes that had taken place over the previous half century. Jerusalem was an Arab and Islamic city but already by the turn of the century this character was under serious threat. The transfer of political and military power marked by the establishment of the British Mandate, added greatly to that threat and hastened its transformation into a more European city both in terms of physical appearance and in demographic composition and culture.

The foundations upon which the modern city of Jerusalem were built can be traced back to the period of the British Mandate. Further historical details will be covered in subsequent chapters, so at this stage in the description of the significance of Jerusalem only a few crucial points need to be made. The creation of the British Mandate for the first time established a political territory approximately congruent with the geographical area known as Palestine: west of the Jordan river, south of the Lebanese mountains and north of the Sinai desert. This political area absorbed parts of the former *sanjaks* of Beirut and Damascus. Not since the Crusader period, 900 years previously, had Jerusalem been the administrative and political capital of such a large and coherent area. Clearly with the location of government offices, legal and religious courts, and organizational headquarters in the city, its economy, its access, and its services all improved. These in turn increased its local and regional importance.

The fusion of the geographical and political during the Mandate had particular significance for the dominant Palestinian Muslim community and the role of the Jerusalemite families. On the one hand they were cut off politically from the Islamic hinterland. In addition, they had lost the support of a sovereign Muslim state and were placed under foreign tutelage. On the other hand, through the establishment of a "Supreme Muslim Council" in 1921, they were given jurisdictional powers over the Muslim religious, or shari'a, courts, and control over the vast array of Islamic waqfs. The separate geographical and political entity of Palestine created by the Mandate allowed for a much greater unitary and centralized administrative system and enhanced the power and influence of the Jerusalem families who dominated these structures.[33] Thus the loss of Muslim dominance over Jerusalem in general political terms was partially offset by a greater direct involvement in the administration at a local level.

When one takes this major development and examines it in the light of two other developments—the growth in the Christian institutional presence and the exponential growth in the Jewish population by the end of the Mandate—one can better understand why Jerusalem was torn in two by the 1948 hostilities. The boom in the construction of churches, Christian hospitals, Christian schools, Christian guest houses for pilgrims, and the employment of Palestinian Christians from the Bethlehem and Ramallah areas led to the construction of Christian quarters outside the walls. The influx of wealth and people these developments entailed all combined to overshadow the Muslim community's attempts not only to represent the Palestinians in their dispute with Britain and the Zionist Jewish immigrants but also to build up their own communal infrastructure. Certainly with reference to the early part of the Mandate period one can say that not since the Crusader period had the Christian influence in Jerusalem been so extensive. The correlation in the rise of its power to the rule of a foreign Christian power could not be overlooked.

Similarly, the trebling of the Jewish population between 1922 and 1946 to slightly less than half the total population of Jerusalem was a direct consequence of British support of Zionism and the establishment of the Jewish "homeland." When, on the eve of the 1939–45 War, Britain seemed to be at the point of changing its mind, it was by then too late to close the floodgates of Jewish immigration and incremental political ascendancy in the city. Disputes over access to Holy Places and the balance of political representation in the Municipal Council became the main flashpoints in the relations between Jews and Palestinian Muslims and also Palestinian Christians whose influence over the British administration was gradually being eclipsed by the increasing number of Jews.

During the fighting that followed the withdrawal of British forces in 1948, Jerusalem was partitioned into Jordanian-held and Israeli-held territories. The partition was a tragedy for the city and it reflected the increasing polarization between the two communities that had developed during the latter stages of the Mandate, and served to entrench the divide separating them. Visitors standing on the Mount of Olives overlooking the eastern part of the city during this period would see below them the Old City standing bold as ever, but appearing drab and neglected. New houses would be visible in the northern suburbs of Shaykh Jarrah, Wadi Joz, and the American Colony and along the main northbound drag from Damascus Gate to Ramallah and El-Bireh. The eastern and southeastern villages of Silwan, Ras al-'Amud, and Abu Tur, clustered in and around the Kidron valley, would be bulging at the seams as their edges gradually merged and formed new suburbs. On the western side, the Israeli-held New City would stretch westward to the edge of the ridges overlooking the road leading down to Jaffa and Tel Aviv. New houses and flats for new immigrants would be seen on the edges of the former Palestinian quarters in the southwest. Struggling to survive, the commercial areas would be seen drifting westward toward the exits of the city and the coastal plain. After the boom years and frenetic energy of the Mandate, this subdued and provincial feel would require explanation. A sharp-sighted visitor would soon spot the reason. Along the western edge of East Jerusalem and the eastern edge of West Jerusalem, the No Man's Land and the Armistice Lines would run like a gash through the city's vitals, severing pipes, cables, roads, alleys, and vistas.

The differences between Jordanian-controlled East Jerusalem and Israeli-controlled West Jerusalem can be usefully if not unfairly compared. During the nineteen years of partition, East Jerusalem remained static in population numbers. Having absorbed thousands of refugees from the western part of the city, any further addition through natural growth was lost by emigration as the Palestinians sought work and security. Poor, strapped for funds itself, the Jordanian government was unwilling to see a "Palestinian" Jerusalem develop at the expense of the Jordanian capital in Amman. It was therefore both unable and reluctant to invest in the economy, the infrastructure, and services of the city. Administrative offices were relocated to Amman and the city fell back onto its traditional economic base of pilgrimage and its post-1948 War equivalent, tourism. Water and electricity remained intermittent right up to 1967. Shorn of its access to the ports and agricultural wealth of the coastal plain and forbidden to develop politically as a center for Palestinian nationalism, East Jerusalem declined into a provincial backwater.

In contrast, Israeli West Jerusalem was made the capital of the new State of Israel. The government sought to overcome the geographic disadvantages of having lost its hinterland and access to the Arabian interior by investing heavily to attract immigrants and employment. Most government offices and national institutions such as the Knesset, the Israeli Parliament, a new university, and the Great Synagogue were built there. Israel had captured the main water supply to Jerusalem and power supplies were made available from sources on the coastal plain. As a result of these activities the population doubled to 200,000 Israeli Jews. Nevertheless, in relation to the development of other Israeli cities like Haifa and Tel Aviv, the future of West Jerusalem was precarious. Its economy was heavily dependent upon government and public sector employment and without access to the Holy Places it had little attraction for tourists or industrial enterprises. On the eve of the 1967 War the Municipality was caught on the horns of a dilemma: in order to secure its future Jerusalem needed to expand, but it was rapidly running out of space for further development. Further development westward would only confirm the advantages of development in the coastal plain.

Thus a visitor standing on the same spot on the Mount of Olives on the eve of the 1967 War would appreciate that neither half of the city was flourishing as a result of the partition. One side was starved of government investment, the other side seemed to survive only through government investment. Neither side was satisfied with the existing situation. The Palestinian Arabs had lost their homes and much of their wealth in West Jerusalem and were not able to create national institutions that would reflect their growing self-conscious-ness as an independent people. The Israeli Jews had not been able to secure the religious heart of their faith, the Western Wall, and were unable to obtain international recognition of their control over West Jerusalem.

The 1967 War dramatically changed the situation. Israeli troops encircled the northern parts of the city and captured the strategic heights from the Jordanian Army before entering the Old City and placing an Israeli flag on the roof of the Dome of the Rock. The Israeli action was decisive and an emphatic assertion of political will and mil-itary power. Nonetheless, acceptance of these actions by the interna-tional community and by their Arab neighbors eluded them. Over the years following the Israeli arrival in East Jerusalem they have consoli-dated and extended their control over both parts of the city. The tragedy remains, however, that the Palestinian Arab inhabitants of the city are no nearer to accepting this position while the Israelis feel no more secure in holding it than they did when the Israeli Municipal Council first discussed what to do on August 13, 1967. In summariz-ing the Council's discussions that evening, the Mayor, Teddy Kollek, concluded:

> I think that there is not much more to be added to the things which have been said. What we all have in common is the feeling of fear and urgency, concern that the tension in the matter of Jerusalem will not subside, and a feeling of responsibility on the part of all of us with regard to Jerusalem. . . .[34]

Let us now examine how that sense of fear and urgency was translated into political decisions taken by the Israeli government and Muni-cipality of Jerusalem in hopes of discovering if after more than thirty years the situation has irrevocably changed or whether in the absence of a peaceful agreement over the future status of Jerusalem, the Israeli Jewish presence continues to remain tenuous and ephemeral as history continues to inexorably unfold.

2 | The Governance of the City

> It also seems to me that everything we are speaking about will
> only be carried out if the Municipality is the initiator and to a
> large extent also the executor. . . . [T]he problem is that the
> government has 'super- worries'—the large international wor-
> ries, the worries of the IDF [Israel Defense Force], worries of
> employment throughout the state, and these are large worries.
> The proportion of Jerusalem in them is indeed important, but
> after all, it is only one problem among many. But for us,
> Jerusalem is Number One on the list of worries. That is why
> we were elected.
> —Teddy Kollek, Mayor of the Israeli Municipal Council of Jerusalem
>   Meeting, August 13, 1967.

Kollek's concern, expressed in the above quotation,
that after the whirlwind victory of 1967 the city
would not figure prominently in the national pri-
orities of the Israeli state not only reflected his knowledge of the Israeli
political system but also expressed his realization that the annexation
of the Jordanian parts of the city and surrounding areas of the West
Bank had completely changed the role of the city in Israeli political,
religious, and cultural life. Henceforward, Jerusalem was no longer to
be solely the Israeli and Jewish city that it had been between 1948 and
1967. It was now also a Muslim city, a Palestinian Christian city, and
an Arab city. It was a city that would attract the attention of people
throughout the world and it was a city many regarded as a symbol of
international and religious peace. The merging of the two parts of the
city under Israeli rule presented its administrators with new realities
and a daunting challenge.

In order to meet this challenge, it was important for the incoming
administrators both to secure Israeli sovereignty over the newly incorporated areas and to depoliticize insofar as possible implications of that
incorporation. Israeli rule over the whole of Jerusalem would be more
tolerable to the Palestinian Arabs and more acceptable to the international community if applied cautiously and without strident nationalism.

This realization has led to simultaneous and contradictory approaches. While Israeli dominance over the city was and continues to
be secured by coercive unilateral measures (such as land expropriations
and demographic and planning policies) designed to ensure an Israeli
Jewish majority on both sides of the city, the Israeli government has
made efforts to blur perceptions of the reality of Israeli military and
political dominance. Questions of citizenship, electoral participation,
and the application of Israeli laws have been answered with qualification and tacit anomaly to smooth the impact of Israeli rule. Indeed, the
city's very boundaries have been obscured: The Armistice Line that
once divided the city has ceased to be prominent as new Israeli settlements now straddle both sides. Municipal services have been provided
to residential areas beyond the extended Israeli municipal borders.
More recently, the ring of settlements outside the new municipal borders of Jerusalem and in the West Bank have created the concept of a
greater Jerusalem or a metropolitan area of Jerusalem served by the
municipal Jerusalem.[1] By blurring the distinction of what is Israel and
what is the West Bank and by blurring the concept and practice of
Israeli sovereignty in this way, incremental change can be introduced
without provoking overwhelming resistance.

I intend to show, by looking at the legal and administrative changes
that have been introduced since 1967, that Israel has attempted both
to establish its control over Jerusalem and make that control more
acceptable by permitting anomalies. Before that, however, I look at the
historical antecedents for the governing of the city, devoting the chapter's first half to the periods preceding Israel's conquest of the city in
1967. I begin with a brief survey of the Ottoman period, when the
first administrative and municipal structures were erected. Already in
these early periods Jerusalem's status as a Holy City conferred administrative arrangements peculiar to it. The administration of the city
during the British Mandate period made possible the decisive shift in
the balance of power from the Muslim and Christian Palestinian Arab
communities to the Jewish community. Finally, the period of the city's
division between 1948 and 1967 is examined.

Arriving at the situation since 1967, the chapter's second half details
the legal, jurisdictional, and administrative changes that have taken
place. The underlying theme, however, derives from the earlier sections: that the uniqueness of Jerusalem presented particular requirements for its administration.

Ottoman and Mandate Periods

Jerusalem has always been a city of religious significance, but it was not until the mid-nineteenth century that it acquired a distinctive legal status both as a city and as a district. In 1840 it was made the administrative capital of the *sanjak* of Jerusalem, which included the *qadas* of Gaza and Jaffa and was given its own *wali*, or governor. The growing importance of Jerusalem was further acknowledged in 1874, when the governor was made directly accountable to the Ottoman Sultan in Istanbul.[2] There were two major reasons for this. The first was the increase in the number of foreigners in the city as a result of Jewish immigration and renewed western interest in the Christian Holy Places. The Ottomans wished to monitor their activities more closely to prevent any undermining of their own position.[3] Second, as a result of the Crimean War the Ottomans were obliged to cede certain jurisdictions and powers to the consuls of the victorious powers. For example, as the Baedecker Guide of 1876 records, British and U.S. consuls in Jerusalem had jurisdiction over any civil problems arising which involved their nationals.[4] Jerusalem was also one of the first cities in the Ottoman Empire to be granted a city council, or *majlis* in Arabic.[5] In 1863 a council consisting of ten members was elected by a male, propertied electorate. Initially its responsibilities were confined to activities in the Old City, such as paving, sanitation, lighting, or building permits, but later, these responsibilities were gradually extended beyond the city walls as new neighborhoods were being built.[6] During this period the territorial boundaries of the council's authority were not strictly defined.

During the late Ottoman Empire considerable religious autonomy was in the hands of the religious hierarchies and institutions of the respective Muslim, Christian, and Jewish communities in Jerusalem. While the Ottoman government took considerable pains to centralize the religious activities of its Muslim subjects, the independent waqf funding of many of the religious institutions in the city and the hereditary nature of many of their key administrative posts meant that the practical imposition of its powers were to a considerable extent constrained.[7] In the same way, the *millet* system throughout the Ottoman Empire protected the activities of the Christian and Jewish communities from state interference in their religious affairs and recognized their control over the administration of their religious sites. The considerable external funding of these two communities weakened the

leverage the Ottomans had over their activities and a degree of autonomous action was permitted. Thus the very nature of Jerusalem as a
Holy City to three religions where there was a concentration both of
institutions and religious personnel placed some constraints on the
application of state power in the city. A modicum of *realpolitik* and the
implicit acceptance of quasi-autonomous religious enclaves in the city
set a precedent for future secular-religious relations and became part
of the fabric and administration of the city.

Following Turkey's withdrawal from the *sanjak*s of Jerusalem and
Acre after its defeat in World War I, British military control over
Jerusalem was legitimized by the League of Nations' establishment of
the British Mandate for Palestine. No specific reference was made to
Jerusalem in the Charter of the Mandate, as it was deemed to be part
and parcel of those former Ottoman and Turkish territories which
became Palestine. But mention was made of the religious sites in
Jerusalem and these were referred to as the "Holy Places." Article 13
of the Mandate Charter specified that:

> All responsibility in connection with the Holy Places ... including
> that of preserving existing rights and of securing free access ... is
> assumed by the Mandatory who shall be responsible solely to the
> League of Nations.... nothing in this Mandate shall be construed as
> conferring upon the Mandatory authority to interfere with the fab-
> ric or management of purely Moslem sacred shrines, the immunities
> of which are granted.[8]

What is highly significant here is that the administration of the Holy
Places was recognized to be of concern and interest to the international community (or to be more exact, the North American and
European states dominating the League of Nations). In doing so, corresponding limits were laid upon the absolute power of the controlling state, in this case Britain.[9]

The Mandate period saw the establishment of the Supreme Muslim
Council for the predominant Muslim community in Palestine. The
council was given autonomy of the administration over the Muslim
Holy Places, the extensive Muslim *waqf*s and other religious property
in Jerusalem.[10] Similarly, the Mandate Charter recognized the *status
quo* arrangements among the Christian churches and the use of the
Western (Wailing) Wall for Jewish believers (see chapter 6). While a
consultative procedure was provided for the Christian community in
the Charter, the Mandate authorities had no powers to enforce its
operation and therefore no Christian equivalent of the Supreme

Muslim Council was created. Jewish affairs were placed in the hands of a Rabbinical Council, but the Mandate authorities made no attempt to alter the status of the Jewish community, and the limited rights of access to their Holy Places which prevailed during the Ottoman period continued as before. The mismatch between their growing demographic presence, economic power, and political influence in Palestine and the restriction on their religious aspirations provided a major cause of friction between the Jewish community, the Mandate authorities and the Palestinian population (see chapter 6).

The administrative status of Jerusalem was also enhanced during the Mandate period. It became the capital of a single geographical area, uniting the *sanjaks* of Jerusalem, Nablus, and Acre. The sitting of government offices and para-state institutions within its confines provided greater employment and commercial prospects than had been the case previously, which led to a sharp increase in the population. In 1927, the municipal boundaries were extended to include neighborhoods and villages in the surrounding area mostly to the west[11] (see map 2.1), although the powers of the Municipality were extremely limited, confined mainly to the provision of basic services. Planning powers and major revenue collection, for example, were retained by the central Mandate authorities. The municipal council, therefore, was very dependent upon government approval for the development schemes and larger initiatives that became increasingly necessary as the city grew. These limitations continue to this day, and are a source of considerable inefficiency and friction between the government and the local bodies.

British policy on the political issues of Jerusalem was as contradictory as it was with regard to Palestine in general. While the British were sympathetic, especially in the later stages of the Mandate, to the Palestinian argument that their demographic dominance in Palestine should be reflected in their continued dominance in the Jerusalem municipal council (Palestinians believed that Jerusalem, as the capital of Palestine, should have a Palestinian mayor), as the demographic balance in the city tilted in favor of the Jews, the argument for Palestinian dominance of the council became harder to sustain in the face of strenuous Jewish opposition.[12] In 1934, an ordinance divided the city into twelve electoral wards in a way that some Israeli scholars maintain was designed to ensure a Palestinian Arab majority on the council.[13] However, as one can see from the peculiar configuration of the municipal borders shown in map 2.1, the British also agreed to a certain degree of gerrymandering in order to incorporate as many new

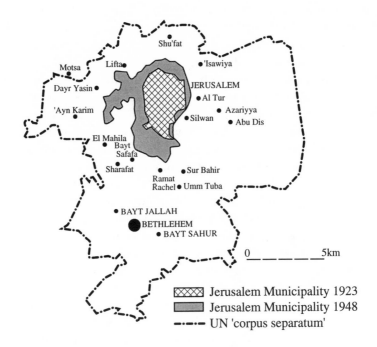

MAP 2.1. Jerusalem in the Mandate Period

Jewish neighborhoods as possible and exclude Arab villages. This is particularly obvious in the way the western border forms a kind of hook to take in the more distant Jewish neighborhoods of Qiryat Moshe, Bet HaKerem, and Bayit Vegan while the eastern borders run tight along the Old City walls to avoid taking in Silwan, Ras al-Amud, Al Tur, and Abu Tur.

Before the end of the Mandate, adjustments to the borders and electoral wards were being discussed. The Fitzgerald Commission, for example, proposed the partition of the city into two boroughs, one Arab the other Jewish, to be coordinated by an administrative council (see map 2.2).[14] The significance of the Fitzgerald proposals was twofold. In the first place, the proposed Arab administrative area included not only the eastern part of the city and all of the Old City but also the southwestern quarters and suburbs (mainly Arab-inhabited) which were subsequently occupied by Israel in 1948. Second, and of particular significance in the light of Israeli claims to the whole of the city, the Zionist leadership accepted the Fitzgerald proposals,

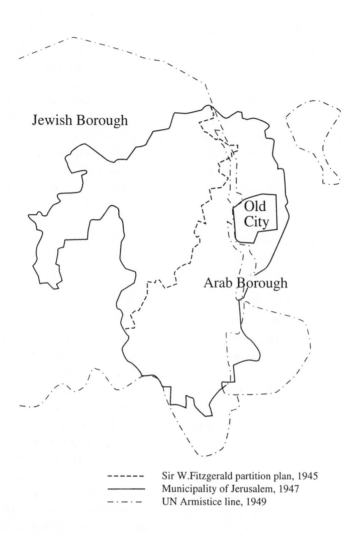

MAP 2.2. The Fitzgerald Plan, 1945

which in fact were very similar to proposals that had been made by the Jewish Agency in 1938.[15]

As Jewish immigration continued to soar, Palestinian anger erupted into the general strike of 1936 that launched the three-year "Great Palestinian Rebellion." In response to the disturbances, the Royal Peel Commission was established by the Mandate authorities in 1937 to determine the causes of the disturbances and make recommendations. The Peel Commission recommended the partition of Palestine into a Jewish and an Arab state with Jerusalem to constitute a separate entity. The Holy Places were held as "a sacred trust of civilization" and should be part of an enclave encompassing Bethlehem and Jerusalem and a corridor to Jaffa. This enclave would be "internationalized" and supervised by the League of Nations.[16] This too was a highly significant development in the thinking concerning the future administration of Jerusalem: the proposed solution underlined how the presence of the Holy Places in Jerusalem, with their concomitant international interest, required a specific type of administration to satisfy the needs of the religious communities and to assure the international community that those needs were being met. The recommendations of the Peel Commission laid the foundations for the clauses of the UN Partition Plan pertaining to Jerusalem and much of the subsequent international diplomacy around the city.

The UN Partition Plan and the Armistice Lines

The Arab outcry triggered by the publication of the Peel Commission's report and the consequent intensification of the rebellion prevented the implementation of the partition recommendations. Attempts to resolve the issue of Palestine's future were put on hold during World War II, but in 1947 Britain in essence turned the problem over to the United Nations. The newly formed world body accordingly appointed a special committee, the UN Special Committee on Palestine (UNSCOP). The majority report recommended the partition of Palestine and, as the Peel Commission had done, the creation of an international enclave for the Jerusalem area (see map 2.2). Jerusalem would be demilitarized and exist as a *corpus separatum* under the aegis of a UN Trusteeship Council. The council would draft a Statute, which would lay down the administrative structures of the enclave. These would remain in force for ten years, after which there would be a reexamination by the council and a referendum by the inhabitants.[17] It is important to note that the "existing rights" of the Holy Places were confirmed and a UN governor was to ensure that no taxation was levied on any Holy Place and was given powers to adjudicate in the event of any disputes between the different religious communities.[18] These proposals were passed by the UN General

Assembly in November 1947 and became known as the UN Partition Plan.

Although the Plan, in the form of a recommendation of the Assembly, lacked the force of international law, it nevertheless carried with it considerable moral and political weight and its sections on the city's internationalization continued for many years to be a prime reference point. Although its limitations have increasingly been recognized since 1967, it is important to note that the Resolution's proposals were consistent with the precedents already set limiting the sovereignty of any single state over Jerusalem. Indeed, the proposals went further and removed Jerusalem completely from the sphere of sovereignty of the successor states of the British Mandate. By mid-century, Jerusalem was recognized as a religious city of international importance, and its internationalization given support in the main international forum for global politics.

The UN Partition Plan, which gave the Jews more than half the country at a time when they formed less than a third of the population and owned only a tiny fraction of the land, was rejected both by the Palestinians and the Arab governments, which continued to call for self-determination and a unitary state. The withdrawal of British forces led to open hostilities between Jewish paramilitary groups, the newly formed Israeli army, and the armies of the neighboring Arab states and Palestinian irregulars. A cease fire was agreed in November 1948 and in April 1949 an Armistice Agreement was signed between the Hashemite Kingdom of Jordan and the newly proclaimed State of Israel. These agreements resulted in the division of Jerusalem into an eastern part held by King Abdullah of Jordan and a western part held by Israel, with the Israeli government holding 84.12% of the total municipal area of mandatory Jerusalem[19] (see map 2.3).

The Armistice Lines run from north to south through Jerusalem and include a band of "no-man's land" in the immediate vicinity of the Old City. There was also an Israeli-held enclave on Mt. Scopus (including the Augusta Victoria Hospital). The former British Government House became a neutral enclave under the jurisdiction of the United Nations and was surrounded by a demilitarized zone. It was used as the headquarters of the UN Truce Supervision Organization and other UN mediating efforts. The Armistice Agreement contained provisions for access to the Holy Places. As it turned out Jordan was reluctant to implement these provisions until there was also

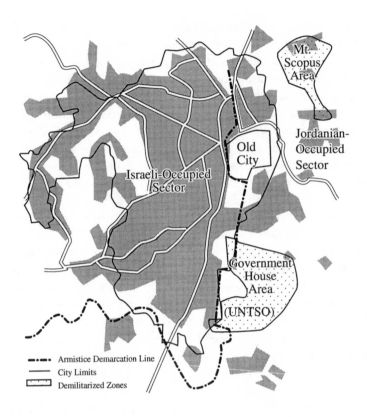

Armistice Demarcation Line
City Limits
Demilitarized Zones

MAP 2.3. Jerusalem According to the General Armistice Agreement, 1949

an agreement on reciprocal access to West Jerusalem and the return of Palestinians to their homes in West Jerusalem.[20]

The Armistice Lines, established by military agreements consecrating the *de facto* division of the city, hold a central role in the debate over the future status of Jerusalem. They became the basis of UN Security Council Resolution 242, which requires Israeli armed forces to withdraw from territories occupied in 1967, but took no account of the internationalization of the city put forward by the UN Partition Plan of 1947. The international community was thus placed in the uncomfortable situation of recognizing the two states between which the Holy City had been divided even while refusing to recognize the division of the city. Thus, states dealing with Jordan and Israel found themselves in the position of having to qualify their dealings with them when it came to Jerusalem (see chapter 8). Finally, the failure of Jordan and Israel to agree on access to the Holy Places strengthened the argument for the necessity of international supervision in some form over the Holy Places to ensure rights of access to them. Most suggested solutions to the problem of Jerusalem comprise some element of extraterritorialization of the Holy Places.

Jordanian East Jerusalem, 1948–1967

Jordanian policy with regard to East Jerusalem, which it had formally annexed along with the rest of the West Bank in 1950, was primarily concerned with integrating it into the Hashemite Kingdom of Jordan on the East Bank. By December 1948, even before the annexation, a municipal council under Transjordanian control had been formed for the eastern part of the city.[21] A military governor remained in place until April 1949, after which date he was replaced by a civilian regime. The borders of the Municipality were extended to six square kilometers to include the surrounding villages of Silwan, Ras al-Amud, Aqabat al-Suwana, 'Ard al-Samar, and the southern portions of Shu'fat.[22] While the municipal council was given powers of taxation and responsibilities for issuing construction permits and for providing services, the government insisted on transferring former Mandate departments, such as education and agriculture, to the capital in Amman, thus curtailing the political status and employment prospects for the city. Indeed, the ruling Hashemite family, anxious to emphasize the primacy of the East Bank and further influenced by its rivalry with the Hussaynis and their supporters based in Jerusalem, did not entertain the possibility of transferring its capital to Jerusalem or even of granting the city a special political status. It is true that in 1953 the Hashemites granted East Jerusalem the status of *amana* (trusteeship) and made it the "second capital" of Jordan,[23] but this was primarily in response to the Israeli government's attempt to force international recognition of West Jerusalem as its own capital by moving the president's official residence to the city in 1952, thus obliging diplomatic credentials to be presented there (see chapter 8). Plans to formalize the status by constructing government offices were never put into action, although in 1959–60 these were discussed in greater detail. Thus, in the absence of any investment in the city or corresponding increase in

the powers of East Jerusalem's Municipality or any permanent location of institutions of national importance, the conferring of this new
status remained largely a cosmetic exercise.[24]

It is important to note that for all Jordan's efforts, its claims over the
eastern part of the city were not recognized by any state—not even by
those like Britain which recognized its annexation of the rest of the
West Bank. The UN continued to press for the internationalization of
the city. Even the Arab League, as of late 1949, shifted its position and
began to support the idea of the internationalization. Jordan continued to resist any suggestions or attempts in that direction.[25] Jordan's
position was that Palestine was entrusted to the Kingdom until such
time as it was able to exercise its self-determination.[26] It therefore
rejected the proposals put forward by both the Trusteeship Council
and the more limited ones suggested by the Conciliation Commission
for Palestine.[27]

In addition to the nonrecognition of the legality of Jordanian rule
over East Jerusalem, a second legal and administrative development during the city's "Jordanian" period also had important implications for
Israeli sovereignty over the Old City and al-Haram al-Sharif compound
in the post-1967 period. This was Jordan's failure to secure absolute
control over the administration of the Muslim Holy Places, in the form
of the shari'a court and waqf systems. Thus, despite the incorporation of
these religious bodies into the Jordanian state structures, they continued, as will be described in chapter 6, to retain a degree of autonomous
action and grew into a religious enclave under Jordanian rule.

The Armistice Agreement specified that Israelis would have access
to the Holy Places but, as already mentioned, Jordan refused to implement this clause because of Israel's refusal to permit the return of
Palestinians to their homes in West Jerusalem.[28] Still, by having signed
an agreement containing this clause, Jordan by implication recognized
the importance of the Holy Places and the need for special arrangements to deal with them. In the matter of the shari'a court and Muslim
waqf systems in Jerusalem, the government was similarly forced to
acknowledge some constraints on its centralizing policies. Initially, the
Jordanian government abolished the British-created Supreme Muslim
Council seen as the stronghold of the Hussayni family, the king's political rivals. Legal supervision of the Muslim Holy Places was placed
under a committee in the prime minister's office, known as the *majlis
al-shu'un al-islamiyya*, or Council for Islamic Affairs.[29] However, the
great prestige of East Jerusalem in the Muslim world and the long-

standing administrative structures of the shari'a court and waqf system ensured that this absorption was not complete. For example, the post of Director-General of Waqf Affairs on the West Bank was established and it was directly accountable to the Chairman of the Council of Islamic Affairs and not to his counterpart in Amman who had responsibility over all other waqf districts. Thus the Director-General was given equal status to his East Bank counterpart and reported directly to the office of the prime minister. Furthermore, not only did the Jerusalem director-general inherit a wide variety of responsibilities from the Supreme Muslim Council, but also by virtue of his oversight of the two great Muslim Holy Places in the Haram compound, the Dome of the Rock and al-Aqsa Mosque, his position attracted greater status and prestige than his Amman counterpart. Accordingly, a number of institutions were set up specifically for Jerusalem. By 1962 a Board of Religious Scholars and a Council for Preaching and Guidance were in place.[30]

It is interesting to note that in comparison with its political status, the religious status of Jerusalem during this period could not be entirely ignored and structures were devised to reflect that status. The administration of the shari'a courts and waqf system were an integral part of the Muslim religious environment of East Jerusalem and could not easily be removed. In effect they served as a buffer or a check against the centralizing policies of the Jordanian state.

Israeli West Jerusalem, 1948–1967

Internationally, Israel's control over West Jerusalem was no more recognized than was Jordan's control over the eastern sector. Notwithstanding, Israel included West Jerusalem in the areas covered by the Law and Administrative Ordinance, one of the first measures promulgated by the new state. Under its provisions, all areas under the control of Israel military forces were henceforth subject to Israeli jurisdiction. Since this included areas designated by the UN as part of the *corpus separatum*, Israel's claimed jurisdiction was not recognized by the international community. Western powers such as the UK and USA acknowledged de facto Israeli authority in those areas it controlled, but withheld de jure recognition "pending a final determination of the status of the area."[31]

Despite opposition, Israel was determined to consolidate its control over western Jerusalem. As early as 1949, while the Armistice Agreement was still being negotiated, government ministries began to be

Table 2.1. Ownership of Land in Israeli-Occupied Area, 1949

Owned by	%
Arabs	33.69
Jews	30.64
Others (Christian institutions)	16.21
Government	2.47
Roads and Railways	18.69

transferred from Tel Aviv to Jerusalem culminating in the establishment of the Israeli legislative chamber, the Knesset, in West Jerusalem
in December 1949. In January 1950, the Knesset declared Jerusalem to
be the capital of Israel. As already noted, the Israeli presidential residence moved to Jerusalem in 1952, after the death of President Chaim
Weizmann,[32] and the foreign ministry followed. These transfers were
partly intended by the Israeli government to place pressure on western governments to recognize Israeli title to West Jerusalem. Most
countries kept their embassies in Tel Aviv.[33]

It is important to note that well over half the land within the Israeli
Municipality of West Jerusalem had not been owned by Jews at the
creation of the state. As can be seen from the following table, taken
from a map based on Mandate sources showing the impact of the
Armistice Lines on land-ownership in Jerusalem, Jews owned just
under 31 percent of the west Jerusalem municipality that fell to their
control (see map 2.4).[34]

Such figures help explain the Palestinian difficulty in accepting Israeli
sovereignty even over parts of West Jerusalem. Many Palestinian
Jerusalemites living today still recognize their family home in West
Jerusalem. Of more importance is the understanding that, through a
network of legislation passed by the Israeli Knesset, this Arab-owned
land was transferred to Israeli Jewish organizations, such as the Jewish
National Fund, and the state's own land-holding bureaucracy, the
Israel-Lands Administration.[35] Development and settlement of this
land is exclusively for Jews.

In addition to the transference of land, internal political and administrative developments also strengthened Israel's hold on West
Jerusalem. When municipal elections were held in 1950, the municipal boundaries were extended to include the depopulated Arab village
of 'Ayn Karim and the new Hadassah complex constructed nearby.[36]
The Municipality remained short of space for housing and utilities and
despite recommendations that the boundaries be extended to include

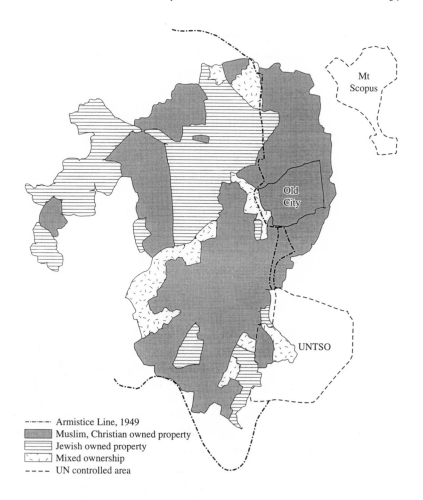

2.4. Land Ownership in Jerusalem, 1948
Derived from: Hadawi, "Map of Jerusalem," Published by Palestine Arab Refugee Office,
New York

parts of the rural settlements of Ora and Aminadav in the Jerusalem
"corridor," this was overruled by the Ministry of Defense.[37] By 1967
the total area of the Municipality of West Jerusalem comprised thirty-
six square kilometers.[38]

Also of great importance was that the most significant holy sites—
the Western Wall (also known as the Wailing Wall), al-Aqsa Mosque, the
Dome of the Rock, and the Holy Sepulcher—as well as most of the
secondary ones were outside Israeli-controlled territory. The chief
religious sites on the west side were the Cenacle, the Tomb of David,
and the Sanhedrin tombs. Conversely, many of the modern Christian

institutions were in the west, but Christian clergy based in the east side were able to gain access by virtue of their non-Arab nationality. One advantage for the Israelis of the absence of holy sites in the territory they controlled was that, unlike the case of the Jordanians, there were far fewer historical impediments to full Israeli control over their part of the city. There was, for example, no strong and well-established indigenous religious structure in its territory to challenge Israeli state jurisdiction,[39] and the issue of control there was less sensitive.

Since the Holy Places were located on the Jordanian side, the Israeli government was able without much difficulty to discuss a limited internationalization of their administration. This concept became known as "functional internationalization." In discussions with the UN Trusteeship Council, Israel declared itself "willing to accept the principle of direct United Nations responsibility for the Holy Places, to participate in discussions on the form and content of a Statute for the Holy Places, and to accept binding declarations or agreements ensuring religious freedom and full liberty for the pursuit of religious education and the protection of religious institutions."[40]

By April 1949 this position had become more specific, and Israel agreed to accept an international regime for the Holy Places in the Old City and its immediate environs (i.e., on the eastern side) provided Israeli sovereignty was assured over the parts of the city under its control.[41] In other words, Israel was willing to agree to the limited internationalization of areas under Jordanian control in exchange for recognition of its own control over West Jerusalem. Despite the clear advantages of such a proposal, by agreeing to some degree of internationalization of the administration of the Holy Places it was accepting at least in principle that limits could be placed on state authority in Jerusalem. As we turn to the post-1967 period this position should be borne in mind when examining both the limits placed upon the Israeli government and its claims to complete control over Jerusalem in the course of the current peace negotiations.

Post-1967 Period

Legal Issues of Annexation

Following the conquest of Jordanian East Jerusalem by Israeli military forces in June 1967, the Israeli government passed legislation incorporating East Jerusalem and adjacent parts of the West Bank into Israel.

While the legislation avoided the term "annexation," semantic ambiguity did not obscure the fact of annexation.[42]

As already noted, Israel's sovereignty over West Jerusalem had not been recognized in international law or by the international community other than through the Armistice Agreements of 1949, which merely confirmed the fact of its presence there. Israel had established its own legal basis for its sovereignty over West Jerusalem through the first law of the Israeli Provisional Government, the Law and Administrative Ordinance of 1948, which applied Israeli jurisdiction over all areas held by Israeli military forces. It was through an amendment of that same law from which Israel in 1967 proceeded to the incorporation of East Jerusalem and adjacent parts of the West Bank.

Thus, on June 27, 1967, the Knesset passed an amendment to the 1948 law stating that "the law, jurisdiction and administration of the state shall extend to any area of Eretz Israel *designated by the Government by order*" (emphasis added).[43] The next day, the Israeli government carried out two important legislative acts. The first was to issue an order designating an area of 30,000 *dunams* of East Jerusalem and the West Bank stretching from Qalandia airport in the north to Sur Bahir in the south, and including the Old City of Jerusalem,[44] for coverage by the amendment of the previous day (see map 2.5). The second was to pass yet another and no less important amendment enabling the Israeli Municipality of West Jerusalem to extend its boundaries over exactly the same area to which the Law and Administrative Ordinance was applied. The amendment empowered the Israeli Minister of Interior "at his discretion and without an enquiry ... to enlarge, by proclamation, the area of a particular municipality by inclusion of an area by order."[45]

The Jordanian East Jerusalem Municipality was ordered to cease activity and was dissolved the very next day, June 29.[46] In these ways Israel was able to sidestep the issue of annexation and its ambassador at the UN was able to term its actions as "the integration of services."[47] No one, however, was fooled.

The response of the international community to the Israeli moves was unequivocal. Two weeks before, on June 14, the UN Security Council had passed a Resolution calling upon Israel to respect the Geneva Conventions in the areas under Israeli military occupation.[48] In July 1967, the UN General Assembly passed two resolutions calling upon Israel to rescind measures affecting the status of Jerusalem.[49] The second resolution led to the UN secretary-general sending a per-

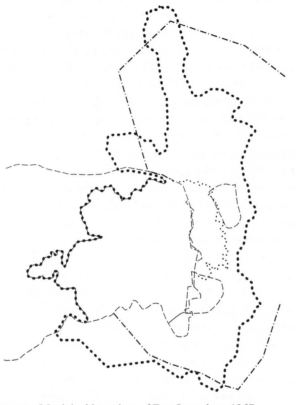

········ Municipal boundary of East Jerusalem, 1967
— ·— ·— Proposed master plan for boundary of East Jerusalem, May 1967
— — — Armistice line, 1949-1967
———— West Jerusalem (Israel) municipal boundary
•••••• Municipal boundary of Jerusalem 28.6.1967

MAP 2.5. Municipal Boundaries of Enlarged Jerusalem, 1967

sonal representative, Ernesto Thalmann, to examine and report back
on the situation. He was informed by the Israeli government that the
integration of East Jerusalem into Israel was "irreversible and not
negotiable."[50] Subsequent resolutions by both the Security Council
and the General Assembly were all concerned to maintain the validity of Jerusalem's status as a *corpus separatum*. Other UN bodies, such

as the UN Educational, Scientific, and Cultural Organization (UNESCO) and the Commission on Human Rights of the Social and Economic Council, also stressed that Israel was obliged to rescind any measures that altered the physical and legal character of Jerusalem[51] (see chapter 8).

Disputes concerning the implications and the legality of Israel's actions have continued. Any diplomatic protocol that could be construed as conferring international recognition of its annexation, such as the location of embassies in Jerusalem, has been avoided. The Israeli government has sought to consolidate its position not only by infrastructural alterations, as will be seen, but also by administrative practice. The Israeli Supreme Court, for example, was moved into the commercial district of East Jerusalem.

The de facto "annexation" wrought politically, legally, and functionally by the steps taken in 1967 was confirmed in August 1980, when a new law was passed entitled "Basic Law: Jerusalem." The law asserted that "complete and united Jerusalem is the capital of Israel" and it is "the seat of the President of the state, the Knesset, the Government and the Supreme Court."[52] Its main purpose, however, was political rather than juridical. It did not legislate any new changes but underlined the political reality of the existing Israeli legislation. The Israeli government, accordingly, moved some of its offices to East Jerusalem.

The law was seen by the international community as a further attempt to prevent and forestall UN recommendations on Jerusalem. It also killed off the post Camp David negotiations between Israel and Egypt over Palestinian autonomy, which in the Egyptian view was to include the future of East Jerusalem. Indeed, the Israeli member of Knesset who submitted the bill, Guela Cohen, affirmed that: "This Bill is designed to ensure that there will never be any compromise over the sovereignty of Jerusalem."[53]

The UN Security Council passed a strongly worded resolution condemning the Israeli action as violation of Israeli law and urged those remaining countries which had diplomatic representation in Jerusalem to remove their embassies.[54] As a result several more countries moved their embassies from Jerusalem to Tel Aviv.[55] Despite this reaction the Israeli government has remained determined to secure its control over both sides of Jerusalem. Planning decisions, the location of new housing settlements, the direction of new immigrants to Israel, the introduction of services and infrastructure, and the allocation and

distribution of resources have all had the overriding aim to absorb and
integrate the eastern areas into the West Jerusalem Municipality.

In fact, the 1980 law was a mere legalism and introduced no changes
in the administration or practical running of the city. The real changes
on the ground dated to 1967. At that time, and prior to the passage of
the laws mentioned above, there was considerable debate as to how the
borders of the new Israeli Municipality were to be drawn. The final
line, a compromise between maximalist and minimalist positions, was
drawn primarily with demographic, economic, and military purposes
in mind.[56] For example, while the new boundaries stretched from
Qalandia in the north to Azariyya in the east and Sur Bahir in the
south, the villages of Abu Dis, Azariyya, Beit Hanina, A-Ram with
their high Arab concentrations were excluded (see map 2.5). Another
aim was to separate economically the annexed areas from the West
Bank. Thus, for example, a cigarette factory in Azariyya and an arak dis-
tillery south of Ramallah were left just outside the limits.[57] Control
over strategic hilltops and defensible valleys also was taken into
account, and boundaries to the north and south adjusted accordingly.
This particularly applied to areas east of Neve Ya'aqov and around Beit
Hanina. The final line also incorporated areas that had been part of the
municipalities of Bayt Jallah, Bethlehem, and al-Birah.[58] Significantly,
there was no extension of the Municipality westward, even though this
would have made sense from a planning standpoint; the kibbutz of
Ramat Rachel was once again exempted, in accordance with the
wishes of its inhabitants, from incorporation into the Municipality.[59]

It is important to note that the annexed areas were entirely congruent with the municipal borders. By extending the Municipality
borders no farther than the areas designated by government order in
accordance with the Law and Administrative Ordinance, the enlargement of the Jerusalem Municipality in 1967 to include East Jerusalem
and adjacent parts of the West Bank could be presented merely as a
unification of the city and an integration of services and administration. A related aspect to this incorporation of East Jerusalem and the
adjacent parts of the West Bank into Israel involved the transfer of
Jordanian-held land to the Israel-Lands Administration.

Despite full military control and the assertion of total Israeli sovereignty over the whole of Jerusalem and the surrounding area, the
Israeli government found that it was obliged to accept restrictions and
ambiguities with regard to the full application of its law and administration. There were a number of areas where the full application of

Israeli law was nominal. This was particularly, but not solely, the case with regard to the administration of the Holy Places. Later chapters will deal with some of these aspects in detail but it is relevant here to draw attention to the key legal and administrative features of these limitations. They highlight how complete sovereignty over the city was not easily attainable and is possibly an unrealistic goal in any peace negotiations. The two crucial areas to be examined are, first, the enforcement of Israeli law, particularly over land and property, and second, the status of the religious affairs of the Muslim community: the control over al-Haram al-Sharif, and the administration of the shari'a courts and waqf system.

Concerning the application of Israeli law, among the problems—rendered more difficult given the largely hostile and uncooperative population—were those involving the status of cases that had been *sub judice* in Jordanian courts, the status of buildings in the process of completion, the registration of companies, and the practice of lawyers. Already in 1968, the government found it necessary to pass the first of a number of laws permitting exemptions to the existing Israeli regulations.[60] For example, it was made illegal to take note of the fact that East Jerusalem Palestinians held Jordanian citizenship, since this would normally have conferred on them enemy status and threatened their rights.[61] Similarly, Jordanian-registered companies with their main offices in Jerusalem were automatically re-registered as Israeli ones to enable them to operate on Israeli territory; the unilateral move was necessary because companies had refused, as part of the resistance to the occupation, to apply for the necessary registration with Israeli ministries, and Israel was anxious to "normalize" the situation as quickly as possible.[62]

One of the most sensitive areas where difficulties arose as a result of the annexation was that of land and property ownership. Technically, the application of Israeli law to East Jerusalem would render owners of private property there "absentee landlords" under the Israeli Absentee Property Law of 1950,[63] which defined "absentees" as anyone who was not "present" in the territory that became Israel between December 29, 1947 and May 19, 1948 and which entitled the state to take custody of their property. Clearly the inhabitants of East Jerusalem were not "present" by this definition, but to have enforced this law would have been counter-productive both with regard to the Palestinian population and internationally, especially with the world's attention focussed on Israel's actions in the wake of the occupation.

Therefore the law was amended to state that the inhabitants of East Jerusalem could not be regarded as "absentee" with respect to their property in "that area"— i.e., East Jerusalem.[64]

The Absentee Property Law had been applied to the waqf system and other religious property in Israel following the establishment of the state in 1948 and could therefore have been expected to be applied to the waqf and other Muslim religious property in East Jerusalem following the 1967 capture of the city. This would have meant that Muslim Holy Places, including al-Haram al-Sharif, one of the three holiest sites in Islam, would have become property under the jurisdiction of the Israeli Custodian of Absentee Property. For reasons of *realpolitik* the Israeli government had to prevent this happening, and one of the articles of the new law exempted the Holy Places from the Absentee Property Law.[65]

Another area where Israel was obliged to restrict the full application of its laws was in education. After 1967, the Israeli government sought initially to impose its own educational system on all the former Jordanian municipality schools. Under the Israeli Law of Supervision of Educational Institutions, the contents of the syllabus, the appointment of the head teacher and other teachers, and the administration of training are all subject to state control. However, Palestinian resistance to the imposition of an Israeli syllabus was intense and pupils were transferred from municipal schools to private and religious schools at a rapid rate. At one point the well-known Rashidiyya Boys School had fewer pupils than teachers![66] In part motivated by the campaign of passive resistance that characterized early Palestinian responses to the Israeli occupation, the strength and durability of the resistance to this educational policy derived largely from Palestinian parents' recognition that an Israeli matriculation certificate would be useless in the higher educational and commercial institutions of the Arab world where most of their children would aspire to.

The final outcome of this standoff was that the Jordanian syllabus was re-adopted by the municipal schools while Hebrew and civics were made compulsory but not examinable. The wider implication of this success by Palestinians was to underscore the Palestinian and Jerusalemite connection with the Arab world. As much as the quasi-autonomous status of the Muslim religious hierarchy and their administration, the presence of a Jordanian syllabus in the Israeli capital was a recognition of the nature of the city. In order to eradicate that cultural presence a complete evacuation of the city would be required.

As for the application of Israeli law with regard to Muslim religious affairs and the Holy Places, in late June 1967, at the same time as the laws effectively annexing East Jerusalem and the adjacent areas were passed, the Protection of Holy Places Law was enacted. This law stated that the Holy Places would be protected "from desecration and any other violation and from anything likely to violate the freedom of access of the members of the different religions to the places sacred to them or to their feelings with regard to those places."[67]

The Israeli Minister of Religious Affairs was charged with the implementation of this law and any further regulations necessary. The most the law conceded to the above-mentioned idea of "functional internationalization" involving limited internationalization of the administration of the Holy Places was that the Israeli Minister of Religious Affairs was permitted to make consultations with the different religious communities before introducing new regulations.[68] Furthermore the law makes no mention of the issue of the status quo assiduously preserved by the British Mandate and given the backing of international law by UN resolutions. The Israeli law was an assertion of Israeli sovereignty over the Holy Places and cut across the internationalizing precedents that had begun during the Ottoman period. While guaranteeing freedom of worship and access, it made such freedom and access subject to Israeli authority and jurisdiction.

Meanwhile, the shari'a courts and waqf system continued to function irrespective of Israeli legislation. Indeed, no new legislation was passed to accommodate the Muslim religious and legal hierarchy or administrative structures. After an initial attempt by the Israeli Ministry of Religious Affairs to assert its jurisdiction over Muslim religious affairs, the government handed the issue over to the Israeli Ministry of Defense, which avoided any direct legal interference.[69] Thus in theory, Israeli sharisa law and the legal writ of the Ministry of Religious Affairs are in existence in East Jerusalem and the adjacent parts of the West Bank, but in practice two parallel Muslim legal systems are in operation in Jerusalem. East Jerusalem Muslims can choose which to apply to according to the circumstances.[70]

Part and parcel of this anomaly was the administration of al-Haram al-Sharif, known to the Israelis as the Temple Mount. During the 1967 War, Israeli troops occupied the Haram area and placed an Israeli flag on the roof of the Dome of the Rock. Aware of Muslim sensitivities, Israeli Chief of Staff Moshe Dayan ordered its removal and kept Israeli soldiers out of the compound pending a final decision over the future

administration of the Haram area. He did, however, confiscate the keys
of the main southeastern gate, Bab al-Magharib, and stationed troops
at the entrance. The troops' spontaneous gesture and Dayan's response
exemplifies Israeli divisions over the course to be followed: while
euphoric Israelis were dreaming of building a synagogue beside or on
the site of the Dome of the Rock or al-Aqsa mosque,[71] the government was anxious to assuage the Western world's fears over the rights
of access to the Holy Places in order to deflect any further attempts to
internationalize the city. The Ministry of Religious Affairs studiously
avoided in its pronouncements any mention of how the Haram area
was to be administered. In fact, since 1967 no law or ordinance has
been passed concerning the status of the Haram area, and a tacit
understanding has been in place since 1967 whereby a Muslim
Council supervises the activities there (see chapter 6). The result was
to allow the evolution of a quasi-autonomous Jordanian-Palestinian
enclave in the heart of an Israeli-controlled city, in which funding,
appointments, and major decisions emanated from Amman. It is too
early to conclude how or if the Israeli Supreme Court's ruling in
September 1993 that Israeli law is applicable to the Haram area will
affect this situation in practice.

The Administration of the City

The administration of Jerusalem is a complex affair. The combination
of its relatively small size and great importance as both a national and
international city makes it particularly vulnerable to numerous
bureaucratic influences. In general, municipalities in Israel are established by and accountable to the Israeli Ministry of Interior. However,
in Jerusalem, the presence there of national ministries and its national
and political significance in Israeli politics draws in the involvement of
other ministries. The Ministry of Foreign Affairs is concerned over the
status and treatment of the Christian communities and with their connections in international forums; the Ministries of Religious Affairs
and Defense are concerned over the use of and access to religious sites;
the Ministry of Housing, the Ministry of Trade and Industry, and the
Ministry of Absorption (immigration) are concerned with the availability of space for development projects promoted by themselves.
Moreover, the role of the Municipality was weakened under the
Mandate, when the British authorities, anxious to maintain some control over the activities of a deeply divided municipal council, had

placed it under the direct authority of a governor, who retained a tight control over the budget of the city. Most of the powers of the governor have since been subsumed by the Ministry of Interior, and there was little expansion in the budgetary responsibilities of the Municipality. This weakened role of the Municipality makes it ill equipped to withstand strong pressures from government ministries. Innovations designed to ease the bureaucratic entanglements that had become characteristic of administration in the city, such as the creation of a Ministry for Jerusalem Affairs, only served to introduce yet another level of bureaucracy.[72]

The small budget at its disposal exacerbates the institutional weakness of the Municipality. As in other Israeli municipalities, revenues are in part locally derived and in part provided by the Ministry of Interior. Jerusalem claims that it should be given extra funds in view of the city's role in the political goals of the nation and the economically and geographically inhospitable environment. In addition, the Municipality carries out a range of services on behalf of the state and has been obliged to cover the costs of providing services to new Israeli settlements across the Green Line, which proved more much more expensive than its own preferred option of upgrading and developing areas closer to the central core of Jerusalem. These additional costs, it argues, should be shared by the government.

In fact, the proportion of the Municipality's budget derived from government sources has steadily declined. In the 1970s 70 percent of the Municipality's funds came from government sources,[73] as compared with a mere 26 percent by 1986. In part, this decline reflected a general ideological reorientation of the government under the Likud Party toward the private sector, but it also reflected the growing role of government ministries, particularly of the Ministry of Housing, in the planning and development of the city. There is also the suggestion that Teddy Kollek, Jerusalem's long-serving mayor, in his frustration with the local and national bureaucracy had diluted the government's financial support for the Municipality by establishing, even before the occupation, the Jerusalem Foundation in 1966. The Foundation, chaired by the mayor, was independent of the Municipality and attracted funds from international sources, but these funds were spent on projects which the Municipality supports. Its disbursements accounted for anywhere from 16 to 20 percent of the Municipality's budget. Between 1966 and 1980, the Foundation disbursed $64 million to projects approved of by the mayor.[74]

One of the main criticisms leveled by Palestinians against the Municipality's administration of the city is the poor level of services provided to their localities in East Jerusalem. Nonetheless, it is necessary to point out that the inequality in services is not unrelated to the lack of Palestinian participation in the political system. Municipal priorities are determined by the Israeli Jewish interests as they are represented in the Council and its committees. It is to this aspect that we should now turn.

When Israel occupied East Jerusalem and incorporated it and parts of the West Bank into the state, it offered citizenship to the 65,000 Palestinians living within the new extended borders of Jerusalem who were counted in the 1967 census. Very few took up the offer, which required forfeiting Jordanian citizenship. To this day, only about 1,500, or 1% of the Palestinian population, have opted for Israeli citizenship.[75] To overcome problems relating to a large community of noncitizens within the new borders of the Israel state, Israel made them permanent residents. Palestinians in Jerusalem were therefore issued Israeli identity cards and allowed to vote in municipal elections. The possession of an Israeli I.D. proved attractive since it entitled the bearers to medical, old age, unemployment, and other welfare benefits.

Palestinian participation in municipal elections has been a highly contentious issue. Communal and political leaders have argued that by participating Palestinians would confer legitimacy upon Israeli rule in the incorporated areas, which at all costs was to be avoided. Some Palestinians, on the other hand, particularly the approximately 1,500 employed by the Municipality, argue for participation on the grounds that the elections constitute a local contest over the equitable allocation of services. In 1969, the first elections after the 1967 War, only 7,150 of the 25,000 eligible Palestinians voted.[76] Since then, the proportion has steadily declined, and at no time has exceeded 20 percent of the Palestinian electorate. There is no doubt that had the Palestinians voted in larger numbers they would have had a considerable impact upon the city's electoral politics. Those who did vote voted for Kollek, but his support for the construction of Israeli settlements in East Jerusalem was a significant factor in Palestinian abstention in municipal elections.

With the Palestinian boycott of elections, the government and Municipality set about trying to secure Palestinian participation in the system through other means: Palestinian involvement, however limited, was seen as a form of engagement and therefore a recognition of the state. First, the Municipality created an Advisor to the Mayor on East Jerusalem Affairs in recognition of the informal and personalized nature of Palestinian politics. The Advisor's office became a key conduit by which the concerns of Palestinian notables were addressed, often going beyond merely municipal affairs. In addition, the Mayor and his Advisor undertook consultations with leaders of the Muslim religious hierarchy in the Awqaf Administration, with the East Jerusalem Chamber of Commerce and other notables.

Second, it breathed new life into the traditional *mukhtar* system, which had been in operation during the Jordanian period. Mukhtars were village heads or leaders of an urban quarter, appointed and paid by the Municipality. They were responsible for signing documents pertaining to landownership or personal status matters such as births, deaths, and marriages and formed the main formal link between the Municipality and the Palestinian community in Jerusalem. There have been approximately 60 mukhtars in Jerusalem at any one time and they have tended to be supporters of the status quo,[77] although during times of tension, particularly the *intifada*, the mukhtars are not only marginalized by the nationalist leaders but their loyalty to the Israeli system is shown to be shallow.[78] At all events, by maintaining this traditional and somewhat anachronistic institution, the Municipality confined its contacts with Palestinian Jerusalemites to a narrow social base and neglected the emerging alternative leadership of educated professionals.

The final means of engaging Palestinians in the political life of the city was the neighborhood council system, or *minhalot* in Hebrew. Started in 1980 as a joint project between a Jewish philanthropic foundation (the Joint Distribution Committee) and the Municipality, neighborhood councils have had some important political implications concerning the future of Jerusalem. In essence, neighborhood councils are designed to encourage local participation in the delivery of municipal and government services through a measure of self-management and the decentralization of decisionmaking.[79] Pilot projects began in eight areas, three in the Palestinian areas of Al-Tur (on the Mount of Olives), Beit Hanina (on the road to Ramallah-al-Bireh), and Bayt Safafa, a village south of Jerusalem that was formerly divided by the Armistice Lines.

For the Municipality, the neighborhood councils were a low-key form of the borough system existing in many Western cities tailored to suit the religious and ethnic composition of Jerusalem. It is an administrative application of the Israeli mayor's conception of Jerusalem as a "mosaic" of different backgrounds. Politically and in the context of the unification of the city, the neighborhood councils serve two roles: by focussing on the delivery of services they constitute municipal authority on a functional level. It is hoped that this self-interest will override the issue of sovereignty. As the Mayor, Teddy Kollek, has said:

> An expanded system of *minhalot* could eventually play a role in a permanent arrangement by becoming the framework for self administration by the different autonomous communities within one municipality.... I believe that a further sharing of functional authority and a greater decentralisation within Jerusalem is possible and very desirable. . . . Israel's sovereignty need not interfere with the Arab community's institutions and economic, cultural and even political life.[80]

The geopolitical principle behind this thinking was that the decentralization of municipal government would make the issue of Israeli sovereignty less contentious to the Palestinian Arab inhabitants in the annexed areas. It is an example of an attempt to blur the issue in order to make it more acceptable. The second political role played by the neighborhood councils is in the way that the very act of participation in the delivery of services from the councils indicate an acceptance and a measure of legitimation of the Israeli Municipality. These two roles clearly have greater significance in the Palestinian areas than in the Israeli Jewish areas.

The neighborhood councils in East Jerusalem and the annexed areas of the West Bank have had mixed results. In Al-tur there has been a pragmatic participation in order to acquire a desperately needed sewage system. It has been a participation much eased by the fact that since Al-Tur had been outside the Jordanian municipal boundaries during the partition period, the village had acquired a council. The new neighborhood council was in effect a revival of the former village council and received the blessing of the Jordanian government and funds from the PLO, Jordanian, and other Arab governments. In Beit Hanina, the suspicions of the Palestinian residents toward the Municipality have been so great that the council operates in a very low-key incremental manner. The Bayt Safafa council initially collapsed as a result of opposition by the existing mukhtars. These have since been co-opted and the council was restructured to accommodate their concerns. Since the beginning of the *intifada*, much of the activity of the councils is in abeyance, although they have not completely collapsed.

Future Trends

By the late 1980s it had become clear that the area of the Israeli Municipality would not be sufficient for the city's projected needs. The existing area was in fact restricting its growth. At the prevailing rate of construction all available land would be used up by the end of the century. The lack of land would both stymie the government's attempts to outpace the Palestinian Arab population growth in the eastern parts of the city and, without development space for industry, would further weaken the city's economic base.[81] In addition, the anticipated conclusion of a peace agreement with the Arab states and the Palestinians and a *de jure* recognition for Jerusalem as Israel's capital would lead to a great demand for space for the construction of embassies and the offices of international institutions. Indeed, an agreement with the Palestinians would lead to the location of many Palestinian, Arab, and Muslim institutions in Jerusalem as well.

In 1988, the Israeli government set up the Kubersky Committee to examine the criteria and options for enlarging the borders of the Jerusalem Municipality. Significantly, the Committee's brief was restricted to considering options only on the western side of the Armistice Lines, of which there were several at the time, ranging from expansion to Bet Shemesh to a tinkering and in-filling of odd permutations in the border.[82] Despite the urban-planning and demographic advantages in an extension northward and eastward, this option was apparently seen at that stage as carrying too many problems. First of all, an expansion in this direction would alter the demography of the city to the detriment of the Israeli Jewish population. Secondly, the international reaction to such a move could damage Israel's attempts to obtain recognition for Jerusalem as its capital. At all events, following the Kubersky Committee's recommendations in 1991, the Municipality in February 1992 enlarged its borders westward by 15,000 *dunams*.

Whatever the strength of the pragmatic arguments in favor of westward expansion, it was almost certainly a concession to the balance of forces ranged against Israel with regard to its attempt to secure control over Jerusalem. Viewed optimistically, it could be interpreted as an indication that Israel, bowing to the inevitable demographically, could be prepared to relinquish parts of the eastern areas for a suitable political price—for example, international recognition of Jerusalem as Israel's capital and control over the Jewish quarter and the Western Wall. The westward expansion could also be seen as an attempt to strengthen the city economically and politically by increasing its links with the coastal plain.

For all the weight of planning considerations, however, it is likely that the determining issue in the future expansion of Jerusalem will be wider strategic factors. The commitment of the previous Labor government to the Israeli settlements in the metropolitan area of Jerusalem to the north, east, and south has been asserted too frequently and consistently to be mere rhetoric. Having been obliged to surrender the Gaza Strip and parts of the West Bank it is likely that the current government will do its utmost to make an Israeli withdrawal from the annexed parts of Jerusalem a virtual impossibility. The future territorial needs of the Municipality for its functional operations and the political commitment of the government to a wide belt around Jerusalem may be combined to produce an additional blurring of the borders that was discussed at the beginning of this chapter. This could be a blurring where the official political borders of the Municipality are one area but the functional borders another, where the Holy Places are administered autonomously but where de facto control in Israeli, and where the Palestinians of Jerusalem are made permanent residents of a greater Jerusalem but not citizens of any state.

3

Running to Stand Still: The Politics of Demography in Jerusalem

"And dare I say frankly that we have to do everything within our power to make Greater Jerusalem the largest Jewish city in the world, a real Jewish city, both in terms of the population numbers and in giving a permanent Jewish character to the whole city."
—Rabbi Cohen, Deputy Mayor of (Jerusalem) Municipal Council Meeting August 13, 1967.

"What is required—and quickly—is Jews, many Jews in Jerusalem. No more trickles of immigration."
—Mordechai Ish-Shalom, former Mayor of Jerusalem, City Councillor, 1967.[1]

Understanding the changes in the demographic composition of Jerusalem is fundamental to understanding the politics of the city. Demography has always been at the heart of the Israeli-Palestinian conflict, and regardless of whether or not the dramatic change wrought by 1948 was by design or a consequence of the war, the fact is that a formerly minority population in what became Israel was transformed into a majority virtually overnight. The situation of Jerusalem following the 1967 War was, of course, more complicated. But the government's policies in Jerusalem have unquestionably been driven by the same logic of control through population shift. Thus, to attain control over East Jerusalem and the annexed areas of the West Bank, the government had not only to increase the Israeli Jewish population substantially, but also to place them in the eastern, Arab-inhabited part of the city in order to prevent any possibility of these areas becoming part of a Jordanian or Palestinian state.

In this context, the demographic policies of the Israeli government and Jerusalem Municipality have been a success. From 1967 to 1990, Jerusalem's population has increased dramatically, from 266,300 to 545,000. Nearly three-quarters of this increase has come from Israeli Jews, and over two-thirds of the increase in the Israeli Jewish population has come from those settled in East Jerusalem and the other areas annexed in 1967. Here we have both an impressive feat of urban development and a vigorous demonstration of the Israeli government's political will. In terms of land utilization, Israeli sovereignty over Jerusalem has never been stronger.

Nevertheless, on another level the very same policies can be considered as less successful. Despite enormous government intervention and investment, the percentage of Israeli Jews has not risen above 72 percent of the total population within the Municipal area—almost identical to what it was in 1967. In addition, it has failed to prevent the increasing transfer of Israeli Jewish population from the west side of the city to the annexed areas of East Jerusalem or the continued out-migration of Jews either to the surrounding hinterland area or other parts of Israel. In the same way, running to stand still, the Israeli government has failed to contain Palestinian Arab population growth. As well as a high natural growth rate amongst the Palestinian Arabs, the absence of any meaningful economic development in other parts of the West Bank has meant that Jerusalem has acted like a magnet attracting scores of Palestinian Arabs from the surrounding areas who move to the Jerusalem region weekly. Indeed, a recent report by the Municipality has concluded that:". . . If Israel does not want to lose the demographic race [in Jerusalem], she must "run faster." She must create the conditions which will enable the Jewish population of Jerusalem to grow at a faster rate than in the past."[2]

Thus, since 1967, while the population of Israeli Jews in Jerusalem has grown by a prodigious 94 percent, the population of Palestinian Arabs has grown by 111 percent. Significantly, the most recent reports show that 50 percent of this Palestinian Arab population is below 18 years of age, that is, just before the peak child-producing years.[3] Striking as the Palestinian Arab growth rate has been, a demographic explosion among Palestinian Arabs in the Jerusalem region is therefore about to occur. This underlying trend, which is poised to jeopardize the Israeli demographic dominance, explains the alarm frequently expressed in Israeli official circles.

Indeed, the government is faced with a troublesome dilemma. If it enlarges the Municipality of Jerusalem further, many thousands more Palestinian Arabs will be included, diluting the "Jewishness" of the city and thereby Israel's claims to sovereignty. If it does not, competition for the available space in the less densely populated annexed area of East Jerusalem by "in-filling" between areas of Arab concentration will exacerbate the already tense relations between the Palestinian and Jewish communities and between the Israeli Jewish secular and orthodox communities. Repeated communal conflict will weaken Israel's claims to the city based upon good government. Moreover, without further space it will not be able to create the economic conditions capable of attracting and retaining new Jewish immigration. Despite the Israeli government's engineering of demographic change in Jerusalem, it has not solved the basic conundrum of Jerusalem's demographic future.

This conundrum has important consequences for the peace negotiations. Despite the centrality of the demographic issue to the future of Jerusalem, its importance must be viewed in the light of the Israeli government's overall strategic aims. The enlargement of Jerusalem's borders in 1967 and the pressures for further extensions have a geostrategic relevance that subsumes the demographic issues indicated above. An enlarged Jerusalem with exclusive Israeli Jewish urban satellites in the hinterland will divide the West Bank into two discrete parts. During the interim period envisaged by the Declaration of Principles signed in September 1993, the consolidation of Israeli control over the hinterland of Jerusalem through land acquisition and migrant settlement will be a major aim. It is this Israeli policy, one aspect of which is the demographic contest, that is the real threat to both an overall peace agreement and the future of Jerusalem. Not only will the West Bank be divided and the Palestinian entity thus gravely weakened, but Jerusalem itself will comprise a large Palestinian minority under Israeli jurisdiction and thus remain inherently unstable. The fact that the Israeli government appears determined to pursue its exclusive and aggrandizing policies in the face of such demographic and political consequences is cause for extreme concern.

Some Definitions

Before examining the political significance of demographic developments in Jerusalem in more detail a number of general points should be made regarding methods and definitions. First, the study of demographic change, as with other aspects of the Palestinian-Israeli conflict, is highly politicized. Methods of enumeration and definition of subject and subject areas can be used to lend weight to one political perspective or another,[4] and the researcher has to be constantly vigilant in determining how and why a particular figure is offered. The categories in Israeli population statistics of "Jew" and "non-Jew," an illustration of the general Israeli policy of not recognizing Palestinians as a distinct people, also has the effect of blurring the demographic profile of the Palestinian Arabs since not all non-Jews are Palestinian Arabs.

Such categorizations can distort a full and clear picture of the demographic changes that have taken place in Jerusalem. This is particularly relevant during the post-1967 period since the absence of any recognized independent, Palestinian or Arab censuses, obliges researchers to rely entirely upon official Israeli statistics without an opportunity to balance them.

One major difficulty in the demographic study of Jerusalem has been the question of its borders. The post-1967 municipal boundaries established by the Israeli government, which have not been accepted by the international community, were drawn up not only with a view toward security and facilitating control, as noted in chapter 2, but also so as to comprise as much land as possible without including the Palestinian Arab population living in the Jerusalem hinterland. The villages of A-Ram, Dahiya al-Barid, Bir Nabala, Beit Hanina, Azariyya, and Abu Dis were all excluded from the new Municipal borders while their lands were included and subjected to expropriations and zoning restrictions. The lines drawn bore no relation to the inhabitants' economic, cultural, or religious ties to the core area of Jerusalem. As Lustick points out the borders followed no agreed or collectively understood lines and their publication required nearly thirty pages of coordinates.[5] Thus a significant proportion of Jerusalem's "daytime" population of Palestinians, that is Palestinians who work and shop in Jerusalem and use the city's services, actually reside outside of the municipal boundaries and consequently do not figure in the statistical data for the city.[6]

A further difficulty is that population change does not take place in neat geographical areas and the differences between changes in two adjacent areas are as revealing as changes within the areas themselves. This is particularly the case in Jerusalem where areas are ethnically and politically segregated. For example, the depopulation of the central business district along the Jaffa Road in West Jerusalem, a secular Jewish area, and the rise in population in the adjacent ultra-orthodox Jewish areas confirms the general statistical trend in Jerusalem of growth among the ultra-orthodox Jews at the expense of secular Jews.

Despite these qualifications, three main features in the growth of Jerusalem's population have received a measure of consensus. First, the Jewish population of Jerusalem increased dramatically during the

Mandate period. The extent and significance of the Jewish proportion of the total population, however, is disputed and will be discussed below. Second, since 1967 Israeli government policies have been designed to establish a permanent Israeli Jewish majority in the city as a whole and in the eastern sector in particular. This target appears to have been attained, although as we have noted in the last chapter there is a question as to whether Israel can continue to sustain a sufficient rate of growth to counter Arab natural growth. This notion of Israeli Jewish demographic superiority is entirely artificial and primarily a result of the way in which the enlarged borders of 1967 were drawn to exclude dense areas of Palestinian Arab settlement. Third, the major source of increase in the Israeli Jewish population of the city within the municipal borders has been immigration. On its own, natural increase would not have been sufficient to maintain an Israeli Jewish demographic superiority over Palestinian Arabs.[7]

It is the constantly shifting relationship between these three salient characteristics of the city's growth—low Israeli-Jewish natural increase, high Palestinian natural increase, and Jewish immigration—that shapes the Israeli government's demographic policies in annexed East Jerusalem and the adjacent parts of the West Bank. The importance to the government of securing and maintaining an Israeli Jewish demographic superiority in the eastern sectors of the city can hardly be overemphasized. It presents the international community, and especially Israel's Palestinian interlocutors in the peace process, with a problematic *fait accompli*. It creates a culture of acceptance of the Israeli presence in the annexed areas and places concrete obstacles to any prospect of withdrawal or partition. This demographic change is Israel's strongest claim to permanent sovereignty in the city, just as its failure to prevent corresponding Palestinian Arab growth places enormous impediments to achieving its goals in the "final status" negotiations. But the government must also consider that achieving Jewish demographic dominance makes the possibility of a stable West Bank and Gaza state more remote.

Demographic Trends up to 1967

Before examining the main features and stages of the Israeli government's demographic policies in the enlarged Jerusalem of 1967, it is useful to provide the historical background to the general trends in population growth and decline in the previous periods. In discussing

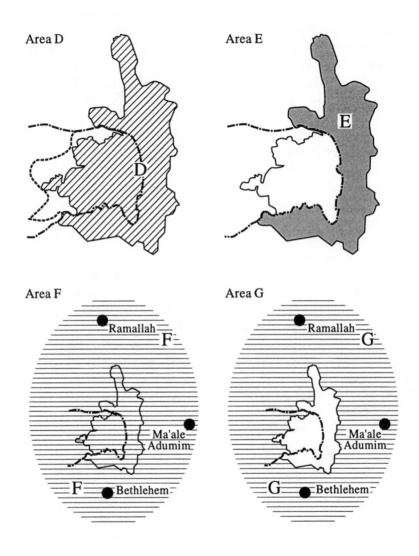

MAP 3.1–3.4 Area D, E, F, G.

these trends and demographic changes in Jerusalem, an understanding of the political and geographic areas referred to is very important. There are six main geo-political areas dating from the Mandate period to bear in mind (see maps 2.1, 2.5, 3.1, 3.2, 3.3, and 3.4).

A.—An area comprising the Municipal boundaries established by the Mandatory authorities, and some of the new Jewish suburbs and

outlying Palestinian villages. This area should be distinguished from
the much larger Mandatory Jerusalem Area subdistrict (see map 2.1).

B.—An area to the west of the Armistice Lines comprising the
Municipality of West Jerusalem between 1948 and 1967 (see map 2.5).

C.—An area to the east of the Armistice Lines comprising the
Municipality of East Jerusalem between 1948 and 1967 (see map 2.5).

D.—An area comprising the boundaries of the enlarged Israeli
Municipality of Jerusalem of 1967, which absorbed East Jerusalem and
adjacent parts of the West Bank, as well as the area west of the city
(from Israel proper) that was incorporated into the Municipality in
1993, indicated on the map by a dotted line (see map 3.1).

E.—An area comprising the former Jordanian municipal boundaries of East Jerusalem (Area C) plus the adjacent areas of the West
Bank absorbed into the Israeli Municipality of Jerusalem in 1967. In
discussing the post-1967 period, these will be referred to as East
Jerusalem and annexed areas (see map 3.2).

F.—An area comprising the post-1967 Municipality area (Area D)
plus outlying areas extending to a 50 kilometers radius from the commercial center of West Jerusalem. In discussing the post 1967 period this
will be referred to as the metropolitan area of Jerusalem (see map 3.3).

G.—An area comprising the part of the post-1967 metropolitan
area outside the borders of the Municipality (i.e., not including the
Municipality itself). This will be referred to as the metropolitan area
outside the Municipality. It is relevant to our discussion when considering the possibility of further Israeli extensions of the Municipality
borders into the metropolitan area where there is a Palestinian Arab
preponderance (see map 3.4).

Ottoman and Mandate Jerusalem

While there is no doubt the Jewish population increased during the
last century of the Ottoman period, precise figures are difficult to
establish. Even the most reliable figures, those of Justin McCarthy, are
not conclusive since they refer to the whole administrative district, the
sanjak, of Jerusalem and not only to the city itself. It is likely that there
was a small majority of Palestinian Arabs in the city at the beginning
of the nineteenth century, but even that is impossible to establish with
any certainty. What is beyond question is that in the late Ottoman years
Jews were beginning to make their presence felt in the city that was to
become the administrative capital of Mandate Palestine, a fact with

important political implications. At the same time, it is important to remember that the increase in the Jewish population did not lead to a corresponding increase in Jewish land-ownership, and Palestinian Arabs continued to own most of the land in and around Jerusalem.

The many discrepancies between sources and methods of enumeration make comparison and evaluation difficult during this period. Different population groups were counted, different geographical areas encompassed and different years surveyed. One salient point in all the estimates of population size in Jerusalem is that the Ottoman censuses typically under-counted women and children, making adjustments for their figures necessary.[8] The Ottoman practice of counting only Ottoman nationals poses a particular problem in Jerusalem, where a large foreign and immigrant community resided.[9] However, Schölch has argued that there has been a tendency by Zionist scholars to exaggerate the undercount of non-Ottoman residents in Jerusalem in order to inflate the size of the Jewish population.[10]

Table 3.1 summarizes the main secondary sources for the population of Jerusalem during the Ottoman era and illustrates the wide range of incompatible data.

It is important to bear in mind that the sources are not strictly comparable since different geographical areas and dates are included, and that many of the widely accepted population figures are based on those of Arthur Ruppin, the head of the World Zionist Organization's Palestine Office in the years before World War I. Ruppin, while claiming to base his figures on Ottoman sources, actually tampered with them to inflate the number of Jews in Palestine.[12] Nonetheless, despite the tendency to overstate the Jewish presence, all the available estimates do indicate a growing Jewish population in the Jerusalem region. At the same time, one can reasonably assume that the Palestinian Arabs at this stage remained a clear majority although the exact proportions are disputed.

The most salient demographic feature concerning Jerusalem during the British Mandate period was the dramatic increase in the total population, Palestinian Arabs and Jews. From the first British census in 1922 to the Mandate government's last estimate in 1946, the total population of the city rose from 62,000 to 164,000 (see table 3.1) a virtual trebling of the population in just over two decades. Immigration by Jews accounted for the largest proportion of the increase, particularly during the thirties.[13] Other important factors

TABLE 3.1: Summary of Jerusalem Population by Different Sources (1840–1914)[a]

	MUSLIMS	CHRISTIANS	JEWS	TOTAL
	1840			
Ben Arieh	4,650	3,350	5,000	13,000
Schölch (1849)	6,148	3,744	1,790	11,682
	1870s			
Ben Arieh	6,500	4,500	11,000	22,000
Schölch (1871)	6,150	4,428	3,780	14,358
McCarthy(1877)	205,016	21,100	6,529	232,645 *sanjak*
	1900			
Ben Arieh	10,000	10,000	35,000	55,000
Schölch (1914)	70,270	32,461	18,190	120,921 *qada*
McCarthy	252,356	14,722	36,216	303,294 *sanjak*

a. Ben Arieh, *Old City*, pp. 279, 358; McCarthy, *Population of Palestine*, p. 7; Schölch, "Jerusalem" in al-'Asali, ed. *Jerusalem in History*, p. 232. 3.1: Summary of Jerusalem population by different sources (1840–1914)[a]

which account for this marked increase include a drop in the mortality rate due to improved hygiene and living conditions: British attention to addressing Jerusalem's endemic water shortage, a critical constraint upon the city's growth, had a direct impact both on the numbers that Jerusalem could sustain and on the living conditions (see chapter 5). Furthermore, the location of large government offices in Jerusalem, the flourishing of Christian institutions, and the opening up of the rural hinterland through the establishment of improved road and rail communication combined to provide greater employment opportunities, stability and security, thereby encouraging population growth (see chapter 7 for a description of Jerusalem's economy during this period).

Table 3.2, giving the population of Jerusalem by religion for this period, is computed from Mandate censuses and estimates.[14] It is now recognized that official British figures require qualification.[15] For example, it is now generally accepted that the 1946 figure for the Jewish population is excessive by a few thousand. The main reason for this was the over-recording of illegal immigrants and of those who arrived in Palestine to live in Jerusalem but subsequently moved to Tel Aviv.[16] A further qualification concerns the restricted nature of the municipal boundaries of Jerusalem. Thus, while the Palestinian Arabs

TABLE 3.2. Population of Jerusalem by Religion, 1922–1946[a]

Year	Muslims	%	Christians	%	Jews	%	Total
1922	13,400	21.4	14,700	23.4	34,100	54.4	62,700
1931	19,900	21.4	19,300	20.8	53,800	57.8	93,100
1946	33,700	20.5	31,300	19.0	99,300	60.4	164,400

a. A category of "Others" amounting to less than 1% of the population is not included.

villages on the periphery such as Lifta, Sheikh Badr, Al-Tur, Silwan, 'Ayn Karim, Dayr Yasin, Shu'fat, al-Malkha, and so on became part of the "daytime population" of a metropolitan Jerusalem area, they were excluded from the population count. Conversely, new Jewish neighborhoods such as Montefiore, Bayit Ha-Kerem, Bet Vegan, Givat Sha'ul, Meqor Hayim, Talpiot, and Ramat Rachel, though outside the Municipality, were regarded as part of the Jerusalem birth registration area and included[17] (see map 3.5).

This selective enumeration distorted the composition of the population of Jerusalem to give an impression of an overwhelming Jewish majority by 1946. If a new metropolitan Jerusalem area had also included the increasingly suburbanized Palestinian Arab villages of the periphery then, some scholars have argued, an approximate parity between the Jewish and the non-Jewish population would be attained.[18] The contrived nature of these borders can be most clearly seen when one examines the map of the municipal borders. A large hook-like feature swings out to the west to include the new Jewish neighborhoods, while in the east, the border hugs the Old City walls to exclude Palestinian suburbanized villages. A more generous spread of the borders would balance out the population in a way that the British Mandate borders did not do.[19] This "gerrymandering" of the municipal borders and the population areas to inflate Jewish population figures should be seen in the light of Britain's commitment to its Jewish National Home policy in Palestine.

In summary, therefore, to obtain an accurate picture of the demographic composition of Jerusalem during the Mandate period further demographic analysis needs to be carried out. Such analysis should adjust the available Mandate figures in three ways: a) scale down the Jewish figures for 1946 by two to three thousand, b) widen the geographical area to include Palestinian Arab settlements on the periphery of the city, such as Lifta, Dayr Yasin, 'Ayn Karim, Maliha, Abu Tur, Silwan, Al Tur, Azariyya, Isawiyya and Anata, and c) separate out the

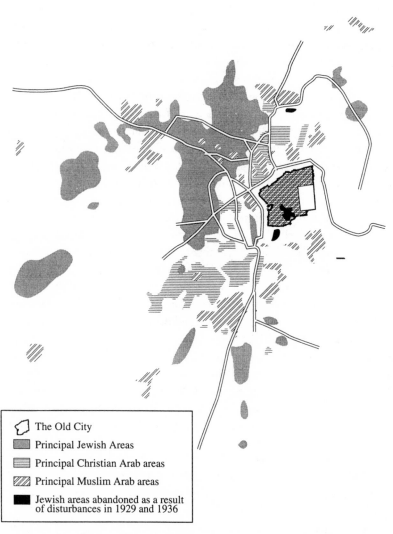

MAP 3.5. Distribution of Jewish and Palestinian Population in Jerusalem, 1945
Source: M. Gilbert, *Jerusalem: Illustrated History Atlas.* Jerusalem: Steimatzky, 1977.

foreign Christians from the totals of Christians. With these amendments one arrives at a figure of approximately 69,000 for Palestinian Arabs and 96–97,000 for Jews for the population of Jerusalem area, as opposed to merely the municipal borders, in 1946.[20]

The geographic distribution of the Palestinian Arab and Jewish population prior to the division of Jerusalem in 1949 and the extension of the Israeli municipal boundaries in 1967 will help explain much of the political impasse over Jerusalem. The north and south of the city were the main areas of Muslim population growth during this period. Areas in the north such as Shaykh Jarrah and American Colony, and in the south such as Abu Tur and Talbiya witnessed the arrival of wealthy and middle-class Muslims engaged in commerce and government service.[21] To the east of the city, villages such as Al-Tur, Silwan, Azariyya (Bethany), and Abu Dis all began to expand and had their numbers supplemented by partially sedentarized Bedouins.[22] To the west of the city the semi-rural Palestinian villages of Lifta, Dayr Yasin, al-Khallaja, al-Malkha, and Sheikh Badr gradually came within Jerusalem's orbit, their population benefitting from the greater employment opportunities available. The Old City also saw a steady increase in the Muslim population, particularly as Jews started to move out in the late thirties and forties due to severe housing congestion and the availability of new housing in the New City.

During the Mandate period wealthy and educated Christian Arab families began to reside in southwestern Jerusalem neighborhoods such as Upper and Lower Baqa'a, Katamon, Talbiyye, and the area known as the German Colony.[23] These were the wealthy quarters of Jerusalem that fell to the Israelis in 1948. Nearly half of the Christian Arab population of Jerusalem lived in the western half of the city.[24] Parts of American Colony, Al-Tur, and Nabi Da'ud in the eastern part of the city were also settled by Christian Arabs. During the Mandate period the Christian community attained the highest numbers ever recorded for Christian residents in the Old City, that is 31,300, 17,528 of whom were Palestinian Arab (see table 3.2). Benvenisti argues that the Christian community had reached "the height of its economic and political power."[25] The Christian Quarter in the Old City was almost entirely Christian.

The main Jewish areas of residence were also in the western parts of the city. Neighborhoods erected along communal lines expanded and in-filling linked them to each other and the central business district along the Jaffa Road running westward from the Old City. In the west areas such as Rehavia, Givat Sha'ul, Kiryat Moshe, Bet HaKerem, and Bayit Vegan were virtually all Jewish. Similarly in the northwest in areas such as Mea She'arim, the Hungarian and Bukharan Quarters and Romema. However, some Jews also lived in or close to predominantly Arab areas such as Talbiyye, Meqor Hayim (adjacent to Baqa'a) in the southwest and in scattered enclaves in the east, such as Shaykh Jarrah and Silwan. The Old City saw a relative decline in the Jewish population as living opportunities increased outside its walls. While the total population of the Old City increased from 22,000 in 1922 to approximately 34,000 in 1944, the Jewish population there dropped from 5,600 in 1922 to approximately 3,000 in the 1940s.[26] By 1947 only 2 percent of the Jewish population of the city was in the Old City.[27] The influx of Palestinian traders and their families from the Hebron area confirmed the Arab and Islamic nature of the Old City. There is no evidence that the British planning authorities deliberately encouraged this residential segregation along ethnic lines. Rather, segregation evolved mainly for reasons of communal assistance and as tensions mounted because of security.

Displacement of Population, 1947–1949

The division of Jerusalem by the 1949 Armistice Agreement was preceded and accompanied by a huge evacuation of the Palestinian Arab population from the western parts of the city to the east and by a much smaller shift of the Jewish population to the west. About 60,000 Palestinian Arabs fled from the New City and from villages west of Jerusalem to Arab-controlled zones.[28] Conversely, approximately 2,000 Jews fled from the eastern part of the city to Jewish-controlled areas.

Even before the fighting began, the Jewish and Arab populations had tended to be separated along ethnic lines. One Israeli demographer, Uri Schmelz, has described the city's demographic situation in the following terms:"Before the end of the Mandate period Jerusalem had been residentially and, to a very large extent, functionally divided de facto into an Arab and a Jewish zone."[29]

But while Schmeltz's description of a divided city is substantially correct, it should be emphasized that this de facto partition was not along East-West lines. Thus, while the only Jews in the eastern sectors were those living in the Old City, some 25,000 Palestinians continued to live in the Arab residential quarters of the New City until the fighting was well underway and were not totally evacuated until the Jewish capture of these areas. In addition, many more thousands of Palestinians lived in the suburbanized villages of the western periphery and in the Jerusalem hinterland beyond.

There were four main phases in the fighting in and around Jerusalem. The period from November 29, 1947, when the UN voted

for the Partition Plan, to the beginning of April 1948, when the
Haganah launched its first formal large-scale military operation,
Operation Nachshon, was marked by quid pro quo attacks in and
around the city by the Haganah and Irgun on the one hand and
Palestinian irregulars on the other. Events during this period that had
a particularly destablizing effect on the city's population included
Haganah's blowing up of the Semiramis Hotel in the heart of
Palestinian residential quarters in West Jerusalem on January 5 (20
civilians killed), Irgun's attack on shops near the Jaffa Gate on January
7 (25 civilians killed), Palestinian explosions at the *Palestine Post* on
February 1 (20 civilians killed), on Ben Yehuda Street on February 22
(57 civilians killed), and the Jewish Agency headquarters (12 civilians
killed).

The second phase coincided largely with Haganah's Operation
Nachshon, launched on April 1 with the aim of carving out a corridor connecting Tel Aviv to Jerusalem, and was marked especially by
fighting to the west of the city. It was during this phase that such mark-
ing events as the death of Palestinian military commander Abd al-
Qadir al-Husseini during the Palestinian counterattack to recapture
the Palestinian village of Castel on April 8 and the massacre at Dayr
Yasin the next day occurred. By the end of the month, the Palestinian
villages on the Western Jerusalem periphery—Saris, Kolonia, Biddu,
Suba, etc.—had been destroyed.

The third phase, involving direct attacks on the Palestinian resi-
dential quarters of West Jerusalem, began with the launching of
Haganah's Operation Jevussi on April 27, part of whose aim was to
capture the entire city. Though the operation as a whole was defeated,
the Haganah occupied the Palestinian neighborhood of Katamon on
April 29 and the remaining Palestinian quarters of West Jerusalem
(Talbiya, Upper Baqa'a, Lower Baqa'a, the "German Colony," and the
"Greek Colony") by April 30.

The final phase commenced on May 14 with Haganah's launching—upon the final withdrawal of British forces and the termination
of the Mandate—of three operations, two of them involving
Jerusalem. Operation Kilshon ("Pitchfork") was to occupy permanently strategic areas in Jerusalem evacuated by departing British
forces, including the Palestinian residential quarters outside the Old
City. Operation Schfifon was aimed at the capture of the Old City
itself. While the Transjordanian Arab Legion, which entered Palestine
on May 15, had reached the northern suburbs of Jerusalem the fol-

lowing day, it held back from advancing despite frantic appeals from the Palestinians barricaded in the Old City. It finally entered on May 19, after the Haganah breached the city walls.[30]

It is difficult to chart with any precision the refugee flows from Jerusalem in the highly fluid situation during the 1948 War. The Palestinian Arab residents of West Jerusalem began to leave on a relatively limited basis during the first months of 1948, spurred by the rising panic that accompanied such events as the blowing up of the Semiramis Hotel and the terror attacks by both sides around the western part of the city. But the first major wave took place during the second phase, when thousands of Palestinian villagers fled or were driven from the villages of West Jerusalem's hinterland; the flow of Arab refugees from the affluent quarters of West Jerusalem also increased during this period as news of Dayr Yasin reverberated among the population, further demoralized by the fall of Tiberias on April 18 and especially of Haifa on the 23rd.[31] A second large wave took place during the third phase of fighting, when the western Arab quarters of the city fell to the Jewish forces. By the end of this phase, virtually the entire Palestinian urban population of some 28,000 had left or been driven from the western quarters, crowding into the Old City and the surrounding Palestinian Arab areas. With the arrival of the Arab Legion, the Jewish quarter in the Old City was evacuated on May 22, 1948 and two thousand Jews left for the Jewish-held western part of the city.[32]

Continuing hostilities affected population levels even after the large movements had ended and immediately prior to the signing of the Armistice Agreement. An Israeli census in the spring of 1948 shows a Jewish population of West Jerusalem of 85,000, down from the official 1946 estimate of 99,300 (see table 3.2). This was further reduced to 58,600 Jews in November 1948, a drop of some 25–30,000 since 1946. Nonetheless, it is important to note that many of these were temporarily residing in Tel Aviv and were able to return to the city at a later stage,[33] and that only some 2,000 Jews from the Old City were actually rendered homeless as a result of the war, as opposed to the tens of thousands of Palestinians who permanently lost their homes in West Jerusalem.

Not all of those fleeing from the West sought refuge in East Jerusalem: many were dispersed to refugee camps to the north and south of the city. Many Christian Arabs stayed with relatives in Bethlehem or Ramallah, while some left the area completely. By the time of the Armistice Agreement in 1949, it has been estimated that approximately half the original Palestinian Arab inhabitants had left the city.[34] Although precise figures are difficult to establish, one researcher has put forward the figure of 7,261 refugees registered as electors in the mid 1950s (the 1954 and 1956 elections).[35] By the early 1960s approximately 12,000 of East Jerusalem's inhabitants were refugees receiving rations from the United Nations Relief and Works Agency for Palestinian Refugees (UNRWA),[36] a figure that did not include, of course, the many thousands of middle-class refugees who never registered as such. No one disputes that the Palestinian population of Jerusalem declined sharply after 1948. A Jordanian census carried out in 1952 estimated the population of East Jerusalem, including Silwan, at 46,700, while the total number of Palestinians in the municipal borders excluding Silwan had been 64,000 in 1946 (See table 3.2.);[37] if Silwan had been excluded in 1952 the drop would have been even more dramatic.

More important than the population decrease in absolute terms, however, is the city's population distribution. As a result of the fighting and the Armistice Agreement, not a single Palestinian remained in the New City, or West Jerusalem, and the only Jews remaining in East Jerusalem were the handful of Jewish women who had married Arabs during the Mandate period.

Jordanian East Jerusalem, 1948–1967

Jordanian-held East Jerusalem was under a cloud of uncertainty in the immediate aftermath of the hostilities as to whether or not the refugees from the New City would be permitted to return to their homes there, when trade and commercial life would resume, what municipal services were to be provided, what political institutions would represent the inhabitants, and so on. As the negotiations among the Israelis, the Arab states, and the Palestinian leadership dragged on, the Armistice Line solidified and Palestinian hopes of an early return to normalcy faded. The annexation of the West Bank and East Jerusalem by Jordan merely served to confirm the lack of progress over any attempts to open up the city and allow the refugees to return. With the Jordanian government determined to build up Amman as the capital of the Kingdom and its reluctance to allow Palestinians much autonomous activity in Jerusalem, employment prospects in the city declined and the population of Jerusalem did not rise significantly. During the nineteen years of Jerusalem's division, the population in the Jordanian municipal borders rose from approximately 45,000 to 70,000.

Demographic changes in Jordanian-held East Jerusalem during the period 1948–1967 were marked by three main features. First, there was only a gradual increase in population and this was below the rate of natural increase. The 1952 census shows that the population of the East Jerusalem Municipality including the adjoining village of Silwan amounted to 46,700 inhabitants. In 1961 this had increased only to 60,500.[38] This gradual increase indicated a considerable outflow of population only partially offset by in-migration from the surrounding hinterland. This emigration can be attributed partly to continuing difficulties over the provision of water and electricity supplies, partly to a Christian Arab exodus, and partly to the development of Amman as the political, administrative, and commercial center of the Kingdom at the expense of Jerusalem, which drew away the professional and middle classes of the city. All these factors severely affected the employment opportunities in the city (see chapter 7).[39]

The second feature of the demographic changes during this period is the disproportionate reduction of Jerusalem's Christian Palestinian Arab population, which suffered most in the mass displacement of the 1948 war. The hostilities and partition of Jerusalem resulted in the loss of their extensive properties in the western part of the city. Some were forced to become refugee squatters in the Old City, others settled in Shaykh Jarrah, the American Colony, or further afield in Ramallah, Beit Hanina, Bayt Jallah, and Bethlehem. Still others made their way to the East Bank of Jordan, Lebanon, and the West. The Jordanian census in 1961 reveals that the Christian (including non-Arab) population in East Jerusalem had dwindled to 11,000, a dramatic drop of 62 percent since 1946.[40] One writer has estimated that between 1948 and 1967 the Christian population of East Jerusalem dropped from 38 percent of the total population to just 15 percent.[41] Many of those left were living in reduced circumstances and unable to leave the city. The Israeli census in 1967 in East Jerusalem showed that while 15.6 percent of the Muslim population of Jerusalem were refugees, as many as 37 percent of Christians in the city were refugees.[42]

The third significant feature to be noted is the in-migration of Palestinian Arabs to Jerusalem particularly from the Hebron region to Jerusalem. In part this development reflected the loss of patronage available to the established Jerusalem families following the 1948 debacle. In part it reflected the political alliances formed by the

Hashemite Royal Family who appointed Hebronites to key positions in Jerusalem. For example, the alliance formed between the al-Ja'abari family and the King ensured Hebronite control over the waqf administration in Jerusalem which in turn led to the leasing of waqf property to Hebronites.[43] Lastly it reflected the departure of Christian Palestinian Arabs and the professional middle classes, creating employment and residential opportunities for Hebronites with connections in Jerusalem.[44]

The main areas that benefitted from this very limited increase in population were the northern and the southeastern parts of East Jerusalem. Wadi Joz and Shaykh Jarrah in the north and Silwan and Abu Tur along the slopes of Mt. Ophel and Wadi Khilwah saw much construction of new homes.[45] Because of the strict planning regulations enforced by the East Jerusalem Municipality, settlement also took place along the edges of the municipal boundaries,[46] where land cost only about 10 percent of what it did inside the boundaries.[47] Because the terrain became increasingly inhospitable and water supplies more and more irregular eastward toward Jericho, housing and commercial growth known as "ribbon development" began northward along the road to Ramallah as far as the airport at Qalandia. Indeed, the former mayor of Arab Jerusalem, Ruhi al-Khatib, estimated the population of the metropolitan area of East Jerusalem to be in the region of 100,000 on the eve of the 1967 War.[48]

Israeli West Jerusalem, 1948–1967

The Armistice Line left Israeli-controlled West Jerusalem as an isolated colony at the end of a political and geographical cul-de-sac. Notwithstanding, the population of the region increased by two and one-half between 1948 and 1967. At the war's end, many Jewish Jerusalemites moved into the Palestinian Arab properties in Upper and Lower Baqa'a, Katamon, Musrara, and Talbiya.[49] Some of the richer depopulated Palestinian Arab villages on the periphery, such as al-Malkha and 'Ayn Karim, were occupied.[50] Later, new immigrants were housed in former British army camps in Talbiyye until public housing was constructed in Katamon and Kiryat HaYovel. In the late fifties housing projects were built in Kiryat Moshe, Bet Hakerem, Bayit Vegan, and Rassco. The Jerusalem "corridor" area was also developed with military agricultural settlements in the north and south receiving approximately 18,000 new people.[51] Of the 41 Palestinian Arab villages in this area, 37 had been totally demolished, while the number of Jewish settlements rose from 6 to 39.[52] Only a handful of Palestinian Arabs with Israeli citizenship lived in West Jerusalem.

By 1966, the Jewish population, which had been estimated at 82,900 in November 1948, had risen to 193,000.[53] This overall increase disguises two significant features of concern to Israeli government and municipal officials. First, compared to the total increase in population in the whole of Israel, Jerusalem was actually in decline. In 1948 Jerusalem comprised 12 percent of the total Israeli population; in 1967 only 8.2 percent.[54] Despite the religious significance of Jerusalem to Judaism, most of the new Jewish immigrants preferred to settle elsewhere.

Second, the increase in Jerusalem's population was not constant, but took place in waves and dips. During and immediately after the 1948 fighting, there was a sharp drop in the population in that area of Jerusalem under Israeli Jewish control. Approximately one quarter of the Jewish population vacated the city.[55] Indeed out-migration to Tel Aviv and emigration abroad became such a serious problem that the new Israeli government was obliged to restrict travel permits from Jerusalem and canceled the food rations of those who left.[56] This situation continued until the mid-fifties; despite massive new immigration, the number of people leaving the city outnumbered the new arrivals (a condition known as negative migratory balance). Indeed the increase in population during this period was more the result of natural increase than of immigration.[57] However, from the mid-fifties onward, migratory balance turned positive because of such factors as improved municipal services, the availability of abandoned Palestinian Arab housing, and increased employment prospects due to the relocation of government ministries in the capital, as well as the perception that the partition of the city had stabilized and that security along the Armistice Line had improved.

Israeli statistics for this period provide a profile of the population, which shows that 99 percent of the population was Jewish with only 1,500 foreign Christians remaining.[58] This is in stark contrast to other Israeli towns such as Haifa, Lydda, and Tel Aviv-Jaffa where significant numbers of Palestinian Arabs remained. None of the Palestinians who fled the Israeli-controlled territory during the fighting had been forbidden to return, and by the time the limited repatriation and family reunion schemes were in operation in the mid-fifties, Palestinian Arab property had been expropriated and passed onto the Jewish National Fund and government agencies concerned exclusively with the absorption of new Jewish immigrants. There was little opportunity for Palestinian Arabs with Israeli citizenship to live in the city.

This did not mean that the Jewish population was homogenous, as 52 percent of new immigrants to the city came from Asian or North African countries, such as Yemen, Iraq, Egypt and the Magharib. A further 30 percent of the population were born in Palestine or Israel.[59] Benvenisti points out the irony in these figures, which suggest that the majority of Jerusalem's population, either from Arab countries or familiar with Arab life, was theoretically well-suited to Jewish-Arab co-existence.[60]

Post-1967 Jerusalem

Within weeks of its victory in June 1967, Israel carried out its de facto annexation of Jordanian East Jerusalem and adjacent parts of the West Bank and incorporated them into an enlarged Israeli Jerusalem Municipality. In so doing, however, the government created a demographic problem: the large Palestinian Arab population diluted the Israeli Jewish demographic dominance and constantly undermined Jerusalem's appearance as an Israeli and Jewish city. To maintain a Jewish demographic superiority, a high rate of Jewish immigration had to be encouraged. At a specially convened Municipal Council meeting in August 1967 Mayor Teddy Kollek, stated that "If we take into account the balance of forces as of today, which is 200,000 Jews and about 70,000 Arabs, plus the natural growth rate of the Arab population which is about twice as high as the already high one in (West) Jerusalem—we must make great efforts to draw further [Jewish] inhabitants to the city."[61]

It was not sufficient simply to encourage Jews to settle in the eastern side since, as Meron Benvenisti, a former Israeli deputy mayor of Jerusalem points out, it would have resulted in the simple transfer of the Jewish population from the west to the east.[62] An absolute increase in the overall Jewish population was necessary,[63] which required an increase in the Israeli Jewish population sufficient to outstrip the Palestinian Arab population. For a quarter of a century the Israeli government had been pursuing this policy which has set the parameters of other related policies relating to economic development, town-planning, and housing construction. As an internal Municipality report expressed it:

> Growth in the Jewish population in Jerusalem stems from three fac-
> tors—natural increase, the balance of migration between the city and
> other settlements in the country and the proportion of immigration
> which Jerusalem receives and its proportion of emigration. It is diffi-
> cult to have any impact on natural increase, but some impact can be had
> on the balance of migration and the ability to attract new immigrants
> in three ways: first, the creation of housing resources to supply the
> needs of the forecast population, second, the creation of work places for
> the population in question, and, three, assuring a high quality of life by
> preserving the quality of the surroundings and providing superior ser-
> vices. . . .[64]

Thus an elaborate program of providing housing at low or interest-
free mortgages and low-cost services was initiated to attract new
immigrants to the city.[65] How seriously the demographic question
was taken can be seen from the fact that one government scheme,
finally abandoned as too ambitious, proposed that 80 percent of all
new immigrants to Israel should be directed to Jerusalem, which
would have entailed the annual addition of 50,000 Jews to the city.[66]
A fourth way to increase the proportion of the Jewish population of
the city not mentioned in the above-cited report was to constrain
Palestinian Arab growth through zoning plans and restrictions upon
construction permits.

The result of all these policies has been an increase in the Israeli
Jewish population from 198,000 in 1967 to 393,000 in 1993. At the
same time, however, the Palestinian Arab population grew from 69,000
to 152,000. Thus, while the Israeli Jewish population almost doubled,
the Palestinian Arab population, despite the vigorous Israeli policies,
more than doubled, keeping the percentage of the city's Arab population much the same, between 25 percent and 28 percent, for more
than a quarter of a century. In this way the basic dilemma of the Israeli
government has not been resolved.

There are three phases in the evolution of Jerusalem's population:
from 1967 to 1976, from 1976 to 1985, and from 1985 to the present.
For clarity, I refer the reader back to the maps and geographical areas
described above (in maps 2.1, 2.5, 3.1, 3.2, 3.3, and 3.4). In the post-
1967 period, the distinction between the municipal area (Area D), the
metropolitan area including the municipal area (Area F), and the metropolitan area alone (excluding the municipal area) (Area G) is especially important.

Phase One: 1967–76

The 1967 War resulted in yet another displacement of the Palestinian Arab population. According to one demographer, 14,000 inhabitants of the former Jordanian Municipality of East Jerusalem fled the country altogether immediately after the war.[67] Another estimate gives the number of Palestinian Arabs who left the country from the area that became the enlarged Israeli Municipality at approximately 20,000.[68] These refugees were joined by a steady trickle of deportations as political resistance to the Israeli occupation mounted. Further displacement involving the population of the annexed areas remained within the occupied territories: the some 650 Palestinian Arabs evicted from the Old City when the Municipality demolished the Magharib quarter on June 10 to make way for a plaza fronting the Western Wall[69] ultimately ended up, after having been temporarily housed in public buildings in East Jerusalem, in the outskirts of the village of Ram north of Jerusalem outside the new municipality boundaries. Similarly, most of the some 4,000–5,000 Palestinians evicted as a result of the later (second half of the 1970s) expropriation of Palestinian Arab property in the area designated as the enlarged Jewish quarter[70] were also obliged to take up residence outside the municipal boundaries.

An Israeli census in September 1967 placed the total population of the enlarged East and West Jerusalem at 267,800 inhabitants[71]— 196,800 Israeli Jews and 71,000 Palestinian Arabs.[72] Assuming that the population of East Jerusalem, including the suburbs of Silwan and Abu Tur, was 66,000 on the eve of the 1967 War, the enlargement of the municipal borders of Jerusalem following the annexation—taking into account the loss of some 20,000 Arabs displaced in the immediate aftermath of the fighting and the careful drawing of municipal boundaries to avoid insofar as possible areas of high Arab population density—added only about 5,000 Arabs to the city.[73] The proportion of Israeli Jews to Palestinian Arabs in the new Municipality of Jerusalem (Area D) was thus 74.2 percent to 25.8 percent. In the metropolitan area of Jerusalem (Area F), the area within daily commuting distance of Jerusalem center,[74] the proportion of Israeli Jews to Palestinian Arabs almost reached parity. Here the Palestinian population was approximately 201,000, or 47.2 percent of the total Palestinian Arab and Jewish population combined.[75] A few years later, in 1970, the Palestinian share had risen slightly to 48 percent while the Jewish share had declined to 52 percent. In this way, despite the departure of up to 20,000 Palestinians from the Jerusalem area and the introduction of new Israeli Jewish residents, the Israeli government was presented with the disturbing fact of a growing Palestinian preponderance in the Jerusalem hinterland.[76] Indeed, in the metropolitan area alone (Area G, outside the municipal boundaries), the proportion of Palestinian Arabs rose from 82.6 percent to 85 percent of the total population.[77]

These important statistics explain the Israeli government's hesitations to consider the enlargement of the Jerusalem municipal boundaries to correspond to either topographical features or residential or commercial integrity. The greater the enlargement the greater the number of Palestinian Arabs to be included. It also explains to a considerable extent the dispute that developed between the Israeli government and the Jerusalem municipality over the construction of Israeli Jewish settlements in the metropolitan area.[78] Creating a Jewish demographic dominance in both the metropolitan area and the enlarged Municipality, Municipal officials argued, would overextend the growth of Jerusalem's Jewish population. The drift of the Israeli Jewish population from within the borders of the Municipality (Area D) to the metropolitan areas outside the Municipal borders (Area G) would result in the "thinning" or outflow of population in some of the central West Jerusalem areas. It is also important to remember that this debate took place as the Palestinian Arab population in both the metropolitan area of Jerusalem and within the Municipality itself continued to rise. Thus already within a year or two of the 1967 War the goal of an Israeli Jewish preponderance in Jerusalem was throwing up difficult dilemmas for the Israelis. The strategy to overcome them was to be threefold: to facilitate the settlement of as many new immigrants as possible, to provide the socioeconomic conditions able to attract and retain the Israeli Jewish population, and to restrict Palestinian growth in and around Jerusalem.

The early seventies saw the first spurt in the growth of the Israeli Jewish population of the city. This was primarily a result of the construction of large housing projects and settlements to the north and east of Jerusalem and of government incentives to settle Israeli Jews in the annexed areas. The fastest growth occurred during the first three years of the decade, yet by 1974 the proportion of Israeli Jews within the municipal boundaries dropped to 72.9 percent and that of the Palestinian Arab rose to 27.1 percent of the total population. This failure to shift the proportions more in favor of the Israeli Jewish population is of particular significance since the Israeli government showed some success in attracting and settling Israeli Jews in Jerusalem. The absolute total of the Israeli Jewish population in the Municipality borders (Area D) grew by 55,000, to 251,000, in 1974. At the same time, the Palestinian Arab population grew by 22,000, to 93,200.[79] The main reasons for the growth in the Palestinian Arab population during this first phase lay in the high natural increase, reduced emigration, high in-migration from the rural hinterland as a result of greater employment opportunities (such as building Israeli Jewish housing estates and settlements), and the gradual return of small numbers of refugees through family reunification schemes.

In the Jerusalem metropolitan area (Area F) there was very little change in the proportion of Israeli Jews to Palestinian Arabs, with 51.4 percent of the population being Israeli Jews.[80] However, in the metropolitan area alone, that is, outside the Municipal boundaries (Area G), the proportion of Palestinian Arabs increased from 82.6 percent in 1967 to 85.4 percent in 1974. In absolute terms the Palestinian Arab population in this area increased by 46,000, while that of the Israeli Jewish population by only 2,000.[81] This is a dramatic statistic revealing the huge increase in the Palestinian Arabs around the edges of the Municipal borders and explains the acceleration of the government's settlement policies in the following decade.

Phase Two: 1976–1985

Two further surges in the growth of Jerusalem's population, particularly that of the Israeli Jewish population, mark the late 1970s and the mid-1980s. The Israeli Jewish population saw an increase of 61,000 people, rising from 266,000 in 1976 to 327,700 in 1985. This was, nevertheless, less than 7,000 a year and below government targets. The implications of this are highlighted when one considers that the proportional increase in the Palestinian Arab population was in fact greater. Between 1976 and 1985, the Palestinian Arab population within the Municipal boundaries (Area D) rose from 100,000 to 130,000. Although only half as great as the increase in the Israeli Jewish population, the Arab increase was from a base figure of two and half times less. Governmental and municipal concern was even greater when statistics revealed that more than half the Muslim population of Jerusalem was under the age of 17.[82]

Again, much of the increase in the Jewish population was due to government incentives. Following the passing of the Basic Law on Jerusalem in 1980, much effort was expended in attempting to attract

TABLE 3.3. Population of Jerusalem by Population Group, Jews and "non-Jews" (mostly Palestinian Arabs)

	JEWS	NON-JEWS	TOTAL	% JEWS	% NON-JEWS
1967	197,700	68,600	266,300	74.2	25.8
1972	230,300	83,500	313,800	73.4	26.6
1983	306,300	122,400	428,700	71.4	28.6
1987	346,100	136,500	482,600	71.7	28.3
1988	353,900	139,600	493,500	71.7	28.3
1989	361,500	142,600	504,100	71.7	28.3
1990	378,200	146,300	524,500	72.1	27.9
1991	393,000	152,000	545,000	72.1	27.9

Source: Years 1967–1990 from M. Choshen and S. Greenbaum, eds. *Statistical Yearbook of Jerusalem*, No. 9, 1990. (Jerusalem: Jerusalem Institute for Israel Studies, 1992), p. 25. Year 1991 from I. Kimhi, "Outline of the Development of Jerusalem, 1988–1993," in *Urban Geography in Jerusalem, 1967–1992*. (Jerusalem: Jerusalem Institute for Israel Studies, 1993), p. 21.[83]

new immigration. Low-cost housing, accompanied by low-interest mortgages and subsidized municipal services, was constructed in huge suburban settlements—at Neve Ya'aqov, Ramot, East Talpiot, and Gilo—ringing the traditional center of Jerusalem. By 1983, the Israeli Jewish population in the annexed parts of the Municipality (i.e., East Jerusalem—Area E), amounted to 51,000 people, approximately one-sixth of the Israeli Jewish population in Jerusalem.[84] But the Palestinian population there was 122,000, so sixteen years after annexation and despite intensive settlement policies, Jews still constituted no more than 40 percent of the total population in the annexed areas. Furthermore, even this gain was achieved at the expense of developing the western side. Thus, while there continued to be a rise in the absolute numbers of Israeli Jews in the entire municipal area (Area D), the transfer of Jewish population from West Jerusalem to the annexed areas (Area E), which Benvenisti feared so much, started during this period.[85] For example, the Israeli Jewish population of the central urban district of Musrara dropped by 50 percent, and that of Nahlaot by 40 percent.[86]

The increase in the Palestinian Arab population during this period (1976–85) was due to much the same factors as in the earlier period: high natural increase, particularly among the Muslims, and internal migration from the rural hinterland, especially from the Hebron area. There were also political factors involved. During this period housing grants were made available by a Joint Jordanian-PLO Committee which encouraged people to settle in the area (see chapter 4). Indeed, the high natural increase was not entirely free of political intentions, as Palestinian political culture supported large families as a counterweight to Jewish immigration. Nonetheless, as a result of government settlement policies, the preponderance of Palestinian Arabs in the Jerusalem metropolitan area including the Municipality (Area F) was held in check. Out of a total population of approximately 650,000, by 1984 52 percent were Israeli Jewish and only 48 percent Palestinian Arabs.[87] On the other hand, within the Jerusalem metropolitan area beyond the Municipal boundaries (Area G), the proportion of Palestinian Arabs rose to an astonishing 91.5 percent in 1985, that is, 182,000 Palestinians to 16,900 Jews.[88] This rise threatened to defeat any gains made by the Israelis in Area E, and plans were drawn up to increase the Israeli demographic presence in this area too. The late Prime Minister Rabin's post-election declaration that the settlements in Area G are security settlements, and therefore non-negotiable, was part of the strategy to head off the political implications attendant upon the Palestinian preponderance in the hinterland of Jerusalem.

Two other features of this change in the Palestinian Arab population during both phases should be mentioned. First, the relative size of the Christian population of Jerusalem continued to decline markedly. In 1967, the Christian population of the city was estimated at 11,960.[89] By 1983 this number had increased only to 13,730, representing a drop in percentage of the total population from 4.4 percent to 3.2 percent.[90] It is worth remembering that in 1946 it was estimated that the Christians constituted 31,300 or 19 percent of the population of the city.[91] The relative decline in the years following the occupation was due to lower natural growth rates than the Muslim population and continued emigration. Moreover, almost 10 percent of Jerusalem's Christians reside in institutions that indicate either the elderly nature of the population or the prevalence of foreign ecclesiaticals or both.[92] Tsimhoni has estimated that 91.6 percent of the Christian population of Jerusalem were Arabic-speaking and therefore, in the main, indigenous Palestinians.[93] A major problem for the Palestinian Christian community during this period was the scarcity of housing. An Israeli census in 1972 estimated that 55.8 percent of the Christian population of Jerusalem lived in the Old City, mostly in the Christian quarter, where they formed 25 percent of the total population.[94] Overcrowding led the Armenian and Roman Catholic Patriarchates to build apartments outside the Old City in Beit Hanina.

The second feature to note is the rapid growth in the size of the religious and orthodox Jewish communities, known as *haredim*, in Jerusalem. Varying definitions of what constitutes a "religious," "orthodox," or "ultra-orthodox" Jew make any accurate assessment of their numbers difficult, but estimates of their numbers in the mid-eighties range from above 20 percent to 38.5 percent of the Israeli Jewish population.[95] Up to 70 percent of these live in religious areas or more strictly defined orthodox neighborhoods (see chapter 6). Schmelz sums up the implications of this feature clearly:

Since the Jewish population of Jerusalem now grows mainly by natural increase and the ultra-orthodox have more children—and are also less prone to migrate from the city—their share seems bound to increase, unless there is a considerable in-migration of other Jews."[96] The growth of this population has led to their expansion out of their traditional areas in the north and west of Jerusalem to adjacent areas and to the establishment of new religious neighborhoods in the annexed areas.[97] The religious beliefs of the orthodox population lead them to forcefully impose their views on culture, entertainment, and Sabbath and Holy Days laws on their secular neighbors.[98] Planners are aware that these activities are contributing to the out-migration of young Jewish professional secular couples from the central areas of West Jerusalem to the annexed areas or the coastal plain.[99] Thus the section of the population that contributes in the most sustainable way to the growth of the Israeli Jewish population, that is through natural growth, is that section which also has a negative effect on the government's and Municipality's efforts to attract more secular Jews to the city and retain them.

Phase Three: 1985 to the Present

The third and most recent phase in the growth of Jerusalem's population comes from the waves of Jewish immigrants resulting from the liberalization of the Soviet Union's emigration policies before its collapse combined with the corresponding tightening of restrictions on entry to the United States. Because of the political sensitivity of settlement in the annexed areas of Jerusalem, exact figures on Soviet Jewish immigration to Jerusalem were withdrawn from the public domain. However, in 1989, the Minister of Absorption stated that 11 percent of the 12,700 Soviet Jewish immigrants—approximately 1,500—had settled in the Jerusalem "area."[100] Assuming this 11 percent to be valid for previous years, one could conclude on the basis of the estimated average annual in-migration of Israeli Jews for those years of about 8,500,[101] that some 900 Soviet Jews a year settled there from 1985 to 1989. This figure seems too low, however, not only because of the high profile of this in-migration to Jerusalem in the Israeli press, but also because of the special facilities for their absorption provided by the Municipality. Indeed, the impact of the immigration was such that the Municipality set up a special body to coordinate the work of the Ministry of Absorption, the Jewish Agency, the Jerusalem Municipality, and voluntary agencies. Employment fairs and cheap furniture rental were arranged to ease their entry into Jerusalem society. The records of the coordinating body show that housing was sought for them in the annexed areas of the Municipality such as Gilo, Ramat Eshkol, Ramot, Neve Ya'aqov and Pisgat Ze'ev.[102] More recent statistics reveal that 30,000 Jews arrived in Jerusalem in the years 1990–1992.[103] However, in the absence of more detail, it is impossible to say whether such immigration was confined only to the Jerusalem municipal area (Area D) or also included the metropolitan area (Area G).

Nonetheless, despite continuing Jewish immigration from abroad, the migratory balance for the Jewish population of Jerusalem has been negative. Between 1982 and 1989, the city lost between 1,400 and 1,800 Jews annually (except for two years, 1986 and 1987). The total deficit over this period was 6,067.[104] But while approximately 22 percent of this total left for Tel Aviv, the highest proportion departed for the surrounding metropolitan area of Jerusalem (Area G) and the West Bank. Municipal officials blamed this drift from Jerusalem to the new outlying settlements on government policies using low-cost housing and low-interest mortgages to attract young couples from Jerusalem itself.[105] According to figures supplied by the Foundation for Middle East Peace, a Washington-based Israeli settlement monitoring unit, approximately 44,000 Israeli Jews lived in Israeli settlements outside the Jerusalem Municipality but within the metropolitan area inside the Green Line (Area G) in September 1992.[106]

Meanwhile, the Palestinian Arab population both in and around Jerusalem continued to rise, not to mention the thousands—estimates range from 10,000 to 20,000[107]—of Palestinians living illegally (because unregistered) within the Municipality boundaries. Thus, by 1993, the total population of Jerusalem was estimated at about 670,000: 400,000 Jews and between 150,000 and 170,000

Palestinians.[108] What is of particular interest in the study of Jerusalem is the spatial distribution of that growth. If growth of the Jewish and Palestinian Arab population had taken place within their pre-1967 areas—that is, Jewish West Jerusalem and Arab East Jerusalem respectively—the political future of Jerusalem would not be as fraught as it is today. It is because Jewish growth has occurred in the eastern sectors of the city that the political aspects of demographic change in Jerusalem are so salient.

Population statistics for the annexed areas vary, but the Jerusalem Institute for Israel Studies estimated 135,000 Jews and 155,000 Palestinians in 1990.[109] According to the *Report on Israeli Settlement in the Occupied Territories*, an Israeli majority was declared for East Jerusalem (Area E) by Deputy Mayor Abraham Kehila in a July 1993 report to Jerusalem's Planning Commission, with 168,000 Israeli Jews and 154,000 Palestinians. But when unregistered Palestinians are included, according to this same report, the number of Palestinians rises to 180,000.[110] Table 3.4 provides a breakdown of population figures by neighborhood, the neighborhoods being shown in maps 3.1, 3.2, 3.3, and 3.4. The discrepancy in totals can be explained by the different dates on which the estimates were made and by the methods of calculation.

To a large extent, the attainment of demographic parity or even superiority in the annexed areas points to the Israeli government's overwhelming success in meeting its strategic aim of making its control over the city irreversible. Given the lack of leverage on the Palestinian side, the chances of prising out new settlements and settlers from Area E as part of a negotiated settlement seem virtually nil. Yet it is also clear that the demographic struggle for Jerusalem is not completely over, and that the Israeli government cannot rest on its laurels. The Israeli Jewish population is bleeding away to the coast, and requires heavy government investment to induce it to stay. Similarly, the municipal area is now congested and requires expansion, which raises the question of how to absorb or neutralize the Palestinian majority in the hinterland. The situation is fluid and dynamic, and the negotiators will have to deal with an ever-changing set of variables.

The demography of Jerusalem since 1967 can be summed up in the following way: The Israeli government's determination to secure its control over Jerusalem has led to a strong commitment to and heavy investment in increasing the Israeli Jewish population of the city. In this it has been assisted by steady Jewish immigration to the city, by the willingness of this population to settle in areas annexed to the city, and by sufficient funds to create employment and services conducive to attracting new population. Conversely, its policies have been hampered by a corresponding steady growth in the Palestinian Arab population not only within the municipal borders itself but also in the immediate hinterland. Low natural growth rate among Israeli Jews, apart from the orthodox section of the community, and a high out-migratory rate have also impeded government policies.

In the short term, the demographic contest has arrived somewhat at an impasse. The demographic balance between Israeli Jews and Palestinian Arabs is much the same today as it was in 1967. However, in the medium term, two key factors have disturbing implications for the Israeli government. First, the high natural growth rate of the orthodox Jewish community is changing the character of Jerusalem and neutralizing efforts by the government and the Municipality to attract and retain the young skilled and productive work force the city needs. The out-migratory trend can be expected to increase, and will only be partially offset by the higher natural growth rate among ortho-dox Jews. Second, by the turn of the century, the available space for housing construction, industry, and services will be exhausted and the government and Municipality will be obliged to consider the further expansion of the municipal borders. To expand westward again after the expansion in that direction in 1992 will send the wrong political signals not only to the Palestinians, the Arab states, and the interna-tional community, but also to the Israeli Jewish population in Jerusalem. But to expand eastward, northward, or southward will mean the absorption of at least another 100,000 Palestinian Arabs into Jerusalem, which will have the effect of contradicting all the efforts and policies of the Israeli government since 1967.

There are some indications of how the Israeli government intends to overcome these dilemmas. By declaring the settlements in the met-ropolitan area of Jerusalem to be "security" settlements and therefore non-negotiable, the government is indicating that the issue is no longer withdrawal to the Armistice Line but control over the wider metropolitan area. Thus the government can be expected to continue to strive for demographic superiority in and around Jerusalem, con-tinuing to direct immigrants to these areas despite the Declaration of Principles signed in Oslo in 1993. By the same token, the legal status of the metropolitan area beyond the municipal boundaries can be expected to remain unchanged; indeed, it would seem likely that the

Municipality's planning and zoning regulations, possibly even Development Area status, will be applied there as well. In practice, then, development of these outlying areas will probably be pursued *as if* they were part of the Municipality without any changes in the borders occurring. In keeping with this scenario, it is interesting to note the way in which the borders of Ma'ale Adumim, the large settlement to the east of Jerusalem along the road to Jericho, have been extended to a point just short of the Jerusalem Municipality.

As indicated at the beginning of the chapter, the Israeli government's determination to assert its control over the Jerusalem region in the face of demographic facts, as well as in face of the range of cultural, religious and political facts, does not auger well for the future of the peace process. An Israeli-controlled Jerusalem metropolitan area will amount to as much as one-third of the West Bank and truncate the emerging Palestinian area further. Even if this were acceptable politically, a West Bank divided in two by an Israeli-controlled zone would hardly be feasible in economic terms. Similarly, an Israeli-controlled zone half of whose population refused to recognize Israeli sovereignty over them would be inherently unstable.

TABLE 3.4 Population in Geographic Areas.

Area A: Mandatory Municipal Borders
As in Table 3.3

Area B: Israeli West Jerusalem, 1948–1967

	Israeli Jews	Palestinians + non Jews
	000's	000's
1948	82.9	2.4
1951	138.6	n/a
1961	165.0	n/a
1966	193.0	n/a

source: U. O. Schmelz, *Modern Jerusalem's Demographic Evolution*, 1987.

Area C: Jordanian East Jerusalem

	Palestinians	Jews
	000's	000's
1952	46.7	—
1961	60.5	—

source: Schmelz, 1987.
Area D: Enlarged Jerusalem, 1967–1992
As in Table 3.3.

Area E: East Jerusalem and the Annexed Areas, 1967–1993

	Israeli Jews	Palestinian Arabs
	000's	000's
1967	—	71.0
1973	51.0	88.1
1985	70.0	130.0
1990	135.0	146.3
1993	152.0	155.0

source: G. Aronson, *Report on Israeli Settlement*, 1994 and statistical abstracts. (Hereinafter *Settlement Report*).

Area F: Metropolitan Area (Enlarged Jerusalem and 10 mile radius)

	Israeli Jews	Palestinians
	000's	000's
1967	225.7	201.4
1970	245.1	226.1
1972	264.7	244.0
1974	284.5	269.1
1984[a]	340.0	310.0

	Israeli Jews	Palestinians
	000's	000's
1985[a]	344.6	312.0
1992	445.8[b]	400.0[c]

source: I. Kimhi, "Aspects of the Urban Ecology of Jerusalem," 1973.
[a] based on I. Kimhi, "Outline of the Development of Jerusalem, 1988–1993, 1993.
[b] based on *Settlement Report*, 1994 and statistical abstracts.
[c] estimated based on previous growth rates.

Area G: Metropolitan Area excluding enlarged Jerusalem, 1967–1992

	Israeli Jews	Palestinians
	000's	000's
1967	28.0	132.8
1972	29.3	159.2
1974	30.6	178.8
1985	16.9	182.0
1992	44.8	245.0

Sources:
Years 1967–74, Kimhi, 1973, but includes larger area then 10 mile radius;
Year 1985, Kimhi, 1993, but area not clearly defined;
Year 1992, *Settlement Report*, 1992, but area defined as 10 mile radius.

4

Planning and Housing Policy: "Conquest by Architectural Means"?

"We desire—and we can say this openly—that Jerusalem will forever have a clear Jewish stamp on it, and that this city will not be one where over time, there will be some sort of 'parity.' There is nothing more dangerous for this city. We did not fight for that, our boys did not fall for that—neither in the war of liberation or in these past days."

—Mordechai Ish Shalom, Council Member and former Mayor of West Jerusalem, Council Meeting, August 13, 1967

The growth of a city, or any other human settlement, is a result of a combination of physical, economic, and social factors. These factors encompass such things as a landscape suitable for urban construction, a productive agricultural hinterland, the availability of sufficient and regular water supply, good access to other urban centers for trade and commerce, and, finally, a defensible terrain. If one were to examine a topographical or geological map of Jerusalem one would soon discover that it lacks many of these advantages. It is, for example, located in rocky highlands, far from both the main trade routes running along the coastal plain and the Levantine ports, and it is on the very edge of a desert terrain with limited water supplies and a narrow agricultural base.[1] Furthermore, its military and strategic value was of no great consequence: occupiers of Palestine from Alexander to Napoleon simply bypassed Jerusalem on their way to the key cities on the coastal plain.

The key to understanding the significance of Jerusalem and its dramatic urban growth in the twentieth century lies not in its trade or strategic location but in its significance for the world's three Abrahamic religions. The presence of priests, religious scholars, rabbis, mystics, ecclesiastical administrators, and jurists all required mosques, synagogues, churches, seminaries, colleges, public and ritual baths, and residential quarters for themselves, their followers, and the lay adherents of their faith and sect. Similarly, the increasing flow of pilgrims, scholars, and tourists required servicing and support systems. Thus hostels, inns, guides, religious paraphernalia, souvenirs, and foods needed to be provided, generating a local economy irrespective of trade connections and indigenous resources. To a large extent, religion acted as a primitive engine for economic and urban development in Jerusalem until the mid-twentieth century (see chapter 7).

The city's physical shape did not change dramatically until the second quarter of the twentieth century. Salah ed-Din, the Muslim liberator of Jerusalem from the Christian Crusaders in the twelfth century, laid the foundations and main urban features of the Old City. His task was taken up with elegance and grace by the Mamluk builders a century later.[2] In the sixteenth century the Ottoman Sultan, Sulayman the Magnificent, built the walls that enclose the Old City to this day. Yet it was not until the end of the nineteenth and the early part of the twentieth centuries that any notable construction took place outside the Old City walls. At this point two additional factors encouraging urban growth came into play: the flow of new Jewish immigrants that had begun in the 1880s but greatly increased in the 1920s as a result of the British government's commitment to a Jewish National Home in Palestine, and the consolidation of Jerusalem as an administrative center for the British Mandatory government. Dispersed and rapid urban growth began in the "New City" outside the city walls during the British Mandate period.

These factors were further emphasized in 1948 after the division of the city, when West Jerusalem was declared the political capital of the new State of Israel and became the site of government offices and other national administrations. Furthermore, having failed to capture the more important tourist sites, which were in Jordanian-held territory, the new Israeli government was compelled to broaden the economic base of the western part of the city to prevent an economic and social decline. It created industrial zones on the urban peripheries for light manufacturing, thereby adding another factor to stimulate the city's growth.

However, it is important to emphasize that while these political and religious factors were prime movers in Jerusalem's urban growth, they were, nonetheless, constrained by the topography of the site and by the availability of water. With a barren, steeply dropping desert terrain on the eastern side of the city, the natural direction for urban development has been along the broad ridges stretching to the west and south-west, and to a lesser extent to the north. Prior to 1967 the main avenues of construction did indeed take place in these directions. On the western side of the city the main Israeli construction followed the ridges toward 'Ayn Karim, while on the eastern side "ribbon" development took place northwards toward Ramallah.[3]

Similarly, the demographics of urban growth largely are determined by the availability of water, and a centralized and competent administration that can construct, distribute, and monitor a complex water system. The rapid population growth of West Jerusalem, in contrast to that in East Jerusalem, was largely possible as a result of government and municipal investment in providing sufficient water from new sources.[4]

The post-1967 period has witnessed an explosion in the urban development of Jerusalem, particularly in the annexed areas in the east. As already mentioned, the eastern areas do not lend themselves to large-scale construction and the provision of urban services. The establishment of new Jewish residential neighborhoods in East Jerusalem and the annexed areas (Area E as defined in chapter 3) can be viewed as a measure of the government's determination to assert physical control over a disputed and inhospitable domain. The explosion in growth is a manifestation of the triumph of political will and the competence of Israeli civil engineers over topographical and environmental factors. In examining the objectives of the Israeli government in the urban development of Jerusalem, one can safely conclude that geopolitical considerations overrode town-planning considerations.

A good example of this is the road system. While the undulating contours of the city make modern mass transit systems unfeasible, the particular configuration of the ring and arterial roads and public transport actually built by the city raises questions on the extent to which their purpose is to serve the urban needs of all the inhabitants as opposed to establishing political and physical control over the Palestinian areas, which previously had been without such an extensively planned system. The consensus among Palestinian Arabs of East Jerusalem and the adjacent area of the West Bank is that the new roads not only integrate the outlying Israeli Jewish settlements into the core areas of Jerusalem but also serve to divide the Palestinian areas, breaking up the physical contiguity of those areas to each other and to the West Bank.

The geopolitical nature of the urban growth in Jerusalem has undoubtedly created a wide array of urban and planning problems. Extending the borders of the municipality of Jerusalem for demo-

graphic reasons, establishing military rule over the West Bank hinterland, and making Jerusalem a national capital of a Jewish state have all
created bottlenecks and shortages, as well as fostering discriminatory
and targeted provision of housing and services. However, not all of the
urban problems can be attributed to the political imperatives of the
Israeli government and it is important to differentiate between the
two. Some problems would accompany rapid growth and modernization whatever the political circumstances and these have to be borne
in mind when assessing those problems that are primarily the result of
the former.[5]

Early Issues in Planning in Jerusalem

Urban development during the British Mandate period occurred
largely in four different locations. First, there was the construction of
approximately forty Jewish neighborhoods and residential areas in the
northwestern part of the city and stretching along the western ridges.
These included neighborhoods such as Bet Ha-Kerem, built in 1922,
Kerem Avraham in 1926, Tel Arza in 1931, and were designed to
accommodate the rising influx of European Jews immigrating to
Palestine as a result of the British Mandate's commitment to a Jewish
National Home.[6] Second was the Palestinian Arab residential con-
struction in the southwest during the 1930s. Neighborhoods such as
Talbiya, Katamon, and Baqa'a were built and settled mainly by wealthy
Palestinian Christians leaving the confines of the Old City and from
Bethlehem (see map 3.5). Third, scattered Palestinian Arab building
also took place to the north of the Old City in suburbs such as Shaykh
Jarrah, Wadi Joz, and Shu'fat and at the western peripheries in the old
villages of Lifta, Dayr Yassin, and Khallat al-Turba. Some Palestinian
Arab construction also took place in areas of high Jewish concentra-
tion such as Sheikh Badr, just south of the Jewish neighborhood of
Romema; there was also some Jewish building in mainly Arab areas,
for example in Neve Ya'aqov, parts of Silwan, and the *kibbutz* Ramet
Rachel. Fourth, new commercial construction of mixed ethnic origin
took place in the "Central Business District" stretching along the Jaffa
Road and tributary streets between New Gate and Herut Square.[7]

As mentioned earlier, the west, southwest, and northwest were the
natural directions for expansion because of the topography of the land
outside of the Old City. Economic factors served to emphasize this
trend. The western approaches of the city were close to the road and

rail links to the increasingly busy port of Jaffa and the coastal cities which were of growing importance to Jerusalem's nascent commercial world. Investment in construction in these areas by wealthy Palestinian Arabs and Jews was understandable. In their desire to protect and enhance the religious and aesthetic characteristics of Jerusalem, the British Mandate authorities were content to encourage this urban development away from the Old City. The main thrust of British planning, therefore, was the channeling of urban development westward through the adoption of a number of urban plans, the latest of which was the Kendall Plan of 1944.[8] The Holy City was regarded as a religious, cultural, and administrative center and its economy was to be based upon the services these functions required. A productive and manufacturing economic base was seen as a detraction from higher characteristics. The same sensibilities led British planners to minimize the space available for industrial development, consigning industrial zones usefully but grudgingly to the extreme peripheries close to the railway station and the road leading to the coast.[9]

In order to establish religious and aesthetic perspectives as guiding principles in the planning of the city it was necessary to preserve the Old City as a religious and cultural monument. This was a theme running throughout the planning history of the Mandate and was responsible for the introduction of regulations to create a park or "green" zone around the city walls and along the slopes to the east, northeast, and southeast. No buildings were allowed close to the walls and many existing buildings were demolished. As the Civic Adviser to the City of Jerusalem, Charles Ashbee, declared of the plan in 1920: "It isolates the Holy City, sets it, so to speak, in the centre of a park thus recognising the appeal it makes to the world; the city of an idea."[10]

The Old City, in this view, was to be preserved as a relic, detached from its immediate environs for both aesthetic and ideological reasons. An Islamic and Arab city sprawling beyond the walls and into the valleys and ridges around it did not appeal to the cultural perceptions of western Christian planners. No allowance was made for the vital interplay between the religious and commercial core of the Old City and the semi-urban and agricultural hinterland. This conception of the Old City as a religious and cultural monument set a disturbing precedent. As will be discussed below, it was used by Israeli planners in their attempts to reduce the Palestinian population of the Old City and detach it from its West Bank hinterland.

The period of Jordanian government rule in the city's eastern part left a distinctive imprint upon Jerusalem's future urban development. The period can best be characterized as a balance between topographical and environmental factors and planning guidelines carried over from the Mandate period. The Armistice Line left the eastern part of the city seriously crippled: only 11 percent of the former Municipal area was in Jordanian hands.[11] While the Jordanians secured control over the prime historical sites in the Old City, Palestinian Arabs had lost their affluent suburbs with good quality housing stock in the New City as well as the main commercial area along the Jaffa road, and many of the key services. For example, the main reservoir was on the western side, so urban development in the Municipal area of East Jerusalem and its immediate hinterland was effectively constrained by the shortage of water supplies. It was not until the early sixties that regular and sufficient water could be provided.[12] Inhabitants of Jordanian East Jerusalem were obliged to resort to old wells and cisterns. These problems, exacerbated by the sudden influx of refugees into the eastern areas as a result of the war, encouraged people to move to Amman or other areas in the environs of Jerusalem where there was less demand on natural springs, wells, and cisterns.

The impact of these factors upon the urban growth of East Jerusalem was heightened by poor economic opportunities. The division of the city had severed the road links between East Jerusalem and Bethlehem, hampering local trade and economic growth. Furthermore the downgrading of Jerusalem as a government administrative center in contrast to the upgrading of Amman as the formal capital of the enlarged Hashemite Kingdom further decreased the economic base of the eastern part of the city. On the other hand the sixties heralded the era of mass tourism in Western Europe and East Jerusalem tourist economy and ancillary services did benefit from the presence of the key Holy Places in the Old City. A perceived threat to the Muslim shrines of the Dome of the Rock and the al-Aqsa mosque from political uncertainties increased the Muslim pilgrimage trade to East Jerusalem. It is important to note that while government investment in East Jerusalem could not match that taking place in Amman, the large religious foundations, or *waqfs*, in Jerusalem invested considerable sums into the commercial development of Jerusalem, especially in the area around Salah ed-Din Street to the north of Herod's Gate.[13]

The Jordanian government was anxious to continue the planning priorities laid down by the British and, in the main, the basic outlines persisted.[14] It is perhaps ironic that as a result of this policy, it was an

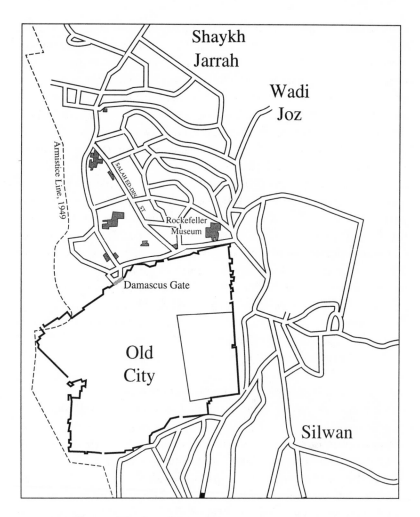

MAP 4.1. Center of East Jerusalem

Arab government that continued the preservation of the Old City as
a cultural monument. The East Jerusalem Arab municipality attempted
to adhere to the British proposals to retain the immediate environs of
the city walls to the east and northeast as green zones and parks.
However, as a result of the influx of refugees, semi-permanent shacks
were erected close to the walls, both inside and outside. In addition,
with the growth in population of Silwan and the eastern villages, the
Dung Gate was made into a major entrance and had to be widened.[15]
Some adaptations to the British plans were essential to compensate for
the loss of the Palestinian Arab commercial, industrial, and residential

districts in West Jerusalem. The area around Bab al-Zahara, or Herod's Gate, became the new Central Business District of East Jerusalem. The western slopes of Wadi Joz to the northeast of the city walls became a small industrial zone that quickly reached its capacity and required new land south of Anata village.[16] The construction of religious institutions was permitted along the tops of the Mount of Olives and the slopes leading up to Mount Scopus.[17] The planting of olive trees continued in the remaining designated green zones themselves.[18]

While planning regulations were enforced inside the municipal area of East Jerusalem, largely uncontrolled residential construction took place on the edges. This was particularly noticeable in the adjacent neighborhoods of Silwan and Abu Tur, to the east and southeast of the Old City. Scattered and longitudinal development took place along the road north to Ramallah and along the new road constructed from East Jerusalem through Abu Dis to Bethlehem. While services to these areas were very limited and often nonexistent, they did have the advantage of being free from the overcrowding and squalor of the Old City. Jordanian plans to incorporate these areas into the Municipality were still being formulated when the 1967 War broke out.[19]

These "extramural" urban developments were to pose two difficult problems for the Israeli government and Municipality in 1967. In enlarging the boundaries of Jerusalem to include parts of the West Bank, Israel incorporated larger concentrations of Palestinian Arabs than it would have wished. In addition, the dispersed nature of Palestinian Arab settlement meant there was a lack of large areas of undeveloped land in the immediate vicinity of Jerusalem. This narrowed the options for future Israeli Jewish housing construction and had political and planning implications in the post-1967 period.

In some ways, the urban development of Israeli West Jerusalem from 1948 to 1967 suffered similar, if less irksome, constraints. Trade and commerce were discouraged by the location of West Jerusalem at a geographical cul-de-sac and its proximity to a hostile border. A major potential growth industry, tourism, was stymied by the lack of access to the main religious sites in the Old City. But Israeli West Jerusalem had important advantages over Jordanian East Jerusalem. First, the main commercial area along the Jaffa road, the wealthy Arab suburbs with high-quality housing stock, the main government and municipal offices, and many of the essential utilities for the functioning of a modern city were located on the west side of the Armistice Line. The main water reservoir for Jerusalem, for example, was in Romema and con-

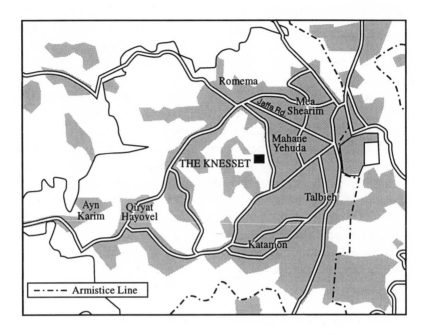

MAP 4.2. Center of West Jerusalem

tinued to supply adequate quantities of water until new sources were
found and pipelines were laid for the expanding population. Second,
the rail and road links, although at times vulnerable to sniper fire, provided good communications with Tel Aviv and the coastal plain. Third,
the broader western ridges were more suitable for urban construction
and residential housing than the steep slopes in the east.

Finally and perhaps most importantly, there was the political will to
expand and develop the western part of the city as the capital of the
new state. Thus the transfer of the new state's administrative functions
from Tel Aviv to Jerusalem and the construction of projects of national
significance, such as the Great Synagogue, the Supreme Court, and a
new University, all served as catalysts for economic and demographic
growth. In addition, during this period the Israeli government, in contrast to the British Mandate authorities and the Jordanian government,
made a commitment to economic diversification (see map 4.2).

Under these conditions, Israeli West Jerusalem was to become a
very different city from the one the British had envisaged. The new
Israeli Municipality was not content simply to adapt the Kendall Plan
of 1944, which, although never implemented, had considerable impact

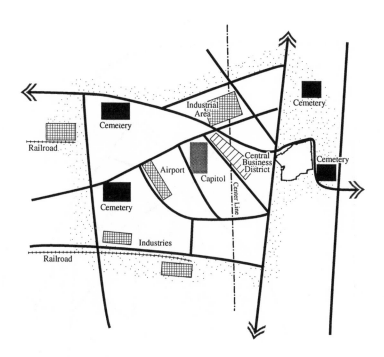

MAP 4.3. Rau Plan, 1948–1949

and has been called by one Israeli planner "the most technically per-
fect of all the plans made for Jerusalem."[20] Political imperatives determined that its Jewish population should greatly expand, and urban-
planning objectives had to be set accordingly. It is important to note
that as a border city security considerations also came into play:
Jerusalem had to be big enough to defend itself. The population target for West Jerusalem set in the years following the city's division was
250,000 people for 1985.[21] Two plans were put forward during this
period with such objectives in mind—the Rau Plan of 1949 and the
Shaviv Plan of 1955.[22] Both plans encouraged the development of
continuous residential areas in the northwestern parts of the city and
along the tops and upper slopes of the western ridges. The valleys
were to be maintained as open spaces and kept free of construction.
The Central Business district was to remain along both sides of the
Jaffa Road (see maps 4.3 and 4.4).

The Rau and Shaviv plans also envisaged a "Capitol"-type zone for
the location of government and cultural activities. The planning area

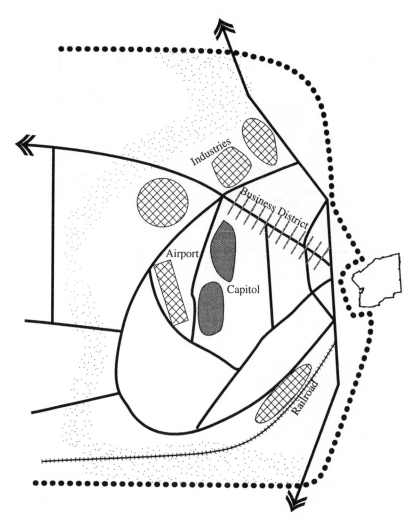

MAP 4.4. Shaviv Plan, 1955–1959

known as the central southern basin became the site for this zone and
the National Museum, the Knesset, the new Givat Ram university
campus, and the Prime Minister's Offices were built there. As noted
above there was an increasing emphasis upon attempts to broaden the
economic base of West Jerusalem by encouraging light industry. While
the Rau plan allocated less than 2 percent of the planned area to industrial zones, by 1955, the Shaviv plan had allocated nearly 5 percent to

industry.[23] Most of this area was in the north close to a proposed railway line, and in the south on the edge of Talbiyya. Finally, there was
an acknowledgment that the development of the Central Business
District westward was an inevitable result of the Armistice Lines.
Traders and shoppers would prefer to be some distance from a volatile
border, a point further west would make the commercial areas more
central relative to the western suburbs, and it would be more convenient for those coming to the city from the coastal plain.[24]

It is worth noting that by 1967, most of the available land reserves
within the Israel Municipality of West Jerusalem had been used up.
The only area available for future expansion was across the Nahal
Shorek, a river running west of Jerusalem below 'Ayn Karim. The
other option was "vertical" expansion—high-rise apartments in the
existing area.[25] Indeed, one outline scheme proposed the setting up of
engineering works, communication centers, industries, and defense
installations as far as six to seven miles to the west.[26] This is not to
imply that *lebensraum* for Israeli West Jerusalem was the catalyst for the
Israeli annexation of East Jerusalem and the adjacent areas of the West
Bank. But it does add an important town-planning dimension to the
political factors that led to the annexation. In addition, it helps explain
the speed and determination with which construction took place after
1967. The greater availability of space suitable for construction in the
annexed areas of Jerusalem was a major impulse behind the Israeli settlement policies.

Urban Planning and the Enlarged Israeli Jerusalem, 1967–1992

Many of the planning problems associated with the development of
Jerusalem in the post-1967 period stem from the political circumstances concerning the annexation of East Jerusalem and parts of the
West Bank. The determination to assert political sovereignty and
demographic dominance over the eastern parts of the city have an
impact upon the rational development of Jerusalem over and above
the problems associated with rapid growth and modernization.
Indeed, the very concept of an enlarged Jerusalem as the capital of a
Jewish state imposes planning priorities of necessity inimical to a third
of its inhabitants, the Palestinian Arabs. As they see it, the major determining factor in the Israeli planning process, overriding any topo-

graphical, environmental, legal, and historical factors, is the issue of
political sovereignty. As the foremost Israeli strategic planner, Yosef
Schweid, has astutely understood:

> Israelis thought that Jewish-Arab coexistence ... would end up leading
> to reconciliation and peace. However, in the eyes of the Arabs, the uni-
> fication of Jerusalem ... was considered to be conquest, and the plan-
> ning of the city and all the actions taken in the city to effect its unifi-
> cation were interpreted as the continuation of the war .... And since
> Israel sees coexistence as the central component in the life of the uni-
> fied city and holds back from imposing on the Arabs of Jerusalem laws
> and plans which are liable to provoke them ..., while the Arabs cling
> to their struggle to establish a separate identity in Jerusalem, any Israeli
> action intended to underline the unification of the city in the Arab
> neighbourhoods only has chances of being carried out if it reinforces
> this separate identity.[27]

Urban planning, a complex process in any circumstances, becomes
many times more difficult when the city is politically, historically, religiously, culturally, and linguistically divided. But before going into the
more explicitly political, or geo-political factors, it is useful to sketch
out some of the other factors which, though less salient in terms of
governmental priorities, have had a considerable bearing on the
implementation of planning policy and hence the development of
Jerusalem since 1967. Such factors include the structures and procedures through which planning policy is applied and the different pressures they are open to, the balance between private and public funding of development projects, the influence of the international community in the formulation of policy, and the degree of public
participation in the planning process.

Planning Structures and Procedures

It is important to note that in this complex area of planning and
implementation the Israeli government does not operate as a single
homogenous unit. One needs to examine the activities of each of the
various departments and ministries in order to understand the process.
No less than in any other modern political system, bureaucratic and
ideological rivalries in Israel impinge upon the formulation of policy.
In the case of Jerusalem, of course, passions are all the more heightened and the identification of a range of perspectives reveals a surprising lack of consensus over specifics in the Israeli polity.

Planning structures and procedures in Jerusalem reveal the interplay among various Israeli government ministries and between those ministries and the Israeli Municipality of Jerusalem itself. Until 1965, Israeli planning procedures and regulations followed the Ordinances laid down by the British Mandate authorities. At that point, in recognition of the fact that rapidly changing urban pressures and administrative amendments had crippled the effectiveness of this law,[28] a new law, the Planning and Building Law, was passed.

The new law altered the responsibilities and the boundaries of the various planning bodies—local, district, and national. Very briefly, the chain of decisionmaking as established in the 1965 law is as follows: Local outline plans are drawn up by a Local Planning Commission whose objectives have been summarized as:

> To control the development of land within the area while preserving the designated agricultural land; to secure proper conditions of health, sanitation, safety, transport and amenity, to demark residential, industrial and commercial zones; to preserve any buildings or objects of historic, architectural or archaeological importance and to preserve and develop places of natural interest or beauty.[29]

The Local Planning Commission is vested with powers to issue building licenses, expropriate land, and enforce building regulations. Regional plans are coordinated by District Planning Commissions composed of representatives from different ministries at district level. District Planning Commissions are required to prepare a "district outline scheme" to implement proposals that should be made by the National Planning Council. However, in the absence of proposals from the National Planning Council, the District Planning Commissions have directed most of their energies to reviewing and approving local plans.[30]

The National Planning Council comes under the aegis of the Ministry of Interior and is composed of representatives from the Ministries of Housing, Transportation, Agriculture, Trade and Industry, and Tourism, and of officials from the primary cities of Israel and other relevant national institutions such as the Parks Authority. The 1965 law made the National Planning Council responsible for the planning of population distribution, location of industries, use of agricultural land, transportation, and waste disposal. Despite or because of this wide remit, interministerial disagreements have paralyzed the functioning of the National Planning Council, so that no clear guidance has been forthcoming from the council with regard to specific local schemes.[31]

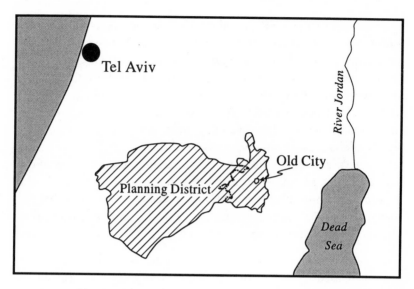

MAP 4.5. Planning District of Jerusalem Region

As we shall see these disagreements and constant delays have important implications for the ability of the Municipality of Jerusalem to secure its planning objectives.

The hierarchy of decisionmaking and its dysfunction at a national and district level has special drawbacks for the city of Jerusalem. It is important to note that the Municipality of Jerusalem constitutes the sole planning authority for the local planning area and therefore acts as the Local Planning Commission. It is also the main and largest planning authority for the Jerusalem planning region (see map 4.5). Therefore, the role of the Municipality's Planning Commission in the planning process is prominent. On one hand this position gives the Municipality considerable authority to initiate, approve, or reject plans, expropriate land, and enforce building regulations. On the other, it means that the Municipality has a direct interface with government ministries on the District Planning Commission and becomes enmeshed in the interministerial rivalries that have choked up the system. It has to operate sometimes in outright opposition to powerful government ministries whose regional perspectives do not always converge with planning priorities of the Municipality.[32] Thus, while the Municipality has day-to-day and direct responsibility for policy formulation and implementation, ministerial officials on the District Planning Commission have ultimate authority over its proposals. The result is one of great frustration for the Municipality.

In a political system of the kind that exists in Israel, where coalition government has rendered certain ministries the virtual fiefdoms of particular parties, the lack of planning convergence can have serious implications. For example, following the election of the Likud party in 1977, the Ministry of Housing became the government's main vehicle for implementing its settlement policies. In the Jerusalem region this has led to the establishment of large urban settlements in the metropolitan region of Jerusalem to which the Municipality has been obliged to provide services at the expense of other projects it sought to undertake. The greater influence of the Housing Ministry on the District Planning Commission has therefore prevailed irrespective of the continuous debate on whether Jerusalem should retain its compact character or be dispersed in response to the government's political and demographic objectives.[33]

Funding

In terms of budget, the Municipality is accountable to the Ministry of Interior, which contributes to the Municipality's "Extraordinary" budget, the section that deals with infrastructural development. However the amounts allocated by the government to the Municipality have declined drastically since 1979, from approximately 76 percent of its infrastructural development budget that year to 29 percent in 1989.[34] Government contributions to the Municipality's town-planning, construction, and maintenance functions have not averaged more than 2.8 percent per annum since 1982.[35] These figures reveal just how reluctant the government is to surrender control over expenditure to the Municipality. As a result the Municipality's urban development priorities and plans are kept on a tight rein.

Rather than ceding control to the Municipality, the government has sought to promote urban development through joint government-Municipality companies and subsidiaries. These include companies such as the construction firm Karta, the Company for the Reconstruction and Development of the Jewish Quarter, the Company for the Development of Yemin Moshe, and the Mamilla Project (set up to develop the area between Jaffa Gate and the Central Business District). While these joint companies are a means by which the Municipality is able to secure additional government funding, they also allow the government ministries to influence the planning and development of Jerusalem and control implementation.

In the public sector, it is the Israel–Lands Administration (ILA) that plays a key role. The ILA, the holding company for the Israeli government, is the largest landowner in the city.[36] In 1948 it acquired approximately 10,000 *dunam*s from the departed British government and refugee Palestinian Arab landlords.[37] In 1967 it acquired at least three times that much in the form of Jordanian government property, other property deemed "absentee" by Israeli law, and expropriations.[38] The ILA, then, owns much of the land available for construction and development in Jerusalem while the Municipality directly owns very little.[39]

The ILA, whose role is of great political significance, shares the Municipality's preference to develop Jerusalem as a compact rather than dispersed city, but for different reasons.[40] It seeks to encourage vertical construction in order to maximize the profit on its holdings in Jerusalem and has no wish to see land values declining through the expansion of Jerusalem's boundaries. In this sense its goals conflict with those of the Housing Ministry and the Ministry of Interior, since these two ministries favor the opposing policy of extending the urban spread through the settlement program. Yet since the early eighties, there has been a certain division within the ILA: officials appointed during the Likud years are sympathetic to the Greater Israel ideology of settlement in the West Bank and therefore also support efforts to settle Jews in a broad swathe around Jerusalem. They were therefore working against the interests of their own institution. At all events, the fact that the ILA management has been integrated with that of the Jewish National Fund, whose charter restricts the development of land and property to the exclusive benefit of Jews,[41] means that virtually all government-supported urban development of Jerusalem in the annexed areas constitutionally excludes the Palestinian inhabitants of Jerusalem.

It should be noted that for all the intensive settlement programs initiated by the government in the annexed areas, there is still considerable private investment stemming from Jerusalem's status as a Holy City. Religious and cultural centers have been funded by international bodies, partly on a philanthropic basis and partly consistent with the age-old tradition of supporting a foothold in the Holy City. This applies to initiatives from a wide range of religious and ethnic groups. The initiatives include the proposed construction of a huge Lubavitcher synagogue in the north of Jerusalem to the establishment of the Mormon Brigham Young University on the slopes of Mount

Scopus, and, less obviously, the restoration program carried out by the Jordanian Awqaf Administration on behalf of the al-Quds Committee of the Islamic Conference Organization.[42]

The Role of the International Community

In recognition of the sensitivities involved due to Jerusalem's importance in the consciousness of the West and the Islamic world, Mayor Teddy Kollek established in 1966 a "Jerusalem Committee" composed of professional architects, town planners, and religious dignitaries, mostly from the West. In setting up such a Committee, whose purpose was to comment on development proposals of the Municipality, Kollek sought not only to avail himself of expert advice but at the same time to draw the teeth of international criticism of the Municipality's policies in changing the character of Jerusalem. Furthermore, by gaining international sanction for his work, Kollek and the Municipality were able to marshal considerable support to withstand ministerial pressures. Ironically, the first public task entrusted to the Jerusalem Committee—evaluating the 1968 Master Plan proposed by the Municipality—resulted in the plan's indefinite shelving.

Notwithstanding this initial negative act, however, the Committee was in general strongly supportive of Municipality initiatives. In particular, it backed the "mosaic" policy Kollek devised in the early 1970s. The policy, designed to establish ethnically segregated residential and commercial areas as a means of acknowledging the divisions between the two communities and within the communities, was under threat by the Ministry of Housing's attempts to support Israeli settlement in areas of dense Palestinian residence, such as the Muslim quarter of the Old City and Silwan.[43] Although Housing's more controversial projects were canceled with the Labor victory of 1992, the victory was short lived. The policy of settling Jews in East Jerusalem in such as way as to disrupt the contiguity of Palestinian areas continued, albeit more discreetly, and the new mayor of Jerusalem elected in 1993, Ehud Olmert, strongly supports Jewish settlement on the Mount of Olives, Shaykh Jarrah, Silwan, and Ras al-Amud—all areas of dense Palestinian residence. While the Jerusalem Committee is still in existence under the continuing chairmanship of former Mayor Kollek, it is uncertain whether it will have any impact at all on the city's direction. In any case, there are indications that Kollek's "mosaic" policy has been dropped.

Public Participation

Public participation in the planning process would probably exist irrespective of the annexation. The degree of public participation provided for under the Planning and Building Law is extremely limited, and the authorities, who vest great confidence in the expertise and impartiality of the professional planners and architects, actually discourage such participation. For example, the law mandated the Ministry of Interior to publish its proposals in two daily newspapers, but until 1973 the only two dailies contracted to print such proposals were minority, small-circulation papers, one belonging to the National Religious Party and the other a Hungarian-language daily![44]

Criticism of the lack of public participation in the planning process led the mayor to introduce a "Public Committee" for the planning of Jerusalem in 1973. However, its members were appointed by the Municipality and their meetings were closed to the general public and press. This served only to highlight the secrecy and lack of accountability of the planning process. Indeed, a prominent member of the first committee, Professor Michael Brown, resigned early on, declaring: "The planning of Jerusalem requires some kind of public participation. This committee is not only not going to provide it, but is creating the misconception that there is this kind of participation."[45] The introduction of neighborhood councils in the mid-1980s may have assisted in informal consultations with planners, but since these councils were concerned mainly with provision of services, their influence on the planning process has been limited.

This issue however, cannot be separated completely from the question of the Israeli enlargement of Jerusalem. It is likely that the primary reason for the reluctance to engage the public in the planning process is the belief that given the diverse nature of Israeli Jewish religious sects and the resistance to Israeli rule by Palestinian Arabs, public debate would serve only to exacerbate divisions rather than encourage consensus. Schweid made this point in a slightly different context but it is still applicable here. Certainly it would provide Palestinian Arabs with a much needed forum to air their grievances and draw attention to the inequalities in the distribution of Municipality services. An authentic process of public participation would allow groups affiliated with the Palestine Liberation Organization and the Jordanian government to influence planning decisions in Jerusalem, which would be unacceptable to the majority of the Israeli Jewish population and the government. At the same time, any attempt to create exemptions that exclude

Palestinian Arabs but allow Israeli Jews to participate freely would have deleterious effects on the Municipality's attempt to present Jerusalem as a harmonious and increasingly integrated city under Israeli sovereignty. The Municipality has evidently decided that it is better to let sleeping dogs lie.

The lack of public—in this case Palestinian Arab—participation in the planning process has implications for the Arab and Islamic character of Jerusalem and the Old City in particular. The concept of "museum city" has already been applied to towns previously inhabited by Palestinian Arabs in Israel, such as Acre, Jaffa, and Safad; with antecedents in Mandate planning policy, it is currently being applied to the Old City and East Jerusalem.[46] The Old City is seen as a tourist site rather than a place to be lived in. Ibrahim Daqqaq, a Palestinian architect and engineer formerly connected with the Committee for the Restoration of Al-Aqsa, sums up the Israeli attitude as follows:

> Probably the fact that the western part of Jerusalem developed in complete isolation from the Old City . . . entrenched the idea of the separation of the two sectors in the minds of Israeli planners. It may have also entrenched their views of the Old City as an embodiment of archaeology rather than a living population centre . . . accentuated in turn by the exaggerated prominence given to the walls of Jerusalem and the severance of relations between it and its immediate environment. In this way, the Old City is being turned into a place to be visited, while West Jerusalem is a place to work and make a living.[47]

Such policies lead to restrictions in the Old City on street vendors, animal markets, and to the increasing regulation of informal religious, economic, and social activity in keeping with modern western concepts of order and ambience.[48] Thus vibrancy and spontaneity are replaced by formality and contrivance and the local inhabitants of the Old City, the Palestinian Arabs, become an exotic backdrop for what a dissenting Israeli architect, Arthur Kutcher, termed a "religious Disneyland."[49]

Planning Problems Directly Resulting from the Enlargement of Jerusalem.

Even before 1967, a debate had been underway among Israeli planners as to the relative merits of a compact or dispersed city, of vertical or horizontal growth. Aesthetics plays a critical role in Jerusalem's status as a national capital and international Holy City, but at the same time the shortage of building space, budgetary pressures to maximize the value of property, and demographic priorities place great strain on any resolve to restrict the vertical and horizontal growth.

The 1967 war and the acquisition of East Jerusalem and the West Bank greatly intensified the debate. Proponents of the "horizontal" development of the city have clearly gained the upper hand, but instead of the intimacy and human scale traditionally associated with such a development option, the purpose has been to settle Israeli Jews in the less densely populated eastern parts of the city and in a belt around the municipal boundaries. Instead of seeking to preserve Jerusalem's unique urban landscape, the aim was to secure political control over the eastern annexed parts of the city. Urban planning principles have been relegated to the second rank. Thus, if urban planning criteria alone had been applied, new housing construction would have been along the western and northern ridges and the wider valley to the north of the city. Instead, there was intensive "public" housing construction almost entirely for Israeli Jews on the east side.

Following the war, Israeli planners argued among themselves about where the natural eastern border of the urban built-up area of Jerusalem should be. Some have even argued that it should include the Palestinian suburbanized villages of Azariyya and Abu Dis but not the northern suburbs from Shu'fat to Ramallah. The exact opposite was what was actually decided upon as the Municipality borders. Most planners have also agreed upon the need of a green belt around the built-up area but could not agree as to the exact line. Developments of the past thirty years have, in any case, overtaken the debate. The establishment of new Israeli settlements and unplanned Palestinian building on the periphery of the borders have eaten away at the remnants of the green areas. From the standpoint of the municipal planners, the dilemma was that while annexing a wider area of the West Bank would have facilitated the considered location of utilities, roads, open spaces etc. and allowed for planning of Jerusalem as a metropolitan region, at the same time it would have brought in more Arabs. As it is, the current borders are designed to provide sufficient space for the housing needed to create a Jewish majority, but are not sufficient to provide at the same time space for industry, services and other institutional developments. As Yosef Schweid argues:

> Even if the first priority of the people drafting the borders of the city had been the intention to ensure control over the shape of the area, they would have had to include within the city's area a much larger amount

of territory than was determined in 1967. If, in spite of this, higher value was given to the question of demographic balance in the city between the Jewish and Arab residents of the city, they would have been better off if they had made the city's area smaller, while deciding that some of the city's needs would be supplied by the area around it.[50]

Clearly hindsight has assisted Schweid in coming to this conclusion. Yet he does identify the contradiction in Israeli policy in Jerusalem since 1967. Packing immigrant and Israeli Jews into Jerusalem will serve no purpose without the industrial and service infrastructure to support them. For that to occur, one needs not only space but also to plan on a regional basis, which in Jerusalem's case includes the city's hinterland inhabited predominantly by Palestinian Arabs.

Another result of the planning policies has been to place enormous strains upon the resources of the Municipality, which is obliged to provide services to satellite service and commercial centers. A Municipality publication reads as follows:

> The Jerusalem Municipality has proclaimed its reservations at this policy of dispersing the development of the city over a wide area and thereby precluding centralised development. The fanning out of the city over a wide expanse creates grave problems concerning the sundry infrastructure systems relating to employment, transportation, public services (health, education, social welfare) and the like . . . . The Municipality has an interest in filling existing suburbs and the intervening empty areas (which are not designated for open spaces) in order to consolidate large suburbs which will make for total community life . . . . The Municipality is against leaving small communities in outlying places.[51]

Huge investment in roads, water, sewage disposal, and electricity supplies has been required to service the new settlements in the annexed areas. Furthermore, at periods when immigration levels were dropping and out-migration was increasing, this horizontal development served simply to reduce the numbers of Israeli Jews in the core areas of the city in order to "thicken" its periphery.[52] Nearly all of the population (98 percent) of the new settlement of Ma'ale Adumim on the road to Jericho is made up of former Jerusalemites.[53] These issues led Mayor Kollek to exclaim in a 1987 interview:

> And the price? Why do people forget the heavy price that every new and unnecessary settlement demands from the Israeli taxpayer? For some reason they argue that the flats in Ma'ale Adumim or in Beitar are

very cheap. Cheap for whom? I can easily prove that these arguments are based upon figures originating from the artificial land prices decided arbitrarily by the Israel-Lands Administration. In reality the building of these settlements is more expensive than inside the city. It is necessary to lay . . . electricity and telephone lines, kilometres of waterpipes, and to pave access roads. In other words, it is necessary to invest many millions in an additional infrastructure that already exists inside Jerusalem.[54]

The Municipality was not against satellite settlements in principle, which in fact conformed nicely to its "mosaic" policy. Rather, the Municipality opposition arises from the construction of such settlements without sufficient thought to the corresponding infrastructural investment and population growth required which leads it to oppose them.

Another result of the emphasis on the horizontal development of Jerusalem for political reasons has been the neglect of urban renewal programs. The division of Jerusalem by an armistice line running through the middle created a corridor of poor and distressed neighborhoods on both sides of the line. After the conquest of East Jerusalem and the removal of the separating walls and barricades, Jerusalem was left with run-down areas right in the new heart of the city. In keeping with trends in inner cities elsewhere in the world, emphasis has moved away from demolition to renewal. But with the priority going to the construction of urban settlements on the periphery, few funds are left over for the public financing of schemes to revitalize the inner city. This is particularly the case when Israeli policy-makers seek to reduce what they perceive as a Palestinian Arab demographic threat to the Israeli Jewish presence in the city.[55]

Another planning issue, already referred to briefly, is whether the very heterogeneous population of Jerusalem should be integrated or permitted to remain in their ethnically and religiously divided neighborhoods. This issue applies not only to the Palestinian Arab and Israeli Jewish communities, but also to divisions among Palestinian Christian denominations, between Palestinian Christians and Muslims, between orthodox and secular Jews, and among the various orthodox and ultra-orthodox Jewish sects. The general policy has been to welcome the diversity of Jerusalem's population and to accept the different housing and service needs of the different communities and is known as the "mosaic" policy much favored by Teddy Kollek. However, such a policy has provided a useful cloak for targeting services to specific communities at the expense of others. Palestinian Arab accusations of discrimination in municipal services are based upon this unequal targeting.[56]

A final issue resulting from the enlargement of Jerusalem and annexation of East Jerusalem and parts of the West Bank is, of course, the whole question of the role of the Palestinian Arab population in Jerusalem. The issue can be summed up in the simple question: Is Jerusalem to be the capital of Israeli Jews alone? The extent to which the Palestinian Arabs of Jerusalem are to be included, consulted, served, and protected may be political questions, but they also have urban-planning implications. A policy committed to including Palestinian Arabs fully within the life and development of Jerusalem would have to also accept external influences on the formulation of policy, certainly from Jordan and the wider Islamic world. How realistic is such an expectation in the political climate that undergirds Israeli occupation of the eastern parts of the city? To some extent this question is answered by the expropriation of Palestinian Arab land, the provision of housing virtually exclusively for Israeli Jews, and the neglect in providing an equal amount of services for Palestinian Arabs.

Housing Policies in Jerusalem, 1967–1992

The last quarter century has been a period of rapid housing construction in Jerusalem. Between 1967 and 1985, more than 81,000 residential units have been built, 80 percent of all housing construction being on the east side of the Armistice Line.[57] Without a doubt, therefore, housing has been one of the key factors in the Israeli government's physical control over the Jerusalem municipal area (Area D) and the major impact upon the character of Palestinian Arab East Jerusalem (Area E).

Israeli Jewish Housing

As we have seen in the previous chapter, the Israeli government and Municipality had set itself the target of maintaining a ratio of Israeli Jews to Palestinian Arabs of at least 2:1. In order to counterbalance the steady growth in the Palestinian Arab population, inducements such as subsidized mortgages and services were introduced to attract a continual stream of new immigrants. While such demographic considerations are clearly the driving force behind housing construction, the exact location of new housing construction reflects the additional political objective of securing physical control over the annexed parts of the enlarged Jerusalem. The former director of the Jerusalem District of the Ministry of Housing, Shmaryahu Cohen, was quite explicit about these objectives:

> After the Six Days War [1967 War] the decision makers remembered two traumatic events: the time when Mount Scopus was cut off from the Western City and the withdrawal from Sinai after the 1956 campaign. The question they faced was: How long will the Americans let us hold the areas we have conquered? Everybody regarded the united Jerusalem as a border city and its boundaries of jurisdiction as the border of the state of Israel. It was necessary to give quick answers to military problems such as: What must be done to prevent the Jordanian guns from taking up again positions in Nabi Samwil? How to ensure a territorial link with the Hadassah hospital on Mount Scopus? The answers were clear: army units are easily transferred from one place to another but a housing project inhabited by Jews is quite another story. Thus it happened that one decision was followed by another and the comprehensive policy was created *post factum*.[58]

Within this political and security framework, it is possible to identify three main stages in the housing construction program in Jerusalem. The first was concerned with "mending the gaps" between the east and west sides of the city; the second dealt with expanding Jewish areas on the east side and surrounding Palestinian Arab residential areas; the third with establishing a strong Israeli Jewish presence in Jerusalem's hinterland.[59]

Before we examine those three stages, let us first note that in its pursuit of physical control over the annexed areas, during the first several months, the Israeli government and the Municipality, fearing the political and diplomatic consequences at a time when the annexation was still under intense international scrutiny, attempted to acquire land without resorting to expropriations. The Municipality was further reluctant to saddle itself with the financial burden of both paying compensation and providing the services the new housing projects would entail.[60] However, by January 1968, the government and the Municipality had decided to embark upon a large-scale confiscation program in order to absorb all the opprobrium at one time and to hasten the process of settlement of Israeli Jews in the annexed areas.[61] By 1970, some 25 percent of the newly annexed areas, or 17,000 *dunam's*, had been expropriated by the Israeli government. This was in addition to the Jordanian state lands acquired by virtue of annexation.[62] As was indicated by the Cohen quotation above, there were no concrete plans as such for all the expropriated land but it was a general view that land would be needed to stop Palestinian Arab growth and to absorb the new immigrants who were to be directed to the city. Financial compensation was offered to the owners but in keeping with the Palestinian spirit of resistance to the Israeli annexation and Jordanian government pressure very few owners accepted it, in order to avoid any hint of recognizing the Israeli government's right to act in this way.

"Mending the Gaps"

This initial stage of the housing construction program, "mending the gaps," was conceived and executed in great haste. As has been already referred to, the partition of the city between 1948 and 1967 had left empty spaces along sections of the Armistice Line. Residential areas close to these spaces were often derelict or neglected. Such spaces were found in the north of the city between Shmuel Hanavi and Shaykh Jarrah, in the center of the city opposite Damascus Gate between Nablus road and the Musrara quarter (known as "the seam"), and in the southern central part of the city known as the Mamilla quarter opposite Jaffa Gate and below Yemin Moshe (see map 4.6). If the city was to be authentically "unified" and cohere under Israeli sovereignty then these areas required revitalization.[63]

Unfortunately, the Israeli government saw the potential in filling these spaces only in terms of meeting its demographic and geopolitical objectives. Proposals by the Municipality to create a commercial area in the Musrara quarter to unite both halves of the city were overruled in favor of increased housing.[64] The open spaces in the north were used to link up Israeli Jewish housing in West Jerusalem to the Israeli enclave on Mount Scopus. A chain of housing projects beginning in Ramot Eshkol and continuing through Givat Hamivkar, Ma'alot Daphna, and French Hill (Givat Shapira) to Mount Scopus straddled all the available open space in this part of the city, enclosing completely what Palestinian Arab houses and gardens that remained.[65] To take advantage of the lack of strong international political pressure on Israel over its annexation of East Jerusalem and parts of the West Bank, premium was placed on speed. Projects designed for other parts of the country were taken off the shelf and implemented in Jerusalem

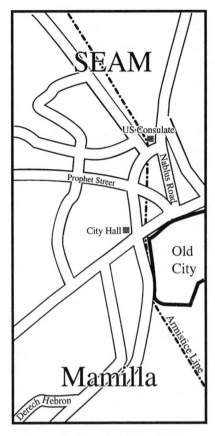

MAP 4.6. The "Seam" and Mamilla Areas

irrespective of the topographical or social differences they were designed for. For example, the plans used for the neighborhood of Ramot Eshkol on one of the northwestern ridges and slopes of Jerusalem were those also used for Holon, outside Tel Aviv on the flat coastal plain.[66]

After construction was completed in the early seventies, energies were devoted to "thickening" the chain and its constituent links. Mount Scopus itself was restored and enlarged to serve 18,000 students and staff, while the Hadassah Hospital was virtually rebuilt to cater for the needs of the population in the north of the city. In the eighties, land adjacent to Mount Scopus that had been expropriated by the government was sold to the Mormon Church to build the Brigham Young University. Land expropriated just below French Hill became the site of the Hyatt Regency Hotel complex.

The demographic and political motivations behind this construction are confirmed by the slow progress made with the other two open areas mentioned—the area between the Damascus Gate and Musrara, and the area between Jaffa Gate and the Central Business District. These were not planned as exclusively residential areas and still have not been completed. The space opposite the Damascus Gate stretching northward along the former No Man's Land was known as the "seam" area dividing the two hearts of the city. Whatever would be created out of this area would be crucial in attempts to unite the city. But in the absence of agreement on what to do with this area, a partial scheme was introduced involving the construction of the main northern arterial road connecting the new neighborhoods in the north with the city center and bypassing the Palestinian commercial district and suburb of Shaykh Jarrah. Opponents of the arterial road argued that it highlights the division of the city, while the residents of the Musrara quarter that used to straddle the area (but which now only comprises a small area on the western side) have objected to the transportation and commercial accretions, such as a bus station and shopping mall, which were part of the plan (see map 4.6). Partly as a result of the difficulties of access to north and eastern parts of Jerusalem caused by the *intifada*, construction of the arterial road began in 1992 and has now been completed.

Similar difficulties and delays occurred with the south-central Mamilla area opposite the Jaffa Gate. The western-most part of this area, known as Yemin Moshe, was inhabited by poor Jewish immigrants primarily from North Africa. As part of the wider development scheme for the Mamilla quarter, the area was expropriated and rehabilitated as secluded luxury houses. The valley running below, running southeast and known as Birket Sultan, was made into a park, an open-air theater, and the site of an arts cinema. However, less progress was made in the area closer to the Old City walls. Buildings abutting or near to the walls themselves were demolished to create a park but debates as to the shape of developments in the Mamilla quarter itself paralyzed progress. The quarter remained abandoned, derelict, and a slum for more than twenty years. When one considers that this occurred at the foot of the gate closest to the Central Business District of Jerusalem and the main point of entry to the Jewish quarter in the Old City, and which also happens to be one of the most attractive gates to the Old City, this neglect is remarkable. In 1991, construction work began on a commercial and residential area intended to link the Old City to the West Jerusalem Central Business District.

Israeli planners themselves are critical of the slow progress of these latter projects. Kroyanker summarizes their views in this way:

> The mending of the gaps in the important areas of the former No-
> Man's Land opposite Jaffa Gate and Damascus Gate deservedly does not
> rank among the great achievements in Jerusalem's planning history or
> the city's development in recent decades.[67]

However, rather than attributing the failure to the greater priority
accorded to housing of Israeli Jews in new housing estates in the
annexed areas, Kroyanker blames the learning process:

> The abandoned houses and the ruins in the Mamilla area and the
> emptiness of the No-Man's Land north of the Damascus Gate indicate
> growing pains and a slow transition from over-ambitiousness and
> impossible plans to modest and realistic ones.[68]

At the same time, it is possible to argue that these plans did not receive
the necessary funding and drive primarily because they lacked a
demographic and housing component and were thus overshadowed
by the great drive to create more and more housing.

Expansion

The second stage of housing construction, which focused on expanding Jewish residence on the eastern side of the city and surrounding
Palestinian areas, began in the early 1970s. This stage went beyond simple demographic considerations to establish physical Israeli control
over the newly annexed areas and can be seen as a reaction to international pressures on the Israeli government to negotiate over the
future of Jerusalem. Romann and Weingrod point out that the second
stage was a direct response to the 1969 Rogers Plan and a later UN
Resolution calling for the Israeli withdrawal from East Jerusalem.[69]
(see chapter 2). It was, in effect, a "military conquest by architectural
means" designed to pre-empt any possibility of withdrawal.[70] It was
probably the Israeli government's single most significant undertaking
aimed at securing the annexed parts of the city.

The main feature of the second stage was the construction of four
large urban settlements in the four corners of the annexed areas, two
in the north, Ramot and Neve Ya'aqov, and two in the south, Gilo and
East Talpiot. As well as establishing Israeli Jewish demographic facts,
each of these urban settlements by their location and layout has a clear
military and strategic value. Neve Ya'acov, for example, is sited along

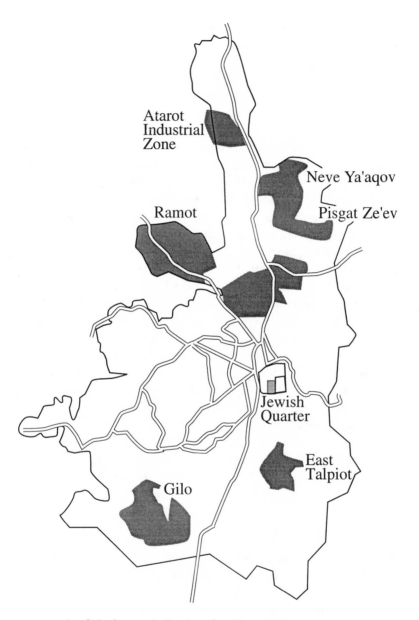

MAP 4.7. Israeli Settlements in East Jerusalem Since 1967

the main traffic axis heading north to Ramallah and Nablus in the
middle of scattered but increasingly dense Palestinian Arab residences.
Its blocks of high-rise apartments, designed to house 4,500 families or
17,000 people, radiate off a central ring road and, seen from the outside, give an imposing fortress-like impression.[71] Similar considerations led to the location and design of Gilo, an extensive urban settlement for approximately 35,000 people. It overlooks the road south to
Bethlehem and Hebron and divides the only Palestinian neighborhood on the south perimeter of Jerusalem, Bayt Safafa, from
Bethlehem and Bayt Jallah. Ramot and East Talpiot, designed to house
30,000 and 15,000 residents respectively, have similar features.[72] These
second stage constructions typify the "fortress Jerusalem" architecture
most associated with post-'67 Israeli planning. The apartments form
rings of imposing blocks on hilltops and upper slopes, acting like sen-
tinels over the neighboring Palestinian Arab residences (see map 4.7).

Although embarked upon a few years later, the urban settlement of
Pisgat Ze'ev is also part of this second stage construction program. The
isolated location of Neve Ya'acov and the social difficulties encountered by the inhabitants led many planners to be concerned about the
future viability of this settlement.[73] In addition, Palestinian housing
construction was continuing apace to its south, threatening to further
increase its geographic and social isolation from other Israeli Jewish
settlements and the center of West Jerusalem. The government, therefore, decided to build Pisgat Ze'ev, which would stretch from Neve
Ya'aqov to French Hill. It was intended to house approximately 15,000
residents, and would divide the Palestinian population areas along the
Jerusalem-Ramallah road from those on the eastern edges of the
Municipality's boundaries.[74]

Creating a Security Belt

The third stage in the housing program had less to do with the actual
housing needs of the city than with security. The placement of smaller
urban settlements for Israeli Jews on ridges, crests, and beside strategic
roads in the metropolitan area surrounding Jerusalem, was intended
both to forestall the spread of the Palestinian Arab housing construction and to inject an Israeli Jewish population into the predominantly
Arab population of the metropolitan region.[75] The former Director of
the Jerusalem District of the Ministry of Housing describes the situation with his usual frankness:

We have made enormous efforts to locate state lands near Jerusalem and we decided to seize them before . . . the Arabs have a hold there. We all know that they remove rocks and plant olive trees instead in order to create facts in the field. What is wrong with trying to get there before them? I know this policy is harmful to Jerusalem in the short run, but it guarantees living space for the future generation. If we don't do it today, our children and grandchildren will travel to Jerusalem through a hostile Arab environment.[76]

Three major settlements were established in this belt—Ma'ale Adumim in the east, Givon in the north, and Efrat in the south. Ma'ale Adumim was purposely situated on an exposed hilltop overlooking the Jericho road for both security reasons and to prevent the creation of a land corridor for Jordanian access to East Jerusalem in the event of a peace agreement[77] (see map 4.8). The presence of the large settlements was consolidated by the creation of smaller satellite settlements such as Givat Ze'ev, Bet Horon, and Tekoa (see map 4.8). It is important to note that the government included the western "Jerusalem corridor," the land to the west of Jerusalem leading down to the coast prior to 1967, inside this security belt. Accordingly the outlying villages and suburbs of Motzsa, Mevassaret Yerushalyim, and Mevasseret Zion were strengthened and developed, particularly through self-build schemes for wealthy Jerusalemites.[78]

Even before these plans were completed, the government and Municipality planning bodies were made aware of the drawbacks in their policy. With a finite number of new immigrants arriving to Jerusalem and the numbers of those out-migrating to the coastal plain increasing, Benvenisti's fear that the increase in the Israeli Jewish population of East Jerusalem (Area E) and in the metropolitan area outside the Municipality (Area G) would not represent real growth but merely a shift in the Jewish population appears to have some foundation. Indeed, as has already been noted, by the 1980s there were indications that this housing program was attracting many people away from the core areas and that the Israeli Jewish population in central Jerusalem was in fact declining. A report in the respected Israeli daily, Ha'aretz, described the situation in 1987:

> The centre of the city is doomed to degeneration. The tourists who visit the Holy City admire the beauty of the Pa'amon Garden and the reconstruction of Mishkenot Sha'ananim, the wonderful parks and the modern architecture of the luxury hotels. Few are aware that there are almost no children in the beautiful parks, that classrooms are being

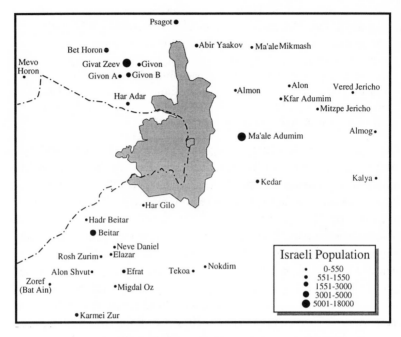

MAP 4.8. Israeli Jewish Settlement in Jerusalem Metropolitan Area
Derived from: Foundation for Middle East Peace

closed in old prestigious neighbourhoods like Rehavia, because there
are not enough pupils, that Mishkenot Sha'ananim is populated by foreign writers and artists, and that young Jewish couples, those who are
not seduced to move to the cheap flats in the new satellite cities, prefer sometimes to make their homes in the cities of the coastal plain.[79]

The tone may be exaggerated but it is clear that the development of
the new settlements has taken place largely at the expense of the
regeneration of the core areas. The Damascus Gate "seam" area and the
Mamilla quarter are only the most obvious examples. Indeed,
Municipality officials fear that Palestinians may start to occupy the
depleted inner-city areas as a result of this depopulation.[80] Schweid
also notes that housing supply for Israeli Jews in Jerusalem has in reality outstripped employment opportunities and that without a greater
investment in the creation of workplaces the increase in population
and housing supply is to no avail.[81]

At the end of 1989, what were from the Israeli standpoint bleak
demographic trends were checked temporarily by a renewed flow of
Soviet Jewish immigrants. As a consequence, the Ministry of Housing

pressed for the creation of new housing zones. Most were located in the annexed areas of the city which had either been designated as open spaces or spaces whose uses had yet to be determined. These included an area between Talbiyya and Gilo in the south, known as Givat Hamatos, and another area between Pisgat Ze'ev and French Hill. Some proposals even involved the establishment of settlements in areas of dense Palestinian Arab housing, such as the Muslim quarters of the Old City, the village-suburb of Silwan and parts of Shaykh Jarrah. Palestinian protestations that the allocation of these spaces for Israeli Jewish housing was particularly unfair in view of the frequent denial of planning permission for Palestinian housing were brushed aside in attempts to absorb as many people as possible from this immigration windfall for Jerusalem.

In October 1990, in order to hasten the construction and occupation of these new settlements, most of which consisted of mobile homes, the Israeli Cabinet made Jerusalem a Class A development area. With that designation the Housing Ministry pays half of the infrastructure costs and the Israel-Lands Administration reduces the price of the land. This allows contractors to reduce prices of apartments and houses by approximately $10,000 each. Similarly, purchasers are eligible for interest-free mortgages ranging from $44,000 to $48,000. Residents of these areas receive free day-care center and kindergarten fees. Loans of up to $7,500 are also available after five years of residency.[82] Despite this energetic push to house new immigrants, the problem identified by Schweid remains: that meeting the housing requirements of new immigrants is not by itself sufficient to assure a Jewish demographic dominance in Jerusalem and the surrounding areas unless the area is secure and provides opportunities for well-paid employment.

Palestinian Arab Housing

By the middle of 1992, 135,000 Israeli Jews lived in urban settlements in East Jerusalem and the adjacent parts of the West Bank (Area E, see chapter 3).[83] This massive flow into an area of less than 20,000 acres clearly had a dramatic impact both upon the Palestinian Arab society in those areas and upon the availability of space for their own housing and development. Since 1967, only 12 percent of all new construction in the city has taken place in the Palestinian Arab areas. The importance of housing and the lack of commercial, industrial, and public-

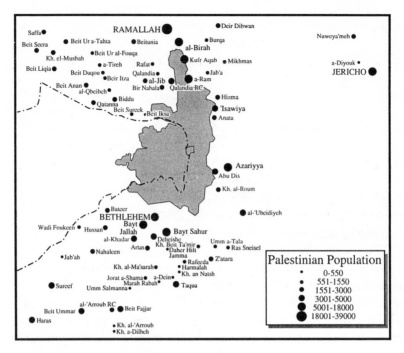

Saffa● RAMALLAH●   ●Deir Dibwan
Beit Seera ● Beit Ur a-Tahta ●Beitunia   ●Burqa   Nuweya'meh ●
●   al-Birah
Kh. el-Musbah ●Beit Ur al-Fouqa
Beit Liqia●   ● a-Tireh Rafat●   Kufr Aqab ● Mikhmas   a-Diyouk ●
●   Beit Duqou ●   Qalandia●   ●Jab'a   JERICHO ●
●Beir Itza ●al-Jib
╷‾╮ Beit Anan ●   Bir Nahala● ●a-Ram
╷ ● al-Qbeibeh●   Qalandia-RC
╵ ╷ ● Biddu   ● Hizma
‾╮ ● Qatanna   ●'Isawiya
╵╯ ●Beit Sureek ●Beit Iksa   ● Anata

                                ● Azariyya
                              Abu Dis
                                ● Kh. al-Roum

      ●Bateer
╷‾╮ BETHLEHEM●   ● al-'Ubeidiyeh
Wadi Foukeen ● Hussan● Bayt
╵   al-Khadar● Jallah ● Bayt Sahur
╷   ●Nahaleen Artas● Deheishe Umm a-Tala
●Jab'ah   Kh. Beit Ta'mir ● ● Ras Sneisel
╵‾   ●Daher Hilt
                Jamma ● Rafeeda● Z'atara
      Kh. al-Ma'sarah● ● Harmalah
      Jorat a-Shama● a-Dein● ● Kh. an Natsh
●Sureef   Marah Rabah●
      Umm Salmanna● ● Taqua

      al-'Arroub RC
Beit Ummar ● ● ● Beit Fajjar
● Haras
      ● Kh. al-'Arroub
      ●Kh. a-Dilbeh

Palestinian Population	
·	0-550
•	551-1550
●	1551-3000
●	3001-5000
●	5001-18000
⬤	18001-39000

MAP 4.9. Palestinian Arab Settlement in Jerusalem Metropolitan Area
Derived from: Foundation for Middle East Peace

service investment can be seen in the fact that of this 12 percent, 82 percent was for housing alone. During the period 1977–83 an average of 90 percent (390,000 square meters) of all new housing construction was for Israeli Jewish housing and only 9.9 percent (43,000 square meters) for Palestinian Arab. This translates into approximately 2,170 apartments for Israeli Jews as opposed for 230 for Palestinian Arabs every year.[84] In the decade between 1980 and 1990, less than 11 percent of the total surface area devoted to housing was for Palestinian Arab housing.[85] A final indicator is that 80 percent of the construction of the Israeli Jewish urban settlements in the annexed areas are publicly funded,[86] whereas virtually nothing has been made available for Palestinian Arab areas.[87] From these indicators, one may infer the presence of a conscious policy of neglecting and restricting Palestinian Arab housing needs in Jerusalem.

One should bear in mind that these figures apply only to those areas within the Municipal boundaries. A more accurate picture of Israeli government bias and discrimination would include those Palestinian Arab residential areas on the periphery of the Municipality in the metropolitan region of Jerusalem (Area G) which is under military rule (see map 4.9). This final portion of the chapter will analyze the situation in both areas.

It has long been common knowledge that Israeli government and Municipality officials have sought to maintain a population ratio of about 72 percent Jews to 28 percent Palestinians and to restrict the population growth of Palestinians accordingly, but it has only recently come to light that this policy involved actual ethnic quotas. Thus, at the end of 1993, a Municipality official, Elinoar Barzaki, inadvertently revealed to the Local Planning Commission that granting planning permission for seventy units in the village-suburb of Sur Bahir southeast of the Old City would exceed the housing quota for the Palestinian Arab sector.[88] Subsequent disclosures and the publication of a Municipality report, "Potential Housing Construction in Jerusalem," showed that the quota system had been in operation for at least twenty years. The quota system ensured that applications for planning permission by Palestinian Arabs were only approved at a rate which corresponded to the 72 percent to 28 percent ratio mentioned above. As a result, the quota allocates only a total of 15,000 new homes for Palestinian Arabs in Jerusalem when, taking into account natural growth only, their housing needs are at least three times that amount.

One consideration Israeli planners have in mind requires some detailed explanation of housing density estimates. At present, despite the smaller families of Israeli Jews, the urbanized Jewish areas are more densely populated than Palestinian areas, with 71 percent of the population (Jewish) concentrated in 52 percent of the city's territory, while 28 percent (Palestinian) is concentrated in 48 percent of the city's territory.[89] The average Israeli Jewish population density is 8.6 housing units per *dunam*, while for the Palestinian Arab population it is 3.3 units per *dunam*, making the average density in the areas populated by Israeli Jews is 2.3 times greater than that in areas populated by Palestinian Arabs. Municipal planners conclude:

> The main and most important conclusion from these data is that within a very short time the land reserves available for Jewish residential building will run out—in contrast to the situation in the Arab sector, where large land reserves of empty ground and low building density will allow the local population to grow to a considerable extent and to building tens of thousands of residential buildings, above and beyond those which exist today.[90]

One can see how the traditional landholding system of the Palestinian

Arab villages absorbed into Jerusalem is having an impact upon future planning. Houses with small fields around them for olive planting and grazing have much more space available for later in-filling. Villages such as Al Tur, Abu Tur, Sur Bahir and parts of Silwan and Ras al-Amud are examples of this pattern. In this way, the Palestinian areas would be able to absorb far greater numbers than currently reside there. Thus, to maintain a demographic balance in favor of Israeli Jews, the Municipality restricts not only the land available for Palestinian housing but also building permission on the land already designated for housing.

There are four elements in the Israeli policy of restricting Palestinian housing development in Jerusalem. First, restrictions are placed upon Palestinian Arabs wishing to settle within the Municipality boundaries. Only those who have residency permits are entitled to live and build within the boundaries. Some estimates say there are 25,000 illegal residents who are living as sub-tenants of permitted residents, particularly in the Muslim quarters of the Old City.[91] Due to their insecure status, these do not make much impact upon the growth in Palestinian housing but simply add to the overcrowding and slum conditions in the Old City. Partitioning, extensions, and conversions of use are frequently resorted to by relatives and landlords to accommodate these people.[92]

Second, Palestinian Arab housing has been restricted by the series of expropriations that have taken place since 1967. Estimates of their extent vary from 25 percent to 72 percent of the total annexed area.[93] The discrepancy is due largely to the fact that some estimates refer only to privately owned property while others refer to Jordanian state lands as well. A high proportion of Israeli Jewish development has taken place upon privately owned Palestinian Arab land, thus removing it from the realm of potential Palestinian Arab housing. These include such areas of the Old City as the Magharib quarter, which has been made part of the enlarged Jewish quarter, as well as the areas expropriated for Israeli Jewish housing already mentioned in the previous section.[94] It should be emphasized that land acquired by the Israeli state is held by the Israel-Lands Administration. As already noted ILA land cannot be sold or leased to or used for Palestinian Arabs.

Third, the Municipality has approved zoning plans that demarcate preservation zones in areas adjacent to Palestinian Arab residence, preventing any expansion out of the existing residential areas. The arbitrariness of such zoning, ostensibly in keeping with the plans laid down by the British, can be seen in the ways these "green" zones have been changed to "red" zones for Israeli Jewish development in the rush to provide housing for the wave of Soviet Jewish immigrants in the late eighties. In an interview, Municipal Councillor and former city planner Sarah Kaminker gave an example:

> Look at Sur Bahir. It is still an Arab neighbourhood. The plan defines it as a few disconnected islands of construction, although it is one village. Most of the land of Jabal al-Mukabber is marked with green lines, which means that this land cannot be built on. When it is ready to be built upon, it will be changed from green to red. This is not [former Minister of Housing] Sharon's emergency procedure, but the regular Municipal procedure.[95]

Kaminker adds: "That means in the future there will be no place for the Arabs to build in Jerusalem. They will need to leave Jerusalem and move to the West Bank."[96] (See map 4.10.)

Similarly, aesthetic considerations have been far more rigorously applied to Palestinian than to Jewish housing. For example, new construction in the Palestinian area of Jabal Mukabbir has been limited to one-story elevations while in French Hill, a new Jewish settlement, apartments of eight stories have been permitted.[97]

The final element in Israeli policy is the absence of Israeli government or municipal funding for Palestinian Arab housing development. Since 1967 only one publicly supported housing development for Palestinian Arabs has taken place, known as the Nuseibeh project in Beit Hanina.[98] Built in 1973, it consisted of a mere 200 units, although Palestinian Arab housing needs by 2025 have been assessed at a total of 122,000 units.[99] In 1981 a Municipal Master Plan submitted to the District Planning Commission proposed 20,000 units for Palestinian Arabs. By 1983 this had been scaled down to 15,000 units in the Beit Hanina and Shu'fat areas. When the plan was finally approved by the District Planning Commission—in the teeth of opposition by the Ministry of Housing—in 1992, it had been scaled back still further to 7,500 units.

This illustrates how procedural delays and amendments obstruct Palestinian Arab housing needs being met. Abu Arafeh has calculated that at the present approval rate of 335 units per year, it will take fifty years for the government to approve the total units allocated to the Palestinian Arab sector by the Master Plan. In contrast 17,400 residential units were approved for Israeli Jews in 1991–1992 alone.[100] Two other points in the plan reflect Israeli policy toward Palestinian Arab

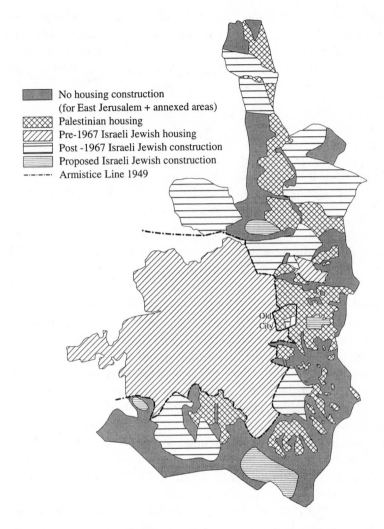

No housing construction
(for East Jerusalem + annexed areas)
Palestinian housing
Pre-1967 Israeli Jewish housing
Post -1967 Israeli Jewish construction
Proposed Israeli Jewish construction
Armistice Line 1949

MAP 4.10. Zoning Areas for Housing Construction in Jerusalem, 1990

housing needs. The approved plans do not open up any new areas for housing development but merely allow Palestinian Arabs to develop the spaces between houses. Finally the plan does not include any commitment for government or municipal spending but provides only the legal framework for approved construction.[101]

Despite the combination of these restrictions, Palestinian Arab housing construction continues to expand at a rapid rate.[102] Before examining the location and nature of this growth, it is necessary to first consider the conditions which have encouraged it. Chapter 3 showed the demographic changes that have taken place in the Palestinian Arab community in Jerusalem and its metropolitan hinterland during the post-1967 period. One impetus to the growth in the Palestinian Arab population was in the in-migration to the annexed and metropolitan areas of Jerusalem of Palestinians from other parts of the West Bank. Their willingness to accept lower wages than Israeli Jews led to the opening up of employment opportunities. Paradoxically, the Israeli Jewish housing program described in the previous section provided a large share of these new jobs.[103] At the same time Jerusalem residents hung onto their Jerusalem residency status. By doing so they were entitled to Israeli National Insurance benefits and to some extent were relieved of the worst excesses of the military occupation experienced in other villages and towns on the West Bank. Despite the restrictions on housing, therefore, Palestinians found it worthwhile to try to remain in the Jerusalem area.

Furthermore, the prolonged Israeli military occupation of the West Bank placed great obstacles in the way of investment and economic development in other regional urban centers such as Hebron and Nablus. As a consequence, the Palestinian areas in and around Jerusalem, with their better access to markets, their better communications, facilities, and infrastructure, attracted both the professional white-collar class and surplus investment funds. Without an independent and vigorous Arab banking system such funds were plowed into housing construction as the safest form of long-term investment in the prevailing political conditions. Such trends were further encouraged by the establishment of a joint Jordanian government and Palestine Liberation Organization "Steadfastness fund," which sought to consolidate Palestinian Arab residence on the West Bank by providing subsidies for housing construction. Up to 25 percent of construction costs could be met from a successful application to this Fund.[104] Israeli planners tend to overstate the significance of these funds whose total contribution to the housing situation was small.[105] More important for financing Palestinian Arab housing construction, at least until the Gulf War in 1990, were the remittances sent by relatives in the Arab Gulf states.[106]

The combined effect, therefore, of Israeli government restrictions and escalating Palestinian Arab growth is twofold. First, there is illegal construction within the boundaries of Jerusalem. Since Palestinians have very little chance of obtaining the necessary building permits, they are often left with little choice but to add stories or extensions to existing structures. And since the Municipality itself is short of building inspectors, many additions go up "overnight," or before the Municipality can do anything about them. This is particularly the case in such areas as Silwan, Sur Bahir, Wadi Joz and Ras al-Amud. Once the Municipality becomes aware of illegal construction, it either imposes fines or demolishes it. The threat of demolition is also an effective way of giving the Israeli authorities some leverage over the family concerned. It should be borne in mind that the total amount of illegal building does not ease the housing shortage for Palestinian Arabs and it receives disproportionate press attention due mainly to a campaign against it by right-wing Israeli political parties.

Second, the Palestinian Arab population is obliged to settle outside the municipal boundaries where building permits are issued either by the municipalities of the area, or by the military government of the West Bank. While these are relatively easier to acquire than from the Jerusalem Municipality, Israeli planners overstate this ease. Many of the residences in the metropolitan region along the periphery of the Municipal borders are built without permits. Some Palestinian Arab suburbs have witnessed spectacular growth. The small village of A-Ram, which had been artificially excluded from the Municipality when its boundaries were drawn in 1967, grew from 800 residents to a population of more than 20,000 inhabitants; Azariyya has doubled in population from 3,000 to 6,000 despite large-scale Christian Arab emigration.[107] Corresponding increases have taken place in other villages close by such as Hizma, Bir Nabala, and al-Jib[108] (see map 4.10).

There are considerable disadvantages in such unplanned developments. For the Israeli government the unplanned dispersal of Palestinian housing serves to underline the rapid decline of available building space for Israeli Jews. It will increase the political pressure for further restrictions, demolitions, expropriations, and re-zoning. It also explains the Israeli government's decision to extend the jurisdiction of the Jerusalem Municipality westward, where there is almost no Palestinian Arab housing to complicate and impede the construction of new Israeli Jewish housing. Finally, the scattered nature of Palestinian Arab housing makes the provision of proper access facilities, service lines and utilities, and other social and welfare amenities much more difficult in the future. Certainly, any future Palestinian planning authority made responsible for East Jerusalem and the metropolitan area outside the Municipal borders will inherit an extremely complex urban planning situation. Without careful planning and investment now, the current ultra-modern and ostensibly luxurious apartment buildings to be seen scattered along the slopes around Jerusalem may become the slums of tomorrow.

In conclusion, it is clear that in planning terms Jerusalem has arrived at a crossroads. Israeli military control over both sides of the city has permitted it to impose Israeli planning procedures and priorities which have given the government immense authority over land use in Jerusalem. Despite interministerial rivalries the overall aim of establishing lasting Israeli control through settlement and infrastructural integration has been largely implemented. However, both the lack of strong economic development and the growth of the Palestinian Arab population brings into question the long-term viability of this control. Without jobs, new immigrants and the skilled population will not stay. Palestinian Arab growth not only extends the demographic targets to be attained but also requires an increasing space for housing, employment, and services for Israeli Jews. Restricting Palestinian Arab housing construction will create tensions and exacerbate resentments against Israeli rule and irretrievably damage the goal of making Israeli sovereignty over Jerusalem acceptable through good municipal government. Extending the borders will only raise the demographic problems identified in chapter 3. The future planning of Jerusalem along lines that will satisfy the housing, employment, and service needs of all its inhabitants very much depends upon the Israeli government realizing that it cannot avoid making hard decisions about the "Jewishness" of the city and that a political compromise is urgently required.

5

Servicing the City

"In my opinion, we have to say it out loud that the Arabs who cannot come to terms with Israeli rule and be a minority—they should draw their own conclusions and leave. As for the services we have to provide for them—on principle I have said that they should receive the same services, but we must act carefully and gradually. . . . We apparently do not understand the Arab mentality very well. We must act step by step."
—S. Z. Druk, Municipal Councillor, Municipal Council Meeting, August 13, 1967.

As a large modern city and metropolitan area, Jerusalem requires an extensive network of water supplies, sewage and waste disposal, drainage, power supply, telephone, and telecommunications. It is almost fatuous to say, yet nevertheless worth making explicit, that contemporary Jerusalem could not function without these utilities and services. Their growth, administration, and political role is an important but often neglected part of any full description and analysis of the history and development of Jerusalem. Of particular interest to this study is the political implications of the degree of control over services exercised by different state or government authorities from the Ottoman period to the present day. In a topographically, ethnically and politically divided city, their location, distribution, and management has great significance for the different communities as they stand today. For example, the protracted struggle between the Israeli government and the Palestinian Arab owned Jerusalem Electricity Company in East Jerusalem was much more than a battle over the corporate assets of a private company. It was more a question of the extent to which the Palestinian Arab community in and around Jerusalem would remain in control of a key strategic utility, and also the extent to which there were limits placed upon the Israeli ability to exercise full sovereignty over East Jerusalem and the annexed areas.

The question of the location, distribution, and control over key utilities has implications for any future agreements on Jerusalem between Israel and the Palestinian Arabs. As Nadav Shragai, the noted Jerusalem correspondent of an Israeli daily, described it: "To the east of Jerusalem, on the road to Ma'ale Adumim, a rubbish dump has been built to replace the Khayriyya rubbish dump. Hundreds of tons of rubbish from Jerusalem are tipped in the territories every week. Where will Jerusalem's rubbish go with the autonomy currently being prepared? And how will the city bury its dead?"[1]

These questions are still applicable whether negotiations center on a repartitioning of Jerusalem or the devolution of functional powers to neighborhood councils. A repartitioning of the city along the Armistice Line would leave East Jerusalem bereft of any of the major utilities, save for a small power generating output. The main water supplies, for example, come from the coastal plain in Israel with the main pumping stations and pipelines situated in the Jerusalem "corridor" and the western part of the city, all areas that Israel held prior to 1967. While some water is available from sources in and around East Jerusalem, it will not by any means be sufficient for the future needs of the East Jerusalem population.[2] In the same way, Jerusalem is connected to its eastern hinterland through a service system that pays little heed to political borders. Water pipes are spread throughout the metropolitan area while sewage is deposited in the valleys and streams running down to the Dead Sea. Similar issues concerning the location and distribution of other utilities and services exist indicating that there would be enormous problems if a simple repartitioning was implemented.[3]

Clearly the lack of a separate utility and service base on the eastern side of the city could be rectified by an intensive program of investment and construction. Yet even if this was possible both logistically and in terms of physical resources, it would take up to ten years for a viable system to be built; in the meantime some transitional arrangements would be necessary. As already mentioned, water supplies from eastern sources would be insufficient, so an agreement with Israel on water sharing would have to be made. These arrangements could be on a commercial basis, similar to that between the Jerusalem Electric Company and the Israel Electricity Company, but with a politically appointed regulatory body making certain that shortages and domestic pressures did not impinge upon the rights of the Palestinian residents of East Jerusalem in a discriminatory way. In this way one can see that, whatever the political structures and boundaries decided upon, the continued functioning of East Jerusalem as an area under Palestinian political authority at the very least during the interim phases will require some cooperation with the Israeli state at a functional level.

If, on the other hand, functional powers are decentralized to local neighborhood councils such considerations would need to be addressed in greater detail. What would be the authority and extent of powers of such a regulatory body? How would the members be appointed, how would disputes be resolved? If these questions can be answered and the appropriate structures created, does this not point to possible areas of political cooperation which would match the functional cooperation? One can re-phrase the question. If there is successful cooperation in the realms of water supply, sewage disposal, and power generation and distribution, essential for the functioning of a post-agreement Jerusalem, how does this differ in substance from a joint Palestinian-Israel control of the utility and service base? Does a cooperation on this level mean that there is joint sovereignty in all but name?

In this way, the control of the city's key utilities and services raises many issues over and above the question of their continued functioning. The way in which they are controlled will help to shape the nature of the future government and administration of Jerusalem. Political issues of sovereignty will no doubt be resolved on the basis of a balance between principle and *realpolitik*. It is important to recognize that the development, administration, and manner of control over the utility and service base will act as an important guide toward a workable formula. It is also a means by which Palestinians are able to secure a foothold over the administration of the city even though the more symbolic issues of sovereignty have not been settled.

These issues make a fundamental contribution to the discussion over the future of Jerusalem. This chapter, therefore, seeks to lay down the basic situation with regard to the utility and service base of Jerusalem. It will concentrate on three areas: water supply, sewage disposal, and power generation and distribution. By examining the historical background to these utilities in Jerusalem and their post-1967 developments, we will be better able to more clearly assess their role in the discussions concerning the future of Jerusalem.

Water Supplies

As the shortage of water and supply difficulties have always been major problems in Jerusalem, water projects have always been among the most impressive engineering enterprises.[4]

Water supply in Jerusalem has always acted like a noose around Jerusalem's neck. The less water available, the greater the constraint on its growth and development. Unable to drink it struggles to survive. Conversely, the greater the supply, the greater the possibilities for expansion and welcoming new residents. Thus the ebb and flow of the water supply has mirrored the rise and fall of successive epochs in Jerusalem's history. Historically, the ancient city of Jerusalem was supplied by the Gihon spring in the Kidron valley, supplemented with wells in Silwan and Bir Ayyub further down the valley.[5] As the city developed and grew on the higher slopes away from the spring, other sources and supplies were required. Private and public cisterns and large pools were built in homes and topographically suitable locations such as Mamilla, 'Ayn al-Sultan, under al-Haram al-Sharif and Hezekiah's Pool in the Christian quarter (also known as the Pool of the Patriarch).[6] These pools and cisterns were fed by a combination of rainfall and an aqueduct bringing spring water from an area south of Bethlehem known as Soloman's Pools. Increased demand for water led to the building of an extension further southwest to the 'Arrub springs. Distribution through the city was by gravity.

During the late Ottoman and Turkish period, water shortages continued to be an acute problem for the population. Commenting on contemporary accounts of the situation, the Israeli scholar, Ben Arieh, notes:

> Jerusalem, wrote[T.] Tobler in the 1840's, was once said to be rich in water yet wanting in water. In his opinion, the city really was well-supplied. Here he appears to be in error. His impressions were probably based on the fact that many methods of supplying water were employed in the city. The opposite, however, seems to have been true: it was the shortage of water that forced Jerusalem's inhabitants to resort to so many ways of assuring continuous supply.[7]

The quest for the diversification of supply is a common and recurring thread running throughout this period. Water sellers continued to draw water from springs and wells in the vicinity of Jerusalem, loading them onto donkeys to do a brisk trade inside the Old City itself, especially in the late summer. The huge public cisterns continued to be an extremely important source. However, their unhygienic state contributed to disease and illnesses in the latter part of the year before they were replenished with fresh rainfall. In 1865 a British engineer, Captain Charles Wilson, graphically described the misuse of cisterns: "When the rain commences all that can be is collected, even from the streets, which, being the common latrine of the city, are by the end of the rainy season in a very filthy state; every duct is opened, and through these all the summer's accumulation of rubbish is carried from the courtyard and the roof to the cistern below. During the early part of summer little evil arises, the heavier particles settling to the bottom; but towards autumn the water gets low, the buckets in descending stir up the deposit, and the mixture which thousands then have to use as their daily beverage is almost too horrible to think of."[8]

All through the Ottoman period one comes across references to the aqueducts leading from Soloman's Pools and the 'Arrub springs.[9] These provided fresh clean water and were constructed to take advantage of the topography to feed both the upper and lower parts of the Old City. However, the aqueducts required constant maintenance, partly as a result of vandalism carried out by Bethlehemites and water sellers who wanted the water for themselves. This was a period when state and municipal authority was weak and the funds and the political will to ensure such maintenance were not always forthcoming. The supplies from this important source were therefore erratic and placed great restrictions upon the growth of Jerusalem.[10]

By the end of the Ottoman period the 'Arrub aqueduct was supplying 40,000 gallons of water a day but this still remained insufficient for the needs of the growing population.[11] More diverse sources were needed. Springs in the greater Jerusalem area as far as the Palestinian village of Lifta were exploited and in 1908 a project to pump water from 'Ayn Fara' in the Wadi Qilt to the east of the city was discussed. It was dropped, however, on the grounds of expense. Instead, a new reservoir was built in Abu Tur to store water for the summer droughts and more efforts were made to encourage conservation of water. The Ottoman Building Law was revised to include a provision that all new residences were required to have a private cistern before a building permit was issued.[12]

These attempts to break through the "noose" of limited water supplies can be contrasted with the initiatives undertaken by the British Mandate authorities, who were well aware that a resolution of the water supply problem was a prerequisite for the urban development of

Jerusalem. They brought with them the immense advantage of a strong centralized and comparatively efficient administration and the technological skills of army engineers. Within six months of the fall of Jerusalem in 1917, the British army had repaired the 'Arrub aqueduct with broader gauge pipes which supplied the city with 1,360 cubic meters of water daily.[13] While bringing great relief this was still not sufficient to meet the needs of the whole population and it was estimated that 36,000 people were still dependent upon cisterns and water from the Kidron valley.[14] The Mandate authorities greatly feared an outbreak of disease in the growing population through the use of these cisterns but recognized their importance in providing water. A survey carried out in 1921 ascertained that there were 7,300 public and private cisterns in use supplying 1,570,000 gallons of water annually. One-third of this capacity was located in al-Haram al-Sharif. In the absence of any immediate alternative sources of water, the Mandate authorities introduced a program of renovation in which the cisterns were emptied, cleaned, renovated, covered, and inspected regularly.

Despite these attempts a severe drought occurred in 1925 and 1926 when the 'Arrub springs failed. The city was forced to transport 100,000 gallons a day by train from Lydda and siphon 40,000 gallons a day from a spring at Urtas which fed Bethlehem.[15] The city authorities were strongly criticized for failing to meet the city's water needs, which were constantly increasing as a result of rapid Jewish immigration. By 1932 the city was being supplied with 400,000 gallons per day yet its needs were estimated to be double that amount.[16] A drought in that year led to the possibility that some of the new suburbs would have to be abandoned.

Efforts which had already been started to secure further sources of water were intensified. Proposals concerning the pumping of water up from the 'Ayn Fashkha springs, beside the northwestern shore of the Dead Sea, were discussed. The expense of such an operation led to protracted negotiations with would-be contractors in the city. The Mandate Water Board also considered pumping water from as far as 'Ayn Duk, halfway up the Jordan Valley, but its use for local irrigation was too important for sufficient amounts to be diverted. Some alleviation of the problem was achieved when pumping operations began at 'Ayn Fara' and 'Ayn Fawwar springs in Wadi Qilt which runs to the east toward Jericho (map 5.1).

Finally the Mandate authorities settled on the Ras al-'Ayn springs at the head of the al-Auja river (now known as the Yarkon river) as the

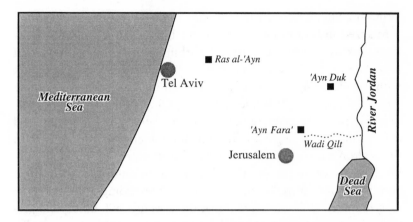

MAP 5.1. Water Supplies in Jerusalem Area During the Mandate Period

main water source for Jerusalem. Over 60 kilometers by road from the city (45 kilometers as the crow flies) it required pumping 800 meters from the coastal plain to the reservoir in the high ground at Romema in the northwestern part of the city. Yet it provided 11,370 cubic meters per day and justified the additional engineering and expense. The pipeline and four pumping stations at Ras al-'Ayn, Latrun, Bab al-Wad, and Saris were inaugurated in January 1936. Jerusalem was "finally liberated from its chronic water shortage."[17]

The British Mandate period marked the introduction of a centralized and integrated water supply system for Jerusalem. The city's localized supplies from springs and cisterns were increasingly supplemented with regular and reliable supplies from the southern aqueducts, the Wadi Qilt springs and the pipeline from Ras al-'Ayn. The extension of this network freed Jerusalem from the constricting "noose" of water shortages and permitted its population to rise in a manner which corresponded to Jerusalem's growing regional and political importance. Nevertheless, it also marked a greater dependency upon external supplies which was sustainable only within the context of a centralized government authority and a safe and accessible hinterland. Thus as Jerusalem grew in size and importance it became functionally more integrated into the region. When the region itself was split into two by the Armistice Agreements, the impact upon the development of Jerusalem was immediate and direct, particularly in the Jordanian eastern half.

Even before the Armistice Agreements were signed, Jordanian-held East Jerusalem suffered severe water shortages. By the summer of

1948, the Ras al-'Ayn springs and pipeline were in Israeli-controlled territory and the 'Ayn Fara' and 'Ayn Fawwar pumping stations had been damaged by the fighting.[18] Later, the Armistice Line cut across the southern lines depriving Jerusalem of water from this source too. In mid-1949, the 'Ayn Fara' pumping station was repaired. In 1951 it was improved to provide 3,000 cubic meters per day of a total supply to Jerusalem of 4,500 cubic meters per day. However, with the influx of refugees from the western part of the city and the Jerusalem corridor combined with the loss of supplies from Ras al-'Ayn and the 'Arrub springs, the Jordanian government was obliged to introduce rationing. With water piped to different neighborhoods and quarters in rotation twice a week and none on Fridays,[19] the dependence on cisterns returned in the Old City, particularly in al-Haram al-Sharif. Residents resorted to using the springs in Silwan and at Sur Bahir. In the mid-sixties, it was estimated that 60 percent of the population of East Jerusalem was without running water.[20]

Because of the shortage of municipal funds the Jordanian Municipality of Jerusalem contracted out the provision of water in some areas to private companies. These companies laid pipelines and sold water direct to customers.[21] Shortages led to high charges which in combination deterred the growth in population. They also contributed to the trend in settling along the road to Ramallah where water was provided by the Ramallah Al-Bireh Water Company who abstracted from the 'Ayn Fara' and 'Ayn Qinya springs and did not experience shortages to the same extent.[22] All these factors led to a very low consumption rate of water in East Jerusalem. On the eve of the 1967 War, the population was consuming only 2,000 cubic meters a day, compared to an estimated 36,000 cubic meters a day in West Jerusalem.[23] Per capita this amounted to a mere 21 percent of the West Jerusalem per capita consumption.[24]

In 1963, the Jordanian government commissioned a report on the future water requirements of East Jerusalem, which projected a minimum requirement of 36 million cubic meters per year.[25] Trial borings were carried out in the 'Ayn Fashkha springs which were considered the most suitable with a flow of 73 million cubic meters a year. However, the water was slightly radioactive and saline and would therefore need treatment before distribution. It would also need pumping more than 1,000 meters up to East Jerusalem and these two factors led to the postponement of the project until sufficient funds were available. The Jordanian government also passed a law in 1966

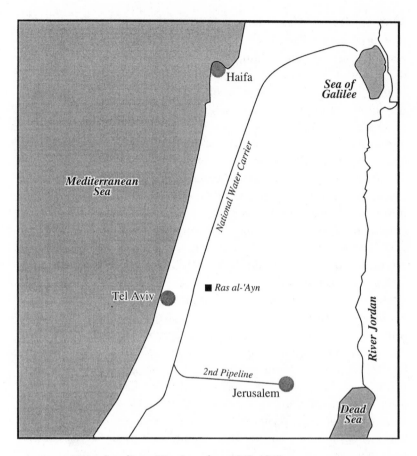

MAP 5.2. Water Supplies to West Jerusalem, 1948–1967

which established the Jerusalem Water Undertaking (Ramallah District) taking over the functions of the Ramallah Al-Bireh Water Company. The JWU continued to sell water to the East Jerusalem Municipality and the villages of Beit Hanina, Shu'fat, Bir Nabala, A-Ram, Hizma, and Qalandiyya were in its service area.[26] Water was abstracted from the 'Ayn Samia spring and a new reservoir was planned. Before these projects could be fully implemented the Israeli army occupied the West Bank and East Jerusalem was connected to the water supply of West Jerusalem.

Although the new state of Israel gained control over the Ras al-'Ayn springs, Israeli West Jerusalem also suffered shortages in the immediate aftermath of the 1948 War, as pipes and pumping stations had been cut and damaged. While the shortages were never as bad as in East Jerusalem, the government's ideological commitment to Jerusalem as the capital of the Israeli state led to a great emphasis on increasing the Jewish population. This in turn led to increasing demand upon the existing water supplies. The Ras al-'Ayn source was sufficient at this stage in absolute terms, but because of the shortage of storage capacity the Israeli Municipality of Jerusalem experienced problems in providing sufficient supplies during peak consumption periods. Two small reservoirs were built at Romema, and in 1955 a larger one was constructed at Bayit Vegan.[27] The Bayit Vegan reservoir was fed by an entirely new pipeline from boreholes made in the Givat Brenner area, south of Rehovot, rising to Jerusalem via Nahshon Junction, Ishtaul, Zova, and 'Ayn Karim as well as a series of underground pumping stations (see map 5.2).[28]

The Municipality was determined to diversify its sources in case of hostilities and to cater for the projected needs of the city. Accordingly a search was undertaken in the Jerusalem region for wells and boreholes. In 1959 a borehole was dug in 'Ayn Karim and further discoveries were made throughout the sixties near Qiryat Anavim, just north of the main Tel Aviv-Jerusalem road, near the Palestinian village of Abu Ghosh.[29] These works were carried out on behalf of the Municipality by Tahal (the Water Planning for Israel Company) and Mekorot (the Israeli Water Company). Mekorot was made the water supply authority within the Municipal boundaries of Jerusalem.

Other attempts at diversification were made. A dam was built near 'Ayn Karim to catch the run-off water of the Nahal Shorek running southwest from Lifta to the coast. The dam's capacity was 1.1 million cubic meters but it was poorly researched and cracks and holes in the bedrock led to much seepage of the water trapped in this way. By the end of May each year the reservoir was usually dry.[30] In 1965 discussions were also conducted concerning the feasibility of recycling the city's waste water but the cost of treatment was regarded as prohibitively high and the project was not implemented.[31]

These attempts at diversification were important since by 1966 West Jerusalem was consuming 12 million cubic meters of water a year while the Ras al-'Ayn spring was producing only 11.5 million cubic meters a year.[32] Indeed the issue became especially acute when the Ras al-'Ayn water was diverted to a burgeoning Tel Aviv and the existing Jerusalem pipelines were connected to the National Water Carrier, the main pipeline running down the coast to the Negev desert from the Sea of Galilee.[33] This meant that West Jerusalem became even more integrated into a national distribution system and more dependent on external supplies.

Within days of the occupation of East Jerusalem and the areas that were subsequently annexed to Israel, the Water Department of the Israeli Municipality of Jerusalem connected pipes between the two systems and repaired the pumps and pipelines damaged during the fighting. This was part of the "integration of services" to which Israel was prepared to admit rather than to accept the term "annexation."[34] The integration of services included the transfer of the offices of the Water Department of the Jordanian Municipality of Jerusalem, along with its archives and personnel, to the West Jerusalem offices, as well as the dismantlement of its motors and pumps.[35] In 1967 and 1968 an inspection of all the cisterns in the Old City and the annexed areas was conducted.

These moves increased the total supply of water to the city by only 16 percent. It is significant that the annexation of the enlarged East Jerusalem and the increase in the total population of the city by approximately 30 percent did not lead to a corresponding increase in water consumption. The Palestinian Arab population had been accustomed to a much lower consumption than the Israeli Jewish population.[36] However, soon after the pipes were connected, the mere availability of regular supplies led to Palestinian Arab consumption increasing by 50 percent.[37]

The Israeli Jerusalem Municipality, at pains to ensure that it was the sole supplier of water to all the residents of Jerusalem, promptly took over pipes and systems operated by independent Palestinian water contractors. It came into dispute with the Military Government of the West Bank over the operations of the Jerusalem Water Undertaking (Ramallah District), the JWU. Because of the enlargement of the municipal borders, the northern suburbs of Jerusalem along the road to Ramallah were supplied by the JWU. Both the JWU and its Palestinian customers inside the enlarged municipality insisted that their agreements should stand. They were supported by the Military Government who did not wish to see the JWU being forced to cease operations in all the Ramallah area simply because of the loss of its main customers to the south.[38] The Municipality of Jerusalem was obliged to back down and negotiated an agreement with the JWU in which it would continue to supply water to existing and new Palestinian customers and be able to purchase water from Mekorot via the Municipality.[39] New Israeli settlements such as Neve Ya'aqov would be the responsibility of the Municipality.

This climb-down is significant since it marked the constraints placed on the full and complete annexation of the enlarged municipal area of Jerusalem and thus the sovereignty of the Israeli state. For logistical and economic reasons the Municipality of Jerusalem was not able to be the sole supplier of water to the residents of Jerusalem. A key strategic utility was not totally in the hands of the Israeli state. Furthermore, from the period 1967 to 1988 the JWU remained accountable to a Jordanian Minister and received funds from the Jordanian-Palestinian Joint Committee as well as other Arab and Islamic sources.[40] A similar state of affairs was also to exist in the provision of electricity to East Jerusalem and the annexed areas. (See section on electricity supply.) It illustrates that without Israel annexing the West Bank the functional links between the annexed areas in the Jerusalem Municipality (Area E by earlier definitions) create obstacles in the way of Israel clinching full control over those annexed areas of Jerusalem.

Very shortly after the Israeli government embarked upon its settlement program it became clear that water consumption in Jerusalem would exceed supply. In 1973, the combination of a dry winter, a heatwave, a higher than normal influx of tourists and new immigrants to the city all contributed to a severe shortage, especially in Beit Hanina in north Jerusalem.[41] Water was also trucked in to parts of West Jerusalem such as Rehavia and Romema. From this drought it was clear that Jerusalem would need additional sources of water and storage capacity in order to meet the demographic objectives of the government. After a period of respite the water "noose" was being felt again.

A third pipeline from the coastal plain was planned and work began in 1976. Twenty kilometers long, it took three years to complete and abstracted water from five boreholes in the Ishtaul area, northeast of Bet Shemesh, and from a borehole near the Modi'in settlements on the West Bank just north of the Jerusalem-Tel Aviv highway.[42] The 36-inch pipeline fed the Romema reservoirs passing beside Zova and Kastel in the Jerusalem corridor. Two pumping stations at Kesalon and David raised the water from 20 meters to 400 meters (see map 5.3).[43]

The Municipality wisely was anxious to avoid a complete dependence upon external water supplies and sought to both increase its storage capacity and abstract water from the immediate locality of Jerusalem. The existing cisterns were insufficient and would require constant maintenance, cleaning, and inspection to retain contemporary standards of water hygiene. The modern equivalent to cisterns in Jerusalem, the reservoirs at Romema and Bayit Vegan, were unable to

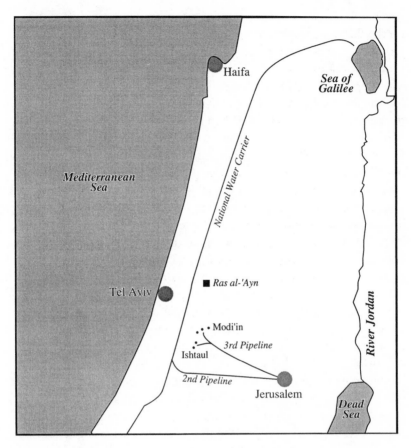

MAP 5.3. Water Supplies to Jerusalem, 1979

meet the surge in demand which occurred in high summer and drought periods. Three more reservoirs were built in the annexed areas. Two were with a capacity of 20,000 cubic meters in French Hill and a smaller on of 5,000 cubic meters in East Talpiot or Abu Tor.[44] By 1979, the Municipality had created a total storage capacity of 250,000 cubic meters. Two more reservoirs are planned in Romema and Har Nov.[45] Following an outbreak of algae bloom at the Bayit Vegan reservoir in 1975, all reservoirs are now covered.[46]

More important than the increase in storage capacity has been the search for additional supplies of water from boreholes both inside the municipal area and on in the metropolitan area outside the municipal border (Area G). Between 1960 and 1975 a program of test drillings carried out by Tahal and the Municipality's own Water Department

established 14 wells near 'Ayn Karim. Six more were established within
the municipal borders.[47] Three were in the annexed areas—at the foot
of Mt. Scopus, in Neve Ya'aqov, and near Shu'fat.[48] By 1973, these wells
were providing 7 million cubic meters of water annually, nearly 25
percent of the city's water consumption for that year. Water engineers
estimated that an astonishing 17 million cubic meters could be
obtained from local sources in this way.[49]

However since these optimistic forecasts the supply of water from
local boreholes has encountered a number of difficulties. The water
from them is subject to seasonal fluctuations and the penetration of
surface flood waters cause contamination. In addition most of the
holes are between 200 to 600 meters deep and are expensive to maintain and repair.[50] Other attempts at diversification included plans to
purify the city's waste water for recycling as irrigation water for agriculture. During the eighties, approximately 20 million cubic meters of
water was siphoned off the Jerusalem pipelines to service agricultural
settlements along the way; 15 million cubic meters were used for
watering crops.[51] The Municipality's Water Department estimates that
by 1992, 11 million cubic meters of water could be saved if these settlements were provided with waste water from the city.[52]

The Municipality has encountered considerable technical problems
in the course of supplying water to Jerusalem. Old pipe work has led
to leakages and wastage and the breakdown of pumps has exacerbated
the shortages of 1973 and 1975. Surges in demand were for at least a
decade difficult to respond to in view of the limited storage capacity.
A dispersed and patchwork distribution system added to the difficulties of management. In 1976 a centralized monitoring station was
built at the Beit Zayit reservoir.[53] A control room monitored the levels of all the reservoirs simultaneously and the supply could be cen-
trally regulated. Malfunctioning of pumps and burst pipes would be
reported and a coordinated action taken. In conjunction with the
Ministry of Environment, pumping stations along the pipelines from
the coast have been partially automated and many have emergency
generators.[54]

Despite all these efforts and improvements, the population growth
of Jerusalem continued to outstrip the capacity to supply it with water.

Projections of growth in the number of water users by the Ministry
of Environment in the whole metropolitan area (Area F) indicate a
population of 750,000 by the end of the century and 930,000 by the
year 2010.[56] The necessity to increase the water supply to Jerusalem

TABLE 5.1. Population and Water Consumption in the Jerusalem Area

Year	Population	Water consumption	consumption per capita
		000 cubic meters	
1972	313,800	19,000	60.5
1978	386,600	33,000	85.4
1982	424,400	37,400	88.1
1988	493,500	41,700	84.5
1990	524,500	41,500	79.1

has, therefore, become a municipal and national priority. Discussions as to the feasibility of a fourth pipeline from the coastal plain began in 1984. To meet the projected demand it was to be a major undertaking, requiring the investment of $70 million, a new power station at Even Saphir in the Jerusalem corridor and four new pumping stations en route. Pipes would range in diameter from 5 inches at the coastal plain to 36 inches higher in the mountains and the water would be raised from 20 meters to 840 meters over a distance of 50 kilometers.[57]

The source for this water would partly be boreholes near Lydda and partly from the National Water Carrier—a 66" pipeline carrying water from the Sea of Galilee to the Negev. The route would follow a line directly south from Lydda to Latrun, then to Nahal Ilan on the north of the Jerusalem-Tel Aviv highway, eastward to Sho'eva, near the Palestinian village of Abu Ghosh and up to 'Ayn Karim where it would divide. One fork would enter the reservoir at Bayit Vegan and the other would carry on farther north through Moza to Ramot. To date only twelve kilometers of this pipeline has been laid at the Jerusalem end of the route and the target date for completion, March 1992, has had to be postponed, possibly for financial reasons. The whole project depends upon the construction of a secondary power station at Even Sappir and this may prove to be difficult to finance from existing budgets.

The decision to invest in a fourth pipeline to Jerusalem demonstrates the strength of the Israeli government's commitment to the growth of the Israeli-Jewish population in Jerusalem and in the surrounding settlements. Confirmation of this view can be found in the way domestic consumption continues to rise well in excess of industrial consumption. Since 1986 domestic consumption has fluctuated between 56.2 percent and 66.7 percent of total demand while industrial consumption has not been greater than 4.5 percent.[58] Capital intensive investment of this sort for largely domestic convenience is quite noteworthy. The strength of the government's commitment, moreover, can be seen in the way in which the construction of new Israeli settlements in and around Jerusalem have continued irrespective of the Municipality's or Mekorot's capacity to furnish them with the appropriate services. The pressure of Israeli Jewish population growth in this way has resulted in poor sanitation and sewage disposal and led to fears of contamination of the very water supplies that the Municipality is hoping to exploit.[59] Drillings have also begun on boreholes in the Herodion region, southeast of Bethlehem, with the view of using this water as an emergency supply to Jerusalem (see table 5.1).[60]

Provision of water to the Palestinian Arab population in the annexed areas and surrounding villages has been extended in line with political and financial reasons. There are strong commercial incentives for Mekorot and the Municipality to increase the quantity of paying customers. Indeed, Municipality pipes have been extended to Anata, Ramallah, Azariyya, Abu Dis, and Bethlehem.[61] This extension of the Municipality's services can be viewed as being consistent with its attempts to be the sole supplier of water in Jerusalem and with the government's attempt to secure control over Jerusalem. As will be discussed similar policies are pursued with respect to the provision of electricity.

The implications of such control could be see during the water shortages of 1973. The residents of Beit Hanina, a Palestinian suburb on the road to Ramallah, suffered shortages many weeks before other parts of Jerusalem were affected because the Municipality cut back on its supplies to the Jerusalem Water Undertaking (Ramallah District), the JWU, which supplied Beit Hanina. The JWU's inability to maintain normal supplies in this situation was largely due to restrictions placed upon its abstraction operations, making it dependent upon purchased supplies from the Jerusalem Municipality. This also increased the cost of the water supplied. Similar dependency can be seen in villages just outside the Municipality borders. Without proper revenue due to the virtual collapse of local government administration on the West Bank, the Abu Dis council was unable to pay the Jerusalem Municipality for its water supplies. This led to the cutting off of the water supplies to the village.[62] During the *intifada*, cutting off the water supply to a particular locality has been used as a means of punishment for anti-Israeli government actions carried out by some of the residents.[63] In this way the Israeli government's control over this key resource in an unbalanced political and economic situation has led to a critical dependency upon the Israeli state.[64]

An important point to consider in any evaluation of a separate water supply for an independent Palestinian East Jerusalem, or functionally decentralized neighborhoods, is the sophistication of the existing system. Despite the Municipality's attempts at diversification, the Jerusalem water supply is, and with the fourth pipeline will become increasingly so, dependent upon the Israeli state network. Supplying the future needs appears to involve a centralized and regional overview for distribution, maintenance, and future investment.

If following a peace agreement East Jerusalem is largely depopulated by Israeli Jews and partially replaced by Palestinian returnees it will require much larger resources traditionally and hitherto available on the eastern side of the city from springs, wells, cisterns, and the Wadi Qilt springs of 'Ayn Fara' and 'Ayn Fawwar. As we saw in the description of the Mandate period, it was not until the British built a pipeline westward to the Ras al-'Ayn spring that Jerusalem's endemic water shortage was temporarily solved. It is possible that new sources will be found higher up from the 'Ayn Fashkha springs near the Dead Sea which will avoid the radioactive contamination that occurs lower down, and a long-term supply will be secured. Research of this sort may show that a separate abstraction system and distribution network is possible for East Jerusalem. To be relevant this decade it will require massive investment and construction at a rapid rate. It does appear that whatever the political arrangements agreed upon concerning the future of Jerusalem, the short and medium term imperatives are that an agreement is made with Mekorot, the Israeli Municipality of Jerusalem, and the Israeli government over the supply of water to Palestinian-controlled parts of East Jerusalem.

It is unlikely that cooperation on this functional level can be wholly effective without political structures which will safeguard the proper implementation of agreements. While the Israeli government is unlikely to accede to anything that hints of a joint Palestinian-Israeli water authority over Jerusalem, the knowledge that some of the water destined for Jerusalem is either derived from or whose pipelines cut across the West Bank gives Palestinian politicians some leverage. It strengthens their case for some form of monitoring body to oversee the management and distribution of water supplies to Jerusalem. Given the wide area from which water to Jerusalem is abstracted, it is hard to see, nevertheless, how an agreement to supply water to Palestinian-controlled areas of East Jerusalem can come about without a wider agreement over the use of water resources in the West Bank and the Sea of Galilee.

Sewage Disposal

As with the question of water supplies, the hygienic and environmentally sensitive disposal of sewage in Jerusalem has long been a problem. Despite its high altitude and wet, cool winters, the accumulation of refuse and sewage became a major cause of disease and epidemic in Jerusalem during the late Ottoman and Turkish periods.[65] A description of the health situation in 1864 published by a British doctor, Dr. Chaplin, gives a colorful account of the desperate state of hygiene in Jerusalem at that time:

> All kinds of animals and vegetable matter are allowed to lie and rot in the streets. If a dog or a cat dies, it putrefies in the roadway, or is eaten by one of its companions ...The remains of horses, donkeys and camels are usually dragged outside the city, and left just under the walls to be devoured by dogs and jackals ... For seven months of the year there is no rain, and the air during this long dry season becomes filled with the loathsome dust and odour which result from so much impurity ...[66]

Another British visitor already mentioned, the engineer Captain Wilson, discovered during his survey of cisterns in the Old City and the Kidron valley evidence of an extensive drainage system which, in his opinion, could have been made usable with a few repairs.[67] Indeed, Ben Arieh points out that rebels against Ibrahim Pasha in the 1830s infiltrated into the Old City via the sewage system, suggesting both their longevity and the extent of their penetration into the heart of the city.

By the second half of the nineteenth century, the Ottoman authorities were carrying out an erratic program of cleaning and refurbishment of the sewage and drainage system in Jerusalem. New canals were dug and old ones repaired. In 1887 special efforts were made around the Damascus Gate with the installation of new pipes and the repair of the old.[68] With the development of neighborhoods outside the Old City walls by Jewish immigrants, some attempts were made to link them to the city's system, but in the main they were provided with their own cesspits and soakaways. Sewage drainage remained confined to the Old City and flowed into the Kidron valley, where it was diverted for irrigation.[69] However, the growth in the population outside the walls began to provoke concern as to the disposal of sewage there. In 1910 and 1912, the Palestinian Mayor of Jerusalem, Husayni al-Husayni, appealed to Diaspora Jewry to help the Jerusalem Municipality fund the construction of a sewage system for the new neighborhoods.[70] In 1914, plans for a new network were completed but were interrupted by the war.

During their administration of Jerusalem, the British showed great concern for the hygiene of the Holy City and tackled the problem with vigor. As part of the water-cleaning strategy, all pools, cisterns, and drains in the city were cleaned, refurbished, covered, and regularly inspected. By the mid-1920s, Jerusalem had acquired the reputation of a healthy city and environment compared to the previous state of affairs and to conditions on the coastal plain.[71] In response to the steady growth of settlement along the western and southern ridges of Jerusalem, the city authorities installed the first drainage network which drained into the Shorek stream, to the west of the city. This in turn flowed into the Mediterranean sea near the modern-day Israeli village of Palmachim. At the same time the city's Water Board expanded and renewed the system in the Old City and extended the outflow pipe to a point further down the Kidron valley. Building regulations with stringent conditions concerning the construction of cesspools, septic tanks, and cisterns were also introduced in order to prevent seepage, accumulation, and contamination.[72]

The partition period between 1948 and 1967 saw few major developments in the sewage disposal system in Jerusalem. The Armistice Line did not cut across any major outflows although residents in the Musrara and Yemin Moshe quarters experienced some difficulties when drainage pipes were cut. In Jordanian East Jerusalem another eight kilometers of piping was added to the system, particularly in Silwan and Wadi Joz; but it continued to flow untreated into the Kidron valley.[73] It became accepted practice for farmers along the valley to irrigate their fields and vegetables by tapping into the outflow.[74] The British regulations concerning the use of cesspools, septic tanks, and cisterns continued to be applied to the best of the ability of the Municipality.

The proportionately faster growth of the population of West Jerusalem did not lead to any greater action on the part of the Israeli

Municipality of Jerusalem on the west side. Sewage continued to be fed into the Shorek and also the Refa'im stream which joined the Shorek a few kilometers west of Jerusalem. In this the planners of West Jerusalem were assisted in the city's growth away from the center in a westerly direction. It was not until 1965 that the Municipality started making plans for the treatment of sewage before disposing of it in the valleys and streams around Jerusalem.[75] By 1967 the daily outflow from West Jerusalem was approximately 28,000 cubic meters, well beyond the capacity of the purification plant planned.

Since the occupation and the annexation of the enlarged East Jerusalem, and despite the tremendous growth in population encouraged by the Israeli government and Municipality, the situation concerning the disposal of Jerusalem's sewage has not improved. It has, in fact, got much worse. In 1991, the Jerusalem Section of the Israeli Ministry of Environment declared in its Annual Report: "Regarding Jerusalem's sewage, the situation is appalling: two streams, Refa'im to the west and Kidron to the east, are flowing with raw sewage, while two other streams, Shorek to the west and Og to the east, are carrying sewage that has been treated only to a minimal extent."[76]

In the last quarter century the sewage outflow of Jerusalem has more than tripled, to an estimated 95,000 cubic meters daily in 1995. By the turn of the century, it is expected to exceed 100,000 cubic meters daily.[77] The only purification plant is the one at 'Ayn Karim which has the capacity of 13,000 cubic meters daily.[78] Other treatment plants are filtration units, which merely break up the solid wastes without treating the bacteria content. According to the Israeli government's State Comptroller's Report of 1991, NIS 7 million (approximately $2.5 million) has been invested in filtration equipment without any noticeable improvement and should not be regarded as tackling the root of the problem, that is, insufficient investment in purification systems.[79]

The result of this neglect is a problem of steadily mounting proportions. Every day, sewage equal to the contents of three Olympic-standard swimming pools is being poured into the streams and *wadis* around Jerusalem. The ecological impact of such action is as yet unknown but deeply disturbing nonetheless. A number of streams are already highly contaminated and there is a danger that the important Yarkon Teninim aquifer, "one of the best sources of water in Israel," may soon be polluted.[80] The proliferation of new Israeli settlements and the expansion of existing Palestinian villages in the Jerusalem area without adequate sewage disposal systems serves to exacerbate this trend.

The Existing System

The sewage disposal system of Jerusalem is divided into four main sewage basins—the Shorek basin (northwest), the Refa'im basin (southwest), the Og basin (northeast), and the Kidron basin (southeast) (see map 5.4). The dividing lines are determined primarily by topography of the city and surrounding area and cut across the Armistice Lines and municipal borders. They also, in most cases, collect sewage from Palestinian and Israeli Jewish neighborhoods without differentiation.

The Shorek sewage basin, for example, comprises the Israeli Jewish neighborhoods of 'Ayn Karim, Hadassah Hospital, Kfar Shaul, Qiryat Moshe, Romema, Ramot, Ramot Eshkol, as well as the Palestinian suburbs and villages of Shu'fat, Beit Hanina, and Dahiya al-Barid. It does not as yet include the Palestinian suburb of A-Ram or the village and refugee camp of Qalandiyya, just outside the municipal borders. At present an extension from part of the Israeli settlement of Neve Ze'ev drains into this basin, but plans have been made to re-direct the sewage to the Og basin in order to decrease the flow to the overworked 'Ayn Karim purification plant.[81] Plans are also being made to collect the sewage from Ramallah and Palestinian areas to the north of Qalandiyya airport in the Shorek basin. The sewage pipes feed into a 28-inch pipe, which enters the 'Ayn Karim purification plant where the solids are separated from the liquid waste. The solids are dried out in sludge beds for fertilizer while the liquid is poured into the Shorek stream and used for agricultural irrigation by Kibbutz Tzara downstream on the coastal plain.[82] Since the purification plant has a limited capacity, the excess sewage, approximately 2,000–3,000 cubic meters a day, is conveyed by pipe to an outflow point west of the Hadassah Hospital, where it is deposited into the Shorek stream and meets up with the sewage from the Refa'im basin a few kilometers further west.

The Refa'im sewage basin is the largest collector of Jerusalem's sewage and stretches from Yir Gonim in the west to Talpiot in the east, Rehavia in the north and Gilo in the south. It also includes the Palestinian suburb and village of Bayt Safafa and collects some sewage from the Israeli settlement at East Talpiot. Approximately 40,000 cubic meters of sewage flows down a 40-inch pipe into a treatment plant beside the Refa'im stream near Beitar. The solid wastes are filtered and

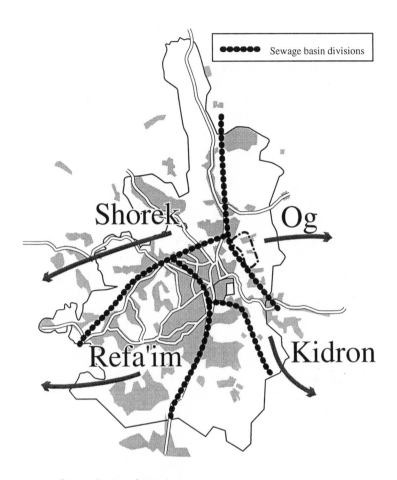

MAP 5.4. Sewage Basins of Jerusalem

broken up before being deposited, without any purification, into the stream. It joins the Shorek stream a few kilometers downstream and receives further filtration at the Bet Shemesh and Kibbutz Tzara plants.

In 1975, the Municipality of Jerusalem received approval for the construction of a purification plant for the Refa'im sewage basin. Land has already been set aside for this purpose and an access road built.[83] The proposed plant would also treat the sewage from Bayt Jallah and the western part of Bethlehem. However, delays have been caused by renewed discussions as to the suitability of constructing a larger plant which would also serve the Shorek basin at the point where the two streams meet. In addition, the mounting problems in the Og and Kidron basins have diverted Municipal energies and funds.

The sewage disposal situation in the northeastern basin, the Og basin, has been and continues to be extremely serious. Approximately 12,000 cubic meters of sewage drain into this basin and projections indicate that this will rise to 44,000 cubic meters by 2000. The basin collects sewage from Palestinian areas such as Abu Tur, Isawiyya, and parts of Anata village and Shu'fat refugee camp. Sewage from Israeli Jewish areas of Givat Sha'ul, French Hill, Pisgat Ze'ev, and Neve Ya'acov also enters this basin. As already mentioned some of the sewage from Neve Ya'aqov feeds into the Shorek basin but this will be phased out. Sewage from Ma'ale Adumim and Kufr Adumim farther to the east, and industrial waste from Mishor Adumim and the Jerusalem Electricity Company generators also drain into the Og stream which descends to the Dead Sea. Of particular concern has been disposal of the contaminated and toxic waste from the laboratories of the Hebrew University on Mount Scopus and the wards of Hadassah Hospital.[84]

A filtration plant has been built just east of Ma'ale Adumim equipped with rotostrainers to break up the solid waste; but the plant does not treat the sewage itself. In addition it has the capacity to filter only 2,500 cubic meters daily. A sewage disposal pipeline is currently being laid to carry the sewage down the al-Mog junction between Jericho and the Dead Sea and some of the sewage will be diverted for agricultural use for Israeli settlements.[85] The rest of the sewage is simply piped out from the residential areas and deposited into the desert, streams, and *wadis* until it drains into the Og stream itself. As early as 1976, the Ministry of Environment was concerned about all this raw and toxic sewage entering the drinking supply and food chain.[86] The Wadi Qilt springs are heavily contaminated and the Society for the Protection of Nature in Israel has issued "no drinking" warnings to hikers. In July 1992, a broken pipe left unrepaired for five days discharged 20,000 cubic meters of raw sewage into the Wadi Qilt itself.[87]

What becomes clear when one examines the situation in the Og basin is the absence of long-term and coordinated planning in view of the steep rise in population in the northeastern parts of Jerusalem. Because of the ambiguity of the Israeli government and municipality to the growth of the Palestinian population both inside and on the edges of the municipal borders little attention was paid to providing essential services such as sewage disposal. It would only serve to encourage Palestinian residency when Israeli policy was to discourage it. In contrast, the lack of adequate sewage disposal for the new Israeli settlements in this area was a result of poor coordination rather than neglect.

According to the Israeli government's State Comptroller's Report for 1991, a dispute between the Municipality of Jerusalem and the Israeli Ministry of Housing contributed to the steadily worsening situation. In return for not paying the Municipality's "sewage tax" when constructing the settlements, the Ministry of Housing agreed to install an adequate sewage infrastructure and contribute half of the costs of a new purification plant in the Og basin. The agreement was broken by the Ministry of Housing and the Municipality has frozen the purification plant project.[88] In addition, the Ministry of Housing ignored another agreement not to allow families to move into Pisgat Ze'ev until an adequate sewage disposal system was provided.[89] The contamination of the Wadi Qilt springs can be directly attributed to the sewage from Neve Ya'aqov. Whenever the pumps which direct the water to the Shorek basin malfunction, the sewage is simply deposited by means of an outflow pipe into the barren land to its east.[90]

Another example of poor planning can be found in the sewage disposal system of Ma'ale Adumim, a community originally planned as a small settlement that would not suffer a contamination problem. When it was decided to transform Ma'ale Adumim into a satellite town of Jerusalem and give it municipal status, no new plans were made for sewage disposal, so that a pool of untreated sewage has built up at the base of the settlement.[91] It may, of course, be contaminating underground water sources. Finally, the industrial waste from the Mishor Adumim industrial estate on the road to Jericho is deposited into the desert around it draining into the Og stream.[92] Hampering the Municipality's plans for dealing with the raw outflow in this basin is not only the dispute with the Ministry of Housing over funding but also objections delivered by the residents of Ma'ale Adumim for a purification plant in their vicinity.[93]

The deposition of raw sewage into the desert and *wadi*s is also a feature of the southeasterly basin, the Kidron sewage basin. This basin collects sewage from the Old City, Wadi Joz, Silwan, Abu Tur, and parts of the new Israeli settlement of East Talpiot. Approximately 24,000 cubic meters of sewage enters the valley daily and descends to the Dead Sea at Nahal Avenat. A sewage outflow pipe extends to the very edge of the municipal borders and some sewage is diverted for agricultural use. A purification plant has been planned for construction at this point but not implemented. There is also a plan to connect parts of East Talpiot, Ramat Rachel, and scattered residences in the southeast to a system collecting sewage from the eastern parts of Bethlehem and

Bayt Sahur. This proposed fifth basin will also flow into the Kidron valley.[94]

The sewage disposal situation for Jerusalem is regarded as scandalous. The national capital of a westernized industrialized country and a city of major international significance is depositing at least 86,000 cubic meters of sewage daily into the natural environment. As the 1991 Annual Report of the Ministry of Environment concluded, "the subject [was] one of great urgency because of the environmental damage that might be caused to the aquifer if the present situation continues, and because of the side effects of treatment activity. . . ."

One should note that the contamination of water sources, the degradation of the environment, and possible long-term ecological damage are being carried out in fulfillment of an ideological commitment to expanding Israeli Jewish population rapidly in the area. This commitment is at the expense of the necessary planning and irrespective of the need to install the required infrastructure. Of particular concern to the Palestinian community is that by contaminating the water aquifers on the eastern side of the city, such neglect on the part of the Israeli government and Municipality of Jerusalem may preempt the development of a Palestinian-controlled water abstraction and distribution system in the future.

It is hard to see how the international community would contemplate a Jerusalem totally controlled by Israel to continue to use the eastern edge of the city as a giant toilet without some regulation. Whatever the specific outcome of the peace negotiations currently underway, some form of Palestinian monitoring of the sewage disposal system of Jerusalem will be vital if those parts of the West Bank between Jerusalem and the Dead Sea are to be freed of further environmental damage. In addition, and in contrast to the Israeli control over water supplies, the vacuum created by Israeli neglect of sewage disposal presents the Palestinian community with an opportunity to introduce a modern comprehensive purifying and recycling system for irrigation or domestic use. Such a system would need to be integrated with the Jerusalem system, which presents another opportunity for Palestinians to influence the development of Jerusalem.

Electricity

Unlike water supplies and sewage disposal, part of the provision of electricity has remained partly in Palestinian hands. Indeed, until 1987, approximately one-third of the customers of the Palestinian company were Israeli Jewish. This was, paradoxically, a direct result of the Israeli government's settlement policies in the annexed areas of Jerusalem. As two Israeli scholars, Professors Michael Romann and Alex Weingrod point out: "This represents one of the rare cases in which the Old East-West dividing line was retained, rather than the now predominant Jewish-Arab ethnic boundary. More significantly, this was the only important instance in which Jewish customers and zones were dependent on an essential public service originating in the Arab sector."[95]

Neither can it be argued that it was the private ownership of the company which inhibited Israeli attempts to control this essential utility. Private Palestinian bus companies and, as we have seen, commercial water contractors were not similarly exempted.[96] The reasons for such favoritism are not entirely clear but probably comprise both a fear of the adverse international reaction that a takeover of a company which has its concession enshrined in international law would engender and a measure of *realpolitik* in recognizing the support of the Jordanian government for the company.

The fact remains that for twenty years important Israeli strategic assets were supplied by a non-Jewish and non-Israeli institution. This points to both limitations on the authority of the Israeli state and also to the possibility of future Palestinian and Israeli cooperation at a functional level. As will be shown, although legal and security grounds were the driving force behind the Israeli takeover of the Palestinian-owned company, it was made possible more on economic and financial grounds than on legal or security grounds.

The first electric lights and generators were installed in Jerusalem at the turn of the century. Private institutions such as the Notre Dame Hostel, the Augusta Victoria Hospital, the Dominican Institute, and a Palestinian Arab pharmacy and hotel bought their own generators and fittings.[97] In the closing phases of the Turkish period, the Jerusalem Municipality began discussions over the possibility of granting concessions to foreign companies for lighting and the construction of tramways.[98] In 1914, a Greek entrepreneur, Mavromattis, secured a concession for the generation and distribution of electric power and the construction of electric tramways.[99] More picturesquely, the concession would have covered an area twenty kilometers in radius from the central point on top of the dome of the Church of the Holy Sepulcher. Due to the onset of the 1914–18 War the concession was not activated.

It is said that General Allenby of the British army ushered in the period of British Mandate rule in Jerusalem with a supply of candles. Certainly fuel shortages and his refusal to recognize the Mavromattis concession delayed the provision of electricity to the general public. Supported by the Greek government, Mavromattis took the British Mandate authorities to the International Court of Justice at the Hague in a celebrated case and won.[100] Subsequently the concession was sold to a British company, Balfour Beatty, who built a power station along the Bethlehem road near the railway station. The thirties saw the gradual extension of power lines to the new suburbs, and in 1948 the British High Commissioner extended the duration of the concession to 1988 with review dates at five-yearly intervals.

After the partition of the city in 1948, the power station and main transmission lines were in the Israeli-held western part of Jerusalem. Consequently East Jerusalem was blacked out for more than a year. Part of the Armistice Agreement signed in 1949 allowed for the provision of electricity from the Bethlehem Road station to East Jerusalem, but failure to implement other parts of the Agreement meant that this never took place.[101] As a result of the "hardening" of the partition the status of the concession held by Balfour Beatty was confusing. The British company continued to supply West Jerusalem and gradually built up its generating capacity on the eastern side of the Armistice Line.

In 1954 the Israel Electricity Company (IEC) bought the concession, including the plant and equipment, as far as it applied to Israeli-held territory.[102] Israeli policy was to site power generating facilities away from the border for security reasons. Investment in steam turbines also required large quantities of water. Consequently, coastal sites were and continue to be used to supply Jerusalem, with power lines and transmission stations along the Jerusalem corridor. The Bethlehem Road power station remained in operation as an emergency back-up station. Following the annexation of East Jerusalem and the adjacent areas in 1967, a new gas turbine was located at the Atarot industrial park, mainly for industrial use.[103] At present there are six transformer stations within the Municipality border supplying West Jerusalem and the new Israeli settlements and one on Har Tuv in the Jerusalem corridor. Plans have been made for the construction of a secondary power station at Even Sappir which is an essential part of the fourth pipeline project. New power lines from the coastal plain generators are being planned which will carry 400 kilowatts and supply the city and settlements in the metropolitan area and in the Jordan Valley.

The only exception to the Israeli state monopoly of the power supply to Jerusalem is the Palestinian-owned Jerusalem Electric Company (JEC).[104] The JEC inherited the Jordanian half of the original concession which was revived when Balfour Beatty installed a generator in Wadi Joz.[105] In 1956, the concession was bought by a consortium of six Palestinian municipalities and 2,000 private shareholders.[106] A year later the Jordanian government purchased the company and its equipment but returned the management of the concession to the original owners. In view of later developments it is important to note that two representatives of the Jordanian Municipality of Jerusalem sat on the JEC's Board of Trustees and it remained accountable to Amman. The area of the concession was extended to a point midway between Jerusalem and Nablus, and midway between Jerusalem and Hebron, which included Bethlehem and surrounding towns, and down to the Jordan River in the east and the Armistice Line in the west.[107] Between 1957 and 1967 the number of electricity customers increased from 7,623 to 22,097.[108] This made the JEC the largest supplier of electricity on the West Bank.

Following the occupation and annexation of East Jerusalem and the surrounding area, the economic absurdity of two electric companies supplying a moderately sized city was clear to all. However, for the Palestinian and Arab community as a whole, the maintenance of an independent Palestinian electricity utility was of great political significance. It was deemed a vital contribution to the survival of the Palestinian and Arab character of the city. It was, in addition, a means by which Israeli sovereignty over the city was tested and rejected. Finally, it was also the largest Palestinian employer on the West Bank. From an Israeli point of view, the area of the concession posed serious legal difficulties: while the JEC's main offices and generators were in the city, most of its customers were not. To take over those parts within the municipal borders as the government believed it was entitled to do would lay it open to accusations that it was deliberately destroying a commercial enterprise.

The Israeli government initially tried to take over the JEC's right to supply Israeli army bases in the West Bank. It also tried to appoint two Israeli officials onto the Board of Trustees as Municipality representatives. In addition the Israeli Custodian of Absentee Property claimed that shares belonging to shareholders no longer resident in Jerusalem should be put in the name of the Custodian.[109] On its part, the JEC resisted vigorously and these initial efforts failed. It is likely that one reason for the failure of these Israeli encroachments was that the Labor government was still hoping to come to an understanding with the Jordanian government over the future of the West Bank and did not wish to antagonize its supporters which were well represented upon the JEC Board.

In return for keeping the concession intact the Board finally agreed to accept two representatives of the Israeli Municipality of Jerusalem on the Board. After further negotiations it agreed to align the price of its electricity with that of the (IEC) and to print electricity bills in Hebrew as well as Arabic and English.[110] With these agreements the JEC retained its position as the sole supplier of electricity to East Jerusalem and the annexed areas and by 1986 it was supplying 30,000 Israeli Jewish customers. Given the emphasis placed by the Israeli government upon securing physical control and sovereignty over the annexed parts of Jerusalem it was an extraordinary achievement and highly symbolic in a political sense.

The whole period of the Israeli occupation has been one of incessant struggle to maintain the administrative and operational independence of the JEC and to keep the concession intact. There has been argument that for much of its post-1967 existence the JEC has not run along modern management lines and its inefficiency and wastefulness have been the cause of much of its problems.[111] In addition, as a "national" institution for the Palestinians, management had to pay close attention to the views of its workforce. Yet these issues were not the overriding ones. The main problem that the JEC faced was that by insisting on retaining all of the concession it had to meet the enormous challenge of providing power to new Israeli settlements and industrial areas constructed in great haste for ideological reasons. It also had to provide for a rapidly expanding Palestinian population inside and outside the municipal borders. Between 1969 and 1977, the JEC underwent an annual growth rate of 25–30 percent.[112] In 1966, the JEC had 22,000 customers, in 1981, 70,000, and in 1986, at its peak it was supplying electricity to 100,000 customers.[113]

To meet with this demand the JEC bought and installed more generators. In 1970 it wished to purchase four more but could not obtain permission from the Israeli government for it to receive a Jordanian government loan on the grounds that the JEC was not economically viable—even though, as a result of the construction of new settlements, the number of the JEC's customers was increasing.[114] It was therefore obliged to purchase power from the (IEC) and links connecting the two systems were established at Gilo and Shu'fat. By 1986, 90 percent of the JEC's power was purchased from the IEC.[115]

In turn this dependence, clearly engineered by the Israeli government, created a further problem. The IEC sold electricity to its own consumers at a subsidized rate, and following earlier agreements with the government, the JEC was obliged to align its price structure with that of the IEC, narrowing its profit margins considerably. The JEC, however, could only buy electricity from the IEC at an inflated rate, reducing further any possible profit.[116] Thus the surplus available to the JEC for investment in new lines and installations was negligible. Yet in order to retain its concession the JEC had to keep abreast of the Israeli settlement program by installing new lines and equipment in all the areas being settled. The net result was an operating loss by 1980 of IS 11.1 million (approximately £3.5 million) and owings by 1986 to the IEC and the Israeli oil company, PAZ, of $12 million.[117] The pressure to keep up with the expansion of the Israeli population in East Jerusalem and the surrounding area led to a lack of investment in Palestinian areas. By 1981, out of the 130 villages in the concession only 50 had been supplied by the JEC.[118] Essential repairs, leaks in the transmission system, and obsolescence of the generating equipment were all neglected.[119] Finally, after letting the JEC spend $12 million on five new generators in the early eighties, the Israeli government reneged on its agreement to grant permission for the assembly of the generators which, as a result, remained in their packing cases.[120]

For a period in the late seventies and eighties, loans from the PLO and Jordanian government were able to keep the JEC afloat.[121] However, the neglect of the Palestinian areas, erratic service, and a growing perception that it was absurd to continue to supply Israeli Jewish settlements at the expense of Palestinian villages when the settlements were held as illegal combined to create deep divisions within the Board of Trustees and dissatisfaction within the workforce and Palestinian community. Indeed, as a Jerusalem Post journalist, Aryeh Wolman, observed of the JEC:

Its tariff and installation charges are fixed by the Israeli government. It is forced to buy Israeli equipment, pay Israeli taxes, abide by Israeli company and labor law, follow Israeli accounting practices, meet Israeli technical standards, and supply Israeli West Bank settlements. On top of everything, the company is suffering large losses, and has to rely on the generosity of the Arab states to keep going."[122]

The question being asked was to what extent was the JEC an independent Palestinian company? Internal arguments among the Board members over the long-term strategic value of retaining the original concession intact combined with the feeling that the Israeli government and settlers were benefitting unfairly from the JEC's limitations weakened the ability of the Board to resist further Israeli encroachments.

No legal attempt to challenge the JEC's concession took place during the Labor government's rule over East Jerusalem and the annexed areas. It was only after the coming to power of the Likud government in 1977 that a move was made. Taking advantage of the company's mounting debts and the dissatisfaction of Israeli Jewish customers in the new settlements over irregular and unreliable supplies of power, the Israeli Ministry of Energy and the Military Administration of the West Bank announced their intention to revoke the concession. This was done under the provisions of the concession which allowed for a five-yearly review and the Israeli government appropriated for itself the role of High Commissioner. The JEC appealed to the Israeli High Court and won a judgment which secured its title over the concession in the West Bank but not in East Jerusalem and the annexed areas.[123] The court opined that since the West Bank part of the concession was inoperable without the East Jerusalem part, the Israeli government should reconsider its decision and granted the JEC leave to appeal if it did not.[124] The legal struggle continued amid the mountains of debts, which finally gave the JEC legal grounds to recover its money.[125] Finally, following a series of breakdowns in negotiations over the future of the company, the Israeli Ministry of Energy unilaterally removed Israeli Jewish areas from the JEC's concession. The JEC was given permission to function and supply Palestinian Arab areas only within the original concession until March 1994.[126]

This protracted battle over the JEC illustrates the importance attached to the concession by the Palestinian community. Although it continues to provide approximately one-third of the electricity consumed domestically in Jerusalem and the surrounding area, it no longer is the sole supplier of power on the eastern side of the Armistice Line.[127] Unlike the situation described by Romann and Weingrod at the beginning of this section, the division of supply is now along ethnic lines. New boundaries have been created which amount to a political defeat for the Palestinians. The loss of the entire concession also provides the Israeli government the basis upon which it can supply to Israeli settlements throughout the West Bank and from which it can encroach further upon the operations of the JEC.

It is worth noting that in the case of power supply what is "done" can be more easily "undone." With the exception of some areas inside the municipal borders a political settlement could easily lead to the reconstituting of the original concession. The legality of the Israeli position is open to question and the extension of the IEC's operations to parts of the West Bank could clearly be halted. Unlike the question of sewage disposal steps taken so far are not necessarily irrevocable.

6

The Politics of Religion in the Holy City

"It seems to me that in order to designate Jerusalem as a Jewish city with the stamp of tradition and sanctity on it, a city which arouses the awe of those who come there—this is a task for which we must all come together. For here we are dealing with 'Jerusalem,' Jerusalem, which, after all, will symbolise for the Jewish people and the whole world the holy city, the Temple city, a city to which people go to obtain spiritual inspiration and religious new birth."
—Rabbi S.Y. Cohen, Deputy Mayor, Municipal Council Meeting, August 13, 1967.

The impact of the Israeli occupation of East Jerusalem can be highlighted by two apparently contradictory but lasting images. The first is of religious revival, of new growth, of bustle and "busy-ness" around the holy shrines and religious buildings. A walk around the Old City or one of the orthodox Jewish quarters of West Jerusalem presents an observer with a constant declaration of activity, renovation, study, prayer, and planning. In Muslim al-Haram al-Sharif, newly cleaned tiles and domes flash blue, silver, and gold, and ornate stone-carved facades stand splendidly repaired and burnished. In the surrounding Muslim quarters, high-domed and dignified Mamluk libraries, law schools, palaces, and mausoleums have been rehabilitated and reoccupied. Students in long religious garb and men sporting the occasional white Islamic turban can be seen making their way between religious book shops, Qur'anic schools, and prayer rooms.

In the Christian areas, pilgrims from all countries of the world abound, buying religious paraphernalia and visiting the myriad churches and chapels. New seminaries, biblical colleges, interdenominational dialogue centers, and monastic retreats periodically decant clusters of clergy and monastic novices in traditional and modern dress. Bishops on sabbatical and theological students stand discussing

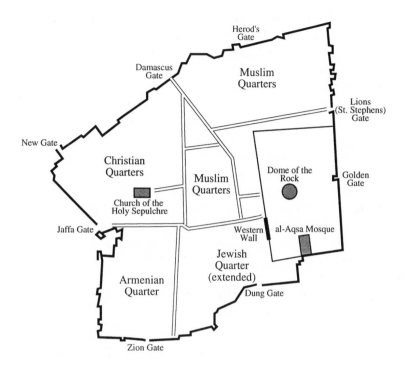

MAP 6.1. The Old City

new insights and revelations. Scores of Jewish *yeshivas*, Torah colleges, and seminaries have been set up in and around the Old City. Groups of black-garbed rabbis and *yeshiva* students hurriedly walk through the winding streets from their studies to the dormitories, stopping only to memorize another passage from the small book in their hands. In the newly cleared plaza, dancing youths celebrate another *bar mitzvah* while families clap and take pictures. Meanwhile the tuneless chanting of prayer emanates from some back room hidden from sight. Some evenings in Jerusalem are a veritable cacophony of religious sounds as the various rituals collide. From such a walk it is clear that, despite inauspicious beginnings, the variety and vitality of religious life in Jerusalem continues at a hectic pace (see map 6.1).

The other, contrasting image is of a scene that took place even before the 1967 hostilities were over. On June 11 the Palestinian inhabitants of the *harat al-magharib*, or Moroccan quarter, beside the Western Wall were ordered to evacuate their houses.[1] Israeli army sappers laid and detonated explosives in their houses and courtyards; bulldozers drove through the Dung Gate and proceeded to clear the rub-

ble. When the dust had settled a large plaza leading to the great
Herodian blocks of the Western Wall was revealed. The only remnant
of the former quarter was a Sufi *zawiya* perched above ground level
and clinging to the entrance to al-Haram al-Sharif, and which was
subsequently demolished for "safety reasons."

To Jews and Israelis, the creation of the plaza was a wonderful sight.
Cut off from their holiest site for years, they could not only return but
also congregate unimpeded and in large numbers. To Muslims and
Palestinians, on the other hand, it left a frightening and sickening feeling. One hundred and thirty-five homes as well as the ancient Buraq
and Afdali mosques had been destroyed. Approximately 650 people
had been evicted without warning.[2] For them, their relatives, and the
Palestinian Arab population of the newly occupied city, the razing of
the Magharib quarter with its two mosques, *zawiya*, and endowed residential and commercial property was a chilling introduction to the
new Israeli era.[3]

It was also in sharp contrast to General Moshe Dayan's broadcast of
June 7, 1967, when he announced:

> We have united Jerusalem, the divided capital of Israel. We have
> returned to the most sacred of our Holy Places, never to part from it
> again. To our Arab neighbours we stretch out, again at this hour—and
> with added emphasis—the hand of peace. And to our Christian and
> Moslem fellow-citizens we solemnly promise religious freedom and
> rights. We came to Jerusalem not to possess ourselves of the Holy Places
> of others, or to interfere with the members of other faiths, but to safe-
> guard the City's integrity and to live in it with others in unity.[4]

International legal opinion held that Israel, as the occupying power,
was obliged to respect the international agreements enshrined in the
Hague and Geneva Conventions. Article 56 of the "Protection of
Cultural Property in Time of War or Military Occupation," annexed
to both the 1899 Hague Convention II and 1907 Hague Convention
IV as Regulations, treats all religious and charitable institutions as pri-
vate property. Destruction and willful damage to such property is
therefore forbidden. In addition, Jordan and Israel had signed and rat-
ified the 1954 Hague Convention for the "Protection of Cultural
Property in the Event of Armed Conflict." This convention covers
both religious buildings and waqf land and property on the West Bank.
Similarly, Article 53 of the 1977 Geneva Protocol I (Protection of
Cultural Objects and Places of Worship) and Article 16 of 1977
Geneva Protocol II (which has the same title) prohibits any act of hos-

tility against cultural properties, as well as their use in any military effort or as targets of reprisal.

The Israeli government, however, insisted that these laws did not apply to East Jerusalem and the other occupied territories. Rejecting the international consensus on their occupation of East Jerusalem and the characterization of itself as "the belligerent occupier of enemy territory,"[5] Israel held that the occupation of East Jerusalem constituted a legitimate extension of Israeli civil law over territory brought under its control as laid down by the Law and Administrative Ordinance announced by the Israel Provisional Government in 1948.[6] There could be no belligerent occupation or annexation of a *terra nullus*, that is, of territory without a sovereign controlling body.

Nonetheless, while not recognizing the applicability of the conventions to East Jerusalem, the Israeli government, which unlike Jordan had not signed the conventions, did to some extent try to work within their ambit. On June 27, 1967, the Knesset passed the Protection of Holy Places Law—the same day it passed legislation effectively annexing Jordanian East Jerusalem and surrounding areas of the West Bank to Israel. The law stated:

1) The Holy Places shall be protected from desecration and any other violation and from anything likely to violate the freedom of access of the members of the different religions to the places sacred to them or their feelings with regard to those places.
2) a) Whosoever desecrates or otherwise violates a Holy Place shall be liable to imprisonment for a term of seven years.
   b) Any person who does anything likely to impair freedom of access to a Holy Place or to hurt the feelings of anyone to whom a place is sacred, shall be liable to imprisonment for a term of five years.
3) This law shall add to and derogate from any other law.
4) The Minister of Religious Affairs is charged with the implementation of the Law, and he may, after consultation with, or upon the proposal of, representatives of the religions concerned and with the consent of the Minister of Justice, make regulations as to any matter relating to such implementation.

An important result of the Protection of Holy Places Law and the occupation in general was the extension of the jurisdiction of the Israeli Ministry of Religious Affairs over East Jerusalem and the other annexed portions of the West Bank. During the early months of the occupation, Israeli policy toward the Muslim and Christian communities and their respective hierarchies was confused. Given their absorption of East Jerusalem and its surroundings, the Israelis were faced with the difficulties of disentangling those parts of the bureaucracy concerned primarily with the annexed areas from those that dealt with the rest of the West Bank. Moreover, given the inevitability of resistance from the Muslim and Christian religious establishments, they knew that this separation of functions would be difficult to achieve without direct intervention, something they had promised not to do (for instance, in Dayan's broadcast).

It is noteworthy that the Protection of Holy Places Law makes no explicit reference to the maintenance of the "Status Quo arrangements" that had regulated questions of access to and custodianship over the Holy Places since the middle of the nineteenth century. As Benvenisti points out, the omission was no accident.[7] While the Status Quo arrangements were of interest primarily to the Christian churches, they placed restrictions upon Jewish access to Judaism's holiest site in East Jerusalem, the Western Wall; these restrictions had been responsible for the 1929 outbreak of intercommunal violence known as "the Wailing Wall Incident," described below. Underlining the new situation shortly after the annexation, the Israeli Minister of Religious Affairs, Zerah Warhaftig, declared that the Temple Mount (to Muslims, al-Haram al-Sharif) "was acquired by our forefathers. King David not only conquered the Mount but also bought it with good money from the Jebusite. There is not the slightest doubt that the Mount belongs to the Jewish people."[8]

The minister simultaneously declared that the government had no intention of replacing the mosques on the Mount with a synagogue, but in light of the destruction only weeks before of the Magharib quarter and the demolition of its mosques, the Muslim leadership was uneasy. The absence of a reference to the Status Quo arrangements also left the Christian community in doubt over the status of their guardianship of the Christian Holy Places.

While Israel's determination to establish physical control and demographic dominance over the city is evident, there is little public documentation shedding light on specific policy positions concerning the various religious communities in Jerusalem. What can be discerned from Israeli actions since 1967, however, is a keen awareness of the role that religion can play in the Holy City. This awareness resulted in the adoption of three overlapping policies, all clearly intended to maintain Israeli rule over the city.

The first of these involved extending Jewish religious rights in East

Jerusalem. These cover a multitude of measures ranging from the creation of the plaza on the ruins of the former Magharib quarter and its
placement under the jurisdiction of the Israeli Ministry of Religious
Affairs, to the refurbishment of damaged synagogues in the Jewish
quarter, to the acquisition of other properties in and around the Old
City. These measures amounted to a unilateral revoking of the Status
Quo arrangements that had hitherto obtained.

The second approach is characterized by a reluctance to antagonize
Western governments and influential ecclesiastical bodies over the
Christian Holy Places. Much is made of the cordial relations that have
been established by Israeli officials with many of the Christian denominations, of the Israeli government's enshrinement of rights of access
to the Holy Places in Israeli law, and of a general policy of noninter-
vention in the internal administration of the Christian denominations.
Avoiding measures that would elicit Christian criticism of the Israeli
government's handling of the Holy Places was considered a necessary
condition for continued Western support for Israel and acquiescence
in its occupation of East Jerusalem. The fact that few sites in Jerusalem
are holy to both Christians and Jews reduces the areas of possible friction.[9] This is not the case with Muslim and Jewish sites in the city.
Jewish claims to al-Haram al-Sharif, holy to Jews and Muslims alike of
Soloman's temple, and the Jewish "Holy of Holies" constitute a major
source of friction between the two communities.

The third policy involves making sure that religious activity does
not evolve into a political force that could undermine Israeli control
of the city. This approach has led to some manipulation of interdenominational and interfaith rivalries in order to prevent the emergence
of a common front against Israeli rule. It has also led to close scrutiny
of senior clergy appointments and in some cases a degree of intervention, particularly with regard to the Christian religious establishment.
Since the Muslim and Christian communities own large tracts of land
in both East and West Jerusalem, the Israeli government naturally wants
sympathetic religious officials and clergy in key positions.

The Muslim Religious Establishment

Historical Background

The Muslim religious establishment of Jerusalem has been deeply
entrenched for centuries. The al-Aqsa mosque and the Dome of the

Rock on the raised platform of al-Haram al-Sharif, regarded as the holiest sites in Islam outside Arabia, attracted both pilgrims and scholars.[10] The religious significance of Jerusalem also grew with the spread of Sufism. Sufi *shaykhs* and their followers set up convents and hostels, known as *zawiyas* in the Old City. The tomb of David, Nabi Da'ud, for example, became a well-known sufi convent.[11] In the attempt to check the spread of Sufism, the Sunni establishment founded a number of law schools and seminaries to train teachers, preachers, and mosque officials.[12]

In order to support this religious activity, waqfs (Muslim religious endowments) were created, and the higher the status of Jerusalem became, the more waqfs were endowed: Jerusalem had more waqfs than any other major Ottoman city, including Istanbul, Cairo, Aleppo, and Bursa.[13] Zâwiyas and takiyas and other hostels, madrasas for scholars and teachers, tombs and mausoleums for wealthy notables, soup-kitchens, orphanages, homes for the poor and needy, public fountains, baths, prayer rooms, and mosques were all supported by endowments drawing income from rented accommodation, markets, and *khans*, as well as from tithes from endowed villages and farms around Jerusalem and other parts of Palestine. Indeed, such was the religious prestige of Jerusalem that waqfs in the city received income from endowed land and property throughout the Arab world.[14] More than two thirds of the Old City was endowed.

Such a concentration of religious institutions produced a plethora of *qadis* (judges), *shaykhs, imams*, a *mufti*, a *bashkatib* (secretary of Haram area), legal jurists, *mutawallis* (overseers) of waqfs, and minor officials responsible for the running of Haram compound. There was no rigid hierarchical structure akin to that of Christian churches. Scions of well-established Jerusalem families or learned jurists were given a status independent of any formal hierarchy, but there was a basic chain of command vis-à-vis the state authorities. This led from the Ottoman Pasha of Jerusalem to the qadi on to the mufti. In addition, many of the posts were hereditary, passed on from father to son or at least kept within a given family. In the latter stages of the Ottoman period, as the powers of the city *majlis* (council) grew and increasingly assumed executive functions, the powers of the religious establishment declined accordingly.

The British Mandate period, when Palestine became a geographical and administrative unit separated from the other remnants of the former Ottoman Empire, saw a revival of the role of the religious establishment. The British established the Supreme Muslim Council to manage the religious affairs of the Muslim community. Headed by the Mufti of Jerusalem and based in Jerusalem, it was a highly centralized structure.[15] Funding for the religious establishment was provided by regularly collected income from the waqf endowments controlled by the new Council. The chief officers of the Supreme Muslim Council were, at least in theory, to be chosen by an electoral college, a provision that at least partially satisfied the growing numbers of Palestinian secularists.[16]

The fact that Jerusalem was the site of the Supreme Muslim Council's main offices and that Jerusalem families and their allies for the most part dominated the administration of waqf properties and the shari'a courts consolidated the religious and political dominance of the city's Muslim religious establishment. When opposition to Britain's Jewish National Home policy—which had crystallized around Hajj Amin al-Husayni, the Mufti of Jerusalem and head of the Supreme Muslim Council—escalated into the Palestinian revolt of 1936–39, the British were obliged to break the Council's power. In Britain's crackdown of the revolt, the most active officials of the Council were deported and the mufti, divested of his functions, escaped abroad. The British in effect took over the administration of the wqafs themselves.[17]

This action, which gravely weakened the Jerusalem religious establishment, had important repercussions when the Hashemites took over the administration of the city's religious affairs following the armistice in 1949. As has been noted in previous chapters, Jordanian policy was to integrate the West Bank, including East Jerusalem, as much as possible into the Hashemite Kingdom. One of the Jordanians' first acts in Jerusalem was to appoint one of their supporters as the new Mufti of Jerusalem and President of the Supreme Muslim Council, and to make the position accountable to the Chief Qadi in Amman.[18]

The Jordanians were also able to undermine the independence and status of the Muslim religious establishment of East Jerusalem by abolishing the hereditary nature of the key religious posts. Thus, posts such as bashkatib, imams of certain mosques, and khatibs, which hitherto provided a lucrative waqf income to their bearers, were thereafter subject to state appointment procedures. This departure from tradition forced the leading religious dignitaries either to make accommodation with the Jordanian government or be swept to the margins of political and religious life in the city. Similarly, the administration of waqf properties was rationalized when waqf funds were paid into a central treasury and then allocated for particular purposes according to a budget set in Amman.[19]

One advantage of this reform was to allow the Awqaf Administration, successor to the Supreme Muslim Council with regard to waqf affairs, to invest heavily in the burgeoning commercial district just beyond the Damascus and Herod Gates. New construction led to an increase in rents which partially offset the losses incurred by the partition of the city in 1949. In 1966, the administration of Muslim religious affairs was further reorganized into five departments to include all activities under a single bureaucratic umbrella.[20] At the same time, there was considerable new endowment activity, increasing the extent of family waqfs. By the end of the Jordanian period, there were 1,240 waqf properties, most of which generated income for charitable purposes. Ninety-three percent of these were located within the Old City and nearly 60 percent were administered directly by the Awqaf Administration.[21]

Since virtually no Muslims remained in Israeli-held West Jerusalem after the 1948 war (see chapter 3), no Muslim religious establishment remained there.[22] Properties formerly under the jurisdiction of the Supreme Muslim Council, including sites such as the Palace Hotel and the Mamilla cemetery, fell under the control of the Israeli Custodian of Absentee Property or the Muslim and Druze Division of the Ministry of Religious Affairs. Works were undertaken, however, to repair war damage to the Ukasha mosque on Strauss Street (although it was not functioning) and to the 'Ayn Karim cemetery.[23] In the fifties, a shari'a Court of Appeal was set up in West Jerusalem for Israel's Muslim population; in the absence of Muslims in the city itself, the court's location there reflected Israel's drive to establish national institutions in Jerusalem.

The Post-1967 Period

In the first few weeks of the occupation in 1967, the Ministry of Defense was placed in charge of relations with the Muslim religious establishment. Following the passage of Israeli legislation incorporating East Jerusalem and its environs into Israel, however, the government transferred that responsibility to the Ministry of Religious Affairs.[24] The latter proceeded to introduce a number of extremely controversial changes in the structure of the Muslim religious establishment to reflect the overall application of Israeli law to these areas.

In the first place, the qadis of East Jerusalem would no longer be allowed to adjudicate on shari'a matters unless they renounced their Jordanian citizenship and pledged allegiance to the State of Israel. Second, even if they accepted these conditions, they would have to accept the amendments in shari'a law enacted by the Knesset and adopted by the qadis in Israel.[25] The ministry would also have the right to censor the Friday sermon delivered in al-Aqsa mosque.

As a first step toward these ends, the ministry tried to set up a Board of Guardians comprising qadis in both Israel and East Jerusalem.[26] The noncompliance of the East Jerusalem qadis ensured the failure of this initiative. Ministry officials also began to pay daily visits to the Awqaf Administration offices in the Old City and tried to persuade the Director-General, Hassan Tahbub, to surrender the relevant files and documents for the administration of waqf and Muslim affairs in East Jerusalem.[27] The ministry wanted waqf land and property to be placed under the jurisdiction of the Custodian of Absentee Property and to administer them as its agent, as was the case inside Israel.[28]

The Awqaf Administration under the *qadi al-quda'*, Sheikh Abdel Hamid al-Sa'ih, rejected these demands and proceeded to establish an independent Muslim supervisory body, the Higher Islamic Board (*al-hay'a al-islamiyya al-'ulya*). The stage was set for a confrontation between the ministry and the Muslim religious establishment. A crisis was precipitated when the Jewish head of the Division for Muslim and Druze Affairs, Dr. Nissim Dana, demanded to see the text of the Friday sermon set for July 14, 1967. The threat of a general boycott of the service and the overwhelming support for the Higher Islamic Board pouring in from all parts of the West Bank obliged the Israeli government to back down over the issue and simply to accept assurances that the sermon would not be inflammatory.[29]

On January 31 the Awqaf Administration was informed that the responsibility for Muslim affairs was being transferred back to the Ministry of Defense. This was a highly significant concession on the part of the Israeli government in that it meant not only that the Awqaf Administration retained its exclusive control over waqf properties in East Jerusalem, but also that it remained institutionally connected to the West Bank. In the years that followed, the Awqaf Administration has been able to build up its organizational base in the Old City to such an extent that it is often perceived as a mini-Jordanian-Palestinian enclave in the heart of the city.

Israel and the Muslim Community

Of Israel's three policies with regard to the various religious communities in Jerusalem described above—extension of Jewish religious rights, reluctance to antagonize Western Christians, and prevention of interconfessional unity that could develop into a political force—the first and the third are most applicable to the Muslim religious establishment. In order to promote the extension of Jewish religious rights and prevent a cohesive religious and political force from arising in opposition to Israel's annexation of East Jerusalem, it was important to contain both the independence of the Awqaf Administration and its range of activities and responsibilities in the city.

The first action of the Higher Islamic Board set up by the Muslim religious establishment during the dispute with the Israeli Ministry of Religious Affairs was to denounce the annexation of East Jerusalem and the adjacent parts of the West Bank and to protest against the demolition of the Magharib quarter.[30] It also proceeded to organize Muslim religious affairs in East Jerusalem and the West Bank under its authority by making the chief qadi the chairman of the board and establishing a shari'a Court of Appeal in East Jerusalem. Other bodies such as the Awqaf Administration and the Committee for the Restoration of al-Aqsa mosque and the Dome of the Rock were also made responsible to the Board.

The representative nature of the Higher Islamic Board was confirmed by the letters of support and recognition it received from Palestinian municipalities, trade unions, cultural associations, and leading individuals in East Jerusalem and throughout the West Bank.[31] In this way the Board became an institutional expression of nonaccommodation on the part of the Muslim population to the unification of Jerusalem under Israeli sovereignty.[32]

The Israelis, on the other hand, refused to have any contact with the Board or to recognize the shari'a Court of Appeal. Instead, hoping to undermine the Board's influence, they expelled many of its leading members from the country in contravention of the Fourth Geneva Convention. Shaykh Abdel Hamid al-Sa'ih, Chairman of the Board and Acting Chief Qadi, was expelled on September 20, 1967, and six other members met the same fate in May 1969.[33]

In an attempt to make the Higher Islamic Board more representative as a West Bank-wide institution, individuals representing other parts of the region were appointed to it, from shari'a courts and the waqf administrative districts outside the East Jerusalem area.[34] The chief result of these appointments was to make the Board more amenable to Jordanian interests, since many of the new members were either supporters of the Jordanian government or, as qadis and *khatib*s, continued to receive their salaries from the Jordanian authorities even though under Israeli occupation. It was not long before the Higher Islamic Board transferred its residual executive powers to the shari'a Court of Appeals based in East Jerusalem but funded and administered by the Ministry of Awqaf in Amman. Thus the Director-General of the Awqaf Administration, Hassan Tahbub, was approved by the Ministry of Awqaf in Amman, and the annual budget of the Awqaf Administration, which had previously been submitted to the Board, was instead submitted to the ministry. In effect the Board retained only an advisory role.

As we have seen, the Israelis conceded de facto administrative control of the Awqaf Administration and Higher Islamic Board over waqf property. By 1970, the Israeli occupation of the city had become sufficiently established for the creation of a new status quo. The government was obliged to recognize the anomalies and its inability to apply full sovereignty over the city with regard to Muslim religious affairs. This situation was reflected in the Legal and Administrative Matters Law, a new law that was intended to regulate the absorption of East Jerusalem and the other annexed areas into Israel (see chapter 2).[35]

Article Two of this law exempted the "Holy Places" from the application of the Absentee Property Law, in effect confirming the jurisdiction of the Awqaf Administration over al-Haram al-Sharif and other mosques, cemeteries, and tombs in East Jerusalem and the other annexed areas. To remove any potential ambiguities over other forms of waqf property, Article 3(a) declared that the residents of East Jerusalem would not "be regarded as [absentees] within the meaning of the Absentee's Property Law, 5710–1950, in respect of property situated in that area."

Thus, by the mid-seventies the Muslim religious establishment in East Jerusalem had regrouped itself under the umbrella of institutions funded and otherwise supported by the Jordanians. Nevertheless, it has always comprised a number of active Palestinian nationalists and Islamists among its employees at all levels. Following the outbreak of the *intifada*, the Board introduced elections for its administrative posts as a concession to grassroots demands for the democratization of Palestinian institutions.[36]

The relative cohesiveness of the Muslim religious establishment posed a serious challenge to Israel's annexation of East Jerusalem and its environs. Parts of the Old City, such as al-Haram al-Sharif compound, were virtually autonomous areas, beyond Israeli civil jurisdiction. Israel endeavored to overcome this challenge by undermining the status of the shari'a court and by curtailing the Awqaf Administration, this last by removing significant areas of the Old City from its control (although the confiscation of waqf property, obviously, had other purposes as well) and by hampering the funding and execution of renovation and educational activities under its auspices.

Concerning the first, while the Israelis had conceded some ground with regard to the status of the Awqaf Administration and the Higher Islamic Board, they were not willing to do so with the East Jerusalem shari'a court. After the 1948 war, shari'a courts had been set up in Israel by the Israeli government, which also appointed their qadis. But with the occupation and annexation, the East Jerusalem qadis refused to allow their courts to be absorbed into the Israeli system and continued to operate as before. Israel countered by refusing to recognize the marriages, divorces, wills, certificates, and waqf property transactions approved by the shari'a court in East Jerusalem, insisting that only the Jaffa shari'a court had jurisdiction in these matters. East Jerusalem Muslims requiring various official permits and execution orders were obliged to obtain the approval of the Jaffa court above and beyond that of the local court. A protracted procedure evolved in which the East Jerusalem court continued to issue the required approvals, which were then taken to the Jaffa court to be stamped by the Israeli-appointed qadi.

In 1988, the Israeli Ministry of Religious Affairs appointed its own qadi for Jerusalem, with a court and residence in West Jerusalem. This step was taken partly to undermine further the position of the East Jerusalem court (by making the Israeli court more accessible) and partly in response to the *intifada*, which made travel to Jaffa exceedingly difficult for West Bankers residing outside Jerusalem's expanded municipal boundaries. It also eased the workload of the Jaffa court, which was experiencing a rise in application requests as a result of the growing Palestinian population in the annexed areas and because of a growing tendency to "play it safe" by having certificates and transactions backed by both courts.

Dr. Yitzhak Reiter, a leading Israeli scholar in Muslim religious affairs in East Jerusalem and former deputy advisor on Arab Affairs in the prime minister's office, has carried out a useful comparison of the

Jaffa and East Jerusalem courts. His work reveals that while Palestinian Muslims from East Jerusalem used the East Jerusalem court twice as often as the Jaffa court, they were not averse to making use of the Israeli court to obtain more favorable judgments.[37] Reiter believes that "The Israeli court represents a [last] resort for the Muslims of East Jerusalem, to which they can turn when they are not satisfied with the decisions of the religious court of East Jerusalem, or when they anticipate from the beginning that the chances of obtaining the support of the East Jerusalem court are nil."[38]

Indeed, Reiter is able to cite examples where the two courts have appointed different *mutawallis* for the same waqf at the instigation of different branches of the family. The opportunities for confusion provided by this situation are only slightly mitigated by the fact that the much higher prestige of the East Jerusalem qadis leads to a measure of deference on the part of the Israeli-appointed qadi.[39]

In this environment of legal and political impasse, the two systems functioned side by side. Some Israeli researchers have gone so far as to interpret this development as an absorption of the East Jerusalem system into the state. For example, the former Deputy Attorney-General, Yoram Bar Sela, argues that

> In this manner, the shari'a court has formally become part of the Israeli administration; but the arrangement is not regulated by legislation and in fact runs counter to the spirit and intent of Israeli law. . . . Though the existence of the [East Jerusalem] shari'a court does not conform to Israeli law, its services have been recognised de facto, and a series of arrangements have been devised to accommodate it within the law.[40]

This conclusion, both an overstatement and simplification of the actual situation, is one with which the East Jerusalem's Muslim religious establishment would certainly not agree. In reality, the opposite had occurred, a fact that has been recognized by many Israeli experts in Islamic affairs.[41]

Concerning the Awqaf Administration, its quasi-autonomous status seemed to make it an obvious candidate for stepping into the vacuum in local municipal affairs that followed the dissolution of the Palestinian municipal council in the immediate wake of the occupation. This vacuum was exacerbated by the failure of the Israeli government and its municipal council to provide adequate services for the Palestinian population of the city and by their fundamental inability to represent them. That the Awqaf Administration failed to take on a representative role or to extend its educational and charitable services to the Palestinian population is partly due to Jordan's desire to keep the Muslim religious leadership in East Jerusalem on a short leash. Especially, however, it is the direct result of Israel's official efforts to prevent it from doing so.[42]

Perhaps the most important means of weakening the Muslim religious establishment and its institutions was through the confiscation of waqf property. The first such confiscation was of the lands of the Magharib quarter—almost exclusively waqf property—after it was razed, which the Awqaf Administration in its confusion and disorganization immediately following the war was in no position to resist.

Some months later, on April 18, 1968, Israeli Finance Minister Pinchas Sapir issued an order expropriating 29 acres (116 *dunums*) of the southern part of the Old City for "public purposes" under a British Ordinance passed in 1943. This was for the reconstitution of the "Jewish Quarter" of the Old City, to reestablish a Jewish presence there.

Before looking at the expropriation order and its direct effects on waqf property in the Old City, it is useful to have some understanding of the size and nature of ownership in the "traditional" Jewish quarter—the precise contours of which are difficult to delineate since boundaries between the quarters of the Old City fluctuated according to immigration and political circumstances.[43] Nonetheless, one can say that the Jewish quarter was small and centered largely in a single area. From the beginning of this century up to 1948, the area was bounded to the west by the Armenian Cathedral and the Armenian residences clustered around it, the Syrian and Maronite convents and their residential communities, and four small quarters named after the Muslim families living there. Its northern side was bordered by the Tariq Bab al-Silsila and the central market area. To the east was the harat ash-Sharaf, located along the slopes overlooking the Magharib quarter. On the south, it was bounded by the city walls and by another small quarter called *harat* Abu Maydun.[44]

The small size of the Jewish quarter was much commented on by Western travelers in the middle of the nineteenth century.[45] Later in the century, Jews began to settle well outside the traditional quarter, in areas to the north near the soup kitchen of Khaski Sultan and along the Tariq al-Wad. It is on the basis of these moves that Israeli settlers have taken over properties in those areas, as will be discussed below.

When one visits the expanded Jewish quarter today, it is difficult to believe that it was once a busy Arab area. Indeed, it was in what was known as the Jewish quarter that the ancient homes of many of the leading Jerusalem families, such as the Khalidi, Abu Su'ud, Hariri, Ja'ouni, Nammari, and Dajani, were located. Most of the Jewish residents in fact were tenants, with most of the properties belonging to Palestinian landlords and waqfs, khayri and dhurri.[46] Benvenisti estimates that no more than 20 percent of the quarter was owned by Jews at the outbreak of the 1948 War.[47]

Following the 1948 War and the evacuation of the Jewish quarter by the Jewish inhabitants, many Palestinian refugees from residential areas of West Jerusalem moved into empty Jewish properties in the quarter. At first their residence was administered by the International Red Cross, but shortly thereafter, and until their eviction in the 1960s and 1970s, their affairs were placed under the jurisdiction of the United Nations Relief and Works Agency (UNRWA).[48] Properties that had been owned by Jews were placed under the control of the Jordanian Custodian of Enemy Property, which rented them out to both individuals and to UNRWA.

The boundaries of the expropriation zone of 1968 as announced by the Israeli Minister of Finance stretched from the Western Wall in the east to the edges of the Armenian Cathedral in the west, and from the Tariq Bab al-Silsila in the north to the walls of the city in the south. The expropriation included 700 stone buildings, of which only 105 had been owned by Jews prior to 1948. Expropriated Palestinian Arab properties included 1,048 flats or apartments housing 6,000 Palestinians, and 437 workshops or commercial stores providing employment to approximately 700 workers.[49]

Of the expropriated properties, 12 belonged to the Awqaf Administration, (of which three to the Muhareb Mosque waqf) and 99 to the Abu Madyan al-Ghauth waqf.[50] Between a quarter and a third of the Arab-owned properties were endowed in some way, amounting to approximately 24 percent of the total expropriated property. No exceptions were made to these expropriations, which underscores the determination of the Israeli state to assert its control over the Old City through its triple policy of land confiscations weakening the waqf system, reducing the Palestinian population of the Old City, and building up the Israeli Jewish population. At the time of the expropriations, the former mayor of Jordanian East Jerusalem during the Jordanian period, Ruhi al-Khatib, declared:

> By these new expropriations Arabs in the City will lose properties which have belonged to them for hundreds of years, and more than

> 6,000 Arabs will be evacuated from the City and dispersed . . . while
> more than 700 employers and workers will be deprived of their means
> of livelihood, and forced to swell the ranks of the homeless. . . . while
> the landlords and beneficiaries of Waqfs, who used to enjoy and live on
> the rent of their properties and Waqfs, will be deprived of their sources
> of livelihood and forced to join the ranks of the needy, if not of the
> refugees.[51]

The eviction of waqf tenants was not carried out in one day, as had
been the case in the Magharib quarter. A new Israeli firm, the
"Company for the Reconstruction and Development of the Jewish
Quarter" (CRDJQ), was created to renovate and rebuild the expropriated area. The CRDJQ, which was directly accountable to the Israeli
prime minister and the interministerial "Committee for Jerusalem
Affairs," notified Palestinian residents of the expropriations and offered
them compensation and help with mortgages for alternative housing.
Some of the Palestinians accepted the terms, but many refused. In
some cases, litigation was initiated, followed by a long process of
harassment and coercion well-documented in the international
press.[52]

The Higher Islamic Board and the Awqaf Administration greatly
weakened their own position by refusing to contest the expropriations
in Israeli civil courts. They refused on principle, arguing that to do so
would confer legitimacy on the occupation and annexation of East
Jerusalem and would constitute a form of recognition of an Israeli role
in the religious affairs of East Jerusalem. There was an additional fear
that to appear in Israeli court as representatives of the Ministry of
Waqfs in Jordan would, under Israeli law, be tantamount to accepting
Israeli-defined "absentee" status, thus paving the way for the Israeli
Ministry of Religious Affairs to take over its functions.[53] However, it
is not clear what the Israeli government could have done if the Awqaf
had continued on this route after its early attempts to incorporate the
functions of the Awqaf Administration in East Jerusalem into the
Israeli state system. Indeed, the Awqaf Administration abandoned its
position twenty years later, in May 1987, at which time it decided to
contest a case.[54]

Nonetheless, the Awqaf Administration's refusal to contest the
expropriations in the late 1960s and 1970s may have reflected an accurate assessment that any such efforts would have had small chance of
success. Similar attempts by Palestinian landlords of private properties
within the expropriation zone were all unsuccessful. In fact, the fail-

ure rate extended even to Israeli petitioners against this law, leading one judge to comment that to the best of his knowledge all attempts to get the expropriation order rescinded had failed.[55]

In addition to weakening the Awqaf Administration by decreasing the amount of land under its control, the Israeli government further erected a number of barriers to its efforts to administer, rehabilitate, and develop the waqf properties that remained. These constitute a good example of the difficulties encountered by the Muslim religious establishment in East Jerusalem. During the early years, the Awqaf Administration was confronted with a wide range of encroachments upon its authority including archaeological excavations, demolitions, and redevelopment work on its properties by various Israeli ministries and other institutions. The Awqaf Administration sought to prevent these measures by sending memoranda to the Israeli Ministry of Defense, cables to the United Nations and, through Jordan, sponsoring resolutions in the United Nations Security Council, the General Assembly, and UNESCO condemning Israeli violations of international law regarding the Holy Places and waqf properties.[56] These protests by the Awqaf Administration had little effect and were not matched by concrete activity on the ground to regain confiscated waqf property or to protect threatened property. This passive posture reflected the general belief that an Israeli withdrawal would not be long in coming and that waqf matters would be addressed in a negotiated political settlement.

By the mid-seventies, however, it had become clear that the Israeli occupation of East Jerusalem would be prolonged. Hence, the Awqaf Administration began to undertake more ambitious initiatives in consolidating its position and protecting its property. It was greatly assisted in this task by the increased availability of funds that had resulted from both the growing pan-Islamic interest in Jerusalem and the rise in oil revenues in other parts of the Arab world. Table 6.1 gives an idea of the sums involved.

As these figures reveal, the overwhelming proportion of funds came from the Jordanian government.[57]

The Awqaf Administration invested considerable effort and funds in order to provide religious instruction in the West Bank. It recognized that a vigorous religious education program would play an important role in maintaining its influence in the Palestinian Muslim community. By educating a new generation of Palestinians about the centrality to Islam and all Arabs of Jerusalem (and, by extension, the importance of Jerusalem's waqf property), the Awqaf Administration

Table 6.1 Financial Participation in the Preservation and Restoration of the Holy Places and Historical Sites in Jerusalem (1967–1987) [1]

	$
Jordanian government	7,500,000
Arab League (Center for the Documentation and Preservation of Historical Sites in Jerusalem)	462,000
Islamic Conference (Joint Jordan-Palestine Committee)	750,000
UNESCO	100,000
Organization of Islamic Capitals and Cities	100,000
Organization of Arab Cities	260,000
Governorate of 'Amman	100,000
ALESCO	25,000
Total	9,297,000

1. Figures compiled by R. Nijm, 'ard tarikhi masawur 'an 'aham al-muqaddisa fi filastin w-al-'ijra'at alati tamat li-siyanat al-turath (Fifth conference on the Holy Places, Tradition and Culture in Palestine, Cairo, 1988) (hereinafter referred to as 'ard tarikhi), p. 37.

hoped that its role would be valued and respected.[58] Of course, it was also interested in expanding facilities for prayer and worship. Table 6.2 gives an idea of the range of activities undertaken by the Awqaf Administration in Jerusalem up to 1982, when the Jerusalem *mudiriyya* (district) had a total of 103 mosques and the Awqaf Administration some 473 employees (a rise from 245 in 1976).[59]

As a result of Israeli expropriations, municipal plans for "slum clearance," and assorted development plans, the Awqaf Administration also embarked upon a renovation and restoration program to encourage the continued residence of Palestinian Muslims in the Old City. In the 1980s this project was placed under the direction of a special new department within the Administration, the Department of Islamic Archaeology.[60] The program benefitted from widespread concern that the Israeli occupation of East Jerusalem was permanently damaging the Islamic character and architectural value of the Old City.[61]

The significance of the work of the Department of Islamic Archaeology lies both in the physical preservation of the buildings under its responsibility and in the political implications of the restoration project for the Old City. There are two facets to this political dimension. First, by preserving historic Islamic buildings, the project focuses on the Islamic and waqf character of the city over the trend toward modernization and "Israelization." Second, it underlines the

Table 6.2 Summary of Construction and Repair Projects Undertaken by the Awqaf Administration in the Jerusalem Province, 1977–1982.

	1977	1978	1979	1980	1981	1982
Mosques	32	20	19	22	13	22
Residential	20	10	15	22	19	30
Dar al Aytam Schools	15	14	4	1	4	12
Other schools	4	7	7	16	6	14
Monuments	6	2	4	4	1	2
Shops	1	1	1	3	–	1
Miscellaneous	15	36	25	28	15	23
TOTAL WORKS	96	93	71	96	58	104

Awqaf Administration's commitment to the presence and vitality of the Palestinian community in the Old City and its determination to avoid marginalization by the Israeli state.[62]

Officials and employees of the Department of Islamic Archaeology emphasize the difficulties created by Israeli institutions, which hamper the department's work. The most frequently cited areas concern tunnelling and the installation of services. The Israeli Ministry of Religious Affairs has carried out excavations underneath the Muslim quarters along the length of Haram wall, causing structural damage to, or even the collapse of, a number of historic waqf properties.[63] Similarly, the installation of modern services such as sewage disposal, drainage, water supplies, and electricity, while welcome in themselves, have nevertheless caused serious damage to waqf properties in the Aqabat Saraya and beside the Tariq Bab al-Hadid.[64] That most of the damaged properties are residences lends credence to the argument that such activities are in keeping with Israeli plans to reduce the Palestinian population of the Old City.[65]

These are the major challenges facing East Jerusalem's Muslim religious establishment, whose role as guardians of the city's Islamic character and as custodians of the Muslim Holy Places has been under constant threat since 1967. The Israeli government does not wish the Muslim establishment to fulfill even this limited role, and certainly seeks to prevent a wider role.

The Jordanian government, the primary financial backer of the various institutions that make up the religious establishment, has found it necessary to limit its expenditure and autonomous organization. Still, when it severed its administrative links with the West Bank in 1988 as a result of the *intifada*, it did preserve its ties with the Higher Islamic Board, the Awqaf Administration, and the shari'a courts. Entirely pragmatic reasons have been cited for this exemption: the Palestine Liberation Organization was in no position to pay the salaries of waqf or shari'a court officials, and the Jordanians did not wish to be accused of allowing the Muslim Holy Places to deteriorate. In the absence of a recognized successor state, the anomaly is dictated by necessity.[66] Nevertheless, with the radical Palestinian nationalism at the height of the *intifada*, the continued connection with the Hashemites did little to promote the popularity of the Muslim religious establishment and the Awqaf Administration, which were already perceived as anachronistic and undemocratic.

Given the political configurations in the Palestinian community, the perceived irrelevance of the Awqaf Administration and the religious hierarchy is not entirely surprising.[67] At the same time, it is perhaps short-sighted. The future of the Awqaf Administration and the shari'a courts is extremely relevant to the ongoing negotiations and the future of East Jerusalem. The Awqaf Administration provides an embryonic administrative structure with elements of territorial control in the form of waqf property, and an independent, albeit insufficient, source of income. Its anomalous position in Israeli law, the manner in which its responsibilities straddle the line between annexed East Jerusalem and the rest of the West Bank, and its control over a holy site of international significance provide a unique opportunity for the Palestinians in the negotiations. It is a structure upon which more powers and responsibilities could be devolved to encompass at least some of the Palestinian demands during the interim phase without jeopardizing the final phase of negotiations.

The Christian Religious Establishment

Historical Background

The history of the Christian community in Jerusalem is overshadowed by the struggle between the Roman Catholic, Greek Orthodox, and Armenian Orthodox clergy over access and custodianship of the holy sites of Christendom. From the Ottoman period onward, the Greek Orthodox church, even while remaining the dominant sect, found its position constantly challenged by the other two main denominations.[68] Moreover, during the latter part of the nineteenth century the growth of the Protestant missions in Jerusalem exacerbated this rivalry as congestion increased and the "availability" of Holy Places that could be sponsored or put under the protection of particular denominations diminished. This incongruous tradition of intra-Christian rivalry has continued into the latter part of this century, with the arrival of Christian fundamentalist and evangelical movements and the Church of the Latter Day Saints (LDS, the Mormons).

The intense rivalry among the church hierarchies over the Holy Places finally obliged the Ottoman authorities to adjudicate and impose arrangements which became known as the "Status Quo Legislation of the Holy Places." Issued in 1852 and 1853, these Ottoman decrees (*firmans*) dealt with the sites and procedures of all the religious communities, but particularly the Christian ones. These arrangements were recognized in international treaties such as the Paris Peace Convention of 1856, the Congress of Berlin in 1878, and the Versailles Peace Treaty of 1919. They were also recognized by the League of Nations and incorporated by the British Mandate authorities into their own ordinances.[69] The Status Quo gave the Greek Orthodox Patriarchate a degree of primacy that was accepted by the other sects even though not regarded by them as permanent and immutable.[70]

In fact, in introducing the Status Quo arrangements, the Ottomans had not been acting on their own initiative but had succumbed to pressures of the great powers, particularly Russia. It will be recalled that one of the causes of the Crimean War was France's attempt to exert countervailing pressure to secure primacy for the Roman Catholics. In this way the Western powers saw that Christian interest in the Holy Places provided them with a pretext for a greater presence in Palestine in general and Jerusalem in particular.

Continued Ottoman military and economic weakness led to further agreements, known as the Capitulations, whereby the Porte allowed the consuls of France, Austria, and Great Britain extensive powers over their nationals in Jerusalem. The cumulative and combined effect of these agreements was extensive restrictions on the powers of the Ottoman pasha of Jerusalem. Ben Arieh has gone so far as to conclude that:

> Jerusalem's progress in the nineteenth century would have been impossible without the special status held by the consuls. . . . The consulates' power and influence grew steadily in the course of the century, with the consuls taking orders from no government except their own and

their offices constituting a sort of miniature government. From their
reports, it seems that the consuls thought of the Holy Land as annexed
territory.[71]

At the same time it appears that Western penetration into Jerusalem
was assisted not only by Ottoman weakness but also by a general
Muslim inactivity. The Islamic revival of the Ayyubid and Mamluk
periods, which led to the great architectural boom of Jerusalem, was
not sustained by the Ottoman religious and political elite beyond the
early period of Ottoman rule. In its stead came Christian expansion
under the protection of Western and Russian consuls. On the other
hand, what amounted to a huge building program by Christians
occurred during the late nineteenth and early twentieth centuries. It
included the construction of the massive Russian Orthodox compound near Jaffa Road, the Lutheran complex in the Muristan district
of the Old City, and other Protestant buildings scattered inside and
outside the walls. The building program was matched by the establishment of respective bishoprics and patriarchies and inevitably led to a
rise in the Christian population of the city.[72]

The British Mandate period saw a further increase in the Christian
population of the city, particularly of Christian Arabs from the
Bethlehem and Ramallah areas and from outside Palestine. It also witnessed a strengthening of Protestant denominations such as the
Anglican Church. While recognizing the primacy of the Muslim community in Palestine, the Mandate authorities removed the Christian
courts from the jurisdiction of the shari'a courts.[73] They also scrupu-
lously adhered to the Status Quo arrangements. Britain's neutrality in
these matters was acknowledged when it interceded in the dispute
between the senior clergy of the Greek Orthodox church (exclusively
mainland Greek or Cypriot) and the laity (mostly Palestinian Arabs).[74]
However, the prevailing Status Quo arrangements continued to cause
friction among the denominations as these last continued to jockey for
changes in their favor and to try to influence the authorities in adju-
dicating disputes. Although the Mandate charter provided for consultative procedures by which adjustments could be made, the failure of
the various church leaders to agree on the composition of the relevant
committees meant that a resolution of the issues in question was
repeatedly postponed.[75] Meanwhile, the Christian "building boom"
that began in the late nineteenth century continued under the
Mandate, with the construction of Christian religious schools and
pilgrim hostels giving the impression of untrammeled growth in

Christian institutions and population. This exacerbated the great uneasiness the dominant Palestinian Muslim society and religious establishment were feeling as a result of the rapid Jewish immigration.

During the 1948–67 period, the churches suffered from the division of their administrative units between two hostile regimes. The main impact of Jordanian policy on the churches in East Jerusalem was the strict limitations placed upon their opportunities to purchase land and develop property.[76] Because Christian churches had sold land to the Jewish National Fund during the Mandate period (especially the Greek Orthodox church with its foreign hierarchy), the Jordanian government passed a law in 1953 restricting the purchase of property "by religious and charitable organizations, which constitute branches of a foreign religious body."[77] In addition, the Jordanian government was at pains to establish its Muslim credentials as guardian of the third holiest site of Islam and in this way sought to check the momentum of Christian development that had been gathering force during the Mandate period. Similarly, greater supervision and some restrictions were imposed upon Christian schools in the city. A ceiling for the number of students was set and amendments made to the curricula which included the teaching of the Qur'an.[78]

As for Israeli-controlled West Jerusalem between the armistice and 1967, while virtually all the Arab Christians had fled from what became West Jerusalem during the 1948 fighting and none had returned, most of the churches had extensive properties in West Jerusalem. The clergies, based in East Jerusalem, needed to cross the armistice lines to attend to their coreligionists in the Galilee and elsewhere in Israel. Since both Israel and Jordan were anxious to avoid antagonizing the west, it soon became possible for clergy to obtain special passes for crossing the Armistice Line. The main change affecting Christians was the introduction of a law banning overt proselytization, aimed at protecting new immigrant Jews from the western Protestant evangelicals who had opened offices in Jerusalem. Nevertheless, Israel was, on the whole, extremely eager to promote good relations with the Western powers. In addition, the protection of Christian pilgrims was essential if tourism was to be made part of the struggling West Jerusalem economy. The visit of Pope Paul VI in 1964 was heralded as a new era in Vatican-Israeli relations, but it was very low key and included no meetings with Israeli officials, and did not in the end help relations much.

Between 1948 and 1967, Israel had officially recognized more than twelve different Christian denominations inside Israel. These were accorded the freedom to appoint their own clergy, to administer their church property independently (save for a number of long-running disputes such as with the Anglican Church, which had not been recognized during this period), and to run their own schools and religious courts. The ecclesiastical superiors based in East Jerusalem had been able to coordinate activities with their coreligionists in Israel only with difficulty, by frequent visits across the line. The physical disappearance of the Armistice Line in 1967 made these contacts much easier.

The Post-1967 Period

When Israel occupied East Jerusalem, Christians were fearful most of all that the new Israeli administration would alter the Status Quo arrangements—which, while a source of friction, were still the "least unacceptable" that could be agreed upon; the worry was that Israel would intervene in favor of one or another of the Christian sects or in their internal affairs. Government pronouncements and actions relating to religious matters were therefore closely scrutinized for clues of any changes. Even before the end of the 1967 War, the Israelis were aware of the need to assuage Christian anxieties on this issue. On June 7, 1967, the Israeli Prime Minister, Levi Eshkol, announced that the Ministry of Religious Affairs had instructions to establish a "council of religious clergymen" to make "arrangements" for the Holy Places.[79] The next day the Minister of Religious Affairs, Dr. Zerah Warhaftig, informed the various religious communities that new regulations concerning the Holy Places were being drawn up.[80] It was never made clear who would establish the council and what its composition would be. In fact it was never set up, nor were the proposed regulations ever published.[81] Instead, the Israeli Knesset passed the Protection of Holy Places Law, mentioned above.

Although church leaders understood from the new law that no drastic changes were imminent, the fact that they were unable to secure an unequivocal commitment from Israel to maintain the Status Quo arrangements and remain clear of their affairs meant that relations with the state were characterized by continuous pressure and piecemeal agreements. Moreover, Israel's determination to promote the interests of the Jewish community, acquire land, and contain the opposition to its annexation of East Jerusalem gave rise to considerable uncertainty among the Christian religious authorities. Ongoing disputes among the Christian denominations intensified that anxiety. The perceived presence, for example, of a pro-Catholic "faction" within Israeli ministries dealing with Christian affairs in the city made the situation unstable.[82] Greek and Armenian Orthodox clergy were concerned that this faction would promote Catholic demands for alterations in the Status Quo arrangements in exchange for Vatican recognition of the State of Israel and its annexation of East Jerusalem. The Vatican's gradually waning support of the internationalization of Jerusalem it had so long championed, and which Israel so opposed, should be seen in this light.[83]

Israel and the Christian Community

The Israeli census of 1967 (see chapter 3) estimated that there were 10,970 Christians in the newly expanded Municipality of Jerusalem, amounting to 17 percent of the Palestinian population and 4.4 percent of the total population.[84] Arab Christian emigration continued to be a feature of the post-1967 period, although a steady natural increase meant that the actual number of Christians, as opposed to their percentage of the total population, did not decrease significantly. A 1992 survey conducted by Dr. Bernard Sabella, a Palestinian sociologist at Bethlehem University, suggests that the Christian population of Jerusalem had decreased since 1967 to 2,620 families, or approximately 10,000 people.[85] The proportion of Christians in the total population of the municipal area decreased even more significantly, from 3.2 percent in 1983 to approximately 2 percent in 1992.[86] These figures illuminate one very important point: although the Christian Holy Places continue to exercise the interest and concern of church hierarchies from all over the world, the actual numbers of indigenous Christians in Jerusalem is very low.[87]

This helps to explain why Israel's policies toward the Christian community have differed from those it pursued toward the Muslim community. First, the indigenous Christian community, by virtue of its small numbers, posed less of a challenge to Israeli rule over annexed East Jerusalem and its surrounding areas. Second, Israel's policies toward the Palestinian Christians in their religious capacity are, by necessity, directed more toward the international Christian community than toward the indigenous congregations. As Mayor Kollek's political biographer writes: "The Israeli authorities all want to make it clear to the outside world not only that Israel maintains freedom of worship and is scrupulous in its protection of the Christian Holy Places, but that the situation of the Christian community under Israel is demonstrably better than it was during King Hussein's regime."[88]

Before proceeding further on Israel's dealings with the Christian churches, it is important to distinguish between those that are deeply rooted in Palestine and those whose presence dates to very recent times, mainly fundamentalist groups that came after 1967. These last have virtually no local followings and are entirely western, and will be addressed later in the chapter. The discussion that follows centers exclusively on the old established churches—the Greek Orthodox, the Armenian Orthodox, the Latin (Roman Catholic), the Greek Catholic, and others—all of which can be characterized by a certain split (greater or lesser depending on the denomination) between a hierarchy answering to the mother church abroad and their indigenous Palestinian congregations.

While Israel sought to establish harmonious relations with the various Christian denominations, it was aware of the church hierarchies' potential for becoming a vehicle for opposition to the occupation. Israel's precautions for preventing this took several forms. First, it was of tactical and strategic importance that a Muslim-Christian religious coalition be avoided that would strengthen and undergird Palestinian nationalism. To this end, additional freedoms and privileges were accorded the Christian clergy that made their experience of Israeli rule significantly different from that of their Muslim counterparts, rendering coordinated and joint positions difficult to achieve. Instances of joint declarations or combined activity—as for example following the 1990 St. John's Hospice incident, which will be discussed below—are therefore rare. Second, it sought to discourage the formation of a united Christian front against Israeli rule. In pursuit of this goal, it took care to avoid antagonizing the churches and used old divisions to play one denomination off against another.[89] Similarly, the senior clergy—most of whom, as mentioned, were foreign—could be courted in an effort to counter the local Christians' Palestinian nationalist sentiments. A third goal was to acquire or lease church-owned property in both East and West Jerusalem, a policy that would not only yield more space in which to pursue its transformation of East Jerusalem into an Israeli Jewish-dominated city, but that had the added benefits of compromising the Church leaderships in the eyes of their own Palestinian congregations and of driving a wedge between the Palestinian

Christian and Muslim populations. Nonetheless, the achievement of these last two goals was not very great.

Central to the relationships with the Christian churches were land transactions, which required that the Israeli government maintain a degree of leverage over senior clergy. Thus, the issuing of visas, discretion over the imposition of taxation, and the granting of permission for new religious buildings were made contingent upon the churches' willingness to sell some of their properties to the Israeli government.

From the beginning of the occupation, the Greek Orthodox Patriarchate sought to preempt any possible changes in the Status Quo arrangements that could undermine its hitherto preeminent position. To this end, it proposed to sign an official memorandum with the Israeli authorities on the subject of their mutual relations. Israel, preferring to keep its options open, declined. Nevertheless, it decided to address a number of grievances concerning the granting of visas to foreign clergy and monks, as well as property and tax matters.[90] In general, relations between the Greek Orthodox Patriarchate and Israel state were cordial and cooperative until the mid-1980s. Indeed, the Patriarchate often consulted with Israeli officials whenever other Christian sects began to organize coordinated protests against Israeli actions.[91] The Patriarchate was also anxious to stave off Jordanian pressure to reform its appointment and accounting procedures by cultivating Israeli support for the existing system.[92] There is evidence to suggest that the municipality attempted to intervene in the appointment of the new Patriarch in 1983.[93]

The most controversial element in this harmonious relationship was the question of land sales and leases by the Patriarchate to the Israeli government. Sales to the Jewish National Fund continued after 1967. In 1977, the Patriarchate received $5 million for approximately 60 *dunams* of land in the area leading down from Jaffa Gate to the Cinemathèque on the road south to Bethlehem.[94] Israel leased the land for 140 years, and the Patriarchate was allowed to build a luxury apartment on it. There is little doubt that other large tracts of undeveloped real estate in West Jerusalem and smaller amounts in East Jerusalem were also sold to the Israel-Lands Administration.[95]

In light of Israel's concerted attempts to secure its territorial base in East Jerusalem and encourage Israeli Jewish in-migration, such transactions had important political implications and were deeply disturbing to the Palestinian Christian congregations. The land issue, which has particular importance since the Greek Orthodox Patriarchate is the legal owner of all the church's property and land in the city, greatly exacerbated the differences—long contentious and disputatious—between the laity (Palestinian) and the clergy (mainland Greek or Cypriot) of the church. To the native Palestinian Orthodox congregation, it was incomprehensible that the Patriarchate could continue to sell land to the Israeli government in the face of the dwindling Palestinian grip on East Jerusalem and the continuing arrival of Jewish immigrants. Indeed, it was the land issue more than any other that precipitated increasingly strident demands by the local congregation for change within the Church: despite reforms within the Greek Orthodox Church elsewhere in the world, until recently there had been no representation of the local population among the Jerusalem Patriarchate's senior clergy.[96]

Since the intifada, calls for a reform of the appointment process and for greater accountability in the financial dealings of the Patriarchate culminated in the establishment of an "Arab Orthodox" Initiative Committee, which regards the Patriarchate as having usurped the rights of the Palestinian Orthodox congregations. A conference convened by the committee in October 1992 in East Jerusalem passed the following resolution:

> The Executive Committee [of the Arab Orthodox Initiative Committee] will work to amend the Laws and Regulations which define the relationship between the Patriarchate and the Arab Orthodox sect, in order to redress the grievances and the injustices suffered by the members of the Arab Orthodox sect and to comply with the new developments at large. In this regard the Conference approves the amendments forwarded by the Arab Orthodox Initiative Committee, to the Laws of the Orthodox Patriarchate (No. 27 of 1958) that would secure the rights and the participation of the Arab Orthodox community in handling the affairs of the Patriarchate and its supervision over the endowments, budgets and buildings of schools.[97]

Church lands were no longer seen as the exclusive province of the Church—and certainly not of a Greek and Greek-Cypriot hierarchy—but part of the Palestinian Arab patrimony. Resolution No. 16 of the conference resolution states that

> The conference will make sure to oversee and protect all church properties in order to curb any attempts at selling religious and physical endowments. Efforts will be made in taking inventories of the properties to be invested for the benefit of the community, for *they are consid-*

ered to be an integral part of the Palestinian land, the tampering of which is considered to be national treason.[98]

A follow-up conference held in Amman received the support and recognition of both the Jordanian government and the Palestine Liberation Organization. Meanwhile, the willingness of the Armenian Orthodox Patriarchate to sell land and property to the Israel Lands Administration prompted the same disquiet within the Armenian community.[99] The Armenians are a close-knit community centered almost entirely on the Monastery of St. James or in the immediate vicinity of the Armenian quarter.[100] While the Jerusalem Patriarchate has been exempted from the democratizing reforms enacted in other parts of the Armenian Orthodox Church, lay influence in the affairs of the Patriarchate is strong because of the close living conditions of the community. Since the Armenian community is reputed to be the largest landowner in the Old City and one of the largest in Jerusalem, government interest, be it Jordanian or Israeli, in the community's affairs is strong. During the Jordanian period, for example, the Jordanian government intervened to ensure the appointment of Patriarch Derderian.[101]

A combination of land issues and Israel's attempts to intervene in the community affairs led to a public rupture between the Patriarchate and the Israeli government in the early 1980s. The Armenian community's financial affairs are handled by the Sacristan, a position occupied in the 1970s by the pro-Israeli Archbishop Shahe Ajamian, who had been responsible for land sales to the Israeli government. Among them were tracts along the western slopes of the city walls from Jaffa Gate to the Dormition Abbey.[102] He maintained extremely good relations with Mayor Teddy Kollek, and was a frequent host to his foreign guests.[103] When the Armenian Patriarchate attempted in 1981 to replace Ajamian with an Australian citizen, Kareki Kazanjian, the Municipality and the Minister of Interior were opposed to the move. Kazanjian's visitor's visa was not renewed, tax exemptions for the Patriarchate were withheld, and repair projects were not permitted. Mayor Kollek himself attempted to get Kazanjian deported.[104] Finally, the public furor over Israel's intervention in the church's internal affairs obliged the government to desist from deporting Kazanjian. However, he remained in East Jerusalem without a residency permit, which made him vulnerable to further Israeli pressures.[105] Subsequent developments revealed that Ajamian and Raphael Levy, the District Governor of Jerusalem, were involved in taking bribes, smuggling, and currency offenses.[106] These events provoked a great deal of tension between the Patriarchate and the Israeli national and municipal governments, and within the Armenian community of Jerusalem itself.[107]

As for the Latin Patriarchate, it could seem ironic, given Israel's attempts to court Western Christendom, that the most Western of the three main churches in Jerusalem is the one with the most problematic relationship with Israel. The reasons for this can be found both in the international plane and in local Israeli-Palestinian politics.[108] The Latin church, as the Roman Catholic Church is called in Jerusalem, acquired much of its property and influence during its dominant position in the Crusader period. The Latins have never completely accepted the restoration of Greek Orthodox preeminence that occurred during the Ottoman period.

The importance of the Vatican's role in Jerusalem derives in general from the influence the church wields worldwide, and in particular from its traditional support for the internationalization of the city under UN auspices and the weight its views on this matter carry with a number of Roman Catholic UN member states. At the same time, long-standing hostility and suspicion between traditional Catholicism and Judaism were not entirely eradicated by Vatican attempts since 1948 to excise perceived anti-Semitic references from its liturgy and dogma. Since 1967 the Vatican's support for the notion of a "territorial internationalization" for the city has gradually waned, yet it continues to insist on some form of international administration of the Holy Places. It does not recognize the Israeli annexation of East Jerusalem and long withheld recognition of the Israeli state entirely.[109] Diplomatic recognition was finally granted in January 1994: after the PLO formally recognized the State of Israel with the Declaration of Principles in Oslo in September 1993, a continuing Vatican stance of nonrecognition would have been *plus royaliste que le roi*. Moreover, the Vatican was well aware that nonrecognition was contributing to its marginalization in the peace process (the Church had not even been invited to the opening session of the Madrid Conference). Pressures from the German and American Catholic bishops (whose provinces are the primary financial backers of the contemporary Catholic church) to recognize Israel may also have had some belated effect. Nonetheless, by granting recognition, the Vatican has now lost the little leverage it had over Israel.

The international dimension has had an impact not only upon relations between the Israeli state and senior Roman Catholic clergy, but also between the clergy and the Palestinian Catholic congregation in Jerusalem. In contrast to the Greek Orthodox Church, clergy-laity relations in the Roman Catholic Church are close and Palestinians are able to rise up in the ranks to become senior clergy. In the late 1980s, for example, a Palestinian, Michel Sabbah, became the Latin Patriarch for Jerusalem.[110]

The influence of the Roman Catholic Church extends beyond that of its own community. The Pontifical Mission for Palestine is one of the largest financial backers of nongovernmental organizations (NGOs) in the occupied Palestinian territories, and many of its projects are devoted to strengthening the Palestinian community on a nonsectarian basis. Like the Greek Orthodox and Armenian Patriarchates, the Latin Patriarchate and the Franciscan Order own large tracts of land in Jerusalem but for the most part resisted selling to the Israeli government. Many years passed before the Patriarchate agreed even to lease the land between the New Gate and the Damascus Gate to the Israelis for a park, and it was only after their planning permits had been repeatedly refused that they finally agreed to sell a small tract of land on French Hill in the annexed area north of the city.[111]

The Vatican's influence can be seen in the dispute over the ownership of the Notre Dame Hostel located on the Armistice Line. Immediately after the 1967 War, this hostel, which had remained empty for nineteen years, was sold by a Catholic ecclesiastical order to the Hebrew University without the Vatican's knowledge. On hearing the news the Vatican put great pressure on the Israelis and managed to have the sale revoked despite strong opposition from both the university and the Municipality.[112] The hostel is now one of the largest and most prestigious hotels in East Jerusalem and the flagship of the Palestinian Christian economy in Jerusalem.

The most important dispute between the Roman Catholic Church and the Israeli Municipality is over the question of tax exemptions for its property, a problem the Latins have in common with other churches. The issue stems from the Mandate period where exemptions were granted to churches for their religious properties. The Jordanians continued this practice, but after the 1967 War, the Israelis argued that the definition of religious property was too wide and should not include profit-making buildings. The Latin Patriarchate in particular refuses to pay tax on such properties on two accounts: first, the UN Partition Plan, accepted by Israel in 1947, included an obligation to continue such exemptions; and second, the payment of these taxes

would imply recognition of Israel as the sovereign authority in East
Jerusalem. As Naomi Shepherd argues, this issue is important in that

> . . . it relates to the all-important question of the overall status of the
> churches in Jerusalem and in all the Holy Land, which is still undefined,
> unsatisfactory and a potential cause of conflict between the churches
> themselves, and between the churches and Israel. All the churches want
> some kind of recognised, independent status, not just a promise of free
> access to the Holy Places. . . . Instead of enjoying a blanket exemption
> from customs duties, for example, the duties are charged, the churches
> apply to the Ministry [of Religious Affairs], and the Ministry (if it
> agrees) pays the duty on the churches behalf. So exemption depends on
> ministerial approval and the state of the Ministry's budget.[113]

In this way the Latin patriarchate and the other churches are left open
to pressures over a wide range of issues: from exemptions, to planning
permission, to visas for new appointments. The scope for Israeli state
intervention is broad indeed.

The Israelis have also been accused of interfering in the dispute
between the Ethiopian and Egyptian Coptic Orthodox churches and
their respective areas in the Deir al-Sultan monastery on top of the
Holy Sepulcher. The Israeli state has been accused of assisting the
Ethiopian takeover of a passageway between two chapels above the
Holy Sepulcher, on account of its desire to promote its relations with
the Ethiopian government and to press Cairo to improve its "cold
peace" with Israel. Evidence for this view is derived from the fact that
while the Israeli Supreme Court decided it was up to the Israeli government to return the control of the passageway to the Copts, the government set up a committee which has yet to make a decision on the
issue after more than nine years of meeting. Further delays in coming
to a decision have extended Ethiopian control of the area.[114]

A number of factors have contributed to an overall worsening of
relations between Israel and the local churches, notwithstanding the
new ties with the Vatican. One such factor is the growing tendency
toward the "Palestinianization" or "Arabization" of the clergy, as
demands for greater involvement in the running of their respective
churches began to be heard from an increasingly educated and politicized Palestinian laity. Similarly, the growing sense that a Palestinian
national identity was replacing the more sectarian one led to further
scrutiny of the clergy's stance on the social and political issues of the
day. As we have seen, the land, property, and administrative structures
are increasingly perceived as belonging to the Palestinian people as an

embryonic nation. The appointment as bishops of Samir Kafity for the Arab Episcopalians (Anglicans), Lutfi Laham for the Greek Catholics, and Michel Sabbah for the Latin Catholics (these last two denominations under the authority of Rome) sent politically aware, articulate, and internationally connected Palestinians to serve as the heads of their respective churches.[115] In addition, these men were the leaders of churches which, in the main, had close contact with and were respected by their congregations.

After decades of uncoordinated relations with the Israeli state, these men were able to draw together the leaders of all the churches in East Jerusalem to issue a series of statements highly critical of the Israeli occupation and government policies during the intifada. For example, on April 27, 1987 a strongly worded statement was issued by the "Heads of the Christian Communities in Jerusalem," part of which declared:

> It is our Christian conviction that as spiritual leaders we have an urgent duty to follow up the developments in this situation and to make known to the world the conditions of life of our people here in the Holy Land. In Jerusalem, on the West Bank and in Gaza our people experience in their daily lives constant deprivation of their fundamental rights because of arbitrary actions deliberately taken by the authorities. Our people are often subjected to unprovoked harassment and hardship. . . . We protest against the frequent shooting incidents in the vicinity of the Holy Places. . . . We demand that the authorities respect the right of believers to enjoy free access to all places of worship on the Holy Days of all religions. . . . we request the international community and the UN to give urgent attention to the plight of the Palestinian people, and to work for a speedy and just resolution of the Palestinian problem.[116]

While in one way these statements can be seen as an astute defensive move by the church leaders to guard their flanks against the criticisms of radical Palestinian nationalists and Islamic fundamentalists during this tense period, it also sent a signal to the Israelis that the Christian community in East Jerusalem could no longer be detached from the main body of Palestinian opinion. The signature of the Greek Orthodox Patriarch, the most politically conservative and pro-Israeli of the Heads of Christian Communities, on these statements was highly significant.

Another key factor in the change in church-state relations has been the shift in the locus of real influence among the various Israeli officials and institutions dealing with the Christian community. In the past, the Israeli government departments responsible for these relations was the mayor's office at the Jerusalem Municipality, the Christian Division of the Ministry of Religious Affairs, the Department of External Christian Relations in the Ministry of Foreign Affairs, and the District Governor of Jerusalem. Representatives of these departments met regularly to coordinate approaches to the churches, in such as way as not to unnecessarily antagonize or provoke the Christian community, while at the same time extracting piecemeal advantage for Israel wherever possible.[117]

Following the inauguration of the Likud coalition in 1977, however, hard-line elements, both secular and religious, were appointed to key positions in the Israel-Lands Administration, the Ministry of Justice, the Ministry of Religious Affairs, and the Ministry of Housing. These were the most important ministries and departments in the Likud's strategic program of ensuring an irrevocable Israeli Jewish dominance over East Jerusalem. However, because the Likud showed less sensitivity to church concerns, they caused the gradual erosion of the cooperative and consultative relationship that had previously been established.[118] For example, in 1979 and 1980 there was a series of arson attacks and acts of vandalism against church property, perpetrated by Israeli extremists. The Dormition Abby on Mount Zion, the Christian Information Center near Jaffa Gate, and the Protestant Bible Bookshop were all damaged, and a Baptist church in West Jerusalem was burned to the ground.[119] While the police investigated the incidents and some people were charged with these crimes, the response of the Israeli government was, on the whole, lukewarm and uninterested.

Coinciding with Likud rule and likewise affecting Israeli-Church relations was the rise of the settler movement, and more particularly increasing settler activity in the Old City, where they began to make their presence felt as of the early 1980s.[120] As the settler groups became increasingly emboldened by covert and overt government funding and political support, they turned their attention to potential sites in the Christian quarters. With this development the complex weave of ad hoc understandings and personal guarantees that constituted the structure of relationships between the churches and the Israeli authorities was put under great strain. This shift in the locus of state power came to a head in April 1990, when the Ateret Cohanim settler group broke into St. John's Hospice, owned by the Greek Orthodox Patriarchate, and set up a yeshiva and residence for its members.[121] The attempt by the Patriarch Diodorus to restore control over the building led to a physical confrontation during which the Patriarch himself was pushed to the floor by the settlers.

The public humiliation of the Patriarch symbolizes the political changes that were taking place within church-state relations in East Jerusalem. Here was the leader of the most ancient Christian community in Jerusalem, who had cooperated with the Israeli state at the risk of his own standing among his community, acceded in the sale and leasing to Israel of precious land in the city, successfully obstructed for many years any concerted Christian opposition to the Israeli annexation of the city, and allowed himself to be paraded by municipal officials as the authentic Christian response to Israeli rule; here he was treated by some North American roughnecks as if he was of no consequence whatsoever, and without any intervention by the Israeli government to restore his dignity and status. At the time of writing there is an impasse over the occupation of St. John's Hospice, while its fate is deliberated by the Israeli courts.

This incident marks the declining influence of those Israeli officials who had sought to maintain the Status Quo arrangements, and the corresponding rise of those committed to a chauvinistic Israeli Jewish agenda for East Jerusalem. It has also prompted a realignment of the Greek Orthodox Palestinians behind the more nationalist church leaders in the Latin Catholic, Greek Catholic, and Anglican churches. There has been a reassessment of the policy of cooperating with Israeli authorities, in the light of the forcible loss of their properties. In fact, relations almost broke down altogether, as evidenced by a bitter public exchange between the Patriarch and the then-president of Israel, Chaim Herzog.[122] From the Patriarch's point of view, there was little incentive to cooperate with Israel against the wishes of the lay Palestinian community, especially when that policy had failed to protect the property of the church from Israeli confiscation and to afford the church any measure of influence over Israel's policy in other matters of direct concern to it.

In summary, the established churches in Jerusalem have always been motivated—no less since 1967 than over past centuries—by their concern to ensure their continued presence in the city. Israel, meanwhile, has sought not so much to alter the churches' position but rather to ensure its own control of the city through cooptation and segmentation of the Christian community. While a relatively stable dynamic appeared to have emerged in the early years of the occupation, by the mid-seventies and especially after the intifada, this stablity was undermined by a radicalization of the Palestinian clergy and the intervention of more chauvinistic Israeli officials, resulting in a closing of ranks on the part of the Christians. It is too early, however, to discern the features of a new dynamic. If it becomes clear that Israel will remain sovereign in all Jerusalem, the hierarchies can be expected to protect their positions and assets through improved relations with the Israeli state. If, on the other hand, the possibility emerges that a Palestinian governing authority may have some administrative or political influence in the city, one can anticipate that the church authorities will continue to be responsive to their local constituencies so as to position themselves better following any transfer of power.

Finally, a word should be mentioned about the growth of new evangelical Christian organizations in Jerusalem since the mid-1980s, which has had a profound impact on church-state relations in Israel. The established churches and their clergy have watched with deep misgivings official Israeli encouragement of groups such as the International Christian Embassy in Jerusalem and other fundamentalist supporters of Israel; the established churches also noticed that some of these settlers moving into the Old City received support from organizations such as the Temple Mount Foundation, which had Christian backing.[123]

In one way, the arrival of the evangelical Christians is part of a long-established tradition in Jerusalem, where the fortunes of the various Christian churches have to an extent reflected international power politics. As noted earlier, the Latins thrived under French protection, the Orthodox enjoyed Russian protection, and the Protestants established themselves during the second half of the nineteenth century as the influence of Protestant Britain and Germany was on the rise. Thus, during the post-1967 period, the emerging influence of Christian Zionist fundamentalist groups and the Mormons reflects Israel's alliances with both the United States and South Africa. What is different about the fundamentalist groups, of course, is that they are entirely foreign, having virtually no local followings.

The evangelical groups have made their presence felt in overtly political ways. Following the storm of international criticism that greeted Israel's Basic Law of Jerualem declaring annexed East Jerusalem as part of the capital of the State of Israel in 1980 (see chapter 2), a group of fundamentalist and evangelical supporters of Israel set up the International Christian Embassy in Jerusalem (ICEJ) to demonstrate their religious and political solidarity with Israel.The primary functions of the ICEJ are to provide information and coordinate pilgrim tours and educational projects. Indicative of the importance attached by the Israeli government to the ICEJ is the fact that the group's annual Feast of the Tabernacles is traditionally attended by the president and prime minister of Israel. However, it is significant to note that while welcoming this Christian fundamentalist backing, the Israeli authorities have not been eager for such groups to establish a greater physical presence in the city. Since 1967, Israel has been governed by coalition alliances dependent upon the support of small orthodox and ultra-orthodox Jewish political parties. The latter are keenly aware that these Christian fundamentalist groups are also active proselytizers and therefore object to their presence in Jerusalem.

Despite this reluctance, however, the Mormons was able to purchase from the Israeli government a piece of prime real estate situated between the Mount of Olives and Mount Scopus, overlooking the Old City. On this site they built the Brigham Young University, the largest non-Jewish development in East Jerusalem since 1967, and which became the focus of great opposition—both Israeli and Palestinian. Palestinians objected to it because it was built upon privately-owned Palestinian waqf land confiscated by the Israelis for "public purposes."[124] Orthodox Jews in Israel opposed the university because they feared it would lead to increased Christian activity in the city (the Mormons have a reputation as active proselytizers) at a time when Israel was still struggling to maintain, through Jewish immigration, its demographic predominance.Violent Jewish Orthodox protests were prevented only when the university principal signed a declaration that the campus would not be used as a base for missionary activities. Finally, both the Palestinian Arab and *haredi* communities feared that the wealth of the Mormons would give them an undue influence in the city.[125]

The Jewish Community

Historical Background

The late Ottoman period saw the grudging acceptance by the dominant Muslim community of the long-established Sephardi Jewish community. The *hakham bashi*, also known in Jewish circles as *rishon-le-zion*, or First in Zion, became a recognized religious post responsi-

ble for liaison between the community and the Ottoman authorities.
When the Ashkenazi Jews began arriving late in the century, they initially accepted the authority of the *rishon-le-zion* but gradually broke
away because of disputes over the distribution of the *halakha* funds,
funds collected in the diaspora for the purpose of maintaining a Jewish
presence in Palestine.[126] Separate ethnic Ashkenazi groups under the
authority of a rabbi set up independent communities; since they were
not recognized by the Ottoman authorities, they sought the protection of foreign consuls.[127] Realizing the extreme vulnerability of their
position, the Ashkenazi sects re-grouped under a General Committee
and appointed a Chief Rabbi to act on their behalf. By the turn of the
century, the position of the Ashkenazi Chief Rabbi was considered on
a par with the Sephardi *rishon-le-zion*. A similar dispute lasting almost
thirty years broke out between the Sephardim and Ma'aravim, or
Moroccan Jews, which often turned violent and resulted in beatings
and jailings.[128] A compromise was finally reached between the two
groups and led to the establishment of a separate communal committee for the Ma'aravim.

The Jewish population of Jerusalem, both Ashkenazi and Sephardi,
was concentrated in what became known as the Jewish quarter of the
Old City. While synagogues and seminaries constituted most of the
monumental buildings, *kollelim* (learning communities centered around
a rabbi, a library, and dormitory accommodation) grew in number. The
main problems facing the Jewish community as a whole were its
poverty and size. By the late nineteenth century, the community constituted approximately half the population of the city but was crammed
into one-sixth of the area. Dedicated to study and prayer, the community was largely unproductive economically, depending on the *halukkah*
funds donated from abroad and upon wealthy benefactors. It was not
until the 1870s that the first Jewish neighborhood was built outside the
walls in defiance of Bedouin raiders.[129] The success of this venture led
to further extramural construction, thus easing the congestion in the
city and absorbing the growing flood of immigrants.[130] The move to
the outlying areas also served to disguise the extent to which Muslim
dominance of Jerusalem, centered upon the Old City, was being overtaken by rapid demographic change on the periphery. This trend accelerated during the British Mandate period, with Jewish neighborhoods
springing up along the safer western ridges.

Among the reforms introduced by the Mandate authorities was the
abolition of the post of the *hakham bashi* and removal of the Jewish

religious courts from the jurisdiction of the shari'a courts.[131] They also established an elected ten-member Rabbinical Council, the *va'ad ha-kehilla*, with two Chief Rabbis, one Sephardi and one Ashkenazi. From 1932 on, the Council was elected under the auspices of the Knesset Israel, the representative body of the Jewish community in Palestine.[132] At the same time, different sects combined to form political parties to lobby for their interests, with the Agudat Israel as the major party of ultra-orthodox Jews.

Meanwhile, the growth of the Jewish religious community in Jerusalem and its emphasis on study and religious devotion had not been matched by a widening productive base. The secular Zionists were investing elsewhere, buying up land in the fertile coastal area. The economic collapse of Europe and North America during the 1930s only exacerbated the poverty of the religious community, with fewer funds coming in to support more and more people; competition among the various sects for existing funds was intense. Increasingly, funds from abroad were going to the secular Zionist groups which had become the dominant force in the country and which wielded considerable influence in British and American political circles; the result was that the *haredi* sects were pushed to the margins of political life in the *yishuv*.

Thus, by the end of the Mandate period, the religious community in Jerusalem was beset by two crises. Economically, it was struggling to survive and needed to come to some agreement with Ben-Gurion, but ideologically it was opposed to the Zionist project of a Jewish state. A partial accommodation was finally achieved that will be discussed below.

While the political course of events in Palestine was shaped by the secular Zionists, the religious community continued to dominate in Jerusalem throughout the Mandate and religious issues continued to play a preeminent role. British adherence to the Status Quo arrangements governing shared Muslim and Jewish sites generated considerable resentment in the Jewish community, particularly with regard to the Western Wall. Revered by Jews as the site of the western wall of Soloman's temple, the wall also became holy for Muslims as the place where the Prophet Muhammad tethered his steed, Buraq, during his mystical journey from Mecca to Jerusalem. Under the Status Quo arrangements, the Jews had permission to use the narrow paved courtyard beside the wall for prayers, provided no fixed furniture blocked the passage of the busy thoroughfare. The Mandatory authorities were at pains to maintain this status quo and in general, an uneasy equilibrium between devout Jews and Muslim passers-by was achieved. However, as Zionist Jews grew in numbers, they began to assert themselves more forcefully along the wall, disturbing Muslim residents and hampering their free passage through the area. Discussions in the Jewish community as to the possibility of buying the wall, the courtyard, and the adjacent Magharib quarter—all of which was Islamic waqf land—led to a sense of alarm among the Muslims.[133]

It was in fact a challenge to the Status Quo arrangements at the Wailing Wall that triggered the most serious intercommunal riots in modern Palestine. The "Wailing Wall Incident," precipitated by a political demonstration at the wall by militant Zionist groups on August 15, 1929, was followed by Palestinian riots in several towns that claimed the lives of 133 Jews and 116 Arabs and that required the use of British troops to quell.[134] The "Wailing Wall incident," which also led to several commissions of inquiry in Palestine, in effect became a test of which religious community would dominate in Jerusalem and indeed Palestine as a whole. The demographic changes taking place in Jerusalem at that time severely strained the existing Status Quo arrangements, which were based upon a different population ratio than that which then existed. At the same time, the British mandatory authorities were aware that any attempt to alter the arrangements would antagonize the Palestinian community even further, at a time when they were seeking Palestinian acquiescence to their "Jewish National Home" policy.

Israel and the Jewish Community

For obvious reasons, it is not possible to discuss the "relationship" between the "Jewish community" in Jerusalem and the Israeli state in the same way as was done with the Muslim and Christian communities. Judaism is not a minority religion whose political role is shaped by relations between its religious leaders and institutions and the occupying state. Rather, the presence of Israeli Jews in the occupied city is representative of the power exercised by the state.

Nevertheless, there are two areas in which Judaism in a religious sense impinges upon the politics of the city: in the extension of Jewish religious rights over the Jewish Holy Places, and in the growing influence of the ultra-orthodox *haredim* community in determining the character of the city sections in which Israeli Jews reside.

When Israel was created, it was the old Jewish *yishuv* that became the religious establishment of the new state. The transformation was not a smooth process. Divisions between the anti-Zionist *haredim* and secular Zionists were profound. The *haredim* considered themselves ideologically and religiously called upon to try to correct the nonobservance of Judaic traditions by secular Jews. More important, to the *haredim* the establishment of a Jewish state before the arrival of the Messiah was an abomination in the eyes of God. The opposition to a Jewish state in principle led them to refuse to serve in the army, pay taxes, or even speak Hebrew. Thus, the vast majority of the *haredim* who comprised the religious establishment in Israel were not only politically anti-Zionist but were also opposed to the secular culture represented by the Zionist leadership.

These issues, which during the Mandate period had been subsumed in the struggle against the British and the Arabs, came to the fore once the state was declared. The secularists were well aware of how damaging a confrontation between themselves and the *haredim* would be to their image in front of the world and the Jewish communities overseas. They also feared it would dissipate their efforts to consolidate control over the territory they had occupied in the recent war.

Accordingly, the new state's first prime minister, David Ben-Gurion, struck a historic bargain with the Council of Torah Sages, which represented the majority of the *haredim*: while Judaism would be the official religion of the state and while the Jewish law of personal status would be adopted, Israel would be a parliamentary democracy. There was not to be a constitutional role for the ultra-Orthodox sects as such, but they could seek representation in the Knesset as religious parties.

These developments on the national stage had important implications for Jewish life in Jerusalem. The agreement struck between the secularists and the ultra-orthodox led to the state funding of the latter's activities.[135] As a result, ultra-orthodox schools, seminaries, synagogues, and ritualistic life in general began to flourish in West Jerusalem, in sharp contrast to the Mandate period. The sabbath was strictly observed, with cafés, restaurants, and places of entertainment closing down completely at Friday sunset. Ultra-orthodox neighborhoods became self-contained areas where a traditional Jewish, mostly Eastern European, lifestyle was observed. One of these neighborhoods, Mea She'arim, expanded northward. In the west, the suburb of Givat Sha'ul became an ultra-orthodox area.[136] Although they have been described as an "inward-looking minority," the ultra-Orthodox sects managed to establish stable enclaves in West Jerusalem. With their high birth rates and cohesive social structures, they became an increasingly dominant feature of Jewish religious life.[137] In the post-1967 period these developments progressed even further and continue to have a significant impact on the politics of the city.

During the period between 1948 and 1967, Jews had no access to the Western Wall or to their synagogues in the Jewish quarter in East Jerusalem, despite provisions in the Armistice Agreement to that effect. The Jewish quarter was occupied by Palestinian refugees, primarily from West Jerusalem, some of whom took up residence in empty synagogues and seminaries.[138] The lack of access to the Jewish Holy Places in East Jerusalem was all the more deeply felt in that there were very few holy sites in West Jerusalem, which was made up primarily of residential neighborhoods. As part of Israel's attempt to consolidate its control over West Jerusalem and establish it as the capital of the state, and also to alleviate the frustration of Israeli Jews resulting from their lack of access to East Jerusalem, the government built the impressive Great Synagogue on King George V Street and made it the seat of the Rabbinical Council.

Access to the Holy Places came with the 1967 occupation of East Jerusalem. The transformation of the Magharib quarter into a vast plaza facing the Western wall has already been discussed. Immediately after the conquest of the Old City by Israeli forces in 1967, the Chief Rabbi of the Israeli army, Brigadier Shlomo Goren, recited prayers in al-Haram al-Sharif compound in an attempt to set a precedent for a Jewish presence in the Haram area.[139] Discussions ensued in Jewish theological circles over the viability of constructing a synagogue alongside the Dome of the Rock. The Ministry of Defense, concerned that civil disorder would result if Jews were seen to be infringing upon the third holiest place of Islam, responded quickly to these developments. The Haram area was returned to the jurisdiction of the Awqaf Administration, with the Ministry of Defense retaining the key to the Moroccan Gate and introducing military foot patrols whenever necessary.

Periodic attempts were made by Rabbi Goren and other Jewish religious militants to establish rights to pray in the Haram area, but these were thwarted by the state authorities and not condoned by the Chief Rabbis of Israel. A consensus was established between the various government ministries and the orthodox and ultra-orthodox sects that while Jews had the right to pray in the Haram area, the circumstances were not appropriate. In this the government was aided by the theological debate over the exact location of the former site of the Holy of Holies which could be desecrated if Jews entered the Haram area to pray. The ancient Jewish religious interdiction against Jews entering the Haram was maintained.[140]

In contrast to the restrictions in the Haram area, there was a wide extension of Jewish religious rights in the Western Wall area. In the vast plaza erected on the ruins of the Magharib quarter, large numbers of Jews congregated to pray and celebrate Jewish rites. The area was declared a Holy Place and put under the jurisdiction of the Holy Sites Division of the Ministry of Religious Affairs. The ministry has sought to extend the area by authorizing excavations in a tunnel along the Western Wall. Structural damage to buildings above the tunnel has led to conflict not only with the Muslim Awqaf Administration, but also with the Israeli Chief Archaeologist for the Old City.[141] Jewish groups have also sought to restore the tomb of Simon Hatzadiq in the Shaykh Jarrah area by evicting Palestinians who live in the caves around the tomb and by taking over the Mosque at Nabi Samwil and erecting a shrine to the Prophet Samuel in the basement.[142] Other attempts to extend Jewish religious rights in East Jerusalem include the acquisition of additional land on the Mount of Olives to extend the cemetery facing the Old City, and attempts by settler groups to take over properties in the Muslim quarters of the Old City.[143]

While these activities have generated considerable attention, reflecting as they do the transformation of Jerusalem from a Muslim-dominated city into a Jewish-dominated one, less notice has been taken of changes within the Jewish community itself. Although this chapter has focused mainly upon the impact of the Israeli occupation on the Palestinian religious communities, the relationship between the largely secular Israeli state and the orthodox Jewish groups is also of interest. It not only provides an obvious point of contrast when discussing Israeli policy, but it also can help explain the pressures to which successive weak coalition governments and coalition municipal administrations in search of crucial swing votes are subjected. In addition, the territorial nature of the growing influence of the orthodox Jewish groups threatens, albeit to a lesser extent, the government's political control over the city, from a somewhat unexpected quarter.

In chapter 3, it was noted that the ultra-orthodox community now comprises approximately one-third of the Israeli Jewish population of

Jerusalem, and in chapter 4 it was further noted that this demographic growth resulted in the expansion of the ultra-orthodox neighborhoods into the adjacent areas and other parts of the city. This continued growth has had considerable impact upon the social and political life of the city, to the extent that some demographers and planners have attributed to it the out-migration of young secular Israeli Jewish families to the coastal plain.[144]

The significance of these developments lies in both the religiously observant lifestyle of these areas and the method by which elements of this lifestyle are imposed upon other Israeli Jews. There is an ideological imperative behind the desire to impose a religiously observant way of life upon secular Jews: namely, it is being done for their own sake.[145] The blocking of roads to motor traffic on the Sabbath, the prohibition of mixed-gender leisure activities, the insistence on certain dress codes for women, and other such structures are sought for what the ultra-orthodox consider the general good of the Jewish inhabitants of Jerusalem. Once an area has been targeted for ultra-orthodox residential expansion, the sect involved collects the required financing and organizes to prevent non-ultra-orthodox families from moving into the area.[146] The final goal is the creation of an *eruv*, an area demarcated as religiously-observant.[147] Current *eruv* boundaries extend from Mea She'arim in the east to the western entrance of Jerusalem, and from Ramban road in the south to a strip north of the former Armistice Line (see map 6.2).

Smaller ultra-Orthodox areas also exist in the new West Bank settlements outside East Jerusalem, in Ramot and Gilo, while a purpose-built settlement, Beitar, has been constructed to the southeast of Jerusalem within the annexed area. Another purpose-built settlement has been planned close to the Palestinian suburban village of Shu'afat, to be called Rekhess Shu'fat.

The geographic spread of the ultra-Orthodox and the religious ideology they seek to impose on Jerusalem has had a significant impact on the less observant and secular life of the city. The opposition to the building of a new Israeli soccer stadium close to the northern ultra-Orthodox areas has forced Jerusalem's only first division team to rent a stadium in Tel Aviv. Every Sabbath, the soccer fans are obliged to travel there from Jerusalem to support their team. Vociferous and often violent opposition has been expressed against mixed swimming pools, cinemas being opened on Friday evenings, certain kinds of advertising, and archaeological excavations.[148] Taken singly, these restrictions

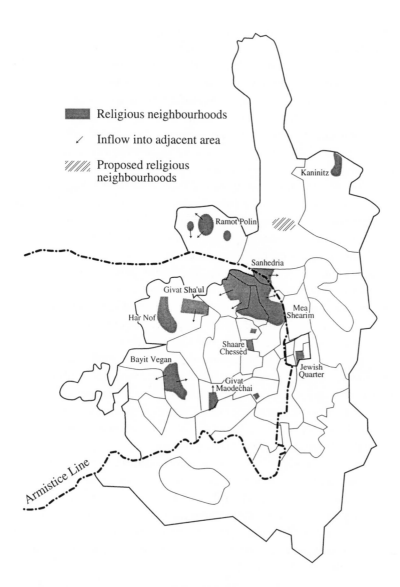

MAP 6.2. Israeli Jewish Religious Neighborhoods

may not be too irksome to secular Israelis, but together they construct a culture which the majority of the more secular population finds inimical. Furthermore they preclude the planning of urban development along the North American and European lines so favored by the Municipality, where leisure amenities and cultural events can occur.

Two related trends that are currently in the process of developing call into question the long-term viability of the expansion of the ultra-orthodox sects in Jerusalem. First, despite a tradition of limited cooperation and ecumenism between the sects, state funding and the growth of rapid communication have led to a growth in "particularism," that is, greater independent sectoral activity. The various sects do not need each other to the same extent as before. They can obtain their own funds directly from the state or from other donors, and they are able to communicate freely and rapidly with other members of their sect in different parts of the world.[149] One result has been the virtual breakdown in the functioning of the Council of Torah Sages and the fragmentation of the *haredi* political party, Agudat Israel, into three parties representing different ethnic and ideological sects. Another result has been the further disengagement of the ultra-orthodox community from other Jewish groupings in Jerusalem.

This result relates to the second developing trend. This is the question of the extent to which less religious and secular populations are willing to continue to subsidize the ultra-orthodox population. With the increase in the ultra-orthodox population continuing unabated, they require not only increased state funding but also greater employment opportunities in fields acceptable to them, such as education and religious services. In order for this to happen the ultra-orthodox sects must first increase their political clout, which is not assisted by their increasing disunity. In the meantime, resentment by the less religious and secular segments of the Israeli Jewish population against the spread of ultra-orthodox residential areas is increasing.

These two trends, which have accelerated in the first few years of the 1990s, contain the seeds of a serious crisis within the Jewish religious community in Jerusalem. To what extent can Jerusalem remain the capital of the Israeli state in the eyes of Israelis if a large proportion of the Jewish population is opposed to that state in all aspects except the funding it receives from it? An interesting conundrum as we approach the new millennium.

7

The Economic Development of Jerusalem

"It is clear that we have to turn Jerusalem into a centre of trade and commerce. Jerusalem was a commercial centre and can be so now, even if we do not know what is going to happen to the West Bank. But we do know one thing . . . we must turn Jerusalem into an industrial centre, a centre of export to the West Bank. We must plan out these things starting from now."
—S. Z. Druk, Council Member, Council Municipal Meeting, August 13, 1967

The geographic location of Jerusalem has been a great hindrance to the economic development of the city. Because of its distance from the ports of Jaffa and Gaza and the main trade routes along the coast, the absence of any exportable raw material in the immediate vicinity, the poverty of its rural hinterland, and an unsuitable landscape for industrial construction, its commercial and industrial development have been seriously handicapped. In many senses it is surprising that there was much economic development in the city at all. As has already been argued, it has been Jerusalem's prominent position in the main monotheistic faiths of the Middle East that gave the city its importance. The presence of holy sites and the opportunity to provide services for the pilgrims they attracted formed the rudimentary basis for its economy and provided its major exportable resource: crafts, religious paraphernalia, and souvenirs.

Aided by the advent of mass transit systems and global communication networks, pilgrimages were transformed into their secular twentieth-century equivalent—tourism—which became a key element in Jerusalem's economy. At the same time, two other branches of the economy became increasingly significant. The consolidation of Jerusalem as a political and administrative center, first under the British Mandate authorities and then under the Israeli government, introduced government service as a major branch of the economy. This was closely followed by the construction industry in providing homes and hostels for government workers, new Jewish immigrants, pilgrims, and tourists as the population and visitors to Jerusalem increased. Nevertheless, it is surprising to discover that these additional branches to the traditional economy did not prevent the general and gradual economic decline of the city in relation to the economic development of other cities in Palestine. In an era of growing materialism and consumerism, religion and piety were to prove insufficient as an economic base for the city.

It is also surprising to discover that this declining trend would continue after 1967. While absolute figures for employment, production, and population have all increased, relative to other urban and industrial centers of Israel, Jerusalem has suffered a decline since 1967. Furthermore, although the decline has occurred in the city as a whole, the decline is greater for the Palestinian Arab sector of the economy of the eastern part of the city which was absorbed into Israel after the 1967 War. By and large, the economic indicators suggest that the occupation of East Jerusalem and the other annexed areas of the West Bank was of greater benefit to the Israeli Jewish economy of Jerusalem than to the Palestinian Arab economy. Despite being politically and administratively unified, the two economies remained divided, which weakened the Palestinian economy. The result was that it became increasingly marginalized and the Palestinian Arab workforce increasingly proletarianized.

Despite some recent improvements, the overall economic picture is bleak. The opening up of the East Jerusalem and West Bank markets, the availability of cheap labor, and the provision of government subsidies and incentives were not sufficient to overcome the somewhat artificial and precarious nature of Jerusalem's economy. It has become clear to Israeli and Palestinian economists alike that in order to be soundly based and compete with the lure of the coastal plain in the long-term, Jerusalem requires access to markets and trade in Jordan, Syria, and the Arabian peninsula. Only extensive and sustained government investment has created the conditions for economic activity.

Ottoman and Mandate Periods

During the nineteenth century the geographical disadvantages of Jerusalem were especially felt. Poor communications with the coast and the main trade routes passing through Ramle limited its attractions as an economic center. Its lack of natural resources and the prevalence of Bedouin raiders, particularly to the east and south of the city, deterred all but the more dedicated and better-armed traders. As the population grew in the latter part of the century, through Jewish immigration and the greater availability of employment in Christian and Western institutions, there was in increase in economic activity. However, the strict religious observances of the ever enlarging Jewish community and their dependence upon a system of external subsidies for their livelihood, known as *halakha,* meant that little trade of crafts developed in the city itself.[1] In 1876, little more than 10 percent of the Jewish population was economically productive.[2] Similarly, the role of Jerusalem in Islam led to the dedication of large estates in Palestine and the Levant as waqfs for the maintenance of Muslim shrines, mosques, Qur'anic schools, orphanages, hostels, and other charitable institutions. This led in turn to a growing number of religious officials, administrators, and workers who derived their income from sources outside the city without necessarily adding to its productive base.[3]

Nevertheless, there was indeed a productive base. Small factories producing olive oil soap and sesame oil and paste (tahini) were well-known and exported to Syria and Egypt.[4] Printing presses set up by Christian institutions to provide literature for pilgrims and tourists employed sufficient numbers of people for a printing workers union to be established. By the end of World War I, 113 workers were employed.[5] (The Jewish presses set up during this period created a tradition that endures to this day, as Jerusalem retains a foremost position in Israel's printing and publishing world.)

As Western penetration into the political and religious life of Jerusalem increased during the twilight years of the Ottoman Empire, more immigrants and pilgrims arrived. New churches, hostels, religious institutions, and residential neighborhoods precipitated a minor construction boom, which created employment for quarrymen, muleteers, masons, and builders. A marked feature of this aspect of economic development was the domination of foreign investment. Indeed, the construction of roads and railways, along with the introduction of postal services and banks, resulted from Western interest in the city.[6] As noted in chapter 5, the first electricity and water concessions were also granted to Western entrepreneurs. It is interesting to note as well that the later arrivals of new Jewish immigrants were more committed to Zionist ideals than to traditional religious observances, and therefore tended to be secular and more economically productive.[7]

The Mandate period highlighted the peculiar dichotomies in Jerusalem's economic development in which absolute growth took place within a context of relative decline. As the foremost economist on Jerusalem, Professor Michael Romann, has observed, during the Mandate period, "Like the rest of the country, Jerusalem went through a process of continuous growth and a consequent broadening of its economic base. However, it lost its pre-eminence as the country's largest city, while its role as the country's capital was confined essentially to the provision of administrative and cultural services, both as concerning the British authorities and the Jewish and Arab sectors."[8]

While the traditional impediments to economic growth in Jerusalem in terms of location and access continued, during the Mandate period a number of others developed. Primary among them was the development of Tel Aviv and Haifa into significant competitors of government and Western investment, the dominance of the municipal government by Palestinian Arabs suspicious of Western and Jewish development projects, the high cost of land and building material as a result of the expansion of government services, an irregular and expensive power supply, and restrictions on land use as a result of a government committed to preserving the religious and cultural features of Jerusalem as a Holy City.[9]

During this period the city also began to see the development of two separate economic sectors—Jewish and Palestinian Arab. In the Jewish sector, the pattern of religious observance resulted in a small workforce, particular among men engaged in religious studies. The lack of a strong entrepreneurial class, which had developed during the Ottoman period, continued to be a problem. Secular and commercially minded Jews tended to base their activities in Tel Aviv. Furthermore, the intentional pursuit of only limited economic contact with the Arab population, combined with the absence of a predominantly Jewish hinterland, placed further obstacles in the way of locally generated trade and commerce for the Jewish sector.[10]

Tel Aviv, as a result of all this, became the center of Jewish banking, commerce, and transportation. Table 7.1 illustrates that although there were more industrial establishments (inclusive of craft workshops) in Jerusalem, they were small units and employed fewer people in absolute terms than their competitors in Tel Aviv.[11]

One can see how nearly four times as much private capital was

TABLE 7.1. Structure of Crafts and Industry in Jerusalem and Tel Aviv-Jaffa, 1928

	Jerusalem	Tel Aviv-Jaffa
Number of establishments	658	543
Number of employed	3,316	4,323
Average employed per establishment	5	8
Total capital invested (LP 000)	365.5	1,145.4

(source: Government of Palestine, *First Census of Industries, 1928*, p. 17)

invested in Tel Aviv than in Jerusalem. However, it should be borne in mind that this concentration of economic growth in Tel Aviv was partly offset by the location of "national" Jewish institutions in Jerusalem such as the Jewish Agency and the Hebrew University.

In contrast, the Palestinian Arab sector benefitted considerably from the opportunities for government service in Jerusalem. Palestinian Arabs dominated the lower and middle ranks of central and local administration and also in large-scale public services and public works projects such as the railways. Two-thirds of municipal employees were Palestinian.[12] Furthermore, the growth of Palestinian institutions such as the Supreme Muslim Council, its related waqf departments, and educational institutions provided an additional indigenous source of employment.[13] The construction boom that marked the Mandate years in which new residential areas, religious institutions, government buildings, post offices, hospitals, and educational and academic institutions were built, also led to the employment of Palestinians, even if the project was initiated by Jewish societies or philanthropists. Indeed, in 1935, the record construction year in the Jewish sector, 40 percent of those employed in that sector were Palestinian.[14]

During World War II, the relative decline of Jerusalem accelerated as economic activity centered around the British army, whose prime location was on the coastal plain. After the war, Jerusalem was badly affected by the intercommunal tensions and attacks on commercial areas. Terrorist activity from both sides culminated in the creation of a security zone, known as Bevingrad, in the main commercial and administrative district between Jaffa Road and the New Gate. Lasting from 1946 to 1948, the zone resulted in the closure of many retail outlets.[15]

Israeli West Jerusalem

The creation of Israeli West Jerusalem as a result of the partition of the city gave it the character of a frontier town and the economic drawbacks of a "regionless" city. It was situated at the end of a cul-de-sac, connected by a long winding road through difficult and often danger-ous terrain. The problems of access were made much worse by the par-tition. The development of the Jerusalem "corridor" agricultural set-tlements were no substitute for the loss of economic interaction with the rest of the West Bank and Jordan Valley. The Armistice Line also passed through the central commercial area of the Mamilla quarter which was then abandoned. Flatland suitable for industrial develop-ment was located near Talbiya but also very close to a hostile border.[16] Under these conditions there was little incentive for the private sector to invest in West Jerusalem rather than the coast lands or the north. In addition, Jerusalem was forced to compete with the new development towns set up by the government to settle the influx of immigrant Jews from Arab countries.

The Israeli government sought to compensate for the disadvantages in a number of ways. It improved the communication and transport links, upgraded water and power supplies, established government offices and ministries in the city, and in the face of a population decline relative to the rest of Israel directed new immigrants to the city.[17] Despite these government policies, gross national investment in Jerusalem, as a percentage of the total investment in Israel, only rose from 3.4 percent in the 1950s to 6 percent in the 1960s. Thirty per-cent of this figure was government investment alone.[18] While sig-nalling a concerted effort on behalf of the government, it also revealed the low priority Jerusalem was given in the wider context of the new state's development. The period of partition did not reverse the over-all pattern already set in the pre-1948 era of relative decline. The estab-lishment of the new state could not alter the fact that Jerusalem was an expensive place to develop.[19]

When one turns to specific branches of Jerusalem's economy dur-ing this period, one can see that it was the location of government offices and services in the city that promoted the greatest growth. In 1946, nearly 40 percent of Jerusalem's workforce found employment in government services, education, and public health, while another 5 percent worked in welfare and national and Zionist institutions.[20] Although this preponderance highlighted the role that West Jerusalem's status as capital of the state played in the city's economy, it should also be noted that there were still more employees in government service in Tel Aviv than in Jerusalem in absolute terms. In 1961, there were 7,600 government employees in Jerusalem as opposed to 10,800 in Tel Aviv.[21]

Realizing the long-term prosperity of Jerusalem would depend upon the expansion of the city's productive base, the government was concerned with building up Jerusalem's industry. Such industries as textiles, metalwork, diamonds, and pharmaceuticals became well-established. The Mandate-period printing industry revived and profited from the additional demand for printing by government and expanded academic institutions. The northern half of Jerusalem became the main industrial zone since it was close to the main road to Tel Aviv. The southeastern zone around the railway station, the normal area of industrial development, suffered form being too close to the border.[22] However, despite the doubling of those employed in this branch to 16 percent of all employed people in West Jerusalem, the industrial base of Jerusalem remained small and declined in every sector relative to developments in the rest of Israel.[23] This limited role played by industry is also reflected in the fact that only 11.8 percent of nonresidential land was devoted to industrial purposes.[24]

In great contrast to the post-1967 period, the other mainstay of the traditional economy of Jerusalem—tourism and pilgrimage—was extremely weak. The location of the prime religious sites in Jordanian East Jerusalem reduced the attraction of the western city as a tourist site. In 1963, only 13 percent of all hotel bookings in Israel were in Jerusalem, compared to 41 percent in Tel Aviv.[25] In addition, this branch of the economy employed no more than 1.2 percent of the city's employed population.[26] The Israeli government was committed to increasing Jerusalem's Jewish population which also helped stimulate economic growth in the city. A primary indicator for this could be seen in the growth of the residential construction industry. In 1963, 80 percent of all government investments in the city was devoted to housing construction, a figure that fell slightly to 72 percent in 1966.[27]

It should be clear from the above that without government intervention, West Jerusalem would have experienced considerable economic hardship. In view of Jerusalem's relatively distant location from the rest of the country, the advantages of the coastal plain and of Haifa in social and economic terms were accentuated during the partition period. The Israeli government's commitment to increasing the population of Jerusalem, establishing national institutions, and widening the productive base of the city ensured that it continued to grow and become a viable municipal entity. At the same time it also created a dependency on government investment and services and failed to address the underlying issue that in comparison to Tel Aviv and Haifa, Israel's capital city continued to experience relative economic decline.

Jordanian East Jerusalem

The partition of Jerusalem into two halves had similar detrimental effects upon the economic life of Jordanian East Jerusalem. There was an immediate loss of water and power supplies and a steady draining away of the more affluent middle-class through emigration. This was despite the great influx of refugees fleeing from the Israeli occupation of Palestinian suburbs in the western half of the city.[28] In addition, the inhabitants of East Jerusalem lost their access to the Central Business District along the Jaffa Road and in the Mamilla quarter. They lost access to coastal outlets for Mediterranean and European trade and they lost control over the coastal plain which had generated income from agricultural tithes and produce for the large waqf-supported institutions and the Palestinian political and religious elite. As a result of this geographic isolation, many wholesalers and suppliers moved to Amman and East Jerusalem retailers became dependent on importers in Amman.[29]

In addition to these disadvantages, which came about as a direct result of the partition of the city, East Jerusalem also suffered from a serious lack of investment in its transport and service infrastructure. For many years the road south to Bethlehem and Hebron was cut off by the Armistice Line. When a new road was eventually built it was a small single lane one, which twisted its way up hillsides and down valleys. Irregular and insufficient water and power supplies did not encourage private investment and government policy was to favor Amman at the expense of East Jerusalem. Indeed, unlike West Jerusalem, the Jordanian government transferred government offices *away* from East Jerusalem to Amman. Nevertheless, also in contrast to Israeli West Jerusalem, East Jerusalem did retain a large hinterland comprising approximately 150,000 people when the nearby towns of Bethlehem, Ramallah, and al-Birah were included. Furthermore, the Armistice Line left all the key religious sites in Jordanian hands, which provided the opportunity for the East Jerusalem tourist industry to grow.

Statistics for the partition period of Jordanian East Jerusalem are scant, but from the 1961 census it appears that at least half of all employed people in East Jerusalem were engaged in trade and service branches of the economy.[30] Less than one-fifth were employed in industrial production which included workshops comprising on average fewer than five persons. There were only two large factories in the East Jerusalem hinterland, a plastics factory in Bethlehem and a cigarette factory in Azariyya.[31] A number of religious institutions maintained their printing presses which received a fillip from the burgeoning tourist industry and growing activities of the Palestinian nationalist movement.

With the loss of the government and public service employment that the Mandate authorities had provided, there is no doubt that the mainstay of the East Jerusalem economy during this period became the tourist industry. It has been estimated that 85 percent of Jordanian tourist income came from tourism in East Jerusalem.[32] In 1966, 617,000 tourists visited Jordan as compared to only 291,000 visiting Israel.[33] There were 51 hotels with 1,891 rooms in East Jerusalem compared to only 1,000 rooms in West Jerusalem.[34] The "spinoff" effects of this tourist trade can be seen in the construction industry, where all the government-recommended hotels in East Jerusalem were built after 1948. It encouraged the growth in bus companies, taxis, travel agencies, entertainment, and food industries.[35] It has been estimated that nearly one-quarter of those employed in East Jerusalem were employed in tourism-related industries.

Despite the transfer of major government offices to Amman, East Jerusalem retained its preeminent status in the West Bank as an administrative center.[36] The office of the Jerusalem District Governor was located there as were small government broadcasting and newspaper operations. A number of key Muslim religious institutions such as various departments of the Awqaf Administration remained in the city. The main hospitals and large Christian educational institutions also continued to function and provide employment for Jerusalemites. While the Jordanian government insisted upon all UN agencies being based in Amman, including the regional headquarters of UNRWA, nevertheless a district office was set up in the northern Jerusalem suburb of Shaykh Jarrah, which coordinated West Bank activities. This retention of Jerusalem's administrative status was perhaps a logical outcome of the fact that Jerusalem has the highest concentration of professionals and educated people in the West Bank. The 1961 census revealed that of the towns of the West Bank, Jerusalem has the greatest number of college graduates.[37]

In addition there were some indications that during the sixties the

TABLE 7.2 Economically Active Persons by Economic Branch, East Jerusalem, Nablus and Hebron, 1961

	Jerusalem	All Nablus	Hebron	W.B.
Economically Active				
Persons (000)	15.1	10.8	7.5	172.1
Percentage	100.0	100.0	100.0	100.0
Agriculture	1.0	2.3	14.9	37.6
Industry (and Quarrying)	19.0	26.4	24.7	11.4
Construction	7.4	8.9	6.3	10.4
VX, water, sanitation	1.4	0.8	0.5	0.4
Commerce	15.7	19.7	16.7	8.1
Transport	5.0	5.1	4.0	2.5
Services	33.0	28.6	22.8	14.4
Undefined	17.5	8.2	10.1	15.2

(source: Hashemite Kingdom of Jordan, *First Census of Population and Housing, 1961*, Final Tables, Vol. II, pp. 24, 26.)

government was about to reconsider its institutional neglect of Jerusalem. It allowed the Awqaf Administration to invest its income in the area just north of the Damascus and Herod's Gates. Many of the shops lining what became the main commercial street of East Jerusalem, Salah ed-Din Street, are owned by the Awqaf Administration, as is the bus station opposite the walls. With the announcement that Jerusalem was to be the second capital of the Kingdom, although more symbolic than practical, King Hussein commenced the construction of a summer palace in Beit Hanina, on the road to Ramallah and may have presaged further government investment which was interrupted by the 1967 War.

Similar to the situation in West Jerusalem, East Jerusalem did not compare well with the other two main cities in the West Bank, Hebron and Nablus. These two cities had greater numbers of people employed in both industry and trade. Table 7.2 gives the relative figures.[38]

According to Israeli estimates made after the 1967 War there were between 2,000 and 2,500 trading companies in Jerusalem and nine bank branches holding 40 percent of the deposits of the West Bank.[39] One can conclude, therefore, that given the lack of government investment and support and given the difficult political and geographical circumstances as a result of the Armistice Lines, the economy of

Jerusalem was thrown back to its pre-Mandate dependence upon servicing religious institutions, pilgrimages, and tourism. This dependency made East Jerusalem especially vulnerable to the political instability in the region.

Post-1967 Jerusalem

Despite the occupation of East Jerusalem and the adjacent parts of the West Bank, the economy of Jerusalem still suffered from some of the disadvantages noted above. Its geographic location, the lack of indigenous exportable resources, and the lack of suitable building space were not conducive to a long-term improvement in trade and industry. The immediate impact of the war brought a loss of employment to the Palestinian Arabs in East Jerusalem. Michael Romann estimates that approximately one-third of those employed before 1967 were rendered unemployed after the war, particularly white-collared workers.[40] The Palestinian economy was affected by the loss of markets in the Arab world, the freeze in investment as a result of the closing down of all the non-Israeli banks, and the requirement to conform to Israeli laws and business regulations that were applied to the annexed areas.[41]

It is clear that despite the difficulties experienced by West Jerusalem during the partition period, its economy was, nevertheless, much more developed than that of East Jerusalem. While the Palestinians constituted 26 percent of the population of the new enlarged city, they only provided 6 percent of the purchasing power.[42] This imbalance was highlighted when, following the combination of Israeli capital investment in large residential settlements and the availability of cheap Palestinian labor, the post 1967 period experienced its first economic boom.

In general, however, the precariousness of Jerusalem's economy continued. The now-established twin features of high government investment with long-term decline relative to other major Israeli cities could only be partially disguised by its rapid geographic and demographic expansion. The post-1967 period was marked by the maintenance of divisions between the Israeli and Palestinian economic sectors despite the military and political unification of the city and cross-sectoral employment patterns, ostensibly to reduce possible flash-points between the Palestinian Arab and Israeli Jewish population, it can be seen as a policy designed to benefit to a large extent Israeli Jewish employment. This led to what has been termed the "proletarianization" of the Palestinian workforce in the annexed areas.[43] Furthermore, since it is the educated white-collar workers who tend to be more nationalistically minded, this proletarianization process had the result of weakening the influence of the nationalistic element in East Jerusalem society.

Public Service

Government and public service continued to remain the principal form of employment for the inhabitants of Jerusalem. The city was, of course, the seat of national and government offices, academic and religious institutions, as well as health and cultural centers. Their location in Jerusalem reflected the city's increased status as the political and administrative center over an increased area of Israeli-held territory. As a proportion of total employed persons, the numbers in government and public service decreased immediately after the war. A major reason for this was that while the Palestinians in government service were by and large incorporated into the workforce, the Jordanian personnel were not. Of the 500 Jordanian government staff who had been in East Jerusalem before annexation, less than one-third were absorbed by Israeli government ministries.[44] Between 1970 and 1975, of the total workforce in Jerusalem, the numbers of those employed in government service increased from 5 percent to 48 percent. The percentage remained in the mid-forties throughout the 1980s.[45] It should also be noted that little more than 5 percent of those employed in this branch were Palestinians.[46] During the last decade the proportion has decreased to 41.7 percent, indicating a trend toward a more evenly balanced employment structure.[47]

Construction

The strength of the Israeli government's commitment to changing the demographic balance in Jerusalem is reflected by the increased activity in the construction branch of the economy. Between 1967 and 1975, there was a staggering 148 percent increase in the registration of development and building contractors, a 70 percent rise in real estate agencies, and a 158 percent rise in architects and engineers.[48] Up to 1983, between 68 percent and 85 percent of the construction in Jerusalem was residential construction alone. While in 1966 and 1967 there were approximately 1,000 residential building starts in West Jerusalem, between 1968 and 1971 the average increased to 4,500 per annum.[49] In the early years, the private sector exceeded the public sector investment in residential construction, but from 1973 onward, housing starts originating from the public sector (government) averaged approximately 70 percent of total housing contractors.[50]

In terms of employment, 43 percent of those employed as building workers were Israeli Jews in 1981. The remainder, however, were not simply Palestinians from East Jerusalem. A high proportion of these Palestinian laborers were and continue to be from the West Bank but outside the areas annexed to Jerusalem. Indeed, two Israeli economists believe that the percentage of Palestinian laborers is much higher than the official figure since there is a high nonregistration rate.[51] The proletarianization of the Palestinian economy is particularly noteworthy in this sector. Tenders by Jewish companies are generally put out to Jewish contractors who then subcontract to Palestinians. Thus, most of the engineering studies, architectural, and legal work is done by Israeli Jews while Palestinians do the laboring.[52]

What these figures do not indicate is the wider picture. Despite the government's commitment to the consolidation of Israeli control over East Jerusalem and the annexed areas, only 10 percent of the national housing effort between 1968 and 1976 was directed toward Jerusalem. This is, in the words of Kimhi and Hyman, "hardly more than the existing proportion of Jews in Jerusalem to Jews in Israel as a whole."[53] In 1983, this proportion actually declined to 7.5 percent. In addition, from these figures we can see how private investors have eschewed the possibility of investing in East Jerusalem housing construction. The level is as high as it is only because of extensive government investment, and that level is itself a low figure compared to the political rhetoric accompanying the settlement program. Kimhi and Hyman conclude with this criticism: "It is apparent, therefore, that in the two areas where the government has direct influence—the construction of housing and the settlement of new immigrants—the declared policy of giving Jerusalem first priority has not been satisfactorily implemented."[54]

As a result of the trends revealed in these figures, the Likud government elected in 1977 sought to extend the incentives for construction available to private investors. In recent years there has been renewed investment in large projects and these are now nearing completion. These include the new Supreme Court, between the Knesset and the Hilton Hotel, the huge Minhat valley shopping mall in the southwest of the city, the new Municipality building on Jaffa Road, a new soccer and sports stadium in the southwest, and the Mamilla complex between Jaffa Gate and the Central Business District.[55]

Industry

A similar picture is revealed when we turn to the third main branch of the economy—industry. Despite a government policy to encourage industrial development in the city, through tax incentives and the provision of improved infrastructural facilities, and despite the opening of new markets in the West Bank as a result of the 1967 War, Jerusalem has declined as an industrial center relative both to other major cities in Israel, and, more significantly, relative to other branches of the economy. Between 1971 and 1983, there was only a 10 percent rise in those employed in industry, while the population rose by 37 percent.[56] 1973 saw a peak of 15 percent in the proportion of the Jerusalem workforce employed in industry, declining to 10 percent in 1983.[57] This can be compared to Tel Aviv and Haifa, where 20 percent and 21 percent respectively worked in industry.

Part of the reason for this decline lies in the traditional limitations placed on Jerusalem by its location. With exports to Europe and North America so crucial to the Israeli economy, the main industrial development continues to be in the coastal areas close to the posts of Ashdod and Haifa. Following the 1967 occupation, however, other limitations on industry have surfaced. The chief of these is the overwhelming importance of the other branch of Jerusalem's economy—tourism. Industrial development is in many ways an anathema to the tourist industry. Noise, industrial waste disposal, unsightly premises, and increased congestion all impinge upon the atmosphere of a place. Nowhere is this more important than in Jerusalem where people come for spiritual and aesthetic values which are easily destroyed by typical mass-production sites. Thus, the pressures to conserve and preserve old buildings and natural features in Jerusalem in order to retain a religious atmosphere places limits upon the types and location of industry.

There is also the simple question of the availability of space. The northwest industrial belt around Givat Shaul, Romema, and Qiryat Moshe has reached the saturation point, while further development outward is difficult due to the steep sided valleys and religious neighborhoods girding these areas. The industrial campus at Talpiot is also full and the new center at Atarot in the annexed areas on the road to

Ramallah is almost full. The most recently constructed campus, at Har Hotzim in the northwest, has developed rapidly and is approaching capacity.[58]

A final limitation on industrial growth has been the Palestinian intifada, which has highlighted the dependence of Jerusalem's industrial development on Palestinian labor. Frequent strikes, curfews over certain Palestinian areas, the long closure of the West Bank during both the Gulf War and in early 1993 for several months has led to a diminished and irregular supply of labor. There are no official figures to fully trace the effects of the intifada on this branch of government.

To overcome these limitations the government has designated an industrial campus at Mishor Adumin, on the road to Jericho and outside the Municipal borders, as the main location for heavy and environmentally sensitive industry. New roads and service infrastructure have been provided in addition to a range of incentives, such as tax-free holidays, to draw industry away from the central areas of Jerusalem while retaining its productive and employment benefits.

A second policy has been the encouragement of science-based industrial development in the Har Hotzim campus. It is held that these industries would conflict less with the tourist and religious needs of the city since there would be much less transportation and processing of raw materials. Noise and waste levels would also be less. Furthermore, the long-established academic traditions of Jerusalem would provide scope for productive joint research projects, and the high-tech to low labor ratio would remove the dependency on Palestinian labor. Indeed, up to 1983, only 1 percent of the labor force in these industries was Palestinian.[59] In recent years the need to ensure that highly trained Jewish immigrants from Russia remain in the city has added a further imperative to this project. A Jerusalem College of Technology has been established with an industrial park adjacent to it to encourage the cross-fertilization of research and development.[60]

The Israeli government has had some success in this endeavor. Between 1979 and 1983, thirty new plants were constructed at the Har Hotzim industrial campus, mostly pharmaceutical and electronic concerns.[61] However, in the late 1980s there was a slowdown in the creation of new enterprises and most of the increase in activity has been due to the expansion of existing enterprises. The lack of success led to intense discussions in government and municipal circles and a report was commissioned by the Hebrew University to analyze the problems and make recommendations.

The report revealed that despite assumptions to the contrary, one obstacle to attracting science-based industries to Jerusalem was the insufficient numbers of academic personnel in the city. In addition, many of the enterprises were still obliged to use high value-added services, such as accountancy, advertising, and market research, based in Tel Aviv. There was also a lack of coordination between government agencies promoting Jerusalem to this branch of the economy. Finally the report pinpointed administrative and management deficiencies in the Har Hotzim site itself. There were problems of ownership rights on the site, insufficient infrastructural services for science-based requirements, poor maintenance, and problems associated with the role of the University in management.[62]

As a result of this and other reports a number of important steps were taken. A Jerusalem Development Authority (JDA) was created to coordinate government activity and private investment. Jerusalem was given Development Area A status, which means investors in business and industry can claim up to 39 percent of investment costs from the government or have a mixture of ten years of allowances and tax-holidays. Additional advantages were available for high-tech businesses and related fields. By 1991, the JDA was responsible for 40 projects worth $500 million.[63] Overall, since 1983, there has been a 4 percent growth in the number of industrial plants and an increase in exports from 30 percent to 42 percent.[64] The Israeli government and municipality can claim a measure of success for its industrial policy. However, it should also be noted that although there may have been improvements in this branch of Jerusalem's economy, it is a low labor-input industry that does not add significantly to Jerusalem's employment opportunities.

Industry in the Palestinian sector has not benefitted from the Israeli occupation and annexation of East Jerusalem and the adjacent areas of the West Bank. In 1973, only 3,700 people were employed in industrial concerns and this figure included commuters from the West Bank.[65] Only three plants employed more than sixteen people—the Jerusalem Electricity Company, the municipal slaughterhouse, and a printing press. Most other enterprises were workshops located in the Old City or in Wadi Joz. As a result, the figures show that while in 1973 East Jerusalem contained 29 percent of the industrial capacity, it constituted only 14 percent of the workforce. Most of the large industrial plants were located in West Jerusalem. In 1983, industrial capacity in East Jerusalem and the annexed areas declined to 17 percent.

However, this overall picture of the Palestinian industrial economy in East Jerusalem requires differentiation. Certain sub-branches saw a greater Palestinian participation. For example, between 30 percent and 37 percent of those employed in light industry, such as vehicle repair, rubber, plastic, leather, textile, or food production were Palestinians. Thus, the location of industrial premises and the stratification of industrial employment highlight once again the proletarianization of the Palestinian economic sector since 1967. Low capital and low labor-input enterprises are situated in the Palestinian sector, while large capital enterprises requiring a larger workforce, predominantly Palestinian, are located in the Israeli sector.

Since 1967, the managerial and white-collar areas of employment for Palestinians have hardly grown at all. In 1983, Palestinians who accounted for one-sixth of all local residents employed and constituted over half the number of unskilled workers in Jerusalem, were hardly represented in managerial occupations. In their study of contemporary social and economic issues in Jerusalem, Professors Romann and Weingrod conclude that "Generally speaking, the process of integration was equally associated with a growing proletarianisation of the Arab labour force, and the parallel upward mobility of the entire structure of Jewish employment."[66]

The main areas for the location of Palestinian industry continue to be in the Old City and Wadi Joz areas although the Municipality has set aside a new area in Ras Hamis, north of French Hill, for future development.[67] During the last fifteen years new industries have, in the main, been established outside the municipal borders because of lower cost of land, lower tax levels, and the greater ease with which it has been possible to obtain building permits.[68] In addition, as we have seen in chapter 3, the concentration of the Palestinian population on the periphery of the municipal borders provides a convenient reservoir of cheap Palestinian labor.

There has also been a measure of economic discrimination against the Palestinian sector, particularly in the marketing of Palestinian products. For example, although the Jerusalem Cigarette Company produces a range of cigarettes that compete in quality and price with Israeli makes, Israeli Jewish wholesalers are reluctant to market an identifiable "Arab product." Similarly, while East Jerusalem stores sell Zionist paraphernalia and Judaica (stars of David and candelabra, etc), one rarely encounters Muslim, Christian, or identifiably Palestinian products in West Jerusalem.

Where Palestinian products, such as shoes or foodstuffs, are marketed in West Jerusalem, they are camouflaged with "neutral" packaging and written in a foreign language.[69] Indeed, licensing laws and operating permits are often used to protect Israeli enterprises against Palestinian competition. The most obvious example of this is the way in which the Israeli cooperative, the Egged Bus Company, is allowed to run on roads served by Palestinian bus companies, but Palestinian companies are restricted only to routes serving Palestinian areas. Restrictions are also placed upon the marketing of Palestinian pharmaceutical and agricultural products.

Tourism

The tourist industry has been described as a "potential goldmine" for the Palestinian sector of the Jerusalem economy.[70] One of the results of the 1967 occupation has been to prevent the full exploitation of this mine by Palestinians. Following 1967, there were no immediately obvious gains as a result of the annexation of East Jerusalem and the adjacent areas. Indeed, there was a decrease in the total bookings for Jerusalem. In 1966, for example, there was a total of 1,500,000 bookings for *both* parts of the city. In 1968, this had dropped to 970,000.[71] By 1972 bookings had begun to rise again to 1,623,000.

What did change quite drastically was the distribution of the bookings between the eastern and western parts of the city. In 1968, 60 percent of hotel rooms were located in East Jerusalem, but by 1979 this had declined to 40 percent.[72] Although between 1969 and 1973 there was a 20 percent rise in income for East Jerusalem, this should be compared to an 80 percent rise over the same period for the Israeli sector.[73] There was a corresponding fall in the Palestinian sector's share of the total income generated by tourism in the city.[74] By the mid-1980s, 80 percent of all bookings were in the Israeli sector.[75] It is worth bearing in mind that despite this overall growth in bookings, length-of-stay, and income, Jerusalem's share of Israel's tourist industry did not rise much above 20 percent in the post-1967 period.

These changes in the tourist trade had a spinoff effect in other areas of the service industry. By 1972, there were only seven new hotels in East Jerusalem, as opposed to fifteen in West Jerusalem. There was a drop in the number of travel agencies from 73 in 1969 to 31 three years later. In West Jerusalem there was a corresponding rise from 17 to 27. Similarly, between 1966 and 1972 those employed in tourist-

related industries in East Jerusalem dropped from 1,100 to 950; in West
Jerusalem that number nearly doubled from 941 to 1,734.[76] The only
area in which East Jerusalem's tourist industry benefitted from the
Israeli occupation and annexation was in the number of souvenir
shops and transport companies, including taxis and bus operators.[77] As
Kimhi and Hyman have argued: "The western part of the city took the
lion's share in the development of tourism that occurred after 1967.
The existing services and the new developments suited the level of
demand promoted by the tourists who came to Jerusalem. Both
tourists and Israelis also demonstrated a clear preference for West
Jerusalem. Moreover, the development of tourist services enjoyed considerable government assistance."[78]

  Israeli economists have frequently attributed this change in the distribution of the tourist industry of Jerusalem to the lower standards of
customer care prevailing in the hotels in East Jerusalem. In some cases
this was an accurate assessment of existing practices but in the main
this is not a particularly significant aspect: the raising of standards can
be easily effected.

  The change in distribution is also due to deeper structural reasons.
The East Jerusalem tourist industry before 1967 was geared to
Christian and Muslim pilgrims from the Middle East and the Islamic
world. After 1967, that market disappeared at a stroke. Palestinian tour
operators were not all able to quickly substitute this market for new
ones. In contrast, Israeli tour operators had good connections with the
European and North American markets. Furthermore, 1967 and the
opening up of the sites in East Jerusalem coincided with the arrival of
the era of mass transit tourism and package tours. These modern tours
did not have the same long-standing connections with hostels, convents, or pilgrim accommodation in churches and Palestinian homes,
as visitors preferred to use familiar Western-style hotels.[79] In addition,
the proportion of Israelis themselves who visited Jerusalem increased.
Israeli tour operators were thus able to capitalize on this combination
of developments and the unification of the city. East Jerusalem hotels
and tour operators did not have a corresponding increase derived from
the Middle East and Islamic market.

  In addition, because of the greater degree of government support
for enterprises within the the Israeli sector, government finance was
available for the construction of four- and five-star hotels.[80] Great
efforts were also made to promote Israeli sites and tours from an Israeli
perspective which neglected Palestinian areas and hotels. For example,

a useful comparison can be made between the renovated Suq al-Qattanin in one of the Muslim quarters of the Old City, and the renovated Cardo in the Jewish quarter.

The Suq is a Mamluk complex built upon Crusader ruins and has been described by a famous historian of Islamic architecture, K. Creswell, as "the finest Bazaar in Syria." Together with the *hamam al-'ayn* at one end and the *hamam al-shifa'* at the other, and the magnificent Bab leading into the Haram itself, the site is of outstanding architectural and historical importance. The restoration of the Suq al-Qattanin by the Awqaf Administration took place in 1974 was designed to regenerate the Suq as a market thoroughfare and attract the tourist trade to a neglected part of the Old City.[81] Despite careful conservation work, the Suq has been a commercial failure. Most of the shops remain shut and it is rarely used as a thoroughfare except on Fridays at noon prayer. The original conception for the restoration project was that the Bab al-Qattanin leading from the Suq to the Haram courtyard would be opened for tourists. The Jerusalem Municipality, however, refused to allow the Bab to be opened to tourists.[82] As a result the passing trade is slight and the shops which were leased cannot pay the rents. This reduced the Awqaf Administration's ability to maintain, clean, and light the Suq, which has, of course, gradually deteriorated.

In contrast, the Cardo is a row of expensive and chic shops along a restored subterranean Roman street in the expanded Jewish quarter. It is well-lit, clean, and attractively laid out. The benefits of government support can be immediately seen. Guided tours are brought there, while clear well-positioned plaques and notices inform passing tourists of its historical interest, thus generating curiosity. The Cardo is promoted in tourist literature—leaflets about it are available in hotel foyers—and its is well integrated into the promotional material sent abroad. These two sites, within a two minutes walk of each other, exemplify why the "potential goldmine" of tourism has not taken place for the Palestinian sector. It is significant to note that employment patterns in this sub-branch of the Jerusalem economy also reflect the proletarianization of the Palestinian sector highlighted by Professors Romann and Weingrod. Palestinians are employed as taxi-drivers, tour bus drivers, waiters, cleaners, and receptionists, rather than having the capability of investing in their own hotels and managing them.

Finally, in recent years, the Gulf War and the Palestinian intifada, which has seen sporadic outbreaks of violence in East Jerusalem, frightened off the package tourist industry. There has been a loss of 2,000 hotel rooms as East Jerusalem has closed down. These will seriously affect any revival in the tourist trade and may result in some tour groups staying in Tel Aviv. On the other hand, the Israeli Municipality has gone to great lengths to increase the number of sites to be visited in Jerusalem to encourage tourists to stay longer. New museums, a biblical zoo, and a promenade offering a dramatic view of the Old City are all projects designed with this in mind.

This overview of developments in the economy of Jerusalem since 1967 indicates a number of interesting points. Apart from relative growth in the tourist branch, and to some extent in government and public service, Jerusalem's economy has been experiencing a gradual but persistent relative decline. One could argue that if it were not for heavy government investment in government and public service and in the housing construction industry, the state of Jerusalem's economy would be much worse. Indeed, it is possible to go further. Without the occupation and annexation of East Jerusalem, Jerusalem would have neither the space for the vast new settlements which constitute the growth in the housing construction branch. Nor would it have the cheap Palestinian labor that allowed this branch of the economy to grow. One could conclude, therefore, that the post-1967 wealth of Jerusalem is generated both by state subsidy and by the prolongation of the occupation.

The Economy of the Two Sectors Compared

In terms of the more specific relationship between the Palestinian and Israeli Jewish sectors, the main characteristic has been the absorption of a less developed economy by a more advanced one. Professors Romann and Weingrod have also argued that even in branches of the economy where Palestinians started with a distinct advantage in 1967, for example in tourism, the Israeli sector benefitted more from the occupation than the Palestinian sector.[83] However, there is evidence to suggest that the Palestinian sector is able to hold its own where Israeli legal restrictions are less, where capital investment is less of a requirement, and where low labor costs are important, such as in transportation.[84]

In general, therefore, Palestinian economic development in the new enlarged Jerusalem has been increasingly marginalized both in terms of what it produces and in terms of geographical location. While there were increasing numbers of Palestinians entering the workforce, there were less and less Palestinian employers. Such dependence upon the Israeli sector, when that sector itself is experiencing decline, does not auger will for the future of the Palestinian economy in Jerusalem. The precedents set by the situation of the Palestinian economic sector inside Israel itself suggest that the Palestinian economy in East Jerusalem and the annexed areas of the West Bank will increasingly be transformed into merely that of unskilled wage labor.

The Palestinian economy of East Jerusalem and the annexed areas was even more greatly affected by decline as a result of the intifada. Strike-days, closures of certain areas, the semi-permanent traders' strike, curfews, disruption of transport systems, and road-blocks all combined to reduce the Palestinian economy to virtual ruins. The closure of at least five large hotels indicates the seriousness of the situation. The intifada has also resulted in strengthening links between the Israeli Jewish settlements and the center of town. Rather than shopping or trading in Palestinian areas, Israeli Jewish shoppers and businesses have turned to other Israeli Jewish areas. In turn this has led Palestinian industrialists and entrepreneurs to seek premises either in the Atarot industrial campus or in West Jerusalem itself as a means to avoid the uncertainties of the Palestinian areas.[85]

In the absence of a comprehensive peace settlement in which Israeli and Palestinian enterprises have access to markets in the Arab world, it is unlikely that the long-term relative decline of Jerusalem can be halted. If political agreements were to lead to the freer exchange of goods, visitors, and finance between Jerusalem and the Arab and Islamic world, it is probable that both Israeli and Palestinian enterprises in East Jerusalem would be well-positioned to take advantage of a more favorable trading climate. It would be important for the Palestinian economy that whatever the nature of those political agreements, they should lead to the lifting of Israeli restrictions on Palestinian commercial and industrial enterprises if the latter are to compete in any meaningful sense.

8

Jerusalem and the International Community

"Two months have passed since the heroes of Israel, the soldiers of the IDF, with the help of God, liberated and unified Jerusalem. We were like people in a dream. We were in a state of shock from the great victory. Now we must rise up with the high historic wave and accustom ourselves to the great reality which we have merited with the kind help of God. After two thousand years of longing and yearning we have merited having the whole of Jerusalem with all its historic parts under Jewish rule. This obliges us to be well equipped to grasp the significance of this historic revolution. We have a great and lofty trust in our hands and the eyes of all of Israel here and abroad lift their eyes towards us."
—Councillor S. Z. Druk, Municipality of Jerusalem Municipal Council Meeting, August 13, 1967.

It is unlikely that there is another city in the world that attracts so much international attention as Jerusalem, despite its comparatively small size: its population even today only slightly exceeds half a million. Neither is Jerusalem a particularly cosmopolitan city such as some of the great ports of the world, nor is it a great cultural center blending a diversity of ethnic origins while at the same time creating a unique indigenous identity. Rather, Jerusalem throughout the nineteenth and twentieth centuries has remained a small, relatively provincial city, fragmented into a dozen religious and ethnic neighborhoods, islands of diversity in one location.

The chief explanation for this apparent contradiction between a small city situated on the borders of a small state at one end of the Mediterranean Sea and one that receives so much international interest lies, as has already been discussed, in the presence of the major holy sites and their attendant religious hierarchies of the three main monotheistic religions of the world. Despite the secularizing trends of the twentieth century, the importance of Jerusalem in doctrine, liturgy, and ritual of these religious communities scattered throughout the world continues to have an impact upon the foreign policies of the modern nation-state. For example, as we have seen in chapter 6, the Vatican takes a close interest in Jerusalem's affairs and is a major player in the discussions concerning its future. The influence it exercises over United Nations votes of many South and Latin American Catholic countries affects the substance of the debate in the United Nations. It is a very contemporary answer to Stalin's pragmatic query as to the number of military divisions possessed by the Pope.

It is also important to consider, irrespective of the residual influence of traditional religion on the temporal councils of state, how political developments since 1945 have combined to thrust the city of Jerusalem into the center of international affairs. The post-1945 polarization of the world into pro-United States and pro-Soviet Union blocs meant that the Arab-Israeli dispute was subsumed under the wider strategic standoff taking place globally. As the epicenter of that dispute, Jerusalem became the focus of international attention. The polarization of the postwar world presented Israel with an opportunity to project itself as the bastion of Westernized democracy against communism, totalitarianism, and feudalism in the Middle East. As a result of U.S. support for this projection, the Israeli state was able to build up formidable military strength and intervene in the Middle East, ostensibly to protect Western interests. However, in the absence of a peace settlement that would allow Israel to be economically integrated into the region, an exponentially rising level of economic and military assistance was required. This in turn impinged upon Western, particularly United States, domestic politics as pro-Israel lobbies sought to solidify government aid to Israel.[1] Recent attempts to recast Israel as the bastion of Western liberal civilization in a sea of Islamic fundamentalism can be seen as a continuation of Israeli policies to secure greater U.S. military and financial aid.

Jerusalem's role in global politics was similarly enhanced by Arab and Islamic attempts to restore control over what was regarded as their city. The loss of East Jerusalem, and al-Haram al-Sharif in particular, to the Israelis in 1967 was a bitter blow to the Arab and Islamic world. The rise in oil prices during the 1973 War gave the Arab states greater financial and political muscle to assert their interests. While physical control over Jerusalem remained with the Israelis, funds were channeled directly to East Jerusalem institutions or multilaterally through organizations such as the al-Quds Committee of the Islamic Conference Organization. Maintaining the Arab or Islamic character of East Jerusalem became the focus of political and educational campaigns in the Middle East. Thus, in a very apt pre-millennial fashion, Jerusalem has once more been reestablished as a key focus in the matrix of international politics.

A useful measurement of the important international role played by Jerusalem in the contemporary period can be seen in the fact that outside Washington D.C., Jerusalem is purported to host the largest accredited press corps in the world. While this may reflect how modern political systems and cultures are increasingly dominated by information technology and media corporations, it is also a strong indication of the tenacity of religious and quasi-religious sentiments.

This chapter focuses upon the role of the international community in the debate and negotiations over the final status of Jerusalem. It argues that while the final outcome of the negotiations will be an agreement between the main protagonists—the Palestinians and the Israelis, there is no doubt that the international community will have a strong interest in the substance of the agreement, particularly those parts pertaining to the Holy Places. In this way this chapter has two main aims. First, it seeks to present the international relations context in which the discussions concerning the final status of Jerusalem occurs. Second, it seeks to indicate the degree of external pressure there is on the protagonists to come up with a solution—and one that satisfies the international community.

The main subject for this chapter is, necessarily, the policies of the United States, which has played a key position in the negotiations over the final status of Jerusalem, largely, as will be seen, through the inaction that has prevented the implementation of United Nations Resolutions on the subject. A brief look is also taken at the role of Great Britain, the United States' chief ally on the question of Jerusalem. During the past decade British policies have increasingly been coordinated with its European Community partners, and the main policy documents of the EC referring to Jerusalem are examined. Finally an overview of the nuances of the Arab and Islamic positions is made illustrating how, despite a semblance of unity over the question of Jerusalem, deep divisions exist. No attempt is made to examine the numerous official and unofficial peace plans presented over the past few decades. They are too numerous to be given proper justice in a general chapter like this one and other researchers have already done much work on this subject.[2]

The United States

United States policy on the question of the final status of Jerusalem should be seen as consisting of two levels: an overarching level of general policy, and a more detailed level dealing with specifics as a result of political developments on the ground. Without such a separation one is left with the distinct impression of overall ambiguity and contradiction, when in fact the general policy has been surprisingly consistent. It is the response to specific developments that have been erratic and ambiguous. At the same time, this division is not always so neat and should not be strictly adhered to on all occasions. Developments on the ground were at times quite dramatic and called for actions that impinged upon the general policy level. In these cases it could be argued that the often bland and ineffectual U.S. responses to unilateral Israeli action in the city amounted to what was in effect a major policy change.

The general policy since the UN Partition Resolution in 1947 has been that Jerusalem should remain a unified city but with its final status to be determined by negotiations. However, over the specific question of the construction of Israeli settlements in East Jerusalem, successive U.S. administrations have either vetoed or abstained from UN General Assembly or Security Council Resolutions demanding an Israeli cessation.[3] For Palestinians this lack of effective action is evidence that the United States is only paying lip-service to its publicly stated general policy of pursuing a negotiated settlement and is, in reality, content to leave the Israelis in control over both sides of the city. De jure recognition of Israeli sovereignty, many Palestinians believe, will come at a judicious political moment for the United States. For the Israelis, while they are aware that a U.S. veto protects them from formal international opprobrium, know that the veto does not amount to U.S. recognition of Jerusalem as the capital of the state of Israel, or, indeed, of their annexation of East Jerusalem and the adjacent parts of the West Bank.

The United States, by refraining from public criticism and effective action on Jerusalem, is able to maintain cordial relations with an essential ally in the region while placating the pro-Israel lobbies in Washington. At the same time by withholding recognition of Jerusalem as the Israeli capital and asserting that Israeli unilateral actions do not affect U.S. policy on the need for a negotiated future for Jerusalem, the United States is also able to maintain its relations with the majority of the Arab states. From the long-term perspective of the U.S. State Department, the question of the future status of Jerusalem will not be resolved in isolation but together with other aspects of the Arab-Israeli conflict. Criticizing the Israeli government for every unilateral measure would not be helpful in building up conditions for serious negotiations.[4] In this situation the general overarching policy is sufficiently vague to allow U.S. officials to sidestep accusations of partiality. Yet, in the face of ongoing developments in Jerusalem this approach has not appeared helpful to either the Palestinians or the Israelis, hence the criticism from both parties.

At the same time, as already mentioned, American policy has not been entirely immutable. While not wishing to respond to every political event, the Israeli occupation of East Jerusalem and annexation of adjacent parts of the West Bank in 1967 constituted a major watershed and did require adjustments in U.S. policy. Changes in U.S. administration led to incremental shifts that were later to have important policy implications. For example, while the United States never recognized Jordanian sovereignty over the West Bank and East Jerusalem, declaring East Jerusalem as "occupied territory," it gradually accepted the notion that East Jerusalemites could participate in elections for a West Bank authority in any autonomy arrangements. This has led, in turn, to U.S. support for the participation of East Jerusalemites in the current peace negotiations, which keeps open the question of the status of Jerusalem under Israeli occupation.

Since the mid-1940s, American policy on the question of the future status of Jerusalem has been shaped by two main considerations: that the Holy Places be protected and there be free access to them, and that the best means to achieve this goal would be through a "unified city whose final status [is] to be determined by negotiations." Evolving political circumstances could dictate exactly how these two considerations might be implemented. The 1947 UN Partition Plan proposed the territorial internationalization of the city, or *corpus separatum*, under a UN administration (see Chapter 2). While the United States had voted in favor of the plan, it did so with considerable misgivings over the practical feasibility of a UN enclave comprising two hostile communities.[5] This skepticism increased during the period of Count Bernadotte's mediation after the termination of the British Mandate. Instead a growing emphasis was placed upon the administration of the Holy Places independently of the municipal arrangements for the city. In talks with the Israeli Foreign Minister, Moshe Sharett, on April 5, 1949, the American Secretary of State, Dean Acheson, declared: "It is recognized that the interest of the international community is primarily in the Holy Places and in the maintenance of orderly conditions around the Holy Places. International interest is not primarily concerned with regulating the day-to-day activity of the inhabitants as such."[6]

The cost of maintaining a UN administration, the problems of policing antagonistic populations, and the unlikelihood of either Israel or Jordan withdrawing from the Armistice Line was the main reasons for U.S. reservations. It was but a small step from this position to the one, supported by the Israeli government, of "functional internationalization," which, in the case of Jerusalem, would recognize the bilateral division of the city between Israel and Jordan but place the administration of the Holy Places under UN supervision.

Aware that support for the functional internationalization of the city would result in the permanent partition of the city, the United States refrained from making it a specific policy commitment. It did nevertheless coordinate this private view with the British government and supported Swedish proposals along these lines at the UN. Here is an example of how the overarching general policy left the United States open to charges of contradiction and ambiguity. Stopping short of publicly endorsing a solution based on functional internationalization and maintaining its belief in the importance of a united city, on a pragmatic level the United States refrained from pushing the UN preference for territorial internationalization vigorously and thus appeared to accept the physical partition of the city. As Slonim concludes: "For American policymakers there was nothing sacred in internationalisation; rather, internationalisation was but a tool to serve what was sacred."[7] In view of later developments it is important to recognize that during the post-Partition Plan Resolution period, the United States refused to acknowledge the sovereignty of either Israel or Jordan over their respective parts of the city.

In 1950, Jordan annexed the West Bank, including Jordan-held East Jerusalem. Only two countries recognized the annexation, Great Britain and Pakistan, but Britain was at pains to exclude East Jerusalem from its act of recognition. For its part and despite British urging, the United States refused to recognize either the West Bank annexation or Jordanian sovereignty over East Jerusalem. The implication being that East Jerusalem was not part of the West Bank but a separate entity. A memorandum of April 17, 1950 stated: "The US has favored the principle of internationalization of Jerusalem to the degree necessary to achieve agreement among the main parties in interest, and has supported the United Nations efforts to achieve this. Since the Jerusalem question is still *sub judice* in the United Nations, we do not recognize any claim to sovereignty on the part of Jordan. . . ."[8]

Following the Jordanian declaration in 1960 that Jerusalem was to be the Second Capital of Jordan, the State Department reaffirmed its opposition to unilateral acts of sovereignty in Jerusalem. A State Department *aide-memoire* delivered to the Prime Minister of Jordan declared that the United States continued

> to adhere to a policy which respects the interest of the United Nations in the status of Jerusalem. The United States Government therefore cannot recognize or associate itself in any way with actions which confer upon Jerusalem the attributes of a seat of government of a sovereign state, and are thus inconsistent with this United Nations interest in the status of that city.[9]

Despite this firmly held position during the 1950s and 1960s, the United States refrained from playing an active role in seeking to impose the UN resolutions and such restraint meant that the international community essentially remained passive in the wake of the partition of the city.

Nevertheless, in contrast to the above passivity in global forums and bilateral relations, in the field of diplomatic protocol the United States strictly adhered to nonrecognition of the partition of the city and territorial internationalization. It is worth turning to look at the practical arrangements adopted by U.S. officials to deal with this juxtaposition of internationalization and de facto partition of the city. To some extent they reflect a greater commitment on behalf of the United States to the UN resolutions concerning a united city than votes and speeches in the UN itself.

Immediately following the Partition Plan Resolution, the United States established the Office of Consulate General for the Jerusalem district.[10] The Office reported directly to the State Department in Washington. After the armistice agreements the Office had premises on either side of the line and coordination was maintained by frequent visits through the Mandelbaum Gate until short-wave radio communication was set up in the 1960s.[11] Despite the declaration by the Israeli government that Jerusalem was the capital of the new state, prompt U.S. recognition of Israel in May 1948 did not lead to the United States establishing its embassy in Jerusalem. The embassy remained in Tel Aviv and continues to this day to handle all affairs with the Israeli government. Initially this was not problematic since the main offices of the Ministry of Foreign Affairs and the President's residence were also located in Tel Aviv. Indeed, even after the Ministry of Foreign Affairs moved to Jerusalem in 1952, the Israeli government was obliged to keep a liaison office in Tel Aviv to overcome the practical difficulties of dealing with diplomats who would not enter Jerusalem on official business.

Ambassadorial visits to Jerusalem were kept to a strict minimum and unofficial social contacts there were discouraged. In Jerusalem the Consulate General and staff were permitted to deal with municipal officials and with officials of the Jerusalem district on both sides, but they were not permitted to have formal contacts with any holders of national office or deal with matters not connected to Jerusalem.[12] Consular staff used special license plates for their official and private cars which merely stated "US Government" and were intended for use only in the proposed area of internationalization.[13] An ambassador for Jordan went so far as to remove the flag from his car when he entered the city to indicate that he was no longer in Jordanian territory.[14]

These moves were all ad hoc responses to the failure of the UN to establish an enclave and the resultant strengthening of national claims on the city by Israel and Jordan. It was inevitable that, in the circumstances of maintaining the de jure fiction of a *corpus separatum*, diplomatic and protocol problems should arise. What is more surprising is that they should be so assiduously adhered to by the United States. There were, however, inconsistencies. For example, the U.S. government refused to send its ambassador to Jerusalem for the official opening of the Israeli Knesset, but when the President's residence was moved to Jerusalem, it was clear that all new ambassadors would be faced with a protocol dilemma. The normal practice was that an ambassador presents his or her credentials at the official residence of the country's Head of State, so a new U.S. ambassador would be obliged to break the diplomatic boycott of Jerusalem. In 1954, when the new United States Ambassador, Edward Lawson, arrived in Israel, the State Department did, indeed, agree to allow him to present his credentials to the Israeli President in Jerusalem. But at the same time it was quick to assure Arab diplomats in Washington that the U.S. government was only conforming to diplomatic protocol and that this move did not mark any change in American policy on the status of Jerusalem.[15]

In the same way, the decision to finally transfer the Israeli Ministry of Foreign Affairs to Jerusalem was met by U.S. censure, albeit of a mild variety:

> The US regrets that the Israeli government has seen fit to move its Foreign Office from Tel Aviv to Jerusalem . . . . You may recall that the presently standing UN resolution about Jerusalem contemplates that it should be to a large extent at least an international city rather than a purely national city. . . . Also, we feel that this particular action by the Government of Israel at this particular time is inopportune in relation to the tensions which exist in the Near East, tensions which are rather extreme, and that this will add to rather than relax any of these tensions.[16]

By these protocol decisions and statements Washington withheld any normalization of the de facto partition of the city. By treating the city as a single unit outside the sovereignty of either Israel or Jordan, the United States affirmed its commitment to Jerusalem as a unified city and to the idea that its status was yet to be decided in negotiations. While U.S. officials were conscious that this position flew in the face of the facts on the ground, it could at the same time be presented as a balanced and even-handed position. By denying recognition to both Israeli and Jordanian sovereignty in the city, the United States was able to call, so to speak, a plague on both houses. After 1967 and the incorporation of East Jerusalem and annexed areas of the West Bank into West Jerusalem, the attempt to maintain this balance was confusing and misleading. Given the balance of forces after 1967 and given the role of the pro-Israel lobby in the United States it was also to some extent disingenuous.

The post-1967 period of U.S. policy toward the future status was marked by apparent and sometimes real contradictions. On the one hand, during the Johnson administration the Permanent U.S. Representative to the UN, Ambassador Goldberg, tried hard to keep American policy aloof from the fray and the United States abstained in UN votes calling for the recision of Israeli measures in East Jerusalem. On the other hand two years later, after Richard Nixon had assumed the presidency, Ambassador Yost spoke in strong terms against Israeli measures and referred to East Jerusalem as "occupied territory." This Goldberg-Yost split is important since it provoked extreme anxiety on the part of the Israeli government and precipitated the acceleration of the settlement program around East Jerusalem described in chapter 4. It is clear that there was a difference in approach between the Johnson and Nixon administrations and although there was not a clear message in support of repartition of the city, there was U.S. resistance to the Israeli unification of the city by force. In the next decade, the Carter administration attempted to encompass both approaches and in view of the role that the Goldberg-Yost speeches played during the Camp David negotiations, the retrospectively perceived common theme between the two speeches should be examined in further detail.

Following the unilateral extension of Israeli civil jurisdiction to East Jerusalem and adjacent parts of the West Bank, the United States issued the following statement:

> The hasty administrative action taken today [by Israel] cannot be regarded as determining the future of the holy places or the status of Jerusalem in relation to them. The US has never recognized such unilateral actions by any of the states in the area as governing the international status of Jerusalem.[17]

Subsequent speeches and statements by Ambassador Goldberg reaffirmed U.S. positions on Israeli actions, but at the same time, the United States refused to vote in favor of motions censuring Israel. In an oft-quoted speech before the Security Council on May 21, 1968, Goldberg gave the following reasons for the U.S. abstention:

> I wish to reaffirm the view of the United States government that the United States, while agreeing that Jerusalem is a most important issue, does not believe that the problem of Jerusalem can be dealt with realistically apart from other aspects of the situation in the Middle East. ... Rather we consider it essential that a peaceful and accepted settlement ... encompass all aspects of the Middle East problem including Jerusalem.[18]

In this way Goldberg's enunciation of U.S. policy followed the traditional line of maintaining Washington's commitment to a negotiated solution without entering into specific condemnations of Israeli policy. It certainly opened up the United States to charges that it was only paying lip-service to that notion of a negotiated solution. It could also be accused of refusing to take into account the major changes that the Israeli government had introduced into East Jerusalem and the adjacent parts of the West Bank and the way in which it was systematically pre-empting any possibility of re-partition or internationalization.

A change in the U.S. government in 1969 brought in a new Secretary of State and a greater willingness to enter into specifics concerning American policy and the future status of Jerusalem. As the expropriation of Palestinian Arab land and the construction of settlements continued, the UN Security Council reviewed the Jerusalem situation in a debate in July 1969. During his speech, the new United States Permanent Representative to the UN, Ambassador Yost, significantly declared:

> The expropriation of land, the construction of housing on such land, the demolition and confiscation of buildings, including those having historic and religious significance and the application of Israeli law to occupied portions of the city are detrimental to our common interests in the city. *The US considers that the part of Jerusalem that came under the control of Israel in the June War, like other areas occupied by Israel, occupied territory and hence subject to the provisions of international law governing the rights and obligations of an occupying Power.* [emphasis added.][19]

This explicit and blunt portrayal of Israel as an occupying power was received with dismay by Israeli officials who interpreted it as a radical departure from U.S. policy as enunciated by Goldberg. In contrast to Goldberg's approach, Yost was explicitly saying that East Jerusalem was occupied territory and that the Geneva Conventions which forbade the alteration of pre-existing laws should apply to it. There was further dismay when, in December 1969, Secretary of State William Rogers made an explicit reference to a Jordanian role in the future of the city:

> Specifically, we believe Jerusalem should be a unified city within which there would no longer be restrictions on the movement of persons and goods. There should be open access to the unified city for persons of all faiths and nationalities. Arrangements for the administration of the unified city should take into account the interests of all its inhabitants and of the Jewish, Islamic and Christian communities. And there should be roles for both Israel and Jordan in the civic, economic, and religious life of the city.[20]

The question to answer, therefore, is: do these references to specific details amount to a fundamental change in the overarching policy of promoting a unified city subject to negotiations? In one sense they do not. Both Ambassador Yost and Secretary of State Rogers revealed a commitment to traditional U.S. policy of the protection of the Holy Places and the unity of the city to be determined by negotiations. In a review of this position in 1971, the U.S. Permanent Representative to the UN, George Bush, said:

> I want to state clearly that we believe Israel's respect for the Holy Places has indeed been exemplary. But an Israeli occupation policy made up

of unilaterally determined practices cannot help promote a just and lasting peace any more than that cause was served by the status quo in Jerusalem prior to June 1967 which, I want to make clear, we did not like and we do not advocate the re-establishing.[21]

In another sense, however, there was, indeed, a shift in policy. In the statements by Rogers and Yost there can be discerned a recognition that a unified Jerusalem with some form of international administration was no longer a viable option and that the future status of Jerusalem could not be left undetermined indefinitely. Furthermore, there was a recognition that by its annexation of East Jerusalem and adjacent parts of the West Bank, Israeli demands that Jerusalem be recognized as its capital were even less likely to be satisfied without a reciprocal recognition of Arab, Palestinian, and Jordanian claims to the city.

In this very complex stew, the U.S. policy shift was not immediately apparent nor did it seem to have been planned. Studies of U.S. policy during this period do not indicate intensive internal consultations or discussions. Rather it appeared to be a response to specific circumstances on the ground that impinged upon the general policy at a later date. Nevertheless, the shift had important implications both for the Camp David Accords and for the post-Madrid Conference peace negotiations.

The whole question of whether East Jerusalem is part of the West Bank and thus part of any yet "to-be-defined" Palestinian autonomous area or state was raised in this way. For Palestinians and the Arab states it was a shift of tectonic proportions—its ramifications not immediately apparent but deeply significant in the long term. Not only did the U.S. position undermine the legitimacy of the Israeli claim to the eastern half of the city, but also implicitly it recognized the link between East Jerusalem and the West Bank hinterland. For the Israelis, the shift in United States policy presented them with a dilemma. The baldly stated Yost speech delegitimized, like no other American statement had done before, their claims to the newly incorporated East Jerusalem and parts of the West Bank. At the same time, by recognizing a possible Jordanian role in East Jerusalem, the United States was implying that under some circumstances it was prepared to formally accept an Israeli role in West Jerusalem.

Although the Israeli government continued to effect the absorption of East Jerusalem into Israel, and the Arab-Israeli dispute flared up on other fronts—notably the war of attrition along the Suez Canal and the 1973 War—the issue of Jerusalem itself remained relatively dormant until the Camp David negotiations in 1977–78. The fact that the issue of Jerusalem was left off the final accord is an eloquent testimony to the intractability of the subject during the negotiations. The Egyptian delegation submitted a plan for the Israeli withdrawal from East Jerusalem and the establishment of Arab sovereignty and administration. This was unacceptable to the Israelis. President Carter, therefore, proposed instead that "the Holy Places of each faith should be under the administration and full authority of their representatives" and that "a municipal council drawn from the inhabitants should supervise essential functions in the city."[22]

The absence of any discrete control by the Palestinians over the municipal administration of East Jerusalem prompted the Egyptian President, Anwar Sadat, to reject Carter's suggestion, which in turn led to the omission from the final accords of any clause concerning Jerusalem. However, at the Egyptian President's insistence, an exchange of letters was made between Egypt and the United States, and from Israel to the United States, each stating their position concerning Jerusalem.[23] Carter's letter to Sadat merely reaffirmed the U.S. position on Jerusalem as that adumbrated by Ambassadors Goldberg and Yost.

In effect the Camp David Accords shelved the issue of Jerusalem and the change of emphasis between the Goldberg and Yost positions was conveniently elided. The postponement of the Jerusalem issue led to considerable confusion as to what the U.S. position actually was and to differences between Secretary of State Cyrus Vance and Carter himself. The difficulty for American policy during the Camp David period was that it was being hoisted by a petard of its own making. The United States was responsible for the conduct of the Camp David Accords and the attempt to get the autonomy talks going. This meant that it had to address specific questions as to the future administration of Jerusalem. At the same time it was also trying to maintain an overall policy position of not recognizing any developments that had not been decided by negotiations. By declaring that the Jerusalem issue could not be settled unless other aspects of the conflict were agreed upon first (Goldberg), the U.S. was suggesting that the Israelis could pre-empt such a settlement if it was based upon some form of withdrawal from Jerusalem (Yost).

In this way the United States refused to recognize that the resolution of other aspects of the conflict was contingent upon specific questions such as whether East Jerusalem was part of the West Bank or not. These aspects could not be dealt with while the United States insisted on keeping Jerusalem any a separate issue to be negotiated at a later stage. Thus the weakness of the American position during the Camp David autonomy negotiations was that by shelving the issue of Jerusalem, an resolution acceptable to all parties of the future of the occupied Palestinian territories was blocked. In many ways, much of the impasse of the early parts of the post-Madrid Conference negotiations can be traced to a similar refusal to include the question of the future status of Jerusalem in the range of topics requiring resolution.

In contrast to the 1970s when, due to U.S. and UN inaction, it was essentially dormant, the 1980s saw the resurfacing of the Jerusalem issue on at least three occasions. The first was the passing of the "Basic Law" on Jerusalem by the Knesset in 1980, which formally annexed East Jerusalem and those parts of the West Bank it had integrated into the Israeli Municipality in 1967. The Basic Law also declared West Jerusalem and the annexed areas as the "eternal" capital of the state of Israel.[24] While the United States disagreed with this law, it did not vote for a censure motion at the UN Security Council. The failure to act at this moment was probably more to do with regional developments than any acquiescence to the Israeli action. The downfall of the Shah of Iran and the assassination of Anwar Sadat of Egypt put U.S. security interests in the region under grave threat. For purposes of *realpolitik* there was no point in antagonizing Israel, the only reliable ally of the United States in the region at that time. However, this reticence meant that Washington's policy on the Jerusalem issue developed no further.

The second occasion was the publication of the Reagan Plan, under which Jerusalem was referred to briefly in the following manner: "We remain convinced that Jerusalem must remain undivided, but its final status should be decided through negotiations."[25]

Again, overall U.S. policy on Jerusalem was not at all advanced by the Reagan Plan. Yet in the small print there were advances that had long-term implications. In replies to the Senate's Foreign Relations Committee, Secretary of State George Shultz reiterated U.S. support for the participation of Palestinian East Jerusalemites in the election of a West Bank and Gaza authority, thereby implicitly confirming a link in the eyes of the United States between East Jerusalem and the Palestinian occupied territories.[26]

The final occasion when Jerusalem rose to prominence in the 1980s was when the U.S. Congress attempted to pass a measure that called on the government to move its embassy from Tel Aviv to Jerusalem. The debate preceding the actual vote prompted vigorous campaigning by members of the Reagan administration, who argued that to tie the administration's hands in this way was not only unconstitutional but also jeopardized its efforts to secure a comprehensive peace in the region.[27] The bill failed in the committee stage and no major policy changes were initiated. It is noteworthy how this insistence upon nonrecognition of the Israeli position was adhered to despite the pressure in favor of the move by right-wing Christian groups and the pro-Israel lobby.

During the latter part of the Bush administration, no changes in the overarching policy were made, although a number of developments occurred that prompted U.S. comment and intervention. Cumulatively, these reactions strengthened the U.S. position on the links between East Jerusalem and the annexed areas of the West Bank to the Palestinian occupied territories. For example, the rapid increase in Soviet Jewish immigration in 1989–1990 and the settlement of a proportion of them in the occupied territories highlighted Israeli and American differences over the definition of East Jerusalem and the annexed areas of the West Bank as "occupied territory." By insisting that East Jerusalem and the annexed areas were part of Israeli Jerusalem, the Israeli government was attempting to obtain Washington's approval for the use of loan guarantees given by the United States for housing in Israel for use in those areas too.

For the Israeli government, the loan guarantee issue was and remains critical. Without the guarantees it could not hope to provide the housing to settle the immigrants needed to outpace the Palestinian demographic growth in the medium and long-term. At the same time the United States government was anxious not to foreclose its options on the future status of Jerusalem and recognized that if it were to entice the Palestinians to the negotiating table, it could not openly approve of the loan guarantees being spent in this way. By refusing to guarantee the loans in 1991, the United States was finally brought to the point of making explicit its rejection of the Israeli position. Following a change in the Israeli government in the summer of 1992, the loan guarantees were approved and the question of whether or not they applied to East Jerusalem and the annexed areas of the West Bank was fudged.

Similarly, when Secretary of State James Baker tried to establish the ground rules for Palestinian-Israeli negotiations, he was repeatedly confronted with the question of East Jerusalemite participation. Israeli

refusal to meet with East Jerusalemite Palestinians as official representatives was countered by Palestinian insistence that they were entitled
to choose who they wished to represent them. A compromise was
reached when it was agreed that East Jerusalemite Palestinians could
be part of the delegation but not be part of the negotiating team that
met with the Israeli team.

These specific responses to developments in Jerusalem did not
essentially change the overarching general policy but they did combine to ensure that it was maintained. The Israeli attempt to make the
question of the future of Jerusalem entirely non-negotiable was not
acceptable to the United States. However, its compliance with Israeli
wishes to postpone discussion of the issue presages further deadlock
across the whole range of issues to be discussed.

In sum, U.S. policy did not go through major changes during the
period under discussion. There was, in the main, a fairly consistent
adherence to the notion that the future of Jerusalem should be determined by negotiations. The U.S. preference was and remains that it
should remain a unified city and that access to the Holy Places should
be secured. In addition the United States believes that the question of
Jerusalem cannot be resolved on its own but must be part of a wider
comprehensive settlement. In practice this has meant that the
Jerusalem issue is shelved while agreement is sought on other issues.

There were along the way changes in emphasis when dealing with
specific political developments in Jerusalem. Cumulatively these
changes pushed at the edges of the general policy creating some anomalies and inconsistencies. The question of whether East Jerusalemites
could participate in the election of the West Bank and Gaza authority
(the proposed Palestinian Interim Self-Governing Authority) is a case
in point. The attempt to keep the issue of Jerusalem separate from
other areas of the Palestinian-Israeli dispute exerts particular pressure
on the general policy and is the one most likely to be overhauled as
the current negotiations progress.

The United Kingdom and the European Community

Since 1967 the impact of U.K. policy on the future status of Jerusalem
has been minimal. Indeed, since the termination of the Mandate,
Britain's role has declined in conjunction with its decline as an international superpower and its gradual integration into the European
Community. Nevertheless, as the former mandatory authority of

Palestine with considerable residual links with individuals and institutions in Jerusalem and whose whole laws, ordinances, and regulations still form the basis of administrative practice of the city, the U.K. has played a somewhat greater role than its current diminished global status would indicate. Furthermore, its close consultation and coordination with the United States on all major issues affecting Jerusalem contributes a breadth and depth to U.S. policy that would otherwise be lacking.

Similar to the United States, the United Kingdom supported the UN Partition Resolution of 1947 which included the internationalization of Jerusalem. It was very much aware of the difficulties of enforcing an administrative structure against the wishes of the inhabitants of the city. Having been forced to abandon the Mandate by Jewish and Palestinian hostility to its policies, it was not willing to reenter the fray on behalf of the United Nations. Once the city had been de facto partitioned into Jewish and Palestinian areas of control, the U.K. was pessimistic with regard to the viability of a UN enclave.[28] Already by the end of 1948, Hugh Dov, the British High Commissioner for Palestine was saying in private that the situation in "Jerusalem was beyond the point where effective UN control could be established," and that in his opinion he saw "no objection to placing these separate areas under the respective sovereignty of the Jewish state and the [Palestinian] Arab state."[29]

Thus the public U.K. line was not supported by the privately held views of Foreign Office officials which in turn led to a lack of effective action to implement the internationalization idea. This discrepancy between public policy and private views continued for many years. In addition, the degree of Anglo–American coordination is significant and reveals the extent to which both countries were willing to accept the status quo. A Foreign Office briefing of September 1949 revealed the following position:

> Meanwhile His Majesty's Government have been in correspondence with the United States Government about the lines on which a final Palestine settlement might be reached. In this correspondence the proposal in regard to Jerusalem was stated as follows: "There should be a partition of Jerusalem for administrative purposes with international supervision particularly of the holy places . . ." The proposal above is now agreed Anglo/US policy, but *this is of course strictly confidential since His Majesty's Government have not ceased to support the principle of full internationalisation in public.* [emphasis added.][30]

The U.K. took a pragmatic view that the Partition Resolution was unfeasible in the prevailing circumstances and that the future status of Jerusalem should not hold up a final settlement of the Palestine question. This view has endured to the present day.

The same Foreign Office document concludes that U.K. policy should be to accept the partition of the city and that any internationalization in the city be restricted to the Holy Places and the Armistice Lines:

> The paramount necessity at present is for a peaceful settlement in Palestine which will restore the situation in the Middle East to normal. This settlement should not be held up owing to the international insistence upon an ideal solution for Jerusalem which is unpractical. . . . There should be international supervision of the holy places and of the line of demarcation between Israel and Jordan in the Jerusalem area. Easy movement between the two parts of Jerusalem should be assured.[31]

This extreme reductionist view of the role of the international community in the future of Jerusalem was not presented, needless to say, at world forums; in public the U.K. continued to support the internationalization of Jerusalem.

Another similarity to the U.S. position on Jerusalem was the establishment of a Consulate-General with offices in both sides of the city and with both offices being directly accountable to the Foreign Office in London. The U.K. embassy in Tel Aviv continued to deal only with Israeli officials in Tel Aviv and the ambassador boycotted the opening of the Israeli Knesset in Jerusalem. "The U.K. Consul-General and staff do not attend Israeli national functions although they do attend municipal functions within pre-1967 borders unless connected with anniversaries such as the unification of Jerusalem."[32] At the same time, the United Kingdom accepted the demands of diplomatic protocol and allowed its new ambassador in 1954 to present his credentials to the Israeli President in Jerusalem.[33] The U.K.'s insistence that the future status of Jerusalem was to be determined by negotiations extended to both sides of the conflict—Israel and Jordan. While the United Kingdom, with Pakistan, was one of the only two countries that recognized the union of the West Bank with Transjordan, it expressly excluded Transjordanian sovereignty of East Jerusalem.[34]

From 1967 onward, U.K. policy on the final status of Jerusalem began to differ considerably in specifics with U.S. policy. The British government was more willing to vote in UN debates against unilateral

Israeli actions in Jerusalem. During the General Assembly debate on June 21, 1967, British Foreign Secretary George Brown warned the Israeli government: ". . . if they purport to annex the Old City or legislate for its annexation, they will be taking a step which will isolate them not only from world opinion but will also lose them the support that they have."[35]

Similarly, in the UN Security Council debate on July 14, the U.K., along with the other European Permanent Member, France, supported UN Resolution 237, which condemned the Israeli annexation of East Jerusalem. The U.K. Permanent Representative declared that Israeli actions in Jerusalem "were invalid because they went beyond the competence of an occupying Power as defined by international law."[36] In 1971, it voted for Security Council Resolution 267, which also censured Israeli actions that altered the status of Jerusalem. Finally in the same year, in a reply to a written question on new Israeli settlements in East Jerusalem and the annexed areas, the U.K. Secretary of State for Foreign Affairs replied that the government "deplored unilateral measures which will prejudice the future status of Jerusalem."[37]

The clearest indication of the consistency of U.K. policy was given by the Lord Privy Seal, Douglas Hurd, in 1981. In a belated response to a Parliamentary Question concerning the passing of the Israeli Basic Law on Jerusalem and Israeli settlement policy in general he said: "We do not accept any unilateral initiatives to change the status of Jerusalem. The future of the city as a whole needs to be resolved in negotiations between the parties concerned as part of a wider peace settlement. East Jerusalem which was occupied by Israel in 1967 remains subject to the provisions of Resolution 242 concerning Israeli withdrawal."[38]

Finally, no doubt in deference to Washington's difficulties over the question of U.S. aid being directed by the Israeli government to new settlements in the late 1980s, the British government forswore to press Israel on the issue itself. However, in response to a written question, Secretary of State of the Foreign and Commonwealth Office David Mellor took the opportunity to spell out British government policy in succinct terms: "The status of the whole Jerusalem area as defined by the UN General Assembly Resolution 303 (iv), 9.12.1949, remains to be determined. All Israeli settlements in the territories occupied since 1967 are illegal."[39]

It should be noted that direct British involvement in the Jerusalem issue appeared to be gradually phased out after the Camp David Accords. "However, it should be noted that the official position that

East Jerusalem is 'Occupied Territory' still remains. Indeed, the U.K. Consul-General's district continues to correspond to the corpus separatum of the UN partition plan although since 1967, he has taken on 'reporting responsibilities' for the West Bank and Gaza Strip."[40] A reluctance to intervene during the autonomy negotiations resulted in the United States government taking the lead in all Arab-Israeli negotiations on the subject.

European Community (EC) policy toward the Jerusalem issue has been marked less by the lack of coordination between the member states it is often accused of exhibiting, than by the lack of "follow up" after various EC positions have been established. In part this has been in deference to the U.S. monopoly over Arab-Israeli mediation, but it has also been a result of the discrepancy between EC policy as such and the policy of the individual member states. This latter point has allowed EC member states to take heed of domestic constraints in the pursuance of their own foreign policy, but at the same time espouse more principled and universalist policies at the EC level without fear of domestic political reaction. Hence, despite protestations of support for the Palestinian views, there is a lack of "follow up." This lack of consistency should not obscure the fact that, in the main, EC policy has been broadly sympathetic to Palestinian and Arab perspectives on Jerusalem, favoring direct Palestinian participation in the discussions over the city's future.

Prior to the Camp David Accords, the EC collectively contributed little to the resolution of the Jerusalem issue. As a result of the stalling of the autonomy talks, EC leaders, meeting in Venice in 1980 for one of their regular summits, issued the Venice Declaration on the Arab-Israeli conflict. The Declaration was an explicit and forthright call for greater Palestinian and PLO participation in any negotiations to resolve the Arab-Israeli conflict. The paragraph on Jerusalem, though, was unspecific and merely concentrated upon the question of access to the Holy Places: "The Nine [member states] recognise the special importance of the role played by the question of Jerusalem for all parties concerned. The Nine stress that they will not accept any unilateral initiative designed to change the status of Jerusalem and that any agreement on the city's status should guarantee freedom of access for everyone to the Holy Places."[41]

Other paragraphs endorsing UN Resolution 242 and 338 firmly put this paragraph in the context of an Israeli withdrawal. The Declaration was met by U.S. disapproval and Israeli opposition and little direct or effective action was taken on the part of the EC to bring about the conditions for the Declaration's aspirations to be fulfilled. One consequence of the Declaration was the introduction of regular visits to the region by the EC "Troika" but no progress was made on the Jerusalem issue as a result of these visits.[42]

Due to the American and Israeli collusion over excluding it from any peace negotiations, the EC was unable to effect any political changes on the ground. It contributed instead to the holding operation being undertaken by the Palestinians to retain the Arab and Islamic character of the city and its integration into the West Bank. EC aid to Palestinian institutions promoting infrastructural development in the West Bank and Gaza Strip was increased, partly through its "Program of Direct Assistance" (PDA) and partly through matching funds provided to European nongovernmental Organizations working in the area. Since 1987 EC contributions to the PDA have increased sixfold. In 1993, 15 million European Currency Units ECUs ($£1 = 1.2$ ECUs) were allocated directly to Palestinian projects. In total, funds worth more than 100 million ECUs were available in 1993.[43] Many of these projects were administered by Palestinian institutions based in, and whose area of operations included, East Jerusalem and the annexed areas of the West Bank.

Despite this lack of political change in Jerusalem, the Venice Declaration was confirmed in subsequent EC summits, notably in Brussels (1987), Madrid (1989), and Dublin (1990). The Madrid communiqué reinforced the European view that East Jerusalem was to be considered as part of the West Bank by endorsing the call for elections in the West Bank and Gaza Strip to include East Jerusalem.[44] The Dublin communiqué reiterated the view that Israeli settlements in East Jerusalem were illegal.

In the early 1990s, the EC has attempted to establish an office in East Jerusalem to coordinate its funding policies in the occupied Palestinian territories. Since it also refuses to submit its projects to the Israeli government for approval, the Israeli government has refused to give it permission to open an office. Until this issue is resolved EC aid operations will be coordinated from Brussels. In 1992, a large grant of 3 million ECUs was allocated to the Council for Palestinian Housing, a new Palestinian coordinating body for housing projects. As was outlined in chapter 4, this is an area of critical need for Palestinians and the inclusion of East Jerusalem and the adjacent areas of the West Bank in the area of disbursement is an important policy initiative.

Jordan, the PLO, and the Arab States

It is a commonly held belief in Europe and North America that the Arab states, including the PLO, form a homogeneous political block against Israel. Similarly, it is presumed that of all the issues confronting the Arab world, the Palestinian issue more than any other is the focus of Arab unity. Students and followers of intra-Arab politics will be well aware that Arab unity is much more the exception than the rule. They will also know that any enhanced degree of unity and coordination over the Palestinian issue is only fragilely held and more to do with the shared perception of Israel as an aggressive expansionist state than with notions of Arab brotherhood and solidarity.

Underlying these disagreements over the most effective way to respond to the Israeli control of Palestinian and Arab land is the question of the degree of involvement Arab states should have both separately and collectively in Palestinian affairs. The balance falls one way or the other depending upon the strength of Arab coordinating efforts and the political and financial strength of the Palestinian nationalist movement and the PLO. The Jerusalem issue further complicates the issue of Arab involvement since its holy nature to both Christian and Muslim Arabs gives it a pan-Arab dimension. Both Jordan and the Palestinians have welcomed this wider Arab involvement in terms of diplomatic support and funding, but at the same time have resisted it in terms of political interference.

The reader will recall from chapter 2 that King Abdullah of Transjordan was adamant in his opposition to the internationalization of Jerusalem. He saw it as a threat to the legitimacy of his dynasty and his "Greater Syria" aspirations and threatened "he would use force if necessary to oppose the implementation of the internationalization of Jerusalem."[45] In contrast, the other Arab states were in favor of internationalization and the Arab League passed a number of resolutions to that effect.[46] Despite this opposition, King Abdullah proceeded to incorporate Jerusalem into Transjordan. The 1949 Palestine Arab Congress in Jericho voted for the union between the West Bank and Transjordan. East Jerusalem was naturally included in this union. The Municipality of Arab Jerusalem and the Governor of Jerusalem were accountable to ministries in Amman and former mandatory government functions were transferred to Amman.

The union between both banks of the Jordan, including East Jerusalem, was recognized only by Pakistan. No other Muslim country recognized the act and certainly all the Arab states refused to support it. It is now known that during this period, Abdullah conducted secret negotiations with the Israeli government. Among the topics discussed was a proposal to exchange uncontrolled access to the Western Wall, the Jewish quarter, and Mt. Scopus for the return of some Palestinian neighborhoods on land held by the Israelis.[47] This would have given East Jerusalem use of the Bethlehem road and access to the southern West Bank. The incorporation of East Jerusalem into Transjordan and the secret negotiations led to mounting Arab suspicions of King Abdullah and in 1950 there were attempts to expel him from the Arab League.[48]

As noted in chapter 2, fear of Palestinian nationalist opposition to annexation led to Jordanian neglect of Jerusalem and the transfer of mandatory government offices to Amman. This policy was not without out its drawbacks in the light of Israeli efforts to bolster its own claims over the city by establishing national institutions there such as the Knesset, the Supreme Court, the president's residence, and the Ministry of Foreign Affairs. In response to these Israeli moves, Jordan held two Cabinet meetings in Jerusalem and one parliamentary debate.[49] In 1960, King Hussein of Jordan announced that Jerusalem had been given 'amana status and would become the Second Capital of Jordan. In 1966, the King began work on the construction of a Summer Palace. This was seen partly as an attempt to oblige foreign diplomats to present their credentials to the King in Jerusalem in the same way as the transfer of the Israeli President's residence to West Jerusalem had obliged diplomats to attend ceremonies there. Jerusalem was also declared the "spiritual capital" of the kingdom and Muslim institutions were invited to hold their conferences and meetings in the city. These remained largely symbolic acts since the proposed parliament and government offices were never built and the Summer Palace was not completed before the 1967 War. Amman therefore remained the administrative and political center of the kingdom.

In terms of the Palestinian national movement, the animosity between the main current headed by Haj Amin al-Husayni and the Hashemite regime meant that the All-Palestine Government was based in Gaza and prominent supporters of Husayni were forbidden to be active in Jerusalem. As the All-Palestine Government began to fade in effectiveness other nationalist groupings appeared. In an attempt to restrain the more militant activities of these groups, the Arab League set up the PLO and the first Palestine National Council held its sessions in Jerusalem in 1964.

As a result of Jordanian insistence on exclusive control over East Jerusalem, the interest of the Arab states in Jerusalem remained largely rhetorical. There were no pan-Arab institutions established there despite its growing importance as a tourist and pilgrimage center for the Arab world. Arab League resolutions did little more than to urge internationalization in the context of an overall peace settlement. In contrast, the Islamic nature of Jerusalem was not deemed to be a threat to Hashemite claims on the city. Indeed the increased religious prestige of Jerusalem would enhance the prestige of its "Guardians," the Hashemites. Accordingly, in December 1953, a World Islamic Congress was held in Jerusalem with delegates from Asia, Africa, China, and the Soviet Union. Significantly, the Congress endorsed Jordanian sovereignty in Jerusalem and established a permanent office there.[50]

Jerusalem was a key military target during the 1967 War, and its occupation by the Israeli army a serious blow to the Hashemites and the Arab states in general. The Israeli view is that King Hussein had been warned not to enter the war to assist the Egyptians. A Jordanian artillery bombardment of West Jerusalem was taken as a *casus belli* by the Israelis who encircled the city and occupied the Old City.[51] The Jordanian view is that they received the Israeli warning too late and that their repeated requests for a cease-fire were turned down.[52] Following the war, Jordan and most other Arab states supported UN Resolution 242, which called for an Israeli withdrawal from the territories it had occupied in June, including East Jerusalem. The PLO, however, argued that the resolution did not go far enough since it did not recognize the Palestinians as a separate people and refused to support it.

For the Arab world, the 1967 War marked the failure of the Nasserist ideology which had espoused the rejection of Western and Israeli influence in the Middle East. For nearly six years thereafter, the Jordanian and Arab role was reduced to submitting formal complaints and protestations to the UN and other world forums about Israeli actions in changing the status quo in East Jerusalem and the adjacent areas of the West Bank. While these complaints and protestations brought little tangible results, they did nevertheless, help to stiffen the resolve of the international community to insist upon a negotiated settlement to the Jerusalem issue. Without them, its is possible to envisage the evolution of a culture of acquiescence to the unilateral Israeli actions in East Jerusalem, particularly by the United States and European countries. The post-1967 period also saw the creation of an Arab consensus over Israeli withdrawal from East Jerusalem and the abandonment of support for the idea for internationalization. By the mid-1970s there was recognition of the need for the Palestinians to have their own capital in East Jerusalem.

In the wake of the 1973 War and the subsequent quadrupling of oil prices, Arab political weakness in face of Israel was halted. In addition, a greater pan-Islamic consciousness of the role of Jerusalem in Islamic culture and Arab history led to the release of large sums of money for Palestinian institutions and groups in Jerusalem. The Arab League, for example, initiated a housing development and restoration project in conjunction with the League of Arab Cities and channeled funds for this purpose through the Awqaf Administration in Jerusalem.[53] The Islamic Conference Organization, backed principally by Saudi Arabia, established the al-Quds Committee, which was devoted to restoration work of Islamic buildings in the Old City and the preservation of Islamic culture. The main recipient of these funds was the Awqaf Administration, but the Jordanian government insisted that they were processed through the Jordanian Royal Committee for the Preservation of Jerusalem based in Amman.[54]

In 1974, the Rabat summit of the Arab League recognized the PLO as the "sole legitimate" representative of the Palestinians. This reflected the growing support for the Palestinian national movement at the expense of Jordan. While King Hussein accepted this shift as an inevitable result of the failure of the Arab states to free even a part of Palestine from the Israelis, he did not relinquish Jordanian political and administrative ties with the West Bank and East Jerusalem. The Higher Islamic Council and the Awqaf Administration, for example, remained under the control and funding of the Ministry of Religious Affairs in Amman.[55] The PLO's position on the future status of Jerusalem was that it would become the capital of the Palestinian state following an Israeli withdrawal to the Armistice Line of 1949.

The next Arab move came as a result of the Camp David Accords signed by Israel, Egypt, and the United States in 1978. President Anwar Sadat shocked the Arab world and the Palestinians when he flew to Jerusalem and formally addressed the Israeli nation from the Knesset rostrum. Here was the leader of the largest Arab nation, whose capital hosted the headquarters of the Arab League and whose armies, although not victorious, had severely damaged the Israeli military standing, conferring recognition on the Israeli occupation of Jerusalem as no other world leader had dared to do. Ultimately, the gesture remained a flamboyant act consistent with Sadat's theatrical style and no lasting change in the Arab position occurred. Following the signing of the Accords, the Egyptian embassy was located in Tel Aviv like other embassies.

It is significant that the negotiations prior to signing nearly collapsed over the Jerusalem issue. While both parties could agree that Jerusalem should remain undivided and that there should be freedom of access to the Holy Places, the Israeli government refused to contemplate any separate Palestinian or Arab administration of the city.[56] In order to proceed with agreements on the Egyptian-Israeli front, and in order not to hold up the proposed negotiations on Palestinian autonomy, President Sadat agreed to drop any mention of Jerusalem in the Accords itself. Instead he insisted upon an exchange of letters between Egypt and the United States confirming the countries' respective position on the future status of the city. As was noted above, the U.S. letter merely reiterated the positions outlined by Ambassadors Goldberg and Yost. In contrast the Egyptian letter was more detailed and explicit. Seven points were outlined:

1. Arab Jerusalem is an integral part of the West Bank. Legal and historical Arab rights in the city must be respected and restored.
2. Arab Jerusalem should be under Arab sovereignty.
3. The Palestinian inhabitants of Arab Jerusalem are entitled to exercise their legitimate national rights, being part of the Palestinian people in the West Bank.
4. Relevant Security Council resolutions, particularly Resolutions 242 and 267, must be applied with regard to Jerusalem. All the measures taken by Israel to alter the status of the city are null and void and should be rescinded.
5. All people must have free access to the city and enjoy the free exercise of worship and the right to visit and transit to the Holy Places without distinction and discrimination.
6. The Holy Places of each faith may be placed under the administration and control of their representatives.
7. Essential functions of the city should be undivided and a joint municipal council composed of an equal number of Arab and Israeli members can supervise the carrying out of these functions. In this way the city shall be undivided.[57]

It is clear that by this letter Sadat was in some way trying to mollify those Arabs and Palestinians who were accusing him of "selling out" the Arab world and the Palestinian cause by signing a separate peace agreement with the Israelis. At the same time, it is important to note that despite his flamboyant gestures, and despite his willingness to make concessions on other fronts, he was not willing or able to depart from the Arab and Palestinian consensus on Jerusalem that had emerged after 1967.

The PLO was adamant in its rejection of the Camp David Accords and its position received a ringing endorsement by the Arab League at the Baghdad Summit in November 1978 where Egypt was also ejected from the League. The Palestinian position was not totally inflexible. Some leading Palestinians in the Palestinian National Council, the Palestinian Parliament, acknowledged the Israeli attachment to the Wailing Wall and parts of the Old City and were willing to consider arrangements which would take that into account. Walid Khalidi, an influential Palestinian strategist and Professor at Harvard University, proposed that:

> An irreversible right of access to the Wailing [Western] Wall would be an integral part of the settlement, while a special regime for the Jewish-owned properties adjacent to the Wailing Wall could be created. These arrangements could be overseen by the grand interfaith council or by a special inter-state Israeli-Palestinian body, under the guarantees of the UN Security council, the Arab League and the Islamic states.[58]

These rights and special regimes remained contingent, nonetheless, on an Israeli withdrawal to the Armistice Line.

From 1978 onward, in the absence of any political and diplomatic movement on the Jerusalem issue, and in the face of Israeli determination to consolidate its hold over the eastern part of the city, Arab efforts were directed toward building up the Palestinian institutional presence in East Jerusalem and the annexed areas. Greater funds were made available through the Arab League, the Islamic Conference Organization, the Islamic Bank, and their subsidiary bodies such as the Arab League Educational, Scientific, and Cultural Organization (ALESCO) and the al-Quds Committee. The Baghdad summit, for example, established the "Joint Committee for the Enhancement of Steadfastness of the Palestinian People in the Occupied Homeland" and, over a decade of activities, directed 37.8 percent of its funds to the Jerusalem area.[59] The Islamic Conference of Foreign Ministers held in Amman in 1978 reaffirmed that the question of Jerusalem was "the paramount cause of Islam and Muslims." Its final communiqué called on Islamic states to contribute to the "al-Quds Fund":

The Conference called upon all the Islamic States to assist in reaching the target of the capital of the al-Quds Fund and its Waqf, amounting to one hundred million dollars. . . . All Islamic States should continue to issue the Palestinian stamp on a permanent basis as long as the question of Palestine and the Holy City of al-Quds remained unresolved and to remit the proceeds to the Palestinian Welfare Society.[60]

With these funds a myriad of Palestinian research centers, media organizations, cultural centers, housing, and restoration projects were created which in turn generated not only employment but also an informal administrative infrastructure for Palestinians in East Jerusalem and the annexed areas of the West Bank.

The major Arab initiative during this period was the approval of the Fahd Plan by the Fez Summit of the Arab League in 1980. The Fahd Plan covered all aspects of the Arab-Israeli conflict but four of the eight points referred to the Jerusalem issue. It proposed:

1. The withdrawal of Israel from all Arab territories occupied in 1967 including Arab al-Quds.
2. The dismantling of settlements established by Israel on the Arab territories after 1967.
3. The guarantee of freedom of worship and practice of religious rites for all religions in the holy shrines . . .
6. The establishment of an independent Palestinian state with al-Quds as its capital.

Subsequent Arab League summits confirmed the Arab commitment to the Fahd Plan, even after the readmission of Egypt to the Arab League. In summary, in deference to Palestinian wishes for a capital city, it signalled the Arab abandonment of its flirtation with the idea of internationalization.

The final major development in the Arab world with regard to the Jerusalem issue took place in 1988 when King Hussein announced that Jordan was severing its political and administrative ties with the West Bank. Often portrayed as an act of pique, it was, in reality, a belated acknowledgement of the influence of the PLO in the occupied Palestinian territories and a recognition that the Palestinian *intifada* had removed what authority and credibility his supporters had retained to that point. As a result of this declaration the West Bank was no longer part of the Hashemite Kingdom of Jordan.[61] The significant point to note is that while administrative links in such spheres as welfare, education, agriculture, and so on were severed, the Jordanians did not cut their links with the Awqaf Administration and shari'a court system in the West Bank. These continued to be funded by and subject to the jurisdiction of the Ministry of Religious Affairs in Amman.

The exemption of the Awqaf Administration and shari'a court system from the King's severance of ties with the West Bank was a consequence of several factors. It was a recognition that the PLO did not have the financial resources to replace the Jordanians in this sphere, and Hussein did not wish to see or be accused of causing the dereliction of the Muslim Holy Places as a result of a handover.[62] He did not wish to abandon his most loyal supporters in Jerusalem and the West Bank, who were to be found in these institutions. At the same time the exemption can also be taken as an act of insurance should political circumstances change and there be a renewal of interest in either a direct Hashemite role in the West Bank or an indirect one through some form of confederation with the PLO. In both cases King Hussein was positioning Jordan well for the future.

Later in the same year, the Palestinian National Council declared the establishment of an independent state of Palestine in the West Bank and Gaza Strip. East Jerusalem was to be its capital. The relevant part of the Declaration said: "The Palestine National Council, in the name of god, and in the name of the Palestine Arab people, hereby proclaims the establishment of the State of Palestine on our Palestinian territory with its capital al-Quds al-Sharif."[63]

Despite the euphoria brought about by these developments and the convening of the Madrid conference in 1990, little concrete movement can be seen on the Jerusalem issue in the current peace negotiations. In the teeth of Palestinian opposition, the Jerusalem issue was kept off the agenda for discussing the interim status of the occupied Palestinian territories. It is not due to be discussed until the third year of the interim period has commenced. Meanwhile, the Israeli government is proceeding with demographic and construction policies in East Jerusalem and the annexed areas of the West Bank.[64]

It is important to note that Israeli demands for U.S. recognition of Jerusalem, East and West, as its capital are unlikely to be met while there is failure to reach a peace agreement with the Palestinians. The risk of alienating the entire Arab and Islamic world is too great—and the rewards too nebulous—for the U.S. government. The most probable moment when Israel will secure American recognition of Jerusalem as its capital will be when the United States also recognizes East Jerusalem or part of East Jerusalem as either Palestinian or

Jordano-Palestinian or as the second capital of Jordan. In the meantime
the United States will attempt to continue its present policy.

It is also important for the Palestinians and Arabs to recognize that
in the absence of other secure and reliable allies in the region, the
United States will not relinquish good relations with Israel. While the
Gulf War of 1990–91 has prompted a rethinking of Israel's strategic
value to the United States, there are few options open to the United
States. In this context it is worthwhile observing Syria's gradual rap-
prochement with the United States and examining its implications for
American-Israeli relations, but at present that relationship remains
essentially unchanged. While this is the case, the question of the future
status of Jerusalem will remain on the back burner. Until U.S. interests
can be secured in another way, whatever the anomalies and inconsistencies, however much it obstructs a resolution of the Palestinian-
Israeli conflict, the United States will not be interested in antagonizing the Israeli state over the question of Jerusalem. The ball, therefore,
is in the court of both the Israelis and the Arab states. In order to have
the Jerusalem issue resolved, either the Israelis will have to amend their
commitment to holding onto the annexed eastern parts or the Arab
states will have to provide the United States with a reliable strategic
alliance that will make it less dependent upon Israel to secure their
interests in the region.

Conclusion

No more the sound of weeping?
"I shall rejoice in Jerusalem,
and be glad in my people:
no more shall be heard the sound of weeping
and the cry of distress.
—Isaiah, 65:19

In November 1993 Mayor Teddy Kollek was swept from office by an alliance of right-wing Likud councilors and ultra-orthodox rabbis who had campaigned on a hawkish and expansionist platform of greater Jewish control over Jerusalem.[1] Kollek's removal as Mayor of Jerusalem marked the end of a very long era—one that spanned three distinct periods: the pre-1967 divided-city period, a middle period marked by the dramatic spread of Israeli Jewish settlement and population growth in the eastern parts of the city, and the post-Madrid conference period where the future of Jerusalem once again surfaced at the conference table.

During the election campaign leading up to Kollek's defeat, the irony of Kollek and his allies appealing to the Palestinian residents of Jerusalem to vote for him as the chief protector of their interests was not lost on Palestinians and Kollek's right-wing critics alike: the man who frequently claimed to have done more than anyone to establish and consolidate the Israeli Jewish hold of the city, who proudly labeled himself a Zionist, and who often made disparaging remarks concerning the Palestinians' lack of political astuteness and organization was now pleading for their support behind him to prevent rivals taking over the Israeli municipal council. At this time, when a Palestinian boycott of the election would have greater political significance than for many years, Kollek's reelection would have the effect of sending a clear signal to the peace negotiators that the Palestinians had rejected Israeli control over the eastern part of the city and that whatever the Israeli assertions were the question of Jerusalem had still not been settled.

The Palestinian reluctance to endorse a further extension of Kollek's hegemony over Jerusalem has been interpreted either as a further example of Palestinian short-sightedness or as taking a principled long-term view that the elections would be a form of recognition of Israeli jurisdiction over the city, which had no validity in international law. Whatever the interpretation, like Banquo's ghost at MacBeth's banquet, the absent but present participants in the municipal election campaign were indeed the Palestinians of Jerusalem. The fact that the question of their participation was a prominent feature in the campaign was a sign that despite twenty-six years of Israeli colonization in East Jerusalem the issues first raised in the specially convened municipal council meeting on August 13, 1967 had not been resolved. Israeli military control over the city, the issues of political legitimacy, of sovereignty, of international recognition, and of the Jewishness of the city still needed to be satisfactorily addressed. The Palestinian refusal to involve themselves in the election, and in this way refuse to recognize the Israeli political system in Jerusalem, meant that the new municipal council was faced with the continuing disturbing fact: it cannot claim to represent all the people of Jerusalem. It is, without a doubt, the local government of the majority of the inhabitants within its enlarged borders, but a politically and numerically significant minority remain outside the system. Despite decades of Israeli government activity on the Palestinian side of the Armistice Line, legitimacy and recognition in East Jerusalem for the Israeli state remain as elusive as ever.

While the defeat of Teddy Kollek marked a political watershed, it was also a culmination of a process of political change that had been lapping round the edges of Jerusalem since the end of the Gulf War in 1991. The U.S. commitment to finally address the Arab-Israeli issue had resulted in the intense pressure placed upon the Likud government of Yitzhak Shamir to participate in negotiations with Palestinians over the future of the occupied Palestinian territories. The Madrid conference in July 1991 brought no resolution to the Jerusalem issue, but it did bring the issue to the negotiating table, to be dealt with at a later stage. Given that a persistent policy of the Israeli government has been to remove discussion of Jerusalem from international forums and from

Israeli-Palestinian negotiations this should be seen as a potentially significant in itself.

Subsequent rounds of negotiations in Washington and the Oslo Accords signed in September 1993 brought formal recognition between the Palestinian Liberation Organization and the Israeli government. One result of these developments has been to place Jerusalem firmly on the agenda of "final" status issues to be resolved. In summary, the Accords decided that Jerusalem will not be negotiated for two years following the interim phase, but it will be negotiated no later than the start of the third year following the signing of the Accords.[2] The Israeli position, therefore, that Jerusalem is non-negotiable has been exposed as vulnerable to international, particularly U.S., pressure.[3] This in itself can be seen also as a watershed and its occurrence during the same year as the political passing away of Teddy Kollek and his replacement by the more hawkish Ehud Olmert brings the issue of sovereignty and borders increasingly to a head.

In view of these developments, the questions that remain to be asked are: now that Jerusalem is on the negotiating table were the election results an indication by the Israeli public that they wish to begin negotiations over the future of the city from a hawkish position? For all his rhetoric, has Ehud Olmert the makings of an Israeli de Gaulle over the Jerusalem issue? With his nationalist credentials secured by his hawkish campaign, can he deliver an Israeli compromise acceptable to the Palestinians? Or is the result more to do with the first flexing of the political muscle of the Jewish ultra-orthodox community reflecting their increasingly dominant demographic status in the city, rather than to do with the future status of Jerusalem. The answers to these questions are beyond the scope of this book, but they do illustrate the rapid process of political change which is taking place in Jerusalem.

Before any speculation over the range of possible futures of Jerusalem, a review of the main issues covered here seems in order. In this way an attempt can be made to draw out the underlying themes which will impinge upon the discussions of Jerusalem's future. It should be appreciated by now that despite its small area and size, Jerusalem is a subject encompassing many different fields and is a subject enriched and complicated by eons of history and by sacred associations. Nevertheless, four arguments or themes have formed a kind of crucible into which most of the relevant details can be poured and which link up historical issues with present-day dilemmas and policy options. The arguments are: international involvement in religious and

political developments in the city cannot be ignored; the unique religious status of the city has placed limitations on sovereign state power
over the city; the politically driven demographic growth and colonization of an ethnically, religiously, and politically divided urban community has created a set of difficult dilemmas for the Israeli government concerning its future expansion and development and, finally,
that a stable and durable resolution of the Jerusalem issue requires the
recognition of Palestinian historical, religious and political aspirations
in the city and a recognition of their demographic presence.

The interest of the international community in Jerusalem has been
referred to at many points throughout the book. Historically this was
expressed in religious terms, over questions of access to the Holy
Places or of establishing an institutional religious presence in the city.
An important manifestation of international concern in the city has
been through pilgrimages to the Holy Places of Jerusalem. These have
been a perennial feature of Jerusalem's religious life but also became
the cornerstone of its rudimentary economy. As we saw in chapter 7,
the evolution of pilgrimages into the mass tourism of the post-World
War II era continues to play an essential role in the city's economy.
Similarly, the constant search for legitimacy and supremacy by state
and temporal authorities led to the support of religious groupings and
movements in the city, such as the Sufis and the Franciscans, leading to
the construction of schools, hostels, hospitals, and other institutional
edifices designed to propagate their views and priorities and to promote the interests of their secular supporters.

Ultimately international interest in the city has been expressed
through invasion and conquest. The Crusades, the advent of the
Ayyubids, the Mamluks, the Ottomans, the British, and finally the
Zionists are all examples of the persistence of Jerusalem's role in the
international arena. During the post-1945 period two other features
express the continuing role Jerusalem plays in international affairs.
Despite its increasing impracticality, the UN proposal for the internationalization of the city remains the formal position of the international community. The proposal is an attempt to assure the integrity of
the city and establish free access to the Holy Places in an impartial a
manner as possible. The reluctance of the great powers to enforce the
proposal meant instead that neither aims were achieved before or after
1967, therefore throwing open their claims to impartiality. The second
feature of the post-1945 period is the role Jerusalem played in the
polarization of the Middle East into pro-U.S. and pro-USSR political

blocs. Seen as the symbolic prize for the main protagonists, the Israelis and the Arabs, the question of which protagonist has legitimate rights over Jerusalem meant that its status throughout this period lacked consensus and was central to the resolution of the Arab-Israeli conflict. Reluctant to antagonize its major ally in a polarized region, the United States refrained from putting pressure on Israel to accede to United Nations resolutions on the city. In the post-Gulf War period, the strategic value of Israel is being questioned and the importance of a regional peace treaty is being emphasized. A resolution of the Jerusalem issue acceptable in some way to the Arab world is therefore also important to U.S. interests. In this light it is no coincidence that the passing of the bipolar world in the 1990s has also seen the issue of Jerusalem becoming once again a subject for formal and serious negotiation.

The second underlying argument that can be identified in this study has been how the unique and specific nature of Jerusalem as a city holy to three religions has framed the nature and degree of the sovereign power of any authority over the city. The power and influence of the religious hierarchies—that is, the Muslim institutions, the churches, and the rabbinates, and their temporal supporters in whatever state structures prevailing internally and externally in a given period—have all combined to influence the nature of political power asserted in the city. Some limitations, traditionally and contemporaneously, have been placed upon the legal, administrative, and coercive jurisdiction of the state. Instances of this pattern repeating itself can be traced down through to the present day. As we saw in previous chapters, the Ottomans were obliged to cede juridical powers over foreign nationals in the city to foreign consuls. The British Mandate authorities accepted the Holy Places Status Quo and ceded considerable powers in Jerusalem to the Supreme Muslim Council. The relevance of this theme to the current situation demands a review of some of the main examples concerning Israeli sovereignty in the city mentioned in earlier chapters.

Despite establishing complete military dominance over the city and its hinterland, and despite the formal extension of Israeli legal jurisdiction over the areas annexed in 1967, Israeli sovereignty over those areas is not complete. A de facto accommodation with both the Jordanian legal system and with the autonomous administration of various Christian denominations and Muslim religious institutions has been in place since 1967. For example, numerous exemptions have been accepted in the field of property laws (particularly the Absentee

Property Law), in the registration of Palestinian companies, the application of employment laws, of health and safety requirements, of taxation on religious property and enterprises, and in the introduction of the Israeli curriculum in East Jerusalem schools.

Of particular importance has been the quasi-independent functioning of the Awqaf Administration. Not only has it been allowed to continue to receive funds from states in a condition of formal belligerence with Israel (such as Jordan, Kuwait, and Saudi Arabia) it has also continued to make appointments, to determine development work in the Old City, and to coordinate its operations as a West Bank-wide institution. As a result it has also retained a remarkable degree of territorial control over significant parts of the Old City and Jerusalem. This administrative control is backed up by a legal system, the Jordanian based shari'a, which runs in parallel and often supersedes the Israeli civil system. The presence of Israeli soldiers on al-Haram al-Sharif does not detract from the Israeli government's acceptance that this area is beyond the jurisdiction of the Israeli state body concerned with such matters, the Ministry of Religious Affairs. It is perceived by both Palestinians and Israelis as an enclave separate from Israeli political control.

In isolation, these exemptions do not amount to dramatic infringements on Israeli sovereignty, but taken in totality they create a network of working practices, of legal and religious relationships, and of social interaction that create a political and moral culture which questions the legitimacy and appropriateness of an Israeli political and legal presence in that part of the city. This questioning is given added force in East Jerusalem when three additional issues are widely recognized by Palestinian residents. First, the more rapid population growth of Jerusalem's Palestinians than its Israeli Jews is beyond Israeli control; second, the level of government services in these areas is such that it appears to free Palestinian residents of any moral or political obligation to the Israeli municipality; and finally, the political sovereignty of Israel in the city is further undermined by the lack of international recognition it has received not only for claiming Jerusalem as its capital city but also for its attempt to annex the eastern parts of the city. Thus the lack of complete and recognized sovereignty combines with these three issues to fundamentally challenge Israeli claims to the city in the eyes of the Palestinians.

The importance of this second argument for the current negotiating process is that by declaring that the PLO should accept Israeli sovereignty for the whole of the city, Israel is in reality demanding more than it already has. It does not have complete sovereignty over the city now. Legal exemptions and territorial enclaves already exist and cannot be wished away. To expect PLO to accept the Israeli position, even if compromises are made in other geographical ways, would be not only to demand extraordinary concessions which the PLO would have great difficulty in delivering but also to demand additional political and geographical confirmation to the Israeli status in Jerusalem. The Israeli claims do not match the reality on the ground.

The third argument in this book is the dilemma posed to the Israeli state by its drive to secure Jerusalem as an Israeli Jewish city—an issue that, while discussed fully in chapters 3 and 4, permeates the whole of the study. In order to establish a Jewish predominance, the Israeli government has sought to increase the Jewish population of the city. This in turn requires further housing construction, the provision of more employment, and the improvement of the service infrastructure. These are vital for the growth of the Jewish population and essential for its long-term economic viability. The dilemma for the Israeli government begins when one understands that there is little or no further space within the existing borders of Jerusalem to provide these facilities. The government is being compelled by the logic of its own policies to extend the municipal border in order to provide additional space. The dilemma is that any geographic extension of the municipal borders eastward, northward, or southward will have to incorporate the Palestinians living in the metropolitan region of Jerusalem but outside its municipal borders. Incorporating these Palestinians into Israeli Jerusalem will simply restore the demographic balance in favor of the Palestinians and the Israeli government will be back at square one in its attempts to create a clear Jewish majority and a Jewish city.

In 1967, this dilemma was addressed by extending the borders of the city in such a way as to exclude areas of Palestinian residence and to provide space for Israeli Jewish housing. This decision gave the Municipality some twenty years of developmental breathing space. In 1991 the same dilemma was addressed by extending the municipal borders westward. While this extension will again give the Municipality some breathing space, it does not address the fundamental root of the dilemma: what to do about the steadily increasing Palestinian population in and around the eastern part of the city. Indeed, the extension westward has the desired effect for the Israeli government of reinforcing the Israeli presence in the Jerusalem "corridor" running down to the coast, so that in the event of a Palestinian state on the West

Bank, Jerusalem is well-connected to the center of Israel. Nevertheless, it is also an accommodation of the "lure" of Tel Aviv for the productive sectors of the city's economy and population. By expanding westward the commuting distance to the coastal plain is thus much reduced, encouraging greater recreational and commercial links with this area. In this way the expansion of the city's borders westward exacerbates the fragility of Israel's hold on the eastern part of the city. In terms of Israel's long-term political objectives for Jerusalem, the expansion should be eastward but it is confronted with the dilemma of an antagonistic population which will not recognize its legitimacy to do so.

The dilemma will grow more acute for the Israeli government and municipal planners. Virtually 25 percent of the Palestinian population of the West Bank live in East Jerusalem, the annexed areas, and the metropolitan area of Jerusalem. It is hard to contemplate an Israeli government attempting to make the necessary jurisdictional extensions over their areas of residence while the peace negotiations are actually in process. It would fail to be accepted both by the PLO and by the international community. It is unlikely that the United States, which has a considerable stake in the successful completion of the negotiations, would countenance such a move. It is also unlikely that the Israeli government has the political capital to expend on the issue in this way. At the same time, the requirements of the urban development drive undertaken by the government continue and it still needs the space to site sewage processing plants, cemeteries, rubbish disposal, industrial plants, or a network of ringroads—to name but a few pressing problems. The questions that need answering, then, are: does this development impetus drive the Israeli government into negotiating in some way with the planned Palestinian authority on the West Bank? Will this lead to coordination between the Palestinian authority and the Municipality? Does this coordination contain the seeds of a direct Palestinian involvement in the administration of the services of Jerusalem? Or, will the Israeli government attempt to obfuscate the issue by applying specific municipality zoning procedures to the metropolitan area without formally extending the municipal borders themselves? Attempts to answer these questions will be made over the next few years and will give us strong indications as to the likely political and administrative structures for Jerusalem in the future.

The final argument in this book is that the prior Israeli government policies, their accelerated building and settlement program during the interim phase of negotiations and their publicly avowed aim of securing the city's hinterland under Israeli control, are not conducive for a stable and durable peaceful resolution of the Jerusalem issue. The temptation to take advantage of their current political domination, of Palestinian weakness, of their support from in the United States and the disarray in the Arab world is not in the long-term interest of the city, of the peace arrangements or, for that matter, of Israel. The issue will not go away just because the Palestinians do not have leverage at present.

A solution to the Jerusalem question must recognize the imperatives of the current situation, that the Palestinians have a strong physical presence in the city and wish to live under Palestinian sovereignty. The Israeli government may be able to assert military control over both halves of the city, but the issue of Jerusalem as a Palestinian, an Arab, a Muslim, and a Christian city will remain in the architecture, the literature, the religious ceremonies, the rituals, and the non-Jewish demographic growth. Indeed, with Jerusalem forming the financial and commercial center of the Palestinian economy in the West Bank and Gaza Strip, with its geographically strategic location in the center of the West Bank, as well as its historical, religious, and political importance, an Israeli imposed solution that does not accommodate these aspects will not only jeopardize the achievements of the peace process so far but also strengthen the arguments of those political and religious groups who argue that a Palestinian and an Israeli state can exist only at the expense of the other. Anti-Israeli sentiment in the Arab and Islamic worlds can only be exacerbated in this way. On the other hand, a generous and magnanimous Israeli offer over the future of Jerusalem would help to seal any peace agreement between Israel and the PLO and Arab states. It would also go a long way toward healing the wounds of 1948 and may help reconcile the Palestinians to the final loss of their homes along the coast and in the Galilee.

The concluding part of this chapter will take this discussion of what can be construed as a "least unacceptable" solution to the Jerusalem question a bit further. There is no shortage of ideas for the city's future.[4] The official Israeli position is that Jerusalem should remain undivided and under Israeli sovereignty. While anxious to assert its support for access to religious sites in the city, the government has not spelled out the kinds of arrangements it envisages. For its part, the official PLO position is that Israel should withdraw from the parts of the city it occupied in 1967 and that East Jerusalem becomes the capital of the state of Palestine. At the same time the PLO has been unspecific as to the nature of the relationship between the two halves of the city, preferring to defer such details until an agreement for withdrawal is achieved. In the absence of any movement on these positions, many individuals and organizations have attempted to devise compromise positions that could satisfy both the Israeli need for access to the Jewish Holy Places, for security, and for international recognition of Jerusalem as its capital, and the Palestinian need for Jerusalem as its capital with free access to it from the West Bank and Gaza Strip.

Part of the difficulty in devising solutions has been that the relationship between the Israeli government and the Palestinians has not been symmetrical. For much of the duration of the conflict the Palestinian component has been subsumed under the wider Arab-Israeli conflict, with the Jordanian government both being given and having assumed the position of the main interlocutor with the Israeli government over the question of Jerusalem. With the outbreak of the intifada in 1987, this aspect has changed somewhat in favor of the PLO as main interlocutor yet the Jordanian government's continued involvement with the Awqaf Administration and the Jerusalem issue in general creates a triangular relationship of awkward dimensions.[5]

Setting aside the UN proposals and the various proposals put forward by the Arab states, either in the Fahd Plan or President Sadat's proposals at Camp David referred to in chapter 8, the plans that have received the most attention are those put forward by Adnan Abu Odeh, Professor Walid Khalidi, Drs. Sari Nuseibeh and Mark Heller, and by the Israel Palestinian Center for Research and Information (IPCRI).[6] What is interesting about these plans is how they all attempt to address the same issue of political sovereignty in different ways. Abu Odeh and Khalidi both attempt to take the sting out of the issue by proposing the "extraterritorialization" or "functional internationalization" of the Old City and the Holy Places by placing their administration in the hands of an international or supra-state religious body. Khalidi differs from Abu Odeh in that he also proposes that while containing two national capitals, the municipal administration of the city should be overseen by a "joint inter-state great municipal council." Abu Odeh is unspecific on this question. Nuseibeh and Heller suggest a "combination of clarity and obfuscation" at different administrative levels which would "satisfy both the aspiration for distinctiveness/ independence and the imperative of integration and unification." In essence some aspects of municipal government would be devolved to both Palestinian and Israeli neighborhoods and at the same time other aspects would be elevated to a "metropolitan" government.[7] IPCRI suggests a similar political symmetry but argue that a demographic parity has also to be established. Their proposal, therefore, is based upon enlarging the municipal borders of Jerusalem to the extent of virtually creating a mini-state of Jerusalem.[8]

In attempting to evaluate these and other proposals Cecilia Albin has produced a "taxonomy" of all the proposals concerning the future of Jerusalem.[9] Her study gives us an idea of the complexity and range of proposals on offer. She classifies all known proposals into four main types: proposals that deal with "resource expansion," "resource contraction" (that is, the size of the city's boundaries), "exchange strategies" (that is, exchange of territory), and "functional strategies" (the sharing of municipal responsibilities). Proposals that suggest an enlargement or reduction of the geographical area of Jerusalem, internationalization of municipal functions or just of the Holy Places or the Old City, the sharing or division of sovereignty or municipal services, etc. are classified accordingly. Clearly the demarcations cannot be rigid and some proposals straddle different categories.

This taxonomy provides two complementary services to understanding the proposals on Jerusalem. First, it acts as a tool for identifying their main characteristics. By determining whether a proposal is essentially one of resource expansion or contraction, or of exchange or functional, one can speculate on its feasibility based on the general feasibility of the classification it falls under. Second, the taxonomy provides a basis for creating new proposals. If, for example, proposals that fall into the "functional strategy" classification appear to provide greater levels of political acceptability to the main protagonists, it would make sense to develop proposals in this area adding the fine-tuning to incorporate various technical, religious, or international concerns as the case may be.

This author does not believe he can add any specifics to the proposals already in circulation. Indeed, the details of any proposal at this stage are too subject to tactical shifts as the negotiations proceed to bear fruit. Nevertheless, in the light of Albin's taxonomy, some general principles can be highlighted. This chapter will conclude with an attempt to delineate what are the main issues that need to be resolved and to draw on precedents from Jerusalem's past which may give indications of how they can be resolved or what difficulties may be encountered in attempting to resolve them.

It should be clear from the preceding chapters and the four underlying arguments outlined above that a number of trends will need to
be accommodated in any political settlement on the future of
Jerusalem. First, the unique religious nature of the city will continue
to provide the city with its economic *raison d'être*. The inappropriate-
ness of Jerusalem as a large manufacturing center will combine with
the persistence and tenacity with which religious movements and
institutions will continue to base themselves in Jerusalem. In the event
of a peace agreement, which will allow greater freedom of access to
Jerusalem, particularly to residents of Muslim countries, the institutional religious interest in Jerusalem will continue to undergird a considerable growth of pilgrimages, study tours, and tourism to the city.[10]
Links between Jerusalem and religious communities regionally and
internationally will take institutionalized forms. These need to be recognized and accommodated in any peace agreement on Jerusalem.

Second, international interest in the city will continue. To some
extent this will be part of the religious trend just mentioned, but secular interest in Jerusalem will also have its separate concerns. The
unfolding of Israel's integration into the Middle East region will continue to be a fractious uneven affair with many crises and confronta-
tions between Israel and its neighbors. Jerusalem's role as both symbol
and microcosm of that process will continue to draw heightened political, diplomatic, and religious interest. Similarly, the unique religious
nature of the city will continue to place significant curbs on whatever
secular authority is established and this should be accepted rather than
marginalized inappropriately.

Third, the issue of political sovereignty cannot be sidestepped.
Palestinian aspirations for part of Jerusalem as their capital will need to
be addressed before any settlement will be deemed acceptable. Israelis
and the international community will need to understand that
Palestinian proposals along the lines of an Israeli withdrawal and joint
sovereignty and municipal administration do not mean the return to a
divided city with closed borders. In the same way, Israeli concerns over
rights of access and personal and military security are based upon their
experiences since 1948 and should not be dismissed. The point that
needs to be grasped is that an agreement need not be at the expense
of the objectives of either party. International recognition of political
sovereignty has strong attractions for both sides. By conceding perhaps
a qualified form of political sovereignty to the Palestinians, the Israelis
may attain international acceptance of an amended version of theirs.

In connection to this, it is also worth asking whether there can be some compromises over the actual geographical area of Jerusalem. Which areas do Israelis and Palestinians have in the minds when they refer to Jerusalem. As Abu Odeh puts it: "Is it the Jerusalem of 1850, of 1910, 1948, 1967 or of 1992? Like other important cities Jerusalem is a living entity that has grown over time, both through natural progress and prosperity and as a result of an increase in population. . . . Is every hectare now called Jerusalem to be considered holy? Does every hectare annexed to the city, due to natural growth, thus become holy?"[11]

Ian Lustick asks the same sort of questions in a ground-breaking article where he dissects what he call the Israeli "fetish of Jerusalem." He is able to collate considerable evidence which points to a measure of official and unofficial Israeli ambiguity over the importance of the current borders.[12] It may be that both Palestinian and Israeli demands for political sovereignty over either all or a part of the city can be reduced to a smaller core that could satisfy both, provided that access to the Holy Places and across the city can be ensured.

The final, and probably foremost point for consideration in any formula on Jerusalem, is this: In the absence of any extreme action of the Israeli government involving the transfer of the Palestinians around Jerusalem to other distant locations, the demographic growth of the Palestinians in the metropolitan area will compel the Israelis to accept the inclusion of Palestinians in the administration of the city in some way. The manner of inclusion may range from the substantive to the nominal. It will depend upon the degree of cooperation established between any Palestinian self-governing authority on the West Bank and both the Israeli and Jordanian governments. Whether the inclusion leads to the evolution of some form of Palestinian political sovereignty in the city will also depend upon such factors as the degree of international support for that development and the economic and political strength of the new Palestinian authority.

My own view is that without this accommodation to the Palestinian population, any formula imposed will remain intrinsically temporary. The view is derived from an awareness of the central paradox at the core of Israeli policies in the city since 1967, which can restated here. Despite the seemingly inexorable advance of Israeli housing projects in East Jerusalem and the annexed areas, despite the electoral swing to the hawkish and expansionist wing of the Israeli municipal polity, and despite the weakness and vacillation of the U.S.

and the international community over the application of UN Resolutions and international law to Jerusalem, it is remarkable that the fate of Jerusalem is still to be decided. Indeed, despite the countless dollars invested in projecting the Israeli presence in Jerusalem, despite the lack of organization, direction, and cohesion of Palestinian institutions and leadership, and despite the imbalance of resources in the two competing communities, the Palestinian presence in the city continues to remain significant.

This paradox cannot be explained by a study of the balance of political forces alone. There is no doubt that the future of the city eventually will be decided on the negotiating table, but one should not overlook the fact that every day it is also being decided by the people who live there. As much as imposed political structures matter, where Palestinians shop, where they work, where they pray, how they tend their gardens, where they go on rest days, who, how, and when they are visited—all these things have determined and continue to determine the nature and culture of the city. Politics can encompass, reflect, radically influence, or attempt to cut across these everyday activities but, at least in the Jerusalem this author has studied, they have not and cannot be ignored. The fact that the issue is still an issue is as much a testament to the daily assertions of belongingness and ownership put forward by the Palestinian inhabitants of the city as all the political programs and well-crafted formulations put forward for the future of the city. In the years since 1967, the Israeli government has not enforced an allegiance to the notion of Israeli sovereignty over the city. Its difficulties in this respect will only increase if or when there is a Palestinian juridisdiction a few hundred yards across the municipal borders. With one-third of the population of the city remaining Palestinian in the foreseeable future, whatever agreements are enforced or recognized by the international community, the Israeli government will have to contend with the fact that a significant proportion of the population of its capital city does not accept its authority and right to be there.

Notes

Introduction

1. See Lustick, "Reinventing Jerusalem," *Foreign Policy*, no. 93 (Winter 1993–94): 42–43. He writes: "By the June 1992 elections that returned the Labor party to power, the only element of the annexationist program that remained part of the Israeli 'national consensus' was opposition to changing the status quo in enlarged Jerusalem."

1. The Significance of Jerusalem

1. The total comes to approximately 600 years and includes the first Israelite period of David and Solomon, the Hasmonean and Maccabean periods, and the period of relative autonomous rule under the early Roman Emperors.

2. H. J. Franken, "Jerusalem in the Bronze Age," in K. al-'Asali, ed. *Jerusalem in History* (London: Scorpion, 1989) (hereinafter referred to as *History*), pp. 15, 23, 27–37. (Franken hereinafter referred to as "Bronze Age.") See also Israel Pocket Library (IPL), *Jerusalem* (Jerusalem: Keter, 1973), pp. 6–8.

3. G. E. Mendenhall, "Jerusalem from 1000–63 B.C." in al-'Asali, *History*, p. 42 (hereinafter referred to as "1000–63 B.C."). Textual historians and archaeologists have found no evidence that the Jebusites were actually expelled from the city. The evidence indicates that they were absorbed into the Israelite kingdom.

4. A siege of Jerusalem by the Assyrians was rebuffed by Hezekiah. This feat led to the doctrine of the "inviolability of Zion." IPL, *Jerusalem*, p. 16.

5. Mendenhall, "1000–63 B.C.," p. 71.

6. J. Wilkinson, "Jerusalem under Rome and Byzantium," in al-'Asali, *History*, p. 86 (hereinafter referred to as "Rome and Byzantium").

7. Ibid., pp. 84–85.

8. Ibid., p. 94.

9. A. A. Duri, "Jerusalem in the Early Islamic Period," in al-'Asali, *History*, p. 106 (hereinafter referred to as "Early Islamic Period").

10. H. S. Karmi, "How Holy is Palestine to the Muslims?" *Islamic Quarterly* 12:2 (April–June 1970): 5. See also H. Lazarus Yafeh's chapter entitled "The Sanctity of Jerusalem in Islam," in *Some Religious Aspects of Islam* (Leiden: Brill, 1981).

11. Duri, "Early Islamic Period," p. 106.

12. M. Burgoyne, *Mamluk Jerusalem: An Architectural Study* (London: World of Islam Trust, 1987), p. 45 (hereinafter referred to as *Mamluk Jerusalem*).

13. Duri details the extensive building work carried out during this period, the construction of the Damascus-Jerusalem highway, the erection of new gates and the relocation of the regime's Mint in Jerusalem. See Duri, "Early Islamic Period," pp. 110–11.

14. Burgoyne, *Mamluk Jerusalem*, p. 46; Duri, "Early Islamic Period," p. 118.

15. Duri, "Early Islamic Period," p. 118.

16. Cited in Burgoyne, *Mamluk Jerusalem*, p. 46; see also F. E. Peters, *Jerusalem* (Princeton: Princeton University Press, 1985), pp. 233–38 on the influence of Christian and Jewish communities.

17. One contemporary account of the slaughter described the scene in the following way: "Now that our men had possession of the walls and the towers, wonderful sights were to be seen. Some of our men—and this was the more merciful course—cut of the heads of their enemies; others shot them with arrows so that they fell from the towers; others tortured them longer by casting them into flames. Piles of heads, hands, and feet were to be seen in the streets of the city. It was necessary to pick one's way over the bodies of men and horses. But these were small matters compared to what happened in the Temple of Solomon [al-Aqsa Mosque], a place where religious services were ordinarily chanted. What happened there? If I tell the truth, it will exceed your powers of belief. So let it suffice to say this much at least, that in the Temple and porch of Solomon men rode in blood up to their knees and bridle reins. Indeed, it was a just and splendid judgement of God that this place should be filled with the blood of unbelievers, since it had suffered so long from their blasphemies. The city was filled with corpses and blood"; cited in Peters, *Jerusalem*, pp. 285–86.

18. Burgoyne, *Mamluk Jerusalem*, p. 47.

19. Peters, *Jerusalem*, pp. 316–17.

20. M. Hiyari, "Crusader Jerusalem," in al-'Asali, *History*, p. 166.

21. Burgoyne, *Mamluk Jerusalem*, pp. 48–8; Hiyari, "Crusader Jerusalem," p. 168.

22. D. Little, "Jerusalem under the Ayyubids and Mamluks," in al-'Asali, *History*, pp. 186–87 (hereinafter referred to as "Ayyubids and Mamluks"). See also Burgoyne, *Mamluk Jerusalem*, p. 61.

23. Silk, cotton, and soap were the other main items of trade or industry in the city.

24. Little, "Ayyubids and Mamlukes," p. 193.

25. Jerusalemites were exempt from taxes due to the city's holiness. See al-'Asali, "Jerusalem under the Ottomans," in al-'Asali, *History*, p. 205.

26. al-'Asali, "Ottomans," p. 221. See also Peters, *Jerusalem*, p. 540; and S. P. Colbi, "The Christian Establishment in Jerusalem," in Kraemer, *Problems and Prospects*, pp. 162–70.

27. To this day the keys of the Holy Sepulcher are held by an ancient Jerusalemite Muslim family, the Nusaybas, since the churches could not agree on which sect had the right to them.

28. See A. Schölch, "Jerusalem in the 19th Century, 1831–1917," in al-'Asali, *History*, p. 229 (hereinafter referred to as "19th Century").

29. In 1877, the powers of the *majlis* were increased.

30. Schölch, "19th Century," p. 230.

31. See R. Kark, *Jerusalem Neighbourhoods: Planning and By-Laws (1855–1930)* (Jerusalem: Magnes Press, 1991) (hereinafter referred to as *Neighbourhoods*) for further details of this important phenomenon.

32. Schölch, "19th Century," p. 244.

33. This development is discussed in M. Dumper, *Islam and Israel: Muslim Religious Endowments and the Jewish State* (Washington, D.C.: Institute for Palestine Studies, 1994), pp. 18–19, 105 (hereinafter referred to as *Islam and Israel*).

34. Council Minutes, Session 34, August 13, 1967.

2. The Governance of the City

1. Prime Minister Rabin's declaration in 1992 that the settlements of metropolitan Jerusalem were non-negotiable "security" settlements, as opposed to the more negotiable "political" settlements can be viewed as preparing the ground for their incorporation into Jerusalem at a later stage. See *Report on Israeli Settlement in the Occupied Territories* (Foundation for Middle East Peace, Washington, D.C.) Special Report. February 1994, p. 8.

2. See A. Schölch, "Jerusalem in the 19th Century (1831–1917)" (hereinafter referred to as "19th Century") in K. al-'Asali ed., *History*, pp. 238–39.

3. Ibid., p. 229.

4. K. Baedecker, *Palestine and Syria, Handbook for Travellers* (Jerusalem: Carta,

1973) (reprint of Leipzig, 1876) (hereinafter referred to as *Palestine and Syria*) cited in Y. Ben-Arieh, *Jerusalem in the 19th Century: The Old City* (New York: St. Martin's Press, 1984), p. 188 (hereinafter referred to as *Old City*).

Ben-Arieh goes on to conclude that "the consulates' power and influence grew steadily in the course of the century, with consuls taking order from no government except their own and their offices constituting a sort of miniature government. From their reports, it seems that the consuls thought of the Holy Land as annexed territory," pp. 188–89. This may be slightly overstating the situation.

5. E. Gutman, "The Beginning of Local Government in Jerusalem," *Public Administration in Israel and Abroad* (Vol. 8, 1967) (hereinafter referred to as "Local Government"), p. 53. See also article by R. Kark, "The Jerusalem Municipality at the End of the Ottoman Rule," *Asian and African Affairs*, 14 (1980): 117–41 (hereinafter referred to as "Ottoman Rule").

6. See Ben-Arieh, *Old City*, p. 123. The last elections for the Ottoman council were held in 1908. Ibid.. p. 53.

7. See M. Dumper, *Islam and Israel*, pp. 14–18, 104–107, for a fuller discussion of this topic.

8. Committee on the Exercise of the Inalienable Rights of the Palestinian People (UNCEIRPP), *The Status of Jerusalem* (New York: United Nations, 1979) (hereinafter referred to as *The Status*) p. 3.

9. Article 14 of the Charter gave teeth to Article 13 by allowing for the establishment of a Special Commission to "study, define and determine the rights and claims in connection with the Holy Places." Ibid., p. 3. The commission was activated after the riots following the Wailing Wall Incident in 1929.

10. U. Kupferschmidt, *The Supreme Muslim Council: Islam Under the British Mandate for Palestine* (Leiden: Brill, 1987) (hereinafter referred to as *Supreme Muslim Council*). For a discussion of the interaction between state power and religious administration see M. Dumper, *Islam and Israel*, pp. 18–24.

11. D. Rubinstein, "The Jerusalem Municipality under the Ottomans, British and Jordanians" (hereinafter referred to as "Jerusalem Municipality"), in J. L. Kraemer ed., *Jerusalem: Problems and Prospects* (New York: Praeger, 1980) (hereinafter referred to as *Problems and Prospects*), p. 80.

12. Before the end of the Mandate, adjustments to the borders and electoral wards were being discussed. The Fizgerald Commission, for example, proposed the partition of the city into two boroughs that were coordinated by an Administrative Council. See W. Fitzgerald, *Report on the Local Administration of Jerusalem* (Government of Palestine, Government Printer, 1945).

13. Rubinstein, "Jerusalem Municipality," pp. 82–83.

14. See W. Fitzgerald, *Report on the Local Administration of Jerusalem* (Government of Palestine, Government Printer, 1945).

15. See M. Gilbert, *Jerusalem*: Illustrated History Atlas, p. 83, for a map of the Jewish Agency proposals.

16. British Government, *Palestine Royal Commission: Report*, Command Paper No. 5479 (London: H.M.S.O., 1937) (hereinafter referred to as *Royal Commission*), pp. 381–82.

17. UNCEIRPP, *The Status*, p. 6.

18. United Nations (UN), *General Assembly Resolution 181 (II)*, 29.11.1947. (hereinafter referred to as *Resolution 181*) Part III, Articles 13, 14.

19. T. Al-Khalil, *Jerusalem from 1947 to 1967* (American University of Beirut: M.A. Dissertation, 1969) (hereinafter referred to as *1947 to 1967*), p. 61.

20. UNCEIRPP, *The Status*, pp. 15–16. The Israeli government interpreted access to mean that Jews had access to the Wailing Wall and the cemetery on the slopes of the Mount of Olives. According to one researcher Jordan was prepared to allow this in return for access to Muslim and Christian sites in West Jerusalem and Nazareth. See al-Khalil, *1947–1967*, pp. 91–92.

21. Al-Khalil, *1947–1967*, p. 85.

22. Rubinstein, "Jerusalem Municipality," p. 91; M. Benvenisti, *Jerusalem: The Torn City* (Minneapolis: Israeli Peset Ltd. and The University of Minneapolis, 1976) (hereinafter referred to as *Torn City*), p. 46.

23. There is some disagreement about the date. Rubinstein, citing Municipal Council minutes, gives it as 1959, while al-Khalil gives it as August 1953.

24. Rubinstein, "Jerusalem Municipality," p. 93.

25. UNCEIRPP, *The Status*, pp. 11–14. See also A. Ginio, "Plans for the Solution of the Jerusalem Problem" (hereinafter referred to as "Plans") in J. L. Kraemer ed. *Problems and Prospects*, p. 65. Bovis, H. E., *The Jerusalem Question 1917–1968* (Stanford: Hoover Institution Press, 1971) (hereinafter referred to as *Jerusalem Question*), pp. 71–76.

26. See *Jordanian Laws and Statutes* (Arabic) (Amman: The Jordanian Bar Association, 1957) (hereinafter referred to as *Jordanian Laws and Statutes*) Vol. 1, p. 4. Al-Khalil, *1947 to 1967*, p. 84.

27. The proposals of the Conciliation Commission for Palestine appeared to legitimize the de facto partition of the city into an Israeli-controlled western part and a Jordanian-controlled eastern part despite qualifications placed upon the exercise of sovereignty and jurisdiction placed upon the two states. See UNCEIRPP, *The Status*, pp. 11–13.

28. See note 15 to this chapter.

29. Kupferschmidt, *Supreme Muslim Council*, p. 258; D. Farhi, "ha-mo'atza ha-muslemit be-mizrah yerushalayim u- vi—yehuda ve shomron me-az milhemet sheshet ha-yamin" (The Muslim Council in East Jerusalem and in Judea and Samaria since the Six Day War—hereinafter "Muslim Council"), *Ha-mizrah Ha-Hedash* (The New East), vol. 28 (1979): 4 (hereinafter referred to as "Muslim Council"). See also M. Dumper, *Islam and Israel*, p. 67.

30. M. Dumper, *Islam and Israel*, p. 68.

31. *Hansard*, House of Lords, UK, 27.4.1950: statement by Lord Henderson; (hereinafter referred to as "statement"), Hassan bin Talal, *A Study on Jerusalem* (London: Longmans, 1979) (hereinafter referred to as *Study*), p. 25.

32. Slonim, p. 203.

33. Bovis, *Jerusalem Question*, pp. 93–94; Benvenisti, *Torn City*, pp. 14–15. The Israeli Foreign Ministry remained in Tel Aviv until 1953 but its subsequent move to Jerusalem had little bearing on this international boycott. For security reasons the Israeli Ministry of Defense remains in Tel Aviv to this day.

34. Sami Hadawi, a former employee in the Department of Land Settlement of the Mandatory government and a specialist adviser to the UN Conciliation Commission, constructed the map from Palestine Survey Maps and Taxation Records; it was published by the Palestine Arab Refugee Office in New York (no date).

35. See D. Peretz, *Israel and the Palestinian Arabs* (Washington D.C.: Middle East Institute, 1958), pp. 137ff; S. Jiryis, *The Arabs in Israel* (New York: Monthly Review Press, 1976), pp. 78f.

36. The pre-1948 kibbutz of Ramat Rachel close to the Armistice Lines and north of Bethlehem remained outside the Municipality.

37. I. Kimhi, S. Reichman, and Y. Schweid, *Greater Jerusalem—Alternative Municipal Frameworks* (Jerusalem: Jerusalem Institute for Israel Studies, 1990) (Hebrew) (hereinafter referred to as *Municipal Frameworks*).

38. R. Westmacott, *Jerusalem: A New Era for a Capital City* (London: The Anglo-Israel Association, 1968) (hereinafter referred to as *A New Era*), p. 15.

39. For the situation of the Muslim community in Israel after the 1948 War see Dumper, *Islam and Israel*, pp. 25–30.

40. UNCEIRPP, *The Status*, p. 14.

41. Ibid., p. 14. Israel's membership in the UN had been conditional upon its agreeing to the internationalization of Jerusalem. Some have viewed this change in the Israeli position as a result of its acceptance into the UN, making any additional concessions on Jerusalem redundant. See bin Talal, *Study*, pp. 20–21.

42. See Speech by Abba Eban to the United Nations, 1967.

43. Law and Administration Ordinance (Amendment No. 11) Law, 5727–1967, Laws of the State of Israel, Vol. 21 (1966/67) (hereinafter referred to as Amendment No. 11), p. 75.

44. The Jordanian East Jerusalem Municipal boundaries had comprised approximately 6,000 *dunams* and the Israeli West Jerusalem Municipality approximately 40,000 *dunams*. The new Municipality comprised approximately 70,000 *dunams*.

45. Municipalities Ordinance (Amendment No. 6) Law, 5727/1967, Laws of the State of Israel, Vol. 21 (1966/67) (hereinafter referred to as Amendment No. 6), pp. 75–76. Jiryis notes that before this amendment the law, which had been designed for the extension of municipal boundaries inside Israel, made

it incumbent upon the Minister of Interior to conduct an investigation to gauge the opinions of the inhabitants of a certain region before any decision was taken. In East Jerusalem the outcome of such an investigation may not have gone in the government's favor. See S. Jiryis, "Israeli Laws as Regards Jerusalem" (hereinafter referred to as "Israeli Laws"), n.d., n.p. (but also to be found in *Shu'un Filistiniyah*, no. 6 (September 1980): pp. 13–24.

46. Benvenisti, *Torn City*, pp. 104–105.

47. See speech by Israel's Ambassador to the UN, Abba Eban, quoted in Benvenisti, *Torn City*, p. 122.

48. UN Security Council Resolution 237, 14.6.67. (hereinafter referred to as Resolution 237).

49. UN General Assembly Resolution 253 (ES-V), UN Document A/6798 (1967) (hereinafter referred to as Resolution 253) and Resolution 2254 (ES-V), UN Document A\6798 (1967)(hereinafter referred to as Resolution 254).

50. Report of the Secretary-General under General Assembly Resolution 254 (ES-V), UN Document S/8146 and A/6793, pp. 36–37.

51. See H. Cattan, *Jerusalem* (London: Croom Helm, 1981) (hereinafter referred to as *Jerusalem*), pp. 190–91 for examples of resolutions.

52. Basic Law: Jerusalem, *Policy Background* (324/1.11.02) (hereinafter referred to as Basic Law) (Jerusalem: Israel Ministry of Foreign Affairs, Information Division, August 17, 1980).

53. *The Times*, June 30, 1980. (All such references are to the *Times* of London.)

54. UNSC Resolution 478.

55. These were the Netherlands, Venezuela, Uruguay, Chile, Ecuador, El Salvador, Costa Rica, Haiti, Panama, Columbia and Bolivia.

56. Benvenisti, *Torn City*, pp. 112–13. See also fuller discussion on this theme in chapter 4 below.

57. Benvenisti, *Torn City*, p. 112.

58. The military and strategic considerations should not be overstated. There were two other strategic high points not incorporated—Gilo in the south and Nabi Samwil in the northwest are the two highest points in the area and both were left outside the extended borders. Indeed, al-Haram al-Sharif area also dominates East Jerusalem and the approaches to the western half of the city and, as we have discussed, this also was free from an Israeli military presence. These points were made by one of Jerusalem's leading planners and strategic thinkers, Yosef Schweid. See his article "The Unification of Jerusalem: The Planning Aspect," *Kivunim*, no. 35 (1987): 110 (hereinafter referred to as "Unification").

59. See Municipality, *Summary*, p. 6.

60. These laws were combined into the Legal and Administrative Matters (Regulation) Law (Consolidated Version), 5730–1970, *Laws of the State of*

Israel, Vol. 24 (1969/70): 144–283 (hereinafter referred to as *Laws of the State* Vol. 24). A Palestinian legal scholar, Sabri Jiryis, has called these laws the "laws of Absorption" as they sought merely to ease the problems of Palestinian integration into the Israeli state and "to secure the basic political objective: the annexation of Jerusalem." See Jiryis, *Israeli Laws*, p. 187.

61. Article 4. This law was passed as a result of very few East Jerusalem Palestinians applying for Israeli citizenship. See A. Mansour, and E. Stock, "Arab Jerusalem after the Annexation," *New Outlook* 14:1 (1971): 24 (hereinafter referred to as "Annexation").

62. Articles 6 to 14.

63. *Laws of the State of Israel*, vol.4 (1949/50), p. 68. (hereinafter referred to as *Laws of the State*, vol.4). For a detailed examination of this law see D. Peretz, *Israel and the Palestine Arabs* (Washington D.C.: Middle East Institute, 1958), pp. 143–52 (hereinafter referred to as *Palestine Arabs*); S. Jiryis, *The Arabs in Israel* (London: Monthly Review Press, 1976), pp. 83–88 (hereinafter referred to as *Arabs in Israel*).

64. Legal and Administrative Matters (Regulation), *Laws of the State*, Article 3a.

65. Ibid., Article 2. While it has little bearing upon the question of the application of full sovereignty over Jerusalem, it is worth noting that East Jerusalem Palestinians were prevented from reclaiming their pre-1948 property in West Jerusalem by another amendment to the Absentee Property Law. They were permitted to claim compensation at 1950s prices between certain dates. Failure to do so allowed the government to pass on ownership rights to existing tenants. Absentee Property (Compensation) Law, 5733–1973, *Laws of the State*, vol. 27 (1972/73): 176–84. See note 60.

66. A. Heshin, "East Jerusalem—Policy versus Reality," in A. Layish ed., "The Arabs in Jerusalem: From the Late Ottoman Period to the Beginning of the 1990's—Religious, Social and Cultural Distinctiveness," *Hamizrah Hehadash*, vol. 34 (1992): 181.

67. Article 1. Protection of the Holy Places Law, 5727, 1967 (hereinafter referred to as Holy Places).

68. Article 4.

69. Benvenisti, *Torn City*, pp. 286–87. See also Bovis, *Jerusalem Question*, p. 108.

70. Benvenisti, *Torn City*, pp. 296–97. See also Y. Bar Sela, "Law Enforcement in the Eastern Sector of Jerusalem" (hereinafter referred to as "Law Enforcement") in O. Ahimeir ed. *Jerusalem—Aspects of Law*, Discussion Paper No. 3 (Jerusalem: Jerusalem Institute for Israel Studies, 1983), p. xxi (hereinafter referred to as *Aspects of Law*).

71. D. Hirst, "Rush to Annexation: Israel in Jerusalem," *Journal of Palestine Studies* 3:4 (Summer 1974): 10–13.

72. This Ministry was a Likud innovation which the Labor government

dropped when it took power in 1992. An Inter-Ministerial Committee on Jerusalem also exists but without a large secretariat that a fully-fledged Ministry would entail. It serves to coordinate the activities of the different ministries without having a mandate for projects of its own.

73. 54% came from the Municipality's property tax, known as the *arnona*, and 20% from other Municipality income. See *Out of Jerusalem* (Magazine of the Jerusalem Committee, Winter 1987/Spring 1988) 6: 1–2, p. 17.

74. S. Shorsky, *What Makes Israel Tick: How Domestic Policymakers Cope with Constraint* (Chicago: Nelson Hall, 1985), p. 106.

75. *Ha'aretz*, July 9, 1992, cited in S. Cohen, *The Politics of Planting: Israeli-Palestinian Competition for Control of Land in the Jerusalem Periphery* (Chicago: University of Chicago, 1993), p. 88.

76. D. Shalem and G. Shamis, *Jerusalem* (Jerusalem: Municipality of Jerusalem, n.d.), p. 30.

77. Heshin, "Policy versus Reality," p. 188.

78. Heshin cites examples from four urbanized villages within Jerusalem where at the height of the intifada mukhtars severed their contacts with the Municipality, and where three mukhtars from Sur Bahir submitted their resignations in writing after they claimed they had been mistreated by Israeli border guards. Ibid., pp. 188–89.

79. See pamphlet issued by the Jerusalem Association for Neighbourhood Management, 10, Shlomtzion Hamalkha Street, Jerusalem 94146, entitled "Jerusalem Association for Neighbourhood Management," no date but acquired in 1992.

80. Cited in S. Hasson, "The Many Faces of Neighbourhood Government," *Israel Studies* (Winter 1991): 13–14.

81. See Report by the City Planning Department of the Municipality of Jerusalem and the Jerusalem Development Authority, *Jerusalem: Extending the Area of Jurisdiction: A Summary*, Jerusalem, April 1991 (hereinafter referred to as *Extending the Jurisdiction*. A more detailed study of the problems can be found in I. Kimhi, et al., *Greater Jerusalem Alternative Municipal Frameworks* (Jerusalem: Jerusalem Institute for Israeli Studies, 1990) (hereinafter referred to as *Municipal Frameworks*).

82. "Committee recommends expansion for Jerusalem," *Jerusalem Post*, August 25, 1991, p. 10.

3. Running to Stand Still

1. Minutes of Council Meeting, Session No. 34, August 13, 1976 This was a special council meeting convened to discuss the role of the Municipality in future of Jerusalem and the annexed areas.

2. Municipality, *Extending the Jurisdiction*, p. 16.

3. Kimhi, "Outline of the Development of Jerusalem," pp. 21–23.

4. Similar difficulties of definition arise when demographers wish to target specific population groups. Official Ottoman statistics, for Jerusalem, for example, only counted Ottoman nationals, leaving aside the large and growing number of foreigners, both Christian and Jew, living in the city. J. McCarthy, *The Population of Palestine: Population Statistics of the Late Ottoman Period and the Mandate* (New York: Columbia University Press, 1990), p. 15 (hereinafter referred to as *Population of Palestine*).

5. I. Lustick, "Re-inventing Jerusalem," *Foreign Policy*, no. 93 (Winter 1993–94): 45–46.

6. See I. Kimhi, S. Reichman, and J. Schweid, *Arab Settlement in the Metropolitan Area of Jerusalem* (Jerusalem Institute for Israel Studies, Jerusalem, 1986) (Hebrew with English summary) and B. Hyman, I. Kimhi, and J. Savitzky, *Jerusalem in Transition: Urban Growth and Change, 1970's and 1980's* (Jerusalem: Jerusalem Institute for Israel Studies, 1985; hereinafter *Transition*) for discussion on this issue.

7. This point is made most forcefully by Kimhi, et al. in *Municipal Frameworks*, 4.3 and 4.4.

8. McCarthy, *Population of Palestine*, p. 4.

9. A. Schölch, "19th Century" in K. al-'Asali, ed., *History*, p. 232.

10. For example, Ben Arieh estimates the Jewish population of Jerusalem between 1890 and 1900 to range between 25,000 and 30,000. These estimates need to be balanced with McCarthy's adjusted figures for the whole of the Jerusalem sanjak, which amounted to no more than 14,000 Jews during the same period while Ottoman statistics themselves indicate that between 1895 and 1899 there were only 5,500 foreigners in the whole of the sanjak. McCarthy based his figures on the most accurate of the Ottoman statistics, corrected them for the under-counting of women and children, then made projections for natural growth. See McCarthy, *Population of Palestine*, pp. 6–7. For figures between 1895–1899, see Schölch, "19th Century," in al-'Asali, ed. *History*, p. 232.

11. Ben Arieh, *Old City*, pp. 279, 358; McCarthy, *Population of Palestine*, p. 7; Schölch, "19th Century" in al-'Asali, ed. *History*, p. 232.

12. See McCarthy's analyses of Ruppin's figures in McCarthy, *Population of Palestine*, pp. 18–19.

13. Schmelz points out that the increase in the Jewish population in Jerusalem was less than in Tel Aviv and Haifa. See U. O. Schmelz, *Modern Jerusalem's Demographic Evolution* (Jerusalem: Jerusalem Institute for Israel Studies, 1987), p. 29 (hereinafter referred to as *Demographic Evolution*).

14. Adapted from Schmelz, *Demographic Evolution*, p. 28.

15. See McCarthy, *Population of Palestine*, pp. 27–33 for a discussion of Mandate statistics in general.

16. See Schmelz, *Demographic Evolution*, p. 28.

17. See McCarthy, *Population of Palestine*, p. 165, citing *Blue Book* (Jerusalem:

Government of Palestine, 1936 and 1937) (herein after referred to as *Blue Book* and date). It is not clear why the Mandate authorities maintained such restricted boundaries particularly since they were at pains to maintain an Arab majority on the municipal council. See chapter 2.

18. See M. Hudson, "The Transformation of Jerusalem, 1917–1987" (hereinafter referred to as "Transformation of Jerusalem") in al-'Asali ed. *History*, p. 258. Schmelz compiles an interesting table giving figures from 1922 onward of the post-1967 municipal borders which confirms this approximate balance but without including Palestinian Arab settlements to the west. See Schmelz, *Demographic Evolution*, p. 72.

19. Indeed, it was partly this geographical and demographic spread of the respective Palestinian Arab and Jewish populations which was recognized by the UN and led to the particular configuration proposed in the internationalization of Jerusalem. The awareness of the Palestinian preponderance in the metropolitan area of Jerusalem persists into the post-67 period and is used to determine strategic planning policy. See Hyman, et al., *Transition*, pp. 36–38.

20. Figures for Lifta (2,550), Maliha (1,940), Dayr Yassin (610) and 'Ayn Karim (3,180) taken from W. Khalidi, ed. *All That Remains* (Washington, D.C.: Institute for Palestine Studies, 1992). Other villages are estimates based upon averages of these.

21. The American Colony was established by a pious American Protestant, Horatio Gates Spafford, in 1881. See Colby, "The Christian Establishment," p. 168.

22. A vivid description of the changes in Azariyya during the Mandate period can be found in Aburish, *Children of Bethany* (London: Bloomsbury Press, 1988).

23. First settled in the late nineteenth century by the pietist sect, the German Templars, who seceded from the German Lutheran church. See Colby, "The Christian Establishment," p. 168.

24. Tsimhoni, "Demographic Trends of the Christian Population in Jerusalem and the West Bank, 1948–1978," *Middle East Journal* 37(1) (Winter 1983): 56 (hereafter referred to as "Christian Population").

25. Benvenisti, *Torn City*, p. 53. A slight exaggeration when one considers the Crusader Kingdoms of the 12th Century, but a useful point to make.

26. Schmelz, *Demographic Evolution*, p. 38.

27. S. Markovitz, "The Development of Modern Jerusalem: An Evaluation of Planning Decisions and the Effectiveness of the Planning Process" (Woodrow Wilson School for Public and International Affairs, Princeton University: Unpublished Thesis, 1982), p. 8 (hereinafter referred to as "Planning Decisions and Processes").

28. Khalidi, ed., *All That Remains*, p. 583. J. Abu-Lughod, in "Demographic Transformation" in Abu-Lughod, *The Transformation of Jerusalem* (hereafter referred to as *Transformation*), p. 159, puts the figure at about 80,000.

29. Schmelz, *Demographic Evolution*, p. 37.

30. For the four phases, see W. Khalidi, *Before Their Diaspora* (Washington, DC: Institute for Palestine Studies, 1984), pp. 316–20; U. Bar-Joseph, *The Best of Enemies: Israel and Transjordan in the War of 1948* (London: Frank Cass, 1987), p. 67; N. Lorch, *The Edge of the Sword, Israel's War of Independence 1947–49* (New York: G. P. Putnam's Sons, 1961); and Sir John Bagot Glubb, *A Soldier with the Arabs* (London: Hodder and Stoughton, 1957).

31. According to Schmelz, approximately 8,700 Palestinians fled east as a result of the fighting along the "Jerusalem corridor" and the fall of Saris, Kolonia, Biddu, etc., while some 20,000 fled following the departure of the Mandate authorities in mid-May. Schmelz, *Demographic Evolution*, p. 42. See also the map in M. Gilbert, *Jerusalem: Illustrated History Atlas* (Jerusalem: Steimatzky, 1977) (hereinafter referred to as *History Atlas*), p. 93.

32. See Hudson, "Transformation of Jerusalem," in al-'Asali, *History*, p. 259.

33. For 1948 census see Schmelz, *Demographic Evolution*, p. 43.

34. Benvenisti, *Torn City*, p. 43.

35. A. Plascov, *The Palestinian Refugees in Jordan, 1948–57* (London: Frank Cass, 1981), p. 109.

36. Benvenisti, *Torn City*, p. 60.

37. For the Jordanian census, see Schmelz, *Demographic Evolution*, p. 44.

38. This was a 2% annual growth rate when the probable rate was between 3 and 3.5% annually. Schmelz, *Demographic Evolution*, p. 60. By including Silwan Schmelz's figures are higher than some other researchers. See for example S. Cohen, *Bridging the Four Walls: A Geopolitical Perspective* (New York: Herzl Press, 1977) (hereinafter referred to as *Four Walls*), p. 69.

39. An Israeli census in 1967 [East Jerusalem Census of Population and Housing (1966/67) (Hebrew and English) (Jerusalem: Central Bureau of Statistics and Jerusalem Municipality, 1968), pp. xi–xii (hereinafter referred to as East Jerusalem Census (1966/67) shows the population within the Jordanian municipal boundaries, including the suburban villages of Abu Tur and Silwan, at 44,369. This marked reduction reflects the further flight of some 15,000–20,000 Palestinian Arabs during the 1967 War as well as a population drift to the peripheries of the municipal boundaries where planning regulations were not so strictly enforced, but the Israeli figure also confirms that there was no sharp increase in the Palestinian Arab population of Jerusalem between 1961 and 1967.

40. Schmelz, *Demographic Evolution*, p. 63, Table 16. In the same year there were only 1,400 Christians in Israeli Jerusalem, probably mostly foreign nationals and non-Arabs.

41. T. Prittie, *Whose Jerusalem* (London: Frederick Muller Ltd, 1981) (hereinafter referred to as *Whose Jerusalem*), p. 71.

42. Benvenisti, *Torn City*, p. 53.

43. See I. Zilberman, "The Hebronite Migration and the Development of

Suburbs in the Metropolitan Area of Jerusalem," in A. Layish, "The Arabs in Jerusalem: From the Late Ottoman Period to the Beginning of the 1990's— Religious, Social and Cultural Distinctiveness," *Hamizrah Hehadash* 34, 1992 (Jerusalem, 1992), pp. 46–48 (hereinafter referred to as "Hebronite Migration").

44. In this context also Tsimhoni refers to the influx of Hebronite shopkeepers, particularly in the Christian quarter. See her "Christian Population," p. 57.

45. Benvenisti, *Torn City*, p. 47.

46. The Jordanian East Jerusalem Municipality retained the services of Henry Kendall, the Mandatory Town Planner who was able to oversee the remnants of his proposed plan submitted in 1948. The plan included the preservation of green areas around the northern and eastern parts of the Old City. See H. Kendall, *Jerusalem City Plan* (London: Her Majesty's Stationary Office, 1948) (hereinafter referred to as *City Plan*).

47. Zilberman, "Hebronite Migration," p. 48.

48. Cited in Al-Khalil, *1947 to 1967*, p. 88. It is not clear how Khatib defines this area, but from the figures they would seem to include Bethlehem, Bayt Jallah, Bayt Sahur, A-Ram, Abu Dis, Azariyya, and Essawiyya. His figure, moreover, is partially confirmed by Israeli estimates, which place the 1961 non-Jewish population of Jerusalem within what became the Municipal boundaries of 1967 at 78,700. Schmelz, *Demographic Evolution*, p. 72, Table 18.

49. Schmelz, *Demographic Evolution*, p. 57.

50. See chapter 4 for further details of housing developments during this period.

51. Ibid., p. 58.

52. B. K. Nijm, ed., *Toward the De-Arabization of Palestine/Israel, 1945–1977* (Dubuque, Iowa: Kendall/Hunt, n.d.), p. 58.

53. See Schmelz, *Demographic Evolution*, p. 48.

54. Benvenisti, *Torn City*, p. 31.

55. Benvenisti, *Torn City*, p. 31.

56. Cohen, *Four Walls*, p. 66.

57. Schmelz, *Demographic Evolution*, pp. 49–50.

58. Ibid., p. 48.

59. Ibid., p. 48.

60. Benvenisti, *Torn City*, p. 32.

61. Minutes and decisions taken at Meeting No. 34 of the City Council held in the Assembly Room, August 13, 1967.

62. A point made by Benvenisti, *Torn City*, p. 250.

63. See M. Romann, *An Economic and Social Survey of Greater Jerusalem* (Maurice Falk Institute for Economic Research in Israel, Jerusalem, 1967) (Hebrew), pp. 53–56, on the calculations he made to project the number of Israeli Jews required to balance Palestinian Arab natural increase and in-

migration over a twenty-year period. Written in 1967, it makes especially interesting reading today, revealing as it does Israeli anxieties of the demographic race from the early days of occupation.

64. Municipality, *Extending the Jurisdiction*, p. 16.

65. A report by Sarah Hogg in *The Economist* was both superficial and inaccurate when it commented on the arrival of new immigrants to Jerusalem: "Israel cannot be accused of pushing Jerusalem on its newcomers: the most it is doing is allowing them to have their way." "Jerusalem: The overburdened magnet," *The Economist*, December 25, 1971, p. 36 (hereinafter referred to as "The overburdened magnet").

66. This scheme was the brainchild of Shimon Peres when Acting Minister of Absorption. See Benvenisti's description of the various plans suggested and how they fared, in *Torn City*, pp. 251–53.

67. See Table 10.1 in J. Abu Lughod, "Demographic Consequences of the Occupation" (hereinafter referred to as "Demographic Consequences") in N. Aruri, *Occupation: Israel over Palestine* (London: Zed Books, 1984), pp. 258–59 (hereinafter referred to as *Occupation*). The figure of 14,000 is arrived at by subtracting the June total from the September total.

68. R. al-Khatib, "The Judaization of Jerusalem and its Demographic Transformation" (hereinafter referred to as "Judaization of Jerusalem") in *Jerusalem: The Key to World Peace* (London: Islamic Council of Europe, 1980), p. 118 (hereinafter referred to as *Key to World Peace*). Ruhi al-Khatib was the Mayor of Jordanian Jerusalem in 1967. Deported by the Israeli government he still officially retains his title.

69. See Tibawi, *The Islamic Pious Foundations of Jerusalem* (London: Islamic Cultural Centre, 1978) (hereinafter referred to as *Pious Foundations*), p. 35; Benvenisti, *Torn City*, p. 306. See also *Jerusalem Post*, June 19, 1967. Dumper, *Islam and Israel*, p. 116 deals with this event in some detail.

70. See Dumper, *Islam and Israel* pp. 117–120 for a description of this event.

71. Israeli statistics distinguish only between Jews and non-Jews, thereby obscuring the profile of Palestinian Arabs who are merged with Greeks, Armenians, Ethiopians, and others. In addition there are three kinds of Palestinians in Jerusalem. Palestinian Arabs with Israeli citizenship from the pre-1967 borders (sometimes referred to as Israeli Palestinians or Israeli Arabs), Palestinian Arabs with Jordanian citizenship but who have Israeli Jerusalem Municipality identity cards and reside in Jerusalem officially, and, finally, Palestinian Arabs who have Jordanian citizenship but who reside in Jerusalem unofficially.

72. Schmelz, *Demographic Evolution*, p. 72.

73. Abu Lughod, "Demographic Consequences" in Aruri, *Occupation*, p. 258.

74. See Jerusalem Institute for Israel Studies, "The Metropolitan Area of Jerusalem," *The Urban Development of Metropolitan Jerusalem*, Publication No. 1 (Jerusalem: The Jerusalem Institute for Israel Studies, 1984) (hereinafter

referred to as "The Metropolitan Area of Jerusalem") for a more detailed definition and analysis.

75. Municipality, *Extending the Jurisdiction*, p. 10.

76. I. Kimhi and B. Hyman, *Socio-economic Survey of Jerusalem, 1957–1977*
(Jerusalem: Jerusalem Committee, 1978), p. 16: See also Hyman, et al., *Transi-
tion:* (hereinafter referred to as *Socio-Economic Survey*), *1970's–1980's*, p. 37
(Jerusalem: Jerusalem Committee, 1985) (hereinafter referred to as *Transition*).

77. Kimhi and Hyman, *Socio-economic Survey*, p. 15.

78. See chapter 4 for further details.

79. Hyman et al. *Transition*, p. 45.

80. See Table 15 in Kimhi and Hyman, *Socio-economic Survey*, p. 16.

81. Ibid., p. 16.

82. Hyman, et al., *Transition*, p. 13.

83. There has been no census on Jerusalem since 1983. All figures since
1983 are extrapolations from that census combined with figures available for
immigration and emigration. Extrapolations for periods over a decade
become increasingly unreliable.

84. Hyman, et al., *Transition*, p. 13.

85. See articles in the *Jerusalem Post*, "HU Professor: Satellite towns bad for
Jerusalem," May 18, 1979, and "Mayor slams Greater Jerusalem Policy," June
22, 1984.

86. Ibid., p. 14.

87. Ibid., p. 37.

88. This figure should be treated with some caution. Although computed
using figures provided by Hyman, et al., *Transition*, p. 37, the proportion of
Palestinian Arabs seems excessive and the total of Israeli Jews seems too low
given the settlement drive that took place during this decade.

89. Tsimhoni, "Christian Population," p. 60. Compared to the figure in the
1961 census of approximately 11,000, this shows only a rise of less than 1,000
people; we can assume that between 2,000–3,000 Palestinian Christians fled
during the 1967 War.

90. Hyman, et al., *Transition*, p. 10.

91. Schmelz, *Demographic Evolution*, p. 28.

92. Most ecclesiasticals residing in institutions would be celibate priests or
monks. See Hyman, Kimhi and Savitsky, *Transition*, p. 13. In addition there is
a surfeit of Christian females in Jerusalem probably due to emigration of
males and interaction of Christian males with visiting females.

93. Tsimhoni, "Christian Population," p. 60.

94. State of Israel, Central Bureau of Statistics, *Census of Population and
Housing, 1972*, part II, no. 10 (Jerusalem, 1979), cited in Tsimhoni, "Christian
Population," p. 63. See also study by the Palestinian sociologist, Dr. Bernard
Sabella, for the al-Liqa' Centre, Jerusalem, entitled "Christian Emigration: A
Comparison of the Jerusalem, Ramallah and the Bethlehem Areas" (1990)

and article entitled "Palestinian Christian Emigration from the Holy Land" (1992).

95. Schmelz, *Demographic Evolution*, pp. 110–11. Also Hyman, Kimhi and Savitzky, *Transition*, p. 20.

96. Schmelz, *Demographic Evolution*, pp. 78, 111.

97. A map illustrates this in Hyman, Kimhi, and Savitzky, *Transition*, p. 21.

98. See descriptions of confrontation with police and Municipality over these issues in N. Shepherd, *The Mayor and the Citadel: Teddy Kollek and Jerusalem* (London: Weidenfeld and Nicholson, 1987), pp. 85ff. (hereinafter referred to as *The Mayor*).

99. See Kimhi, Reichman and Shweid, *Municipal Frameworks*, 4.6.2. and Municipality, *Extending the Jurisdiction*, p. 7.

100. G. Aronson, "Soviet Jewish Emigration, the United States and the Occupied Territories," *Journal of Palestine Studies* 19, no.4 (Summer 1990):38 (hereinafter referred to as "Soviet Jewish Emigration").

101. Jerusalem Institute for Israel Studies, *Statistical Yearbook of Jerusalem*, No. 8, 1989 (Jerusalem: Jerusalem Institute for Israel Studies, 1991), p. 28. (hereinafter referred to as *Yearbook* followed by date [1989]).

102. See for example Municipality of Jerusalem, *Immigration Absorption Project* (Jerusalem, December 1991). An unconfirmed report in the *Jerusalem Post*, June 18, 1992 claims that many of the Soviet immigrants leave Jerusalem after a year of fruitless job-seeking.

103. *Jerusalem Post*, May 25, 1992, p. 3.

104. M. Choshen, and I. Kimhi, *Migration To and From Jerusalem* (Jerusalem: Jerusalem Institute for Israel Studies, 1991), p. 8 (hereinafter referred to as *Migration*).

105. The Deputy Mayor Amos Mar-Haim was quoted as saying that "the figures are worrisome. The population of Jerusalem has been growing, on the one hand, but on the other, year after year we are losing the best of our young people." *Jerusalem Post*, May 25, 1992. Article entitled "Jerusalem losing best of its young people," by Bill Hutman, p. 3.

106. The figures are compiled from those supplied by the Israeli peace movement, Peace Now, and the Council of Jewish Communities in Judea, Samaria and Gaza. The total for East Jerusalem and the metropolitan area inside the Green Line is 184,878; for East Jerusalem only: 140,000. "The new Greater Jerusalem," *Report on Israeli Settlement in the Occupied Territories*, 2:6 (November 1992): 4.

107. Official figures are 10,000. See *Jerusalem Post*, April 29, 1992. Internal Municipality estimates go up to 20,000. See Municipality, *Extending the Jurisdiction*, p. 17.

108. Latest figures obtained in July 1994.

109. N. Shragai, "Demography before everything," *Ha'aretz*, May 31, 1992.

110. *Report on Israeli Settlement in the Occupied Territories*, Washington, D.C. February 1994.

4. Planning and Housing Policy

1. See D. H. K. Amiran, "The Development of Jerusalem, 1860–1970" (hereinafter referred to as "Development"), in D. H. K. Amiran, A. Shachar, and I. Kimhi, *Urban Geography of Jerusalem: A Companion Volume to the Atlas of Jerusalem* (Jerusalem: Dept. of Geography, Hebrew University of Jerusalem, 1973), pp. 20–23 (hereinafter referred to as *Urban Geography*). Amiran gives some useful climatic and topographical background to the urban development of Jerusalem. However, he does suggest that the trade arteries from Beersheva to Nablus and Jaffa to Jericho crossing at Jerusalem were factors contributing to its development.

2. See D. Little, "Jerusalem under the Ayyubids and Mamluks, 1197–1516 A.D." (hereinafter referred to as "Ayyubids and Mamluks") in K. al-'Asali, ed., *History*, pp. 177–99 for a brief but useful introduction to the post-Crusader period. See also M. Burgoyne, *Mamluk Jerusalem* for descriptions of post-Ayyubid construction.

3. Amiran, "Development," pp. 20ff. See also I. Kimhi, "Aspects of the Urban Ecology of Jerusalem," in Amiran, Shachar and Kimhi, *Urban Geography*, p. 109.

4. See chapter 5 for a discussion of Jerusalem's endemic water problem.

5. N. Shragai, "Demography Above Anything," in *Ha'aretz*, May 31, 1992.

6. See Gilbert, *History Atlas*, Map 41, p. 77.

7. Herut Square is the contemporary name. I do not know the Mandate name.

8. See in particular, the 1930 Outline Scheme. H. Kendall, *City Plan*, pp. 18ff. There were also plans put forward in 1918, 1919, and 1922 which, although not enforced, acted as important guidance. The Kendall Plan, put forward during the waning years of the Mandate, was not implemented either, but it had the greatest impact in terms of future planning. Its overall aim was to integrate the transportation routes in a way that responded to the urban growth of the city to the southwest, west, and north and to extend the small industrial areas to the southwest and northwest. It also introduced the idea, which has persisted until the present day, of retaining the valleys as continuous open spaces while confining construction to the slopes and crests.

9. See S. Shapiro, "Planning Jerusalem: The First Generation, 1917–1968" (hereinafter referred to as "Planning Jerusalem") in Amiran, *Urban Geography*, pp. 143–47. See also H. Kendall, *City Plan* for the evolution of British planning objectives.

10. Cited in Shapiro, "Planning Jerusalem," pp. 141–42.

11. See table 2.1

12. See chapter 5 for further details.

13. Dumper, *Islam and Israel*, p. 69. This was despite the loss of their holdings in Israel.

14. This may have largely been due to the fact that Henry Kendall, Planning

Officer during the British Mandate, returned to his former post in Jerusalem between 1963 and 1966. (Dates supplied by Professor Anthony Coon, Centre for Planning, University of Strathclyde.)

15. Unfortunately it was widened simply by inserting a concrete beam destroying the character of the gate. See Report by Brown Engineering International, presented to Arab Jerusalem City Council, 1963; cited in M. Turner, "The Old City and its Walls," *Out of Jerusalem* 3:4 (Winter 1982/83): 29.

16. See M. Kendall, *The Planning of Jerusalem (Jordan) and Region* (Jerusalem, October 1965), p. 3.

17. E. Efrat, "Changes in the Town Planning Concepts of Jerusalem (1919–1969)," *Environmental Planning* (The Israeli Association for Environmental Planning Quarterly), July–Sept. 1971, p. 58.

18. See Shapiro, "Planning Jerusalem," p. 153, note 20.

19. See Kendall, *Planning*, for details of the proposals.

20. Shapiro, "Planning Jerusalem." Shachar Shapir was a former planner with the Israel Lands Administration. Partly because of the wealth of data the Plan provided and partly because of the coherence of its approach and the consolidation of existing recommendations, both Israeli and Jordanian planners have drawn on the Kendall Plan for ideas and assumptions.

21. Efrat, "Changes," p. 57.

22. See Shapiro, "Planning Jerusalem," pp. 148–51.

23. See Tables VIII and IX in ibid., pp. 149 and 150.

24. These points are made by Yosef Schweid in "The Unification of Jerusalem: The Planning Aspect," *Kivunim*, No. 35, 1987 (Hebrew), p. 113.

25. Ibid., p. 6.

26. Efrat, "Changes," p. 57.

27. Schweid, "Unification," p. 119.

28. S. Markovitz, "Planning Decisions and Processes," pp. 62–63.

29. Ibid., pp. 64–65 (citing Planning and Building Law, 1965, Article III, Section 61).

30. Ibid., p. 64.

31. Ibid., pp. 88–89.

32. See D. Kroyanker, *Developing Jerusalem, 1967–75: The Planning Processs and Its Problems Reflected in Some Minor Projects*, n.p. n.d., pp. 78–80.

33. Another aspect of the Municipality's dual role as planning authority and Local Planning Commission which affects the planning process are the divisions which occur within the Municipality itself. The Town Planning Department is in frequent disagreement with the Finance Department over the question of aesthetics and economics. Disputes that should more appropriately be resolved within a forum once removed from the Municipality instead permeate its workings and hamper its smooth functioning. In the absence of strong guidelines and proposals emanating from the national and

regional bodies, planning policy in Jerusalem is forged in the hotbed of political rivalries and inter-departmental squabbles; ibid., p. 70.

34. *Statistical Yearbook of Jerusalem*, 1989, p. 303.

35. *Yearbook (1989) of Jerusalem*, p. 305. The average would be much lower
if it were not for a contribution of 9.9% in 1984/5.

36. "Planning Problems," p. 80.

37. Calculations based on figures supplied by map 2.4, p. 37. See chapter 2.

38. Shepherd, *The Mayor*, p. 28.

39. Ibid., p. 17.

40. "Planning Problems," p. 80; see also Markovitz, "Planning Decisions and
Processes," p. 377.

41. See D. S. Michelson, "Physical Development Patterns of New
Neighbourhoods in Jerusalem since 1967," *Engineering and Architecture–Journal
of the Association of Engineers and Architects in Israel* (Nos. 11–12, 1977) (hereinafter referred to as *Engineering and Architecture*), p. 73. See also W. Lehn and
U. Davis, *The Jewish National Fund* (London: Kegan Paul International, 1988),
pp. 58–59. See A. Granott, *Land Problems of Palestine* (New York: Bloch, 1940),
pp. 2–3 for an exposition of this principle from the former chairman of the
Jewish National Fund.

42. See Dumper, *Islam and Israel*, p. 115, for contributions made by Arab and
Islamic bodies between 1967 and 1987. In addition, between 1979 and 1988,
the Jordanian-Palestinian Joint Committee directed JD 1,285,031 (approximately US $8 million) to the Awqaf Administration. See *Achievements Report,
1979–88* (Amman, Oct. 1988).

43. See M. Dumper, "Israeli Settlements in the Old City of Jerusalem,"
Journal of Palestine Studies 21 (4) (Summer 1992): 41ff. (hereinafter "Israeli
Settlements").

44. Markovitz, "Planning Decisions and Processes," p. 101. Palestinian Arabs
who complain about the lack of formal notification of planning proposals
would be surprised to learn that Israeli Jews in Jerusalem make similar complaints. See article by A. Rabinovich, "Announcements in Chinese was all the
public knew of impending plans," *Jerusalem Post*, March 21, 1974. (hereinafter
referred to as "Announcements in Chinese").

45. Abraham Rabinovich, "Professor Resigns from Jerusalem Planning
Committee," *Jerusalem Post*, February 2, 1973, cited in Markovitz, p. 103.

46. For details on Acre see E. Cohen, *Integration and Separation in the
Planning of a Mixed Jewish-Arab City in Israel* (Jerusalem: Hebrew University,
1973), pp. 6–16 (hereinafter referred to as *Integration and Separation*). See also
Abdullah Schlieffer's comments on Jaffa in A. Schlieffer, "Islamic Jerusalem as
Archetype of a Harmonious Urban Development," *Saqqaf* 172: 149–75, cited
in al-'Asali, ed., *History*, p. 273. He writes: "I must confess that I now fear for
Islamic Jerusalem what has happened to the traditional quarters of Jaffa—a
brilliant restoration job and technically worthy of study—the physical frame

of Jaffa's Islamic core brilliantly preserved, the inner structure rewired, reinforced, replastered. But the moral implications are, to say the least, deeply disturbing—the transfer of a once vital but morally conservative Arab quarter into a Muslim-free bohemian artistic quarter and red-light district. May God spare Jerusalem such a restoration."

47. I. Daqqaq, "Transformation," in Abu Lughod, *Transformation*, p. 88.

48. In 1968 David Amiran, an Israeli urban geographer, wrote: "Anyone coming to visit the Old City after twenty years will be very impressed by the renewal of many shops in the main business streets which changed their facades and interiors to become modern and pleasant, and no longer reminiscent of the old 'oriental' shops of the past." See Amiran, "Development," p. 50.

49. See A. Kutcher, *The New Jerusalem: Planning and Politics* (London: Thames and Hudson, 1973), p. 106.

50. Schweid, "Unification," p. 116.

51. "Planning Problems," pp. 78–79.

52. See chapter 3.

53. Shepherd, *The Mayor*, p. 62.

54. See article by Roman Priester, "Two voices crying the wilderness," *Ha'aretz*, April 8, 1987.

55. See discussion in Dumper, "Israeli settlement," pp. 38–41.

56. The Municipality refuses to publish figures that show the different levels of spending in Palestinian Arab areas and Israeli Jewish areas so it is difficult to be specific. But observation and the candid admission of the Municipality itself in setting up a Committee for the Equalization of Services attests to the prevalence of this practice. See the view of the Mayor's Advisor on Arab Affairs in A. Cheshin, "East Jerusalem: Policy versus Reality," in A. Layish ed., *The Arabs in Jerusalem: From the Late Ottoman Period to the Beginning of the 1990's– Religious, Social and Cultural Distinctiveness, Hamizrachi Hahedash* (Special Edition) vol. 34 (Jerusalem: 1992), pp. 187f. See also D. Aronson, "The Politics of Social Welfare: The Case of East Jerusalem," *Middle East Report*, May–June 1987, pp. 33–35. See also Shepherd, *The Mayor*, p. 53.

57. M. Romann and A. Weingrod, *Living Together Separately: Arabs and Jews in Contemporary Jerusalem* (Princeton: Princeton University Press, 1991), p. 59 (hereinafter referred to as *Living Together*). They give a figure of 65,000 units until 1985. Kimhi, Reichman and Schweid, *Greater Jerusalem*, 4.3.1., estimate that since 1980 an average of 2,300 units have been built each year. If one multiplies this by seven for the years between 1986 and 1993 and total to 65,000, you get approximately 81,100 units.

58. Article by Priester, *Ha'aretz*, April 3, 1987. Romann and Weingrod argue the same point more sedately: "The overall policy had as its main axiom the prevention of any possible future attempt to again divide the city or to cut off the occupied East Jerusalem territory from sovereign Israeli control"; Romann and Weingrod, *Living Together*, p. 54.

59. David Kroyanker, the Municipality's Chief Planner, has spelled out these three phases clearly in D. Kroyanker, "The Face of the City" in J. Prawer, and O. Ahimeir eds., *Twenty Years in Jerusalem, 1967–1987* (Jerusalem: Ministry of Defence Publishing House and Jerusalem Institute for Israel Studies, 1988) (hereinafter referred to as *Twenty Years*).

60. Compensation was to be paid in government bonds redeemable after 15 years. G. Weigert, *Israel's Presence in East Jerusalem* (Jerusalem, 1973), p. 151. See Kroyanker, "Face of the City."

61. Kroyanker writes: "Because of objective needs—and in order to somewhat soften the bitter feelings that had been aroused by the confiscation of the Arab-owned sites—the government confiscated also Jewish-owned ones—the Jewish shema quarter in Gai Ben Hinom (today's site of the Cinematheque), the Mamilla area opposite Jaffa Gate, parts of French Hill, large parts of the old Jewish settlement off Neve Ya'aqov which had been abandoned by its residents in 1948, and nearby Atarot." D. Kroyanker, "Face of the City."

62. No precise figures of the quantities of the land were available at the time of writing.

63. See *Jerusalem Post*, May 25, 1979, "Slum areas in the heart of unified city."

64. Schweid, "Unification," p. 112.

65. See interview with Sarah Kaminker in which she reveals that the houses in French Hill were originally designed to be four stories, but government pressure increased them to eight in *challenge* 3, no. 1, p.12.

66. See article by Roman Priester, "Jerusalem 1987: Wall and Tower," in *Ha'aretz*, April 3, 1987.

67. Kroyanker, "Face of the City."

68. Ibid.

69. Romann and Weingrod, *Living Together*, p. 56.

70. A phrase, taken out of context it has to be admitted, used by Hillel Halkin in "Building Jerusalem," *Commentary*, 52 (September 1971), p. 60; cited in Markovitz, "Planning Decisions and Processes," p. 102.

71. Michelson, "Physical Development Patterns," pp. 62, 68.

72. See Shapiro, "Planning Jerusalem," pp. 61, 63, and 68.

73. The main problems stemmed from a preponderance of evacuees from slum areas and new Israeli Jewish immigrants from Soviet Georgia. Combined with a lack of veteran Israelis a socially divided and unstable community was created in Neve Ya'aqov.

74. See Kroyanker, "Face of the City." The role of this settlement was to "rescue Neve Ya'aqov from its isolation and to create a physical dividing line between Arab neighbourhoods alongside the Jerusalem-Ramallah road on the one side and the desert on the eastern side."

75. See chapter 3.

76. Quoted in article by Priester, *Ha'aretz*, April 8, 1987. Further details of the struggle over land uses can be found in S. Cohen, *The Politics of Planting: Israeli-Palestinian Competition for Control of Land in the Jerusalem Periphery* (Chicago and London: University of Chicago, 1993), Geography Research Paper, No. 236.

77. Moshe Dayan, , one of the initiators of the idea of settlement along this road, is reported to have said "between the Jordan and Jerusalem there is no obstacle that could stop the Jordanian armour in the next war." See article by Roman Priester, "Two voices crying the wilderness," *Ha'aretz*, April 8, 1987.

78. Kroyanker, "Face of the City," p. .

79. See article by Priester, *Ha'aretz*, April 8, 1987. A recent study made by Israel Kimhi reveals that 60% of new apartment buyers in Bet Shemesh are from Jerusalem. Kimhi, "Outline of the Development of Jerusalem, 1988–1993," in *Urban Geography*, p. 19 (hereinafter "Outline").

80. Municipality, *Extending the Jurisdiction*, p. 16.

81. Schweid, "Unification," p. 114.

82. *Kol Ha'ir*, October 19, 1990; cited in *News from Within*, October 6, 1990, p. 13. These benefits are open, unusually, to those who have not undergone military service themselves but have had a father or brother who has served in the army—a definition which includes many orthodox Jews but which continues to exclude most Palestinian Arabs from inside Israel.

83. Shragai, "Demography Above Anything," *Ha'aretz*, May 31, 1992.

84. Ibid.

85. See A. R. Abu Arafeh, *The Housing Situation in Jerusalem* (Jerusalem: Arab Thought Forum, 1992) (Arabic and English) (al-waqa' al-sukan fi madinat al-quds), p. 7 (hereinafter referred to as *Housing Situation*). The surface area of completed buildings amounted to 4,600,000 square meters of which 2,925,000 square meters were for housing. All completions including housing in the Palestinian Arab sector came to 470,000 square meters.

86. Romann and Weingrod, *Living Together*, p. 59. See also Hyman, et al., *Transition*, p. 7 who say that private sector investment was concentrated mostly in the western part of the city.

87. No figures differentiating between public funding for Palestinian Arabs and Israeli Jews are publicly available. See D. Aronson for the difficulties in obtaining data on government and Municipality expenditure in Palestinian Arab areas.

88. Article by B. Hutman, "Housing Quotas for Arabs," *Jerusalem Post*, December 3, 1993.

89. Municipality, *Extending the Jurisdiction*, p. 10.

90. Ibid., p. 10.

91. This is the most recent estimate. See Kimhi, "Outline," p. 93.

92. M. Dumper, "Property Restoration for Community Development in the Old City of Jerusalem," unpublished report to the Welfare Association,

Geneva, 1987 (hereinafter referred to as "Property Restoration"), Section A, Chapter Five. See also Romann and Weingrod, *Living Together*, p. 59 on official neglect of the Muslim quarters. See also K. Khatib, *The Conservation of Jerusalem* (East Jerusalem: PASSIA, 1993), pp. 18–44 for a detailed analysis of living conditions in the Old City.

93. I. Mattar, "From Palestinian to Israeli: Jerusalem, 1948–1982," *Journal of Palestine Studies* 12 (1983): 62 (hereinafter referred to as "Palestinian to Israeli") estimates that from 1967–1982 approximately 5,600 *dunams* were expropriated. Abu Arafeh gives a figure of 72% although it is not clear how he arrives at it. See Abu Arafeh, *Housing Situation*, p. 5.

94. See M. Dumper, "Israeli Settlement," for details of Old City expropriations.

95. Interview with Sarah Kaminker, *Challenge* 3, no.1, pp. 10–11.

96. Ibid., p. 10.

97. Ibid., p. 12; see also Benvenisti, *Torn City*, pp. 243–44.

98. Benvenisti, *Torn City*.

99. Kaminker, and *Jerusalem Post*, June 19, 1987.

100. Abu Arafeh, *Housing Situation*, p. 10–11.

101. See article by B. Hutman, "Plan without a hope," *Jerusalem Post*, February 28, 1992. (hereinafter referred to as "Plan"). Since the approval of this plan the European Community has pledged assistance for the housing needs of Palestinians. It remains to be seen what proportion of these funds will be used in Jerusalem.

102. See Kimhi, et al. *Municipal Frameworks*.

103. See Romann and Weingrod, *Living Together*, p. 118.

104. As an effective but crude instrument for urban development these funds were open to abuse. Latterly an approved Municipality building permit was necessary before payments were made. See Romann and Weingrod, *Living Together*, p. 58. See also I. Kimhi, S. Reichman, and J. Schweid, *Arab Settlement in the Metropolitan Area of Jerusalem* (The Jerusalem Institute for Israeli Studies, 1986) (hereinafter referred to as *Arab Settlement*).

105. Between 1979 and 1988, $112 million was spent by the fund on housing in the Jerusalem area, approximately $10 million per annum. For funding purposes the Fund defines the Jerusalem area in such a way as to include Jerusalem, Ramallah and al-Birah, Jericho, Bethlehem, Bayt Jallah and settlements in between.

106. Apart from the Shu'fat refugee camp, Jerusalem is noteworthy for the lack of shanty towns and bidonvilles on its outskirts. These are a common feature of a rapidly expanding city without proper government investment. As Professor Anthony Coon commented in reviewing an earlier draft of this chapter most shanty towns spring up on government-owned land. Strict Israeli government control over the land around Jerusalem rules out this possibility.

107. T. Sawicki, "The Land Competition—Growth of Arab Settlement in the Jerusalem Region," *Israel Studies* (Jerusalem Institute for Israel Studies, Spring 1988), pp. 19–20 (hereinafter referred to as "Land Competition"). Professor Coon has supplied figures for building permits in al-Azariyya. In 1987, twenty-four were given, in 1988, nine, and in 1989, only six. Not all these were for housing. It has been estimated that Azariyya needs 25 permits for residential construction per annum to keep up with natural increase.

108. To put these increases in context, one should recall that the population of the West Bank more than doubled between 1967 and 1987.

5. Servicing the City

1. Nadav Shragai, "A Metropolis on the Border," *Ha'aretz*, July 17, 1992 (Unofficial translation).

2. For example, one can hypothetically assume that following a peace agreement, up to one-half of the Israeli Jewish population of East Jerusalem will leave East Jerusalem and the annexed areas. They would be replaced partially by Palestinian "returnees" and in-migration from the West Bank. The total population of East Jerusalem and the annexed areas can be estimated to reach 200,000 people.

3. See article by N. Shragai, "A Metropolis on the Border," *Ha'aretz*, July 17, 1992, in which he reports on discussions within the Municipality and the Israeli government on the impact of the autonomy proposals on the administration of Jerusalem and the metropolitan area.

4. Amiran, "Development," p. 21.

5. Wilkinson, "Ancient Jerusalem: Its Water Supply and Population" (hereinafter referred to as "Water Supply") in *Palestine Exploration Quarterly* 106: 33–36; also Ben Arieh, *Old City*, pp. 59–67. I am very indebted to Richard Sexton, of the University of East Anglia, for the sight of his research notes on the water supply to Jerusalem during the periods prior to 1967.

6. The potential for collecting water in cisterns was very great. A survey carried out by the Mandate authorities in 1921 concluded that there were 7,300 cisterns in Jerusalem with a combined capacity of 445,000 cubic meters. The network of cisterns under al-Haram al-Sharif had the capacity of 15,900 cubic meters. See Amiran, "Development," p. 34.

7. Ben Arieh, *Old City*, p. 59.

8. C. Wilson, *Ordnance Survey of Jerusalem*, Her Majesty's Treasury, 1865. (Facsimile Edition: Ariel Publishing House, Jerusalem, 1980) (hereinafter referred to as *Ordnance Survey*), p. 86.

9. See for example U. Heyd, "Waqf and Public Works" (hereinafter referred to as "Waqf") in *Ottoman Documents on Palestine 1552–1615* (London: Oxford University Press, 1960) (hereinafter referred to as *Ottoman Documents*), pp. 139–53.

10. See R. Kark, "The Jerusalem Municipality at the End of Ottoman Rule," *Asian Affairs*, no.14 (1980): 34–36 (hereinafter referred to as "Ottoman Rule").

11. See Ben Arieh, *Old City*, p. 86.

12. Amiran, "Development," p. 34.

13. Ben Arieh, *Old City*, p. 88.

14. Amiran, "Development," p. 34.

15. Information derived from research notes made by Richard Sexton from material at the Public Records Office.

16. *The Times*, "Another Drought in Palestine—Jerusalem Water Supply" May 17, 1932 (hereinafter referred to as "Another Drought").

17. Amiran, "Development," p. 34.

18. Benvenisti, *Torn City*, p. 44; Khalil, *1947 to 1967*, p. 86.

19. *Jerusalem Post*, May 4, 1979.

20. Benvenisti, *Torn City*, p. 135; see also A. Rabinovich, "There's water in those hills," *Jerusalem Post*, February 23, 1973. (hereinafter referred to as *Jerusalem Post*, February 23, 1973).

21. Benvenisti, *Torn City*, p. 136.

22. Jerusalem Water Undertaking (Ramallah District), *Annual Preview, 1991* (Ramallah: Jerusalem Water Undertaking, 1991), p. 6.

23. A. Rabinovich, "1,500 J'lem families suffer heat wave with serious dearth of water," *Jerusalem Post*, July 23, 1973 (hereinafter referred to as *Jerusalem Post*, July 23, 1973).

24. *Jerusalem Post*, May 4, 1979.

25. Rofe and Rafferty, *Jerusalem and District Water Supply: Geological Hydrological Report* (July 1963, n.p.). Details supplied by Richard Sexton.

26. The Jerusalem Water Undertaking (Ramallah district) was responsible to the Jordanian Minister of Municipal and Rural Affairs. See JWU, *Annual Preview*, pp. 56–61. Jordanian government involvement continued up to the severance of administrative ties with the West Bank in 1988.

27. The reservoir at Bayit Vegan had the capacity of 90,000 cubic meters. O. Berry, "Water's fine as reservoir near capacity," *Jerusalem Post*, September 26, 1986.

28. Ministry of Environment, Jerusalem District, *Annual Report, 1991/ 1992* (hereinafter referred to as *Annual Report*), Paragraph 2.218.

29. Ministry of Environment, *Annual Report*, Paragraph 2.218.

30. D. Gross, "How to make a lake (temporary)," *Jerusalem Post*, February 13, 1974 (hereinafter referred to as *Jerusalem Post*, February 13, 1974) and *Jerusalem Post*, February 23, 1973.

31. *Jerusalem Post*, July 12, 1974; see also al-Khalil, *1947 to 1967*, p. 82.

32. Municipality of Jerusalem, Department of Information and Public Relations, *Jerusalem*, no date (probably 1989) (hereinafter referred to as *Jerusalem*).

33. See Gilbert, *History Atlas*, Map 62.

34. See chapter 2, Note 34, for description made by Abba Eban, Israel's Ambassador to the United Nations in 1967.

35. Khatib, *Judaisation of Jerusalem*, p. 121.

36. See Amiran, "Development," p. 51, n.44.

37. Benvenisti, *Torn City*, p. 134.

38. Benvenisti, *Torn City*, p. 136.

39. *Jerusalem Post*, July 23, 1973.

40. The Joint Committee provided $1.5 million. Other sources are as follows: OPEC, $250,000; Islamic Bank $420,000; UN Development Program, $750,000; Save the Children Fund, $1,400,000; European Community, Ecu 570,000; Arab Fund for Economic and Social Development, 100,000 Kuwaiti Dinars.

41. *Jerusalem Post*, July 23, 1973; A. Rabinovich, "Jerusalem runs short of water," *Jerusalem Post*, July 25, 1973 (hereinafter referred to as *Jerusalem Post*, July 25, 1973), and "Water trucks supply parts of Jerusalem," *Jerusalem Post*, July 27, 1973.

42. The Ishtaul borehole produced 2,500 cubic meters per hour and the Modi'in borehole produced 1,500 cubic meters per hour. Municipality of Jerusalem, Information and Public Relations Department, "Water," Brochure (Hebrew) (Jerusalem, no date but probably 1989) (hereinafter referred to as "Water").

43. The pumps had the capacity to shift water at 5,000 cubic meters per hour. Municipality of Jerusalem, "Water."

44. *Jerusalem Post*, July 25, 1973, and O. Berry, "Water-saving Plan pays off," *Jerusalem Post*, September 18, 1986.

45. Municipality of Jerusalem, Water Supply Department, Information and Public Relations Section, "Water in Jerusalem," Leaflet (Hebrew) (Jerusalem, no date but probably 1989).

46. J. Siegel, "Putting the Lid on spoiled water in J'lem reservoir," *Jerusalem Post*, May 21, 1976.

47. Municipality of Jerusalem, Brochure, "Water."

48. "Jerusalem drinks its own water," *Jerusalem Post*, February 25, 1973; and *Jerusalem Post*, February 23, 1973.

49. *Jerusalem Post*, February 28, 1973.

50. *State Comptroller's Annual Report*, No. 38, 1988, p. 374.

51. Ibid., p. 376.

52. Municipality of Jerusalem, Brochure, "Water." See also *Jerusalem Post*, July 12, 1974.

53. A. Rabinovich, "J'lem can now control its water supply," *Jerusalem Post*, August 12, 1976 (hereinafter referred to as *Jerusalem Post*, August 12, 1976).

54. Ministry of Environment, *Annual Report, 1991/92*.

55. Compiled from Municipality of Jerusalem, "Water" (Brochure) and

Statistical Yearbook of Jerusalem, 1990 (hereinafter referred to as *Yearbook (1990)*), p. 186.

56. Ministry of Environment, *Annual Report*, Paragraph 2.218.

57. Ibid.

58. Municipality of Jerusalem, *Yearbook (1990)*, p. 186.

59. *Jerusalem Post*, July 12, 1974; see also *Press Statement* by Co-ordinating Committee of International Non-Governmental Organizations, "Update: Water Crisis in the Occupied Territories," February 21, 1992.

60. State Comptroller, *Annual Report, 1988*, p. 375.

61. Municipality of Jerusalem, *Yearbook (1990)*, p. 186.

62. *Jerusalem Post*, August 27, 1976.

63. See the description of measures taken against Azariyya in S. Aburish, *Cry Palestine: Inside the West Bank* (London: Bloomsbury, 1991).

64. The Mayor's Advisor on Arab Affairs denies that the Municipality uses the provision of services for political reasons, although he concedes that members of the security services have argued for this to happen. See A. Cheshin, "East Jerusalem: Policy versus Reality," in A. Layish, ed., *The Arabs in Jerusalem: From the Late Ottoman Period to the Beginning of the 1990's—Religious, Social and Cultural Distinctiveness, Hamizrachi Hahedash* (Special Edition) 34, 1992 (Jerusalem: 1992), pp. 188–89.

65. Ben Arieh, *Old City*, p. 90.

66. Cited in Ben Arieh, *Old City*, pp. 90–91.

67. See Wilson, *Ordnance Survey*, p. 65.

68. Kark, *Ottoman Rule*, p. 131; Ben Arieh, *Old City*, p. 91.

69. Kark, *Ottoman Rule*, p. 131.

70. Ibid., p. 131.

71. Amiran, "Development," p. 28.

72. See for example Kendall, *City Plan*, pp. 80–88.

73. Khalil, *1947 to 1967*, p. 87.

74. Benvenisti, *Torn City*, p. 137.

75. A. Rabinovich, "Diplomacy decides where the sewage should go," *Jerusalem Post*, July 12, 1974 (hereinafter referred to as *Jerusalem Post*, July 12, 1974).

76. Ministry of Environment, *Annual Report*, Paragraph 2.22.

77. *Ibid.*, Paragraph 2.4. and Map produced by Balasha Jalon Consulting Engineers on sewage outflows in Jerusalem. See also estimates by Tahal cited in State Comptroller's Report, 1991, in G.F. Cashman, "Something smells in the Holy City," *Jerusalem Post*, May 1, 1992 (hereinafter referred to as *Jerusalem Post*, May 1, 1992).

78. *Jerusalem Post*, May 1, 1992; see also Ministry of Environment, *Annual Report*, Paragraph 3.322 that states that the plant actually deals with a sewage outflow 20,000 cubic meters daily, 7,000 in excess of capacity.

79. Cited in *Jerusalem Post*, May 1, 1992.

80. Ministry of Environment, *Annual Report*, Paragraph 2.3.

81. Municipality of Jerusalem, *Map of Sewage Masterplan, 1989*, Sheet No. 2 (September 1989) (hereinafter referred to as *Masterplan, 1989*).

82. *Jerusalem Post*, July 17, 1974 and December 16, 1985.

83. Ministry of Environment, *Annual Report*, Paragraph 5.2; see also *Jerusalem Post*, December 6, 1986.

84. Ministry of Interior, Environment Protection Services, *Fourth Annual Report: Environment in Israel* (1976) p. 16.

85. P. Golan and A. Bar-Am, "City's sewage is poisoning Judean desert beauty spot," *Jerusalem Post*, May 3, 1985 (hereinafter referred to as *Jerusalem Post*, May 3, 1985).

86. Ministry of Interior, *Fourth Annual Report: Environment in Israel, 1976* (Ministry of Interior, 1976), p. 16.

87. Article by Udi Arnon, "Sewage from the city polluted Wadi Qilt," *Kol Ha'ir*, 10, 1992.

88. State Comptroller's Report, 1991, cited in *Jerusalem Post*, May 1, 1992.

89. P. Golan, "City's sewage continues to poison wadis," *Jerusalem Post*, December 6, 1985 and *Jerusalem Post*, May 3, 1985.

90. *Jerusalem Post*, December 6, 1985. At one point when the odor of the sewage provoked too many complaints from the residents it was merely extended further away from the settlement.

91. *Jerusalem Post*, May 3, 1985.

92. *Jerusalem Post*, December 6, 1985.

93. *Jerusalem Post*, May 1, 1992.

94. Municipality of Jerusalem, *Master Plan Map, Balasha Jalon, Map*, and Ministry of Environment, *Annual Report*, Paragraph 2.2.

95. Romann and Weingrod, *Living Together*, p. 46.

96. Ibid., p. 45.

97. Ben Arieh, *Old City*, p. 36; Y. Ben Arieh, *Jerusalem in the 19th Century: Emergence of the New City* (Yad Izhak Ben-Zvi: Jerusalem, St. Martins Press: New York, 1989), p. 375 (hereinafter referred to as *New City*) Kark, "Ottoman Rule," p. 137.

98. Kark, "Ottoman Rule," p. 137.

99. *Jerusalem Post*, February 23, 1979.

100. Ibid.

101. See Benvenisti, *Torn City*, p. 45; and al-Khalil, *1947 to 1967*, pp. 90–92 for different views of the applicability of Article 8 of the Armistice Agreement to the supply of electricity across the Armistice Line.

102. Benvenisti, *Torn City*, p. 190.

103. Ministry of Environment, *Annual Report*, Paragraph 2.220.

104. The JEC is variously known as the Jerusalem District Electricity Company, the Jerusalem Arab Electricity Company, and the East Jerusalem Electricity Company.

105. Benvenisti, *Torn City*, p. 191.

106. Material supplied by the JEC in 1992.

107. D. Richardson, "Court ruling in electricity case," *Jerusalem Post*, February 17, 1981 (hereinafter referred to as *Jerusalem Post*, February 17, 1981) and J. Greenberg, "Electrical breakdown," *Jerusalem Post*, March 28, 1986 (hereinafter referred to as *Jerusalem Post*, March 28, 1986).

108. al-Khalil, *1947 to 1967*, p. 86.

109. Benvenisti, *Torn City*, p. 192.

110. A. Wolman, "Current affairs," *Jerusalem Post*, March 13, 1981 (hereinafter referred to as *Jerusalem Post*, March 13, 1981). It continued to use Arabic place names instead of Israeli ones, e.g., Jabal Mukabbir instead of East Talpiot. See Romann and Weingrod, *Living Together*, p. 49.

111. Many reforms were undertaken to improve the management structures and work practices of the JEC. Recommendations put forward by Rand Corporation consultants brought in by the former chairman, Anwar Nusayba, were also introduced; see *Jerusalem Post*, March 13, 1981.

112. This compares to the Israel Electricity Company who grew by 8% over the same period, in itself regarded as high. *Jerusalem Post*, February 23, 1979.

113. *Jerusalem Post*, February 17, 1981 and March 28, 1986.

114. Material supplied by the JEC in 1992. See also *Jerusalem Post*, February 23, 1979.

115. *Jerusalem Post*, March 28, 1986.

116. See discussions concerning rates in *Jerusalem Post*, March 28, 1986.

117. *Jerusalem Post*, March 13, 1981 and March 28, 1986.

118. Benvenisti, *Torn City*, p. 194; T. Prittie, *Whose Jerusalem* (London: Frederick Muller Ltd, 1981), p. 199. JEC officials defend this lack by pointing out there are numerous Palestinian villages in Israel that are still not supplied with electricity by the IEC decades after the establishment of the state of Israel.

119. *Jerusalem Post*, March 28, 1986.

120. Material supplied by the JEC in 1992.

121. The Jordanian-Palestinian Joint Committee, or Steadfastness Fund, has provided JD 9 million (approximately $60 million) over a ten-year period from 1979–88. See Joint Committee, *Achievements Report*, Table 10, p. 66.

122. *Jerusalem Post*, March 13, 1981.

123. *Jerusalem Post*, March 13, 1981.

124. *Jerusalem Post*, February 17, 1981.

125. *Jerusalem Post*, March 28, 1986.

126. Material supplied by the JEC in 1992.

127. Municipality of Jerusalem, *Yearbook (1990)*, p. 189.

6. The Politics of Religion in the Holy City

1. Benvenisti, *Torn City*, p. 81; D. Hirst, "Rush to Annexation: Israel in

Jerusalem," *Journal of Palestine Studies* 3:4 (Summer 1974): 4 (hereinafter referred to as "Annexation").

2. A. L. Tibawi, *The Islamic Pious Foundations in Jerusalem: Origin, History and Usurpation by Israel* (London: Iraqi Cultural Foundation, 1978), p. 35; R. Khatib, "The Judaization of Jerusalem and its Demographic Transformation," in *Jerusalem: The Key to World Peace* (London: Council of Europe, 1980), p. 114 (hereinafter referred to as "Judaization"). A survey carried out by George Dib and Fuad Jabber calculated that 290 rooms had been demolished; see G. Dib and F. Jabber, *Israel's Violation of Human Rights in the Occupied Territories: A Documented Report* (Beirut: Institute for Palestine Studies, 1970), pp. 217–27 (hereinafter referred to as *Violation*); Benvenisti, *Torn City*, p. 306, gives a figure of 619 people evicted and Hirst, "Annexation," p. 10 mentions 1,000 or 129 families. Dib and Jabber, *Violation*, p. 227 and the *Jerusalem Post*, June 19, 1967 estimate the number at 220 and 200 families respectively.

3. Israeli responses to this act are interesting. Benvenisti, for example, justified it in the following terms: "The move was the settling of an historic account with those who had harassed the Jewish people over the centuries, restricting it and humiliating it at its holiest place, as well as with those who had prevented access to the wall for nineteen years. The displaced inhabitants of the Mugrabi Quarter were not personally to blame, but it was their fate to be additional victims of the Arab-Israeli conflict." *Torn City*, p. 307.

Yosef Schweid, the municipal architect and town planner, expresses it similarly: "It was not just the practical aspect—the need to absorb large numbers of people [in front of the Wall], which was the deciding factor here; even more important was the sense of the historic necessity of the act, a sense of expiation and restitution, and that was what motivated the decision." "Unification," p. 111.

Teddy Kollek has admitted that he ordered the demolition of the Magharib quarter to be carried out quickly before international bodies like UNESCO and the UN could intervene. Shepherd, *The Mayor*, p. 21.

4. Cited in W. Zander, *Israel and the Holy Places of Christendom* (London: Weidenfeld and Nicholson, 1971), p. 98.

5. For a fuller discussion on this issue, see A. Gershon, *Israel, the West Bank and International Law* (London: Frank Cass, 1978), pp. 78–82; E. R. Cohen, *Human Rights in the Israeli-occupied Territories* (Manchester: Manchester University Press, 1985), pp. 37–56; and R. Shehadi, *The West Bank and the Rule of Law* (New York: International Jurists and Law in the Service of Man, 1980), pp. 10ff (hereinafter referred to as *Rule of Law*).

6. See chapter 2.

7. Benvenisti, *Torn City*, p. 263.

8. *Ha'aretz*, August 18, 1967; cited in E. Offenbacher, "Prayer on the Temple Mount," *The Jerusalem Quarterly*, no. 36 (Summer 1985): 132.

9. The only major site which both religions have in common in Jerusalem is the Tomb of David. There is a Christian chapel but the entire site is under the jurisdiction of the Ministry of Religious Affairs. Until 1948, the site was a waqf under the custodianship of the Dajani family who have sought a restoration of their rights. Interview with Awni Dajani, beneficiary of the Dajani waqf, international lawyer and former legal advisor to King Idris of Libya, November 22, 1989.

10. As a voluntary second leg of the main *haj* to Mecca and Medina a *ziyâra* to Jerusalem became a lesser but still important act of piety. See H. Lazarus-Yafeh, "The Sanctity of Jerusalem in Islam," in *Some Religious Aspects of Islam* (Leiden: Brill, 1981), pp. 58ff.; and H. S. Karmi, "How Holy is Palestine to the Muslims?" *Islamic Quarterly* 12:2 (April–June 1970): 5–6. For a discussion on the reasons for the enhanced status of Jerusalem as a pilgrimage center, see S. D. Goitein, "The Sanctity of Jerusalem and Palestine in Early Islam," in *Studies in Islamic History and Institutions* (Leiden: Brill, 1968). Goitein disagrees with many of the points made by Lazarus-Yafeh. See also Peters, *Jerusalem*, on the growth of the sanctity of Jerusalem and its pilgrimage traditions, pp. 374–75. For a somewhat more ambiguous view of these traditions see also his later book, Peters, *Jerusalem and Mecca: The Typology of the Holy City in the Near East* (New York: New York University Press, 1986), pp. 44–45.

11. Kupferschmidt, *Supreme Muslim Council*, p. 105; Massignon, "Documents," pp. 82–84; Trimingham, *Sufi Orders*, pp. 16–17.

12. Peters, *Jerusalem*, p. 335; for the role of Sufis in Jerusalem during the Mamluk period, see Burgoyne, *Mamluk Jerusalem*, p. 63. See also Barron, *Mohammedan Wakfs*, pp. 7–8, who writes that many Sufi institutions in Jerusalem were supported by the Khaski Sultan waqf. The Sinan Pasha waqf had properties throughout the eastern Mediterranean and a reader of the Qur'an in the Mosque of Omar was paid for out of funds from this waqf's property in Egypt, *ibid.*, p. 62 *n*17.

13. Dumper, *Islam and Israel*, p. 105.

14. See for example the waqf of Khaski Sultan which had villages in Lebanon and property in Tripoli endowed for the soup-kitchen in Jerusalem, S. H. Stephan, "An endowment deed of Khasseki el-Sultan, dated 24th May, 1922," *Quarterly of the Department of Antiquities in Palestine* 10 (1944): 183–86 (hereinafter referred to as "Khasseki el-Sultan"), and O. Peri, "The Waqf as an Instrument to Increase and Consolidate Political Power: The Case of Khasseki Sultan Waqf in Late 18th Century Ottoman Jerusalem," in G. Gilhar and J. Warburg, *Studies in Islamic Society* (Haifa: Haifa University Press, 1989), pp. 48–49.

15. Extremely important was the transfer of the powers of the top legal position in the Ottoman Empire to a Jerusalem Court of Appeal. See F. M. Goadby, "Religious Communities and Courts in Palestine," *Tulane Law*

Review 8:2 (1934): 225; R. H. Eisenman, *Islamic Law in Palestine and Israel: A History of the Tanzimat and the Shari'a in the British Mandate and the Jewish State* (Leiden: Brill, 1978), pp. 17–18; Khayat, "Waqfs in Palestine and Israel—From the Ottoman Reforms to the Present," Ph.D. Dissertation, the Americn University, Washington, D.C, 1982, pp. 91–92. For a history of the incorporation of Islamic law into Mandate and Israeli legislation, and for the changes in *shari'a* law itself, see Eisenman, *Islamic Law*, and A. Layish, "Muslim Religious Jurisdiction in Israel," *Asian and African Studies* (Journal of the Israel Oriental Society) 1 (1965) (hereinafter referred to as "Religious Jurisdiction"). For the political aspects of these changes see Y. Porath, *The Emergence of the Palestinian Arab National Movement, 1918–1929* (London: Frank Cass, 1977) (hereinafter referred to as *Emergence*), pp. 187–88 and 194–95. The authority to appoint *muftis* was also transferred to the Supreme Muslim Council; see *Committee for Moslem Religious Affairs*, p. 7.

16. See Barron, *Mohammedan Wakfs*, pp. 49–50 for details of the formation of the electoral college.

17. Defence (Muslim Awkaf) Regulations, 1937. See also Lesch, *Arab Politics*, pp. 121–23; Porath, *National Movement*, p. 172.

18. This is a view shared by Kupferschmidt, *Supreme Muslim Council*, p. 258. See also A. Layish, "Mahkama," *Encyclopedia Islamica* (forthcoming) (hereinafter referred to as "Mahkama"); and Y. Reitter, *Waqf in Jerusalem, 1948–1990* (Jerusalem: Jerusalem Institute for Israel Studies, 1991) (hereinafter referred to as *Waqf*), p. 12.

19. Reitter, *Waqf*, pp. 12–13.

20. Official Gazette, Law No 26 (Amman 1966). Regulation No. 142 Article 8, iii–v, Article 9, iii, iv, vi, Article 47.

21. A. Layish, "The Muslim Waqf in Jerusalem since 1967: Beneficiaries and Management," in "The Arabs in Jerusalem: From the Late Ottoman Period to the Beginning of the 1990's—Religious, Social and Cultural Distinctiveness," in *Hamizrah Hehadash* 34 (1992): 97–98.

22. However, the Palestinian Muslim community of Israel did have a formal recognized hierarchy. See Dumper, *Islam and Israel*, chapters 3 and 4.

23. See L. Mayer, and J. Pinkerfield, *Some Principal Muslim Religious Buildings in Israel* (Jerusalem: Government Printer, 1950) pp. 14 and 16; Reiter, *Waqf*, p. 31.

24. Benvenisti, *Torn City*, pp. 91–92.

25. See Farhi, "Muslim Council," and also Reiter, *Waqf*, pp. 15–16.

26. Benvenisti, *Torn City*, p. 91.

27. Interview with Hassan Tahbub, Director-General of Awqaf Administration, 1960–1983, October 4, 1988.

28. For a full exposition of the legal status of waqf property and administration in Israel, see A. Layish, "The Muslim Waqf in Israel," *Asian and African Studies* (Journal of the Israel Oriental Society) 2 (1966): 41–76; and R. H.

Eisenman, *Islamic Law*, pp. 224ff. For a critique of Israeli policies with regard to the waqf system see Dumper, *Islam and Israel*, chapters 3 and 4.

29. Benvenisti, *Torn City*, p. 284.

30. The full text of the protest sent to the Israeli government can be found in Institute for Palestine Studies, *Resistance of the Western Bank of Jordan to Israeli Occupation* (Beirut: Institute for Palestine Studies, 1967), pp. 11–14.

31. For example, prominent Muslim clergy, *'ulama'*, from the Nablus region wrote: "The residents and *qadis* of the city of Nablus declare their support for your insistence on the Arab character of Jerusalem, which is an integral part of the West Bank of the Kingdom of Jordan, and endorse the contents of the memorandum submitted by the inhabitants of Jerusalem on 24th July, 1967 in which they reject, together with all the people of this country, all measures taken by the Israeli authorities to detach the city of Jerusalem from Arab territory and to place it under Israeli control." Cited in ibid., p. 22.

32. Layish, "Waqf in Jerusalem," p. 111.

33. See *Bayan, 1967–76* (Jerusalem: al-awqaf al-islamiyya, no date), p. 6; and Daqqaq, "Square One," p. 72.

34. Interview with Hassan Tahbub, May 3, 1989; see also Daqqaq, "Square One," p. 72, and Farhi, "Muslim Council," pp. 7f, who implies that this step was taken to assuage the "rebelliousness" of regional religious leaders.

35. Legal and Administrative Matters (Regulation) Law (Consolidated Version), 1970, *Laws of the State of Israel* 24 (1969–1970): 144–52.

36. Reiter, *Waqf*, p. 34.

37. Ibid., p. 17.

38. Ibid., p. 18.

39. It is fairly comic for an outsider to learn that the Israeli *qadi* has confirmed the officially unrecognized Jordanian-salaried Director of the (East Jerusalem) Awqaf Administration as the official *mutawalli* of the Khanqah al-Salahiyya, a waqf in the Old City. Reiter, *Waqf*, p. 17.

40. Y. Bar Sela, "Law Enforcement in the Eastern Sector of Jerusalem," in O. Ahimeir, *Jerusalem—Aspects of Law* (Jerusalem: Jerusalem Institute for Israel Studies, 1983) Discussion Paper No.3, Second revised Edition, pp. xx–xxi.

41. See for example, Layish, "Waqf in Jerusalem," and Reiter, *Waqf*.

42. See Dumper, *Islam and Israel*, pp. 107–123 for an extended exploration of this theme.

43. See for example the description of the quarter made by the Muslim historian Mujir id-din, cited in Peters, *Jerusalem*, p. 392.

44. Tibawi, *Pious Foundations*, pp. 45–46. Ben Arieh, *Old City*, pp. 316ff.

45. See for example, T. Tobler, *Denkblatter Aus Jerusalem* (Constance, 1853), pp. 125–26, and J. T. Barclay, *The City of the Great King: or Jerusalem as it was, as it is, as it is to be* (Philadelphia, 1858), pp. 432–44; cited in Y. Ben Arieh, *Jerusalem in the 19th Century: The Old City* (New York: St. Martin's Press, 1984), pp. 317–18.

46. See 'Arif al-'Arif, *mufassal tarikh al-quds* (Jerusalem: Ma'aari Printers, 1986), pp. 431–32. See also C. Ritter, *The Comparative Geography of Palestine and the Sinaitic Peninsula* (Edinburgh, 1866), p. 191, cited in Tibawi, *Pious Foundations*, p. 44. Ben Arieh is quite explicit about this too and attributes the *khazaka* system of rental in the Jewish quarter to this fact. The *khazaka* system was set up to prevent Palestinian Arab landlords and waqf administrators from exploiting the great pressure on housing, as a result of continual immigration, by preventing Jews from competing with each other over rents. Ben Arieh, *Old City*, pp. 327–28.

47. It is not entirely clear from the text whether he means 20 percent of the traditional smaller quarter or 20 percent of the larger expanded post-1968 quarter. By referring to the pre-1948 quarter it is assumed he means the smaller version. Benvenisti, *Torn City*, p. 239.

48. Interview with Antony Bakrijian, historian, former UNRWA official and resident of the Old City, March 10, 1989. See also Graham-Brown, "Jerusalem," *Middle East*, no. 136 (February 1986), p. 48; Benvenisti, *Torn City*, p. 44; Tibawi, *Pious Foundations*, p. 38. See also Plascov, *The Palestinian Refugees in Jordan, 1948–1957* (London: Frank Cass, 1981), pp. 68, 109, 112.

49. Statement by R. Khatib, deported Mayor of Jerusalem, published in Dib and Jabber, *Violation*. Document no. 67, p. 176.

50. See Dib and Jabber, *Violation*, p. 176. Figures for *waqf dhurri* are harder to ascertain but from my own fieldwork at least fifty-five properties of this kind were expropriated, including sixteen from the Khalidi family, thirteen from the al-'Asali family, and eight from the Ja'ouni family. Other figures for *waqf dhurri* are Dajani—three, Hariri—one, Daqqaq—one, Abdo—one, Hallaq—one, Khatib—two, Husayni (one branch)—one, Quttayni—three. No claim as to the completeness of these figures, therefore, is being made. For example, there are certainly more *waqf dhurri* properties than have been counted by this researcher.

51. Cited in Dib and Jabber, *Violation*, p. 178.

52. See for example, *The Christian Science Monitor*, March 5, 1975, "A bulldozer battle for Jerusalem"; *International Herald Tribune*, April 21, 1975, "Arabs fighting ouster in Jerusalem Old City"; *Tages-Anzeiger*, June 2, 1975, "Planners drive Arabs out of Jerusalem"; *Jerusalem Post*, January 16, 1977, "The case of the hole in the wall"; and the letter by Anglican clergy in Jerusalem that this latter article prompted in *Jerusalem Post*, January 31, 1977. In some cases where tenants refused to leave they found that access to their homes was cut off, excavations carried out around them, courtyard and house walls demolished, and that they had to live with the constant noise of drilling and banging and the danger of falling masonry. In the end nearly all the Palestinians left.

53. Interview with 'Isam Anani, July 30, 1985.

54. *al-Fajr* (English weekly) May 17, 1987, p. 14.

55. *Jerusalem Post*, January 5, 1975, "Law Report" (Sapolinsky v. Minister of Finance).

56. See for example resolution No. 15C/3.343 of October–November 1968, calling on Israel to preserve cultural properties especially in the Old City of Jerusalem, or UNESCO Decision No. 88 Ex/4.3.1. of 1971, calling upon Israel to preserve cultural properties, especially Christian and Islamic sites in the Old City of Jerusalem, and UNESCO Decision No. 89, Ex/4.4.1 of June 1972, deploring the continuation of Israeli archaeological excavations in Jerusalem. *UN Resolutions on Palestine, 1947–72* (Beirut: Institute for Palestine Studies, 1974), pp. 141ff. See also memoranda and letters sent to the Israeli Military Commander by the Higher Islamic Board in Shaykh Sa'd al-Din al-'Alami, ed., *al-hay'at al-islamiyya al-'ulya—watha'iq* (Jerusalem: Dar al-Tabi'a al-'Arabiyya, n.d.).

57. Figures supplied by the Jordanian-Palestinian Joint Committee show that 1,285,031 Jordanian Dinars (approximately $10 million) were transferred from their funds to the Awqaf Administration's Jerusalem District. The huge discrepancy between this figure and table 6.1 can be explained by the fact that the Joint Committee funds were used for more general purposes. For example, nearly one-fifth of the funds (330,000 JDs) were spent on salaries of guards in al-Haram al-Sharif. Joint Committee, *Achievements Report, 1979–1988*, table 7, p. 60.

58. This emphasis on education is exemplified by the Jerusalem *mudiriyya* where the Awqaf Administration runs a number of elementary schools and secondary schools, supports religious instruction in other non-Awqaf Administration secondary schools, and has established a *shari'a* college and several *dur al-qur'an* and *dur al-hadith*. See '*Idarat al-awqaf al-islamiyya al-'ama, bayan: al-awqaf al-islamiyya ti al-dafa al-gharbiyaa, 1967–1976 (Jerusalem: da'ira al-awqaf al-islamiyya, n.d.), pp. 20–25 (hereinafter Bayan I)*, and ibid., *1977–1982*, pp. 12, 14 (hereinafter *Bayan II*). One very important spinoff from these activities has been that since many of these institutions are located in or around al-Haram al-Sharif significant numbers of young men have been attracted to the Old City and the Haram courtyard and their very physical presence serves as a deterrent against attempts by militant Israeli nationalists to establish some kind of Israeli foothold in the Haram courtyard. See *Jerusalem Post*, May 22, 1987, article entitled "Police investigate al-Aqsa college."

59. *Bayan II*, pp. 51–54, 60–63, 68–71, 74–78, 81–83, 87–91.

60. See Nijm, *'ard tarikhi*, pp. 29–30.

61. Two surveys, one by the British School of Archaeology in Jerusalem and another under the auspices of the Arab League, drew attention to the poor condition of many of these waqf properties. British School of Archaeology in Jerusalem, *The Architecture of Islamic Jerusalem* (London: British School of Archaeology in Jerusalem, 1976); and M. Burgoyne, *Mamluk Jerusalem: An*

Architectural Study (London: World of Islam Trust, 1987); also R. Nijm ed., *Kunuz al-Quds* (Amman, 1983).

62. The work of the Department is divided into several parts: a) an historical research unit that delves into the *shari'a* court records and the Haram Library archives to discover the foundation, development, and use of a particular building; b) a photographic and surveying unit that draws up detailed maps of the main features and structural history of the building; and c) a material and design unit that prepares the different stages of the restoration work—including, for example, finding the correct existing sources of stone so that the restoration masonry work is authentic. Interviews with Yusuf Natshe, July 27 and August 8, 1985. See also Y. Natshe, *al-turba al-kilaniyya* (The Kilaniyya Mausoleum) (Jerusalem: Islamic Waqf Department, 1979); see Nijm, *'ard tarikhi*, p. 33, who says the department was set up in 1983.

The department consists of three archaeologists and two architects as well as a number of photographers and surveyors. This excludes the contract laborers and two or three stone masons who have been trained in Mamluk and Ottoman masonry design by the department. The necessity for skilled labor and for specialist equipment and materials makes the program an expensive one. For example, al-Muzhiriyya cost JD 17,000 and al-Kilaniyya cost JD 30,000. Interview with Yusuf Natshe, August 8, 1985.

63. Interview with Adnan Hussayni, July 27, 1985; see also, M. Burgoyne, "The Continued Survey of the Ribat Kurd/Madrasa Jawhariya Complex in Tariq Bab al-Hadid, Jerusalem," *Levant* 6 (1974), p. 51. The Israeli Chief Archaeologist in Jerusalem argues that such damage is caused by the drying-out of the soil brought about by the proper drainage and sewage disposal introduced by the Israeli Jerusalem Municipality. Interview with Dan Bahat, Chief Archaeologist of Jerusalem for the Israeli government, March 19, 1987.

64. Interview with Adnan Hussayni, March 31, 1987; see also S. Graham-Brown, "Jerusalem," *Middle East*, No. 136 (February 1986) p. 49.

65. See R. Thomas, "Demography and Settler Politics in the Old City of Jerusalem," *Khamsin* 1 (1989): 82–92, for a more detailed exposition of this argument. The question of the legality of the Department of Islamic Archaeology work, for example, has practical implications for its restoration program. By declaring the Old City an antiquities site (as did the British Mandate government) all restoration work must have the consent and approval of the Israeli Chief Archaeologist for the Old City, Law of Antiquities, *Government Gazette*, August 31, 1967, p. 2159.

66. Interview with Ambassador Awn Khasawneh, Legal Advisor to H.R.H. Crown Prince Hassan of Jordan, March 31, 1993, Amman.

67. It should be noted that none of the current Palestinian back-up teams for the peace delegation comprise any significant Muslim religious leaders. More recently, with despair and frustration with the peace process growing,

and with King Hussein continuing his tentative steps toward greater democracy, greater Jordanian involvement in the final arrangements for the Muslim Holy Places has not been ruled out by Palestinians.

68. In very generalized terms, the Latins, or Roman Catholics, were favored during the Crusader period, while the Armenians were dominant during the Ayyubid and Mamluk periods. See K. Hintlian, *History of the Armenians in the Holy Land* (Jerusalem: Armenian Patriarchate Printing Press, 1989), p. 39.

69. Palestine Order in Council of 1992 stipulated that "It is well understood that no alterations can be made in the Status Quo of the Holy Places."

70. See examples in S. P. Colbi, "The Christian Establishment in Jerusalem," in Kraemer, *Problems and Prospects*, pp. 162–70 (hereinafter referred to as "Christian Establishment)."

71. Ben Arieh, *Old City*, pp. 188–89.

72. See Chapter 3 for figures.

73. Colbi, "Christian Establishment," p. 171.

74. Ibid., p. 172.

75. Ibid., p. 171; see also W. Zander, *Holy Places*, pp. 68–71.

76. Interview with Naomi Teasdale, Advisor to the Mayor on Christian Affairs, March 30, 1993. See also Shepherd, *The Mayor*, p. 70.

77. G. Talhami, "Between Development and Preservation: Jerusalem under Three Regimes," *American-Arab Affairs* (Spring 1986), p. 103. In 1965, the purchase of land by churches was completely forbidden. Without presenting her sources Talhami argues that acquisitions by the churches continued surreptitiously, since in 1949 it was estimated that 91 plots of commercial land belonged to the Christian churches but by 1969 they owned 392 plots.

78. Colbi, "Christian Establishment," p. 174. Interview with Naomi Teasdale, March 30, 1993.

79. Benvenisti, *Torn City*, p. 267.

80. Ibid., p. 101.

81. These regulations should not be confused with the "code of behavior" regulations one often sees at Holy Places issued by the Ministry of Religious Affairs. See ibid., p. 104.

82. Very crudely, the Department of External Christian Relations in the Ministry of Foreign Affairs is felt to be more concerned with reaching an accommodation with the Vatican than other Israeli bodies due to the Vatican's influence in the Third World, Latin America, Central America, and in the United Nations.

83. Patient Israeli diplomacy has succeeded in diluting this position to a call for "international guarantees" for the Holy Places. Benvenisti, *Torn City*, pp. 266–70.

84. See *Census of Population and Housing, 1967* (Jerusalem: Central Bureau of Statistics, 1968), table 4, p. 10.

85. These figures exclude clergy (religious?) students, and foreign

Christians. B. Sabella, "Christian emigration: A Comparison of the Jerusalem, Ramallah and Bethlehem areas." Unpublished survey for the al-Liqa Institute, Jerusalem, 1992, p. 3.

86. 1983 figures are taken from Kimhi, Hyman, and Savitzky, *Transition*, p. 10; 1992 figures are based upon Sabella's estimates.

87. The decline in numbers of Christians in Jerusalem is the subject of many Middle East Council of Churches discussions and international Christian conferences. See for example the declaration of the Cumberland Lodge Conference, "Christians in the Holy Land," May 28–30, 1993; cited in *Middle East International*, No. 452, June 11, 1993.

88. Shepherd, *The Mayor*, pp. 69–70.

89. It should be borne in mind that in this the government was in turn greatly assisted by the continuation of age-old disputes over precedence, custodianship and access. Interview with Daniel Rossing, former Director of the Christian Division of the Ministry of Religious Affairs, January 14, 1993.

90. Benvenisti, *Torn City*, p. 271.

91. Shepherd, *The Mayor*, p. 77.

92. Interview with Naomi Teasdale, March 30, 1993.

93. Shepherd, *The Mayor*, p. 75.

94. Shepherd, *The Mayor*, p. 72.

95. Benvenisti, *Torn City*, p. 260. Some members of the Palestinian congregation suspect that the land around Mar Elias, close to the Tantur Institute, which was expropriated by the Israelis was actually sold to them but an expropriation announced to cover the Patriarchate.

96. During the Mandate period this point caused a number serious disputes which led the Mandate authorities to make a special study of the situation.

97. Recommendations and Resolutions of the Arab Orthodox conference held in Jerusalem on October 23, 1992.

98. Ibid.

99. Ibid.

100. See V. Azarya, *The Armenian Quarter of Jerusalem* (London: University of California Press, 1984) chapters 4 and 5. See also Hintlian, *Armenians*, pp. 46–50.

101. Azarya, *Armenian Quarter*, pp. 114–17.

102. Shepherd, *The Mayor*, p. 75.

103. One can imagine how useful it was to have a senior dignitary from one of the Eastern Orthodox churches extolling the virtues of an Israeli administration over a unified city. Ajamian also voted against World Council of Churches conference resolutions that were critical of Israel and was hailed by Israelis as a good friend of Israel.

104. Ibid., p. 76.

105. Despite being deposed Ajamian continued to appear at Israeli receptions and was granted passage to Jordan without customs checks.

106. Shepherd, *The Mayor*, pp. 160–62.

107. See Azarya, *Armenian Quarter*, p. 218, *n*18. See also Shepherd, *The Mayor*, p. 76.

108. For further detail of Vatican-Israeli relations see F. J. Khoury, "The Jerusalem Question and the Vatican," in H. F. Ellis, ed., *The Vatican, Islam and the Middle East* (Syracuse, New York: Syracuse University Press, 1987), pp. 143–62; G. E. Irani, *Papacy and the Middle East: The Role of the Papacy in the Arab-Israeli conflict, 1962–1984* (Notre Dame, Indiana: University of Notre Dame, 1986); and L. Rokach, *The Catholic Church and the Question of Palestine* (London: al-Saqi, 1987).

109. See discussion of this theme in F. Khouri, "The Jerusalem Question and the Vatican," in Ellis ed., *The Vatican, Islam and the Middle East*; Irani, *The Papacy and the Middle East* chapter 2.

110. A short profile on Sabbah can be found in D. Tsimhoni, "The Latin Patriarchate of Jerusalem from the First Half of the 19th Century to Present Times: Institutional and Social Aspects," in Layish, *Arabs*, p. 127. For his role in the intifada, see pp. 133ff.

111. Shepherd, *The Mayor*, p. 73.

112. Benvenisti, *Torn City*, p. 260; see also Shepherd, *The Mayor*, p. 73.

113. Shepherd, *The Mayor*, p. 71.

114. In 1992, the Coptic Orthodox Church initiated proceedings again, this time to obtain an injunction that the Israeli government had to decide whether to enforce the Supreme Court ruling. The high court ruled that the court cannot force the government to decide. In January 1993 the government established a new committee to look into the matter. Further pressure will be placed upon the government when, as it seems likely, the Coptic Orthodox church will apply to the Supreme Court to obtain the injunction it seeks.

115. See Tsimhoni, "The Latin Patriarchate," pp. 126ff.

116. See Documentation Section, *MECC Perspectives*, no. 8, July 1990, pp. 75–76. The statement was signed by: His Beatitude (HB) Diadorus, Greek Orthodox Patriarch of Jerusalem; HB Michel Sabbah, Latin Patriarch of Jerusalem; Bishop Samir Kafity, President Bishop, Episcopal Church in Jerusalem and the Middle East; Archbishop Lutfi Laham, Patriarchal Vicar, Greek Catholic Patriarchate of Jerusalem; HB Yeghishe Derderian, Armenian Orthodox Patriarch of Jerusalem; Bishop Naim Nassar, Evangelical Lutheran Church in Jordan; HB Basilios, Coptic Orthodox Patriarch of Jerusalem; Archbishop Dionysios Behnam Jijjawi, Syrian Orthodox Patriarchal Vicar of Jerusalem; Most Reverend Father Cechitelli (Order of the Franciscan Monks), Custos of the Holy Land.

117. Interview with Naomi Teasdale, March 30, 1993.

118. Initially the good rapport between Mayor Kollek and the then-Foreign Minister, Moshe Dayan, meant that the Municipality and the District

Governor, Raphael Levy, were given a free rein in their dealings with the churches; see Shepherd, *The Mayor*, p. 74.

119. Shepherd, *The Mayor*, p. 70.

120. See M. Dumper, "Israeli Settlement," pp. 32–53.

121. They claimed that the property had been sold to them by an Armenian tenant via a Panamanian company. See *Jerusalem Post*, "Casualties reported over Old City settlement," April 17, 1990.

122. An open letter from the President to the Patriarch was published in the *Jerusalem Post*, May 18, 1990. The Patriarch's reply was issued in a press release of May 28, 1990, but not published. The dispute also spilled over into the diplomatic domain when the Patriarch called on the Greek government to suspend attempts to improve Greek-Israeli relations. See *Jerusalem Post*, May 16, 1990.

123. See G. Halsell, *Prophecy and Politics: Militant Evangelists on the Road to Nuclear War* (Westport: Lawrence Hill, 1986), pp. 96ff.

124. Some this land was a Khalidi family waqf; interview with Haider Khalidi, *mutawalli* of the Khalidi waqf in Jerusalem, May 23, 1985.

125. Among the areas of contention was the way the campus itself is lighted. At night the lights of the stairwell bisect those of the main campus thoroughfare making the sign of a crucifix. Much ingenuity was spent devising a system of blinds to break up the continuity of the lines so both the Muslim and Jewish religious communities would not be offended. See D. Rossing, "Interfaith Relations in Israel Today," *1988 Waley-Cohen Lecture* (London: Council of Christians and Jews, 1988), p. 2. It should also be mentioned that prior to receiving permission to build the campus, the Mormon church had donated a large sum of money to the Jerusalem Foundation which supports the work of the Municipality.

126. All Jews residing in Palestine were entitled to a proportion of these funds. Allocation was in the hands of the *rishon-le-zion* and since many of the Jews were impoverished it acted as a powerful form of religious, political and social control. See Ben Arieh, *Old City*, pp. 283–84; see also p. 360. A brief summary of the system can be found in R. Nyrop, *Israel: A Country Study* (Washington, D.C.: The American University, 1979), pp. 66–67.

127. Ben Arieh, *Old City*, p. 290.

128. J. Halper, "Jewish Ethnicity in Jerusalem," in A. L. Eckhardt, ed., *Jerusalem: City of the Ages* (New York: University Press of America, 1987), p. 186.

129. See Kark's monograph on this subject. R. Kark, *Jerusalem Neighbourhoods: Planning and By-Laws (1855–1930)* (Jerusalem: Magnes Press, 1991). See also reservations expressed in my review in *Journal of Palestine Studies* 22:1 (Autumn 1992): 108–109.

130. Ashkenazi-Sephardi divisions were also reflected in these new neighborhoods. For example, the first construction, Mishkenot Sha'ananim, was a

row of twenty apartments divided in half, so that one side was Ashkenazi and the other was Sephardi. See Halper, "Ethnicity," p. 188.

131. Nyrop, *Israel: A Country Study*, p. 73.

132. Israel Pocket Library, *Jerusalem*, p. 147.

133. Ben Arieh, *Old City*, pp. 374–75.

134. Details of this incident can be found in Porath, *Emergence*, pp. 259–73; P. Mattar, *The Mufti of Jerusalem* (New York: Columbia University Press, 1988) (hereinafter referred to as *The Mufti*), pp. 33–49. Mattar argues that the Mufti became involved only after the incident had already flared up and during the course of the whole affair was reluctant to antagonize the government. See also A. Lesch, *Arab Politics in Palestine, 1917–1939: The Frustration of a Nationalist Movement* (London: Cornell University Press, 1979), pp. 208–12; E. Lundsten, "Wall Politics: Zionist and Palestinian Strategies in Jerusalem, 1928," *Journal of Palestine Studies* 8:1 (Autumn 1978).

135. While some ultra-Orthodox refused to accept such funding from a "heretical" state, the majority of the sects did. The best known of the sects that did not accept state funding are the Eda Haredit, or Haredi Community, comprising mostly Satmar hassidim, of which a small branch are the notorious anti-Zionists, Neturei Karta. Ironically, this sect, or collectivity of sects, is able to survive financially only because other ultra-orthodox sects do accept state funding thereby reducing the demand on the funds available for ultra-orthodox groups from non-state sources. See M. Friedman, *The Haredi (Ultra-Orthodox) Society: Sources, Trends and Processes* (Jerusalem: Jerusalem Institute for Israel Studies, 1991).

136. Israel Pocket Library, *Jerusalem*, p. 183.

137. Shepherd, *The Mayor*, p. 85.

138. The desecration of these synagogues and also of the cemeteries on the Mount of Olives is often cited by Israelis as evidence of Jordanian government anti-Semitism. In turn, the Jordanians say that such acts were not government policy but the acts of individuals. They also argue that much of the damage was caused by the positioning of machine-gun batteries in the synagogues and by later Israeli shelling. In much the same way, Palestinian Muslims in Israel highlight the conversion of mosques into nightclubs and cemeteries into shopping complexes which occurred inside Israel after 1948.

139. See W. Zander, "Truce on the Temple Mount," *New Outlook* 19 (July/ August 1976): 15.

140. Zander, "Truce," p. 15. The reason for the Jewish interdiction was to prevent Jews from unwittingly committing an act of sacrilege by stepping on the Holy of Holies, the precise location of which was not known.

141. Interviews with Adnan al-Hussayni, former Director of Department of Engineering and Maintenance, Awaqf Administration, July 27, 1985, and Dan Bahat, former Chief Archaeologist of Jerusalem, Israeli Ministry of Education, March 19, 1987.

142. Personal observations, March 1993.

143. See Dumper, "Israeli Settlement," pp. 41–51.

144. See Kimhi, Reichman, and Schweid, "Greater Jerusalem," 4.6.2.

145. See Yosseph Shilhav's example of the use of elevators in Y. Shilhav, "Spatial Strategies of the 'Haredi' Population in Jerusalem," *Socio-Economic Planning and Science* 18:6 (1984): 412.

146. Ibid., p. 412.

147. See Shepherd, *The Mayor*, pp. 80–81.

148. Shepherd, *The Mayor*, p. 85.

149. Friedman, *Haredi Society*, pp. vi–vii.

7. The Economic Development of Jerusalem

1. Ben Arieh, *New City*, p. 391.

2. M. Romann, "The Economic Development of Jerusalem in Recent Times," in Amiran, Shachar, and Kimhi, *Urban Geography* (hereinafter referred to as "Economic Development"), p. 92.

3. See Dumper, *Islam and Israel*, chapter 6 for the role of Muslim waqfs in the economic development of Jerusalem.

4. Ben Arieh, *Old City*, p. 39.

5. Ben Arieh, *New City*, p. 396.

6. Ben Arieh, *New City*, pp. 366ff., 380.

7. Roman, "Economic Development," p. 93.

8. Ibid.

9. Ibid., p. 97. See also the discussion of Mandate plans for preserving the character of Jerusalem in chapter 3 above.

10. Ibid., p. 97.

11. Cited in ibid., p. 94.

12. Ibid., p. 94.

13. See Dumper, *Islam and Israel* for examples.

14. Romann, "Economic Development," p. 94. Despite this relative boom for Jerusalem, field data indicate that there was still a greater concentration of construction activity in the Jewish sectors in Haifa and Tel Aviv, idem., p. 97.

15. Ibid., p. 98.

16. A. Shachar, "The Functional Structure of Jerusalem," in Amiran, Shachar and Kimhi, *Urban Geography*, pp. 87, 89.

17. Romann, "Economic Development," p. 101.

18. Kimhi and Hyman, *Socio-Economic Development*, p. 66.

19. Romann, "Economic Development," p. 103.

20. Central Bureau of Statistics, *Population and Housing Census, 1961*, Publication No. 24; cited in Romann, "Economic Development," p. 98. In 1967, the government employed 12,500 workers (excluding teachers, judges and police) and the Hebrew University had approximately 4,500 staff. Other

large employers included that Hadassah Hospital and the Jewish Agency offices. M. Romann, *An Economic and Social Survey of Greater Jerusalem* (Jerusalem: Maurice Falk Institute for Economic Research, Dec. 1967), p. 16 (hereinafter referred to as *Greater Jerusalem*).

21. Romann, "Economic Development," p. 101.

22. Shachar, "Functional Structure," p. 98.

23. See Tables xiii and xv in Romann, "Economic Development," pp. 102–103.

24. Shachar, "Functional Structure," p. 87.

25. Romann, "Economic Development," p. 100.

26. Ibid., p. 100.

27. Kimhi and Hyman, *Socio-Economic Development*, p. 67. In 1965, a peak year for housing construction, there were 3,070 housing starts.

28. The Municipality of Arab Jerusalem only constituted 7.5% of the population of the West Bank. Romann, *Greater Jerusalem*, p. 18.

29. Efrat, p. 58.

30. Romann, "Economic Development," p. 104.

31. Kimhi and Hyman, *Socio-Economic Development*, p. 48.

32. Kimhi and Hyman, *Socio-Economic Survey*, p. 58.

33. More than 500,000 came from Arab and Muslim countries. See Romann, *Greater Jerusalem*, p. 21.

34. Ibid., p. 58.

35. Romann, "Economic Development," p. 105.

36. The Jordanian government only employed approximately 500 people during this period. See Romann, *Greater Jerusalem*, p. 22.

37. Romann, *Greater Jerusalem*, pp. 18–19.

38. Cited in Romann, "Economic Development," p. 104.

39. Romann, *Greater Jerusalem*, pp. 22–23.

40. Romann, *Greater Jerusalem*, pp. 8, 42–43. See also Romann and Weingrod, *Living Together Separately*, p. 100.

41. Romann, *Greater Jerusalem*, pp. 113, 159.

42. Ibid., p. 100.

43. Ibid., *Greater Jerusalem*, p. 10.

44. Ibid., p. 47. Most of these were given employment in the lower echelon of the bureaucracy.

45. Kimhi and Hyman, *Socio-Economic Survey*, p. 31. See also Kimhi, Hyman, and Savitzky, *Transition*, p. 25.

46. See Kimhi, Hyman, and Savitzky, *Transition*, figure 14, p. 26.

47. It is worth noting that during the same period only 21 percent of employed people in Tel Aviv were employed in the government and public sector. See I. Kimhi, "Outline of the Development of Jerusalem, 1988–1993," in *Urban Geography* (hereafter referred to as "Outline)".

48. Kimhi and Hyman, *Socio-Economic Survey*, p. 39.

49. Ibid., p. 44.

50. Ibid., pp. 44–45; see also Kimhi, Hyman, and Savitzky, *Transition*, p. 34.

51. Kimhi and Hyman, *Socio-Economic Survey*, p. 27.

52. M. Romann, "Centre versus Periphery: The Development of the Jewish and Arab Sector in Unified Jerusalem since 1967," *The Economic Quarterly* 33, no. 128 (in Hebrew), p. 509.

53. I. Kimhi and B. Hyman. "Demographic and Economic Developments in Jerusalem since 1967," in J. Kraemer, *Jerusalem: Problems and Prospects* (New York: Praeger, 1980) (hereinafter referred to as "Demographic and Economic Developments"), p. 143.

54. Kimhi and Hyman, "Demographic and Economic Developments," p. 143.

55. Kimhi, "Outline," p. 20.

56. Kimhi, Hyman, and Savitzky, *Transition*, pp. 10, 27–28.

57. Ibid., figure 15, p. 27.

58. Kimhi, Hyman, and Savitzky, *Transition*, p. 30.

59. Ibid., p. 28.

60. See *Jerusalem Post*, August 7, 1992, p. 21.

61. Kimhi, Hyman, and Savitzky, *Transition*, p. 28. See also the article by Evelyn Gordon, "High-Tech on the Mount," *Jerusalem Post*, August 7, 1992 (magazine section).

62. D. Felsenstein, *The Development of Science-based Industries in Jerusalem* (Jerusalem: Jerusalem Institute for Israel Studies, 1988) Research Report No. 1 (Hebrew). An English summary can be found in *Israel Studies* (Review of the Jerusalem Institute for Israel Studies) (Fall 1988): 40–41.

63. Jerusalem Promotional Supplement, "Jerusalem Development Authority—an address for nearly everything," *Israeli Business and Technology* (Sept.–Oct. 1991), pp. 11–16.

64. Kimhi, "Outline," p. 28.

65. Kimhi and Hyman, *Socio-Economic Survey*, p. 50.

66. Romann and Weingrod, *Living Together Separately*, p. 122.

67. Kimhi, Hyman, and Savitzky, *Transition*, p. 30.

68. Romann and Weingrod, *Living Together Separately*, p. 119.

69. Romann, "Centre versus Periphery," p. 509.

70. Interview with Palestinian economist, Ibrahim Mattar, February 1992.

71. Kimhi and Hyman, *Socio-Economic Survey*, p. 58.

72. Kimhi and Hyman, "Demographic and Economic Development," p. 148.

73. Kimhi and Hyman, *Socio-Economic Survey*, p. 80.

74. Ibid., p. 82.

75. Kimhi, Hyman, and Savitzky, *Transition*, p. 35.

76. Kimhi and Hyman, *Socio-Economic Survey*, p. 60.

77. Ibid., p. 37; see also Romann and Wiengrod, *Living Together Separately*,

p. 114, who argue that Palestinian competition with Israeli Jewish enterprises in these fields was possible since it involved less capital outlay and cheaper labor costs.

78. Kimhi and Hyman, *Socioeconomic Survey*, p. 59.

79. See the description of how Palestinian families in the Old City used to cram into a few rooms in order to rent out the rest of the house to Easter pilgrims in L. Ekin, "From Pilgrimage to Packaged Tours: Jerusalem and tourism," *MECC Perspectives*, pp. 26–27.

80. Kimhi, Hyman, and Savitzky, *Transition*, p. 36.

81. The proposals for the Suq al-Qattanin are contained in a document entitled *suq al-qattanin—dirasat muqadima l-lsayid mudir al-awqaf al-'am* (Jerusalem: Awqaf Administration, November 20, 1972). See also *Bayan I*, pp. 38–43.

82. R. Nijm, *'ard tarikhi*, p. 3.

83. Ibid., p. 119.

84. Romann and Weingrod, *Living Together Separately*, p. 114.

85. I. Kimhi, "Outline," p. 19.

8. Jerusalem and the International Community

1. There are numerous works examining the impact of pro-Israel lobbies on U.S. domestic politics. See for example, E. Tivnan, *The Lobby: Jewish Political Power and American Foreign Policy* (New York: Simon and Schuster, 1987).

2. See for example, C. Albin, "Strategies and Options in the Jerusalem Conflict," presented at a workshop on "Society and Politics in Jerusalem" at the Truman Research Institute, Hebrew University, Jerusalem, in June 1992; and N. Chazan, "Negotiating the Non-Negotiable: Jerusalem in the Framework of an Israeli- Palestinian Settlement," *Occasional Paper*, No. 7, March 1991 (Cambridge, Mass.: American Academy of Arts and Sciences).

3. See IPS list.

4. The chief proponent of this view has been Ambassador Goldberg, the U.S. Permanent Representative to the UN during and after the 1967 War. His views will be dealt with in greater detail below.

5. Slonim, "Status of Jerusalem," pp. 183–85. See also M. Kaufman, "Jerusalem Policy," and Feintuch, "U.S. Policy," p. 19.

6. *Foreign Relations of the United States, 1949, Vol. 6: The Near East, South Asia and Africa* (Washington D.C.: Government Printing Office, 1977) p. 891, cited in Slonim, "Status of Jerusalem," p. 191.

7. Slonim, "Status of Jerusalem," p. 202.

8. *Foreign Relations of the United States, 1950*, pp. 1096–97, cited in Slonim, "Status of Jerusalem," pp. 206–207.

9. Cited in Slonim, "Status of Jerusalem," p. 207.

10. The Jerusalem district also included the unrecognized West Bank. See Feintuch, *U.S. Policy*, p. 118.

11. Ibid., p. 118.

12. See Dean Acheson's instructions to the U.S. Embassy in Tel Aviv on January 13, 1950. *Foreign Relations, 1950*, pp. 667–68, cited in Slonim, "Status of Jerusalem," p. 198.

13. Feintuch, *U.S. Policy*, p. 118.

14. S. Adler, "The United States and the Jerusalem Issue," *Middle East Review* 17, no.4 (Summer 1985) (hereinafter referred to as "Jerusalem Issue"), p. 48.

15. Department of State, *Bulletin*, November 22nd, 1954, p. 776, cited in Slonim, "Status of Jerusalem," p. 203.

16. Secretary of State John Foster Dulles, *Press Release*, July 28, 1953, in Department of State, *Bulletin* 29, no.737 (August 10, 1953), pp. 177–78, cited in Institute for Palestine Studies, *Jerusalem*, p. 10.

17. State Department, *Bulletin* 57, no.1464 (July 17, 1967), p. 60, cited in Institute for Palestine Studies, *Jerusalem*, p. 20.

18. Ibid., p. 28.

19. UN Security Council, July 1st, 1969, (Provisional Verbatim Record of 1483 meeting, pp. 56–61; cited in Institute for Palestine Studies, *Jerusalem*, p. 32. The speech contained some remarkably strong denunciations of Israeli actions, at one point comparing them to terrorist bombs. For example, "[A just and lasting peace] will not be found through terror bombings, which inevitably harm innocent civilians, any more than it will through unilateral attempts to alter the status of Jerusalem," ibid., p. 33.

20. State Department, *Bulletin* 62, no.1593 (January 5, 1970), p. 10, cited in Institute for Palestine Studies, *Jerusalem*, p. 35.

21. UN Security Council (Provisional Verbatim Record of 1582nd Meeting, pp. 166–67, cited in Institute for Palestine Studies, *Jerusalem*, p. 39.

22. J. Carter, *Keeping Faith: Memoirs of a President*, (New York, Bantam Books, 1982) pp. 374, 388; cited in Slonim, "Status of Jerusalem," pp. 231–32. Slonim points out that these proposals were similar to those put forward by a Brookings Institute Study Group on the Middle East. Some of the participants of the Study Group, such as Zbigniew Brzezinski and William Quandt, were also present during the Camp David discussions.

23. The letters are reproduced verbatim in Slonim, "Status of Jerusalem," pp. 180–81.

24. See chapter 2 for further details.

25. Department of State, *Bulletin* 82, no.2066 (September 1982), p. 25, cited in Institute for Palestine Studies, *Jerusalem*, p. 66.

26. Department of State, *Current Policy*, no.418, pp. 2–3, cited in Institute for Palestine Studies, *Jerusalem*, p. 66.

27. See Institute for Palestine Studies, *Jerusalem*, pp. 68–76; also Slonim, "Status of Jerusalem," pp. 246–50.

28. See Feintuch, p. 52 on discussions which took place with the UN mediator Count Bernadotte on Rhodes island in September 1948.

29. *FRUS* (1948): 1440; cited in Slonim, "Status of Jerusalem," p. 188.

30. Foreign Office Document 371/75343; cited in Slonim, "Status of Jerusalem," p.195 n.56.

31. Ibid.

32. Slonim, "Status of Jerusalem," p. 203. Letter from FCO to author, August 9, 1993.

33. Feintuch, p. 116.

34. This finely nuanced position was bound to lead to anomalies such as the signing of the Anglo-Jordanian Treaty of Alliance which expressly included East Jerusalem. See Slonim, "Status of Jerusalem," p. 206; and Bovis, *Jerusalem Question*, p. 88.

35. UN General Assembly, 5th Emergency Special Session, 21 June 1967, cited in Feintuch, p. 127.

36. Cited in Benvenisti, *Torn City*, p. 123.

37. *Hansard*, 1–4–71, 814, 443–444.

38. *Hansard*, December 16, 1981, vol. 15, col 134.

39. *Hansard*, March 8, 1988, vol. 29, 126w.

40. Letter from FCO to author, August 9, 1993.

41. Venice Declaration, June 13, 1980.

42. The Troika compromised the three foreign ministers of the EC states who were the current, former and designated chairs of the EC Council of Ministers of any given year.

43. A. Brown, R. Heacock, and F. la Torre, eds., *Palestine: Development for Peace* (Proceedings of the ECCP-NENGOOT Conference, Brussels, September 28–October 1, 1992.) (Jerusalem: ECCP-NENGOOT, no date) Speech by Juan Prat, Director General of the Foreign Affairs Division of the European Community, p. 219.

44. European Community Declaration on the Middle East, Madrid, 27 June 1989; cited in Documents and Source material, *Journal of Palestine Studies* 19:1 (Autumn 1989): 122.

45. *Jerusalem Post*, December 12, 1949; cited in Slonim, "Status of Jerusalem," p. 196.

46. See Bovis, *Jerusalem*, pp. 71–76. Abdullah was prepared to accept the Arab consensus on Jerusalem at given moments without necessarily changing his policy. See A. Shlaim, *The Politics of Partition: King Abdullah, the Zionists and Palestine, 1921–1951* (Oxford: Oxford University Press, 1990), p. 198 (hereinafter referred to as *Partition*).

47. See Shlaim, *Partition*, pp. 360ff. See also G. Padon, "The Divided City: 1948–1967," in A. L. Eckhardt, ed., *Jerusalem: City of the Ages* (Lanham: University Press of America, 1987), pp. 130–31 (hereinafter referred to as "Divided City"). In view of the protracted contemporary impasse over the

question of territorial concessions in Jerusalem, this suggestion is of particular interest.

48. Padon, "Divided City," p. 131.

49. Ibid., p. 132

50. *Filastin*, December 10, 1953; *al-Difa'a* December 3, 1954; cited in Padon, "Divided City," p. 133. The Congress met again in Jerusalem in 1960 and 1961.

51. M. Brecher, "Jerusalem: Israel's Political Decisions, 1947–1977," *Middle East Journal* 32 no.1 (1978), p. 23.

52. See King Hussein, *My War With Israel* (Paris: Albin Michel, 1968), p. 78.

53. Photocopy of project outline in author's possession.

54. See Dumper, "Islam and Israel," p. 442. Established in 1972 and attached to the Royal Court of Jordan, the Committee's management body comprises representatives of five Jordanian Ministers, including Education, Religious Affairs, and Foreign Affairs, and representatives of the Qadi al-Quda,' the Greek Orthodox Patriarch and the former Mayor of Arab Jerusalem, Ruhi al-Khatib. They issue a monthly bulletin and supply the Royal Court with a full report on developments in Jerusalem. Interview with the Director-General, Brigadier-General Fa'iz Fahd Jaaber, April 6, 1993.

55. See discussions concerning these development in I. Daqqaq, "Back to Square One," in A. Schölch, ed., *Palestinians Over the Green Line* (London: Zed Press, 1983), pp. 64–101.

56. J. Carter, *Keeping Faith: Memoirs of a President*, pp. 325, 340–41, 354, cited in Slonim, "Status of Jerusalem," p. 231.

57. Cited in Slonim, "Status of Jerusalem," p. 180. Begin's letter to Carter tersely summed up the Israeli position: "I have the honour to inform you, Mr President, that on 28th June, 1967—Israel's Parliament (the Knesset) promulgated and adopted a law to the effect: 'The Government is empowered by a decree to apply the law, the jurisdiction and administration of the state to any part of Eretz Israel (Land of Israel-Palestine), as stated in that decree.'

"On the basis of this law, the Government of Israel decreed in July 1967 that Jerusalem is one city indivisible, the capital of the state of Israel."

58. W. Khalidi, "Thinking the Unthinkable: A Sovereign Palestinian State," *Foreign Affairs*, 56 (1978): 706.

59. Jordanian-Palestinian Joint Committee, "Achievements Report," Table 19, p. 75. The Committee was variously known as the "Joint Committee," the "Steadfastness Committee" or the "Sumud" Committee.

60. Final communiqué of the 17th Islamic Conference of Foreign Ministers on the Question of Jerusalem (al-Quds), March 21–25, 1978, Amman, Jordan.

61. King Hussein's announcement and address to the nation,, with subsequent interviews can be found in Documents and Source material, *Journal of Palestine Studies* 18:1 (Autumn 1988): 279f.

62. Interview with Ambassador Awn al-Khasawneh, Legal Advisor, Office of His Royal Highness the Crown Prince, Royal Court, Amman, March 13, 1993. Ambassador al-Khasawneh also added that the exemption was not seen as permanent. Once Palestinian state structures are in place Jordan would be willing to surrender jurisdiction over the Holy Places to the Palestinians.

63. Full text can be found in Documents and Source Material, *Journal of Palestine Studies* 18:2 (Winter 1989): 213f.

64. A fuller discussion of events since the convening the Madrid conference will be the subject of a further research by the same author.

Conclusion

1. Kollek's One Jerusalem list obtained 19 percent of the votes cast. The *haredim* coalition received 21 percent. The new mayor's list, "United Jerusalem," received only 17 percent but in the vote for the Mayor's position itself, Ehud Olmert also received the majority of the *haredim* vote. The United Jerusalem list and the *haredim* coalition have decided upon a joint program to run the municipal council. Figures from M. Choshen, S. Greenbaum, and N. Shahar, *Statistical Yearbook of Jerusalem*, No. 11, 1992 (Jerusalem: Jerusalem Institute for Israel Studies, 1994) pp. 354–55.

2. A full text of the Oslo Accords can be found in *JPS*.

3. In view of the extent of international support for Israel in other areas, the continued lack of recognition of Israeli sovereignty over Jerusalem is quite remarkable. Rashid Khalidi has identified it as a much neglected "asset" in the Palestinian case for sharing the city. See his remarks at a PASSIA meeting, June 1992. Summarized in the *PASSIA Annual Report*, 1992 (Jerusalem: Palestine Academic Society for the Study of International Affairs, 1993), p. 37.

4. A useful but somewhat dated tabulation of a number of proposals for the future of Jerusalem can be found in Benvenisti, *Torn City*. See also N. Chazan, "Negotiating the Non-Negotiable: Jerusalem in the Framework of the Israeli-Palestinian Settlement."

5. The Washington Agreement in July 1994 between Israel and Jordan recognized a Jordanian role in the administration of the Holy Places.

6. A. Abu Odeh, "Two Capitals in an Undivided Jerusalem," *Foreign Affairs* 71:2 (Spring 1992): 183–88 (hereinafter referred to as "Two Capitals"). W. Khalidi, "Thinking the Unthinkable: A Sovereign Palestinian State," *Foreign Affairs* 56:3 (1978): 705–707. S. Nuseibeh, and M. Heller, *No Trumpets, No Drums: A Two-State Settlement of the Israeli- Palestinian Conflict* (London: I. B. Tauris, 1991), pp. 114–24 (hereinafter referred to as *No Trumpets*). IPCRI proposals have appeared in various forms. See for example M. Amirav, and H. Siniora, *Jerusalem: Resolving the Unresolvable* (Jerusalem: IPCRI, 1991/1992) pamphlet (hereinafter referred to as *Jerusalem*.

7. Nuseibeh and Heller, *No Trumpets*, pp. 120ff.

8. See Amirav and Siniora, *Jerusalem*, pp. 12–14. IPCRI's proposals are continually in the process of revision and the latest drafts should be consulted.

9. See C. Albin, "Negotiating Indivisible Goods: The Case of Jerusalem," *Israel Journal of International Relations*, 13 (1991): 45–76.

10. The problem will be more a question of its regulation so that the reliance on such activity does not destroy the very character which has proved such an attraction down the ages. The regulations governing access to Venice are probably relevant here.

11. Abu Odeh, "Two Capitals," pp. 185–86.

12. Lustick, "Reinventing Jerusalem," pp. 46–54.

Bibliography

Abu Arafeh, A. R. *The Housing Situation in Jerusalem*. Jerusalem: Arab Thought Forum, 1992.

Abu-Lughod, I., ed. *The Transformation of Palestine*. Evanston: Northwestern University Press, 1971.

Abu-Lughod, J. "Demographic Consequences of the Occupation," in Aruri, ed. (1984).

———. "Demographic Transformation," in Abu-Lughod, I., ed. *Transformation of Jerusalem*.

Abu Odeh, A. "Two Capitals in an Undivided Jerusalem," *Foreign Affairs* 71, no. 2 (Spring 1992).

Adler, S. "The United States and the Jerusalem Issue," *Middle East Review* 17, no. 4 (Summer 1985).

Ahimeir, O., ed. *Jerusalem—Aspects of Law*. Discussion Paper no. 3. Jerusalem: Jerusalem Institute for Israel Studies, 1983.

Ahurish. S. *Children of Bethany*. London: Bloomsbury Press.

———. *Cry Palestine: Inside the West Bank*. London: Bloomsbury, 1991.

al-'Alami, Shaykh Sa'd al-Din, ed. *al-hay'at al-islamiya al-'ulya — watha'iq*. Jerusalem: Dar al-Tabi'a al-'Arabiyya, n.d.

Amiran, D. H. K. "The Development of Jerusalem, 1860–1970," in Amiran et al., eds. (1973).

Amiran, D. H. K., A. Shachar, and I. Kimhi, *Urban Geography of Jerusalem: A*

Companion Volume to the Atlas of Jerusalem. Jerusalem: Dept. of Geography, Hebrew University of Jerusalem, 1973.

Amirav, M., and H. Siniora. *Jerusalem: Resolving the Unresolvable.* Jerusalem: IPCRI, Winter 1991/1992.

al-'Arif, 'Arif. *Mufassal tarikh al-quds.* Jerusalem: Ma'aari Printers, 1986.

Aronson, D. "The Politics of Social Welfare: The Case of East Jerusalem," *Middle East Report* (May–June 1987).

Aronson, G. "Soviet Jewish Emigration, the United States and the Occupied Territories," *Journal of Palestine Studies* 19, no. 4 (Summer 1990).

———., ed. *Report on Israeli Settlement in the Occupied Territories.* Washington, D.C.: Foundation for Middle East Peace.

Aruri, N., ed. *Occupation: Israel over Palestine.* London: Zed Books, 1984.

al-'Asali, K., ed. *Jerusalem in History.* London: Scorpion, 1989.

———. "Jerusalem under the Ottomans," in al-'Asali, ed. (1989).

Azarya, V. *The Armenian Quarter of Jerusalem.* Berkeley and London: University of California Press, 1984.

Bar-Joseph, U. *The Best of Enemies: Israel and Transjordan in the War of 1948.* London: Frank Cass, 1987.

Bar Sela, Y. "Law Enforcement in the Eastern Sector of Jerusalem," in O. Ahimeir, ed. (1983).

Barron, *Mohammedan Wakfs in Palestine.* Jerusalem: Greek Convent Press, 1922.

Bayan 'Idarat al-awqaf al-islamiyya al-'ama, bayan: al-awqaf al-islamiyya ti al-dafa al-gharbiyaa, 1967–1976. Jerusalem: da'ira al-awqaf al-islamiyya, n.d.

———. *1977–1982.*

Ben Arieh, Y. *Jerusalem in the 19th Century: Emergence of the New City.* Jerusalem: Yad Izhak Ben-Zvi; New York: St. Martins Press, 1989.

———. *Jerusalem in the 19th Century: The Old City.* New York: St. Martins Press, 1984.

Benvenisti, M. *Jerusalem: The Torn City.* Minneapolis: Israeli Typeset Ltd. and The University of Minneapolis, 1976.

Bovis, H. E. *The Jerusalem Question 1917–1968.* Stanford: Hoover Institution Press, 1971.

Brecher, M. "Jerusalem: Israel's Political Decisions, 1947–1977," *Middle East Journal* 32, no. 1 (1978).

British School of Archaeology in Jerusalem. *The Architecture of Islamic Jerusalem.* London: British School of Archaeology in Jerusalem, 1976.

Brown, A., R. Heacock, and F. la Torre, eds. *Palestine: Development for Peace.* Proceedings of the ECCP-NENGOOT Conference, Brussels, 28 September-1 October 1992. Jerusalem: NENGOOT, n.d.

Burgoyne, M. "The Continued Survey of the Ribat Kurd/Madrasa Jawhariya Complex in Tariq Bab al-Hadid, Jerusalem," *Levant* 6 (1974).

———. *Mamluk Jerusalem: An Architectural Study*. London: World of Islam Trust, 1987.

Carter, J. *Keeping Faith: Memoirs of a President*. New York: Bantam Books, 1982.

Cattan, H. *Jerusalem*. London: Croom Helm, 1981.

Chazan, N. *Negotiating the Non-Negotiable: Jerusalem in the Framework of an Israeli-Palestinian Settlement*. American Academy of Arts and Sciences Occasional Paper no. 7. Cambridge, MA: American Academy of Arts and Sciences, 1991.

Cheshin, A. "East Jerusalem: Policy versus Reality," in A. Layish, ed. (1992).

Choshen, M., and I. Kimhi. *Migration To and From Jerusalem*. Jerusalem: Jerusalem Institute for Israel Studies, 1991.

Cohen, E. *Integration and Separation in the Planning of a Mixed Jewish-Arab City in Israel*. Jerusalem: Hebrew University, 1973.

Cohen, E. R. *Human Rights in the Israeli-occupied Territories*. Manchester: Manchester University Press, 1985.

Cohen, Saul. *Bridging the Four Walls: A Geopolitical Perspective*. New York: Herzl Press, 1977.

Cohen, Shaul. *The Politics of Planting: Israeli-Palestinian Competition for Control of Land in the Jerusalem Periphery*. Chicago: University of Chicago, 1993.

Colbi, S. P. "The Christian Establishment in Jerusalem," in Kraemer, ed. (1980).

Daqqaq, I. "Back to Square One," in Schölch, ed. (1983).

———. "Jerusalem's Via Dolorosa," in Abu-Lughod, I., ed.

Dib, G., and F. Jabber. *Israel's Violation of Human Rights in the Occupied Territories: A Documented Report*. Beirut: Institute for Palestine Studies, 1970.

Dumper, M. *Islam and Israel: Muslim Religious Endowments and the Jewish State*. Washington, D.C.: Institute for Palestine Studies, 1994.

———. "Israeli Settlement in the Old City of Jerusalem," *Journal of Palestine Studies* 21, no. 4 (Summer 1992).

———. "Property Restoration for Community Development in the Old City of Jerusalem." Unpublished report to the Welfare Association, Geneva, 1987, Section A, Chapter Five.

Duri, A. A. "Jerusalem in the Early Islamic Period," in al-'Asali, ed. (1989).

Eckhardt, A. L. , ed. *Jerusalem: City of the Ages*. New York: University Press of America, 1987.

Efrat, E. "Changes in the Town Planning Concepts of Jerusalem, (1919–1969)," *Environmental Planning* (July–September 1971).

Eisenman, R. H. *Islamic Law in Palestine and Israel: A History of the Tanzimat and the Shari'a in the British Mandate and the Jewish State*. Leiden: Brill, 1978.

Ekin, L. "From Pilgrimage to Packaged Tours: Jerusalem and Tourism," *MECC Perspectives*, no. 8 (July 1990).

Ellis, H. F. *The Vatican, Islam and the Middle East*. New York: Syracuse University Press, 1987.

Farhi, D. "ha-mo'atza ha-muslemit be-mizrah yerushalayim u-vi —yehuda ve shomron me-az milhemet sheshet ha-yamin" [The Muslim Council in East Jerusalem and in Judea and Samaria since the Six Day War], *Ha-mizrah Ha-Hedash* [The New East] 28 (1979).

Felsenstein, D. *The Development of Science-based Industries in Jerusalem*. Research report no. 1. Jerusalem: Jerusalem Institute for Israel Studies, 1988 [in Hebrew].

Fitzgerald, W. *Report on the Local Administration of Jerusalem*. Government of Palestine, Government Printer, 1945.

Franken, H. J. "Jerusalem in the Bronze Age," in al-'Asali, ed. (1989).

Friedman, M. *The Haredi (Ultra-Orthodox) Society: Sources, Trends and Processes*. Jerusalem: Jerusalem Institute for Israel Studies, 1991.

Gershon, A. *Israel, the West Bank and International Law*. London: Frank Cass, 1978.

Gilbert, M. *Jerusalem: Illustrated History Atlas*. Jerusalem: Steimatzky, 1977.

Ginio, A. "Plans for the Solution of the Jerusalem Problem," in Kraemer, ed. (1980).

Glubb, Sir J. B. *A Soldier with the Arabs*. London: Hodder and Stoughton, 1957.

Goadby, F. M. "Religious Communities and Courts in Palestine," *Tulane Law Review* 8, no. 2 (1934).

Goitein, S. D. "The Sanctity of Jerusalem and Palestine in Early Islam," in Goiten, ed. *Studies in Islamic History and Institutions*. Leiden: Brill, 1968.

Graham-Brown, S. "Jerusalem," *Middle East* no. 136 (February 1986).

Granott, A. *Land Problems of Palestine*. New York: Bloch, 1940.

Gutman, E. "The Beginning of Local Government in Jerusalem," *Public Administration in Israel and Abroad* 8 (1967).

Halkin, H. "Building Jerusalem," *Commentary* 52 (September 1971).

Halper, J. "Jewish Ethnicity in Jerusalem," in Eckhardt, ed. (1987).

Halsell, G. *Prophecy and Politics: Militant Evangelists on the Road to Nuclear War*. Westport, CT: Lawrence Hill, 1986.

Hasson, S. "The Many Faces of Neighbourhood Government," *Israel Studies* (Winter 1991).

Heshin, A. "East Jerusalem-Policy versus Reality," in A. Layish, ed. (1992).

Heyd, U. "Waqf and Public Works," *Ottoman Documents on Palestine 1552–1615*. Oxford: Oxford University Press, 1960.

Hintlian, K. *History of the Armenians in the Holy Land*. Jerusalem: Armenian Patriarchate Printing Press, 1989.

Hirst, D. "Rush to Annexation: Israel in Jerusalem," *Journal of Palestine Studies* 3, no. 4 (Summer 1974).

Hiyari, M. "Crusader Jerusalem," in al-'Asali, ed. (1989).

Hudson, M. "The Transformation of Jerusalem, 1917–1987," in al-'Asali, ed. (1989).

Hyman, B., I. Kimhi, and J. Savitzky. *Jerusalem in Transition: Urban Growth and Change, 1970's and 1980's.* Jerusalem: Jerusalem Institute for Israel Studies, 1985.

Irani, G. E. *Papacy and the Middle East: The Role of the Papacy in the Arab-Israeli Conflict, 1962–1984.* Notre Dame: University of Notre Dame, 1986.

Israel Pocket Library. *Jerusalem.* Jerusalem: Keter, 1973.

"Jerusalem Development Authority — an address for nearly everything," *Israeli Business and Technology.* (September–October 1991).

Jerusalem Institute for Israel Studies. "The Metropolitan Area of Jerusalem," *The Urban Development of Metropolitan Jerusalem.* Publication no. 1. Jerusalem: The Jerusalem Institute for Israel Studies, 1984.

Jiryis, S. *The Arabs in Israel.* New York: Monthly Review Press, 1976.

———. "Israeli Laws as Regards Jerusalem." In H. Kochler, ed. *The Legal Aspects of the Palestine Problem with Special Regard to the Question of Jerusalem.* Vienna: Wilhelm Braumuller, 1981, pp. 181–191.

Kaminker, Sarah. Interview. *Challenge* 3, no.1.

Kark, R. "The Jerusalem Municipality at the End of the Ottoman Rule," *Asian and African Affairs* no. 14 (1980).

———. *Jerusalem Neighbourhoods: Planning and By-Laws (1855–1930).* Jerusalem: Magnes Press, 1991.

Karmi, H. S. "How Holy is Palestine to the Muslims?" *Islamic Quarterly* 12, no.2 (April-June 1970).

Kaufman, M. *America's Jerusalem Policy, 1947–1948.* Jerusalem: Hebrew University of Jerusalem, 1985.

Kendall, H. *Jerusalem City Plan.* London: Her Majesty's Stationary Office, 1948.

Kendall. *The Planning of Jerusalem (Jordan) and Region.* Jerusalem: October 1965.

Khalidi, W. *Before Their Diaspora: A Photographic History of the Palestinians 1876–1948.* Washington, D.C.: Institute for Palestine Studies, 1984.

———. "Thinking the Unthinkable: A Sovereign Palestinian State," *Foreign Affairs* 56 (1978).

———., ed. *All That Remains: The Palestinian Villages Occupied and Depopulated by Israel in 1948.* Washington, D.C.: Institute for Palestine Studies, 1992.

al-Khalil. "Jerusalem from 1947 to 1967." Unpublished M.A. dissertation, American University of Beirut, 1969.

Khatib, K. *The Conservation of Jerusalem.* East Jerusalem: PASSIA, 1993.

Khayat, "Waqfs in Palestine and Israel—From the Ottoman Reforms to the Present." Ph.D. Dissertation, the Americn University, Washington, D.C, 1982.

al-Khatib, R. "The Judaization of Jerusalem and its Demographic Transformation," in *Jerusalem: The Key to World Peace.* London: Islamic Council of Europe, 1980.

Khoury, F. J. "The Jerusalem Question and the Vatican," in Ellis, ed. (1987).

Kimhi, I. "Aspects of the Urban Ecology of Jerusalem," in Amiran et al., eds. (1973).

————. "Outline of the Development of Jerusalem, 1988–1993," in *Urban Geography in Jerusalem, 1967–1992.* Jerusalem: Jerusalem Institute for Israel Studies, 1993.

Kimhi, I., and B. Hyman. "Demographic and Economic Developments in Jerusalem since 1967," in Kraemer, ed. (1980).

————. *A Socio-economic Survey of Jerusalem, 1967–1975.* Jerusalem: Jerusalem Committee, 1978.

Kimhi, I., S. Reichman, and Y. Schweid. *Arab Settlement in the Metropolitan Area of Jerusalem* [in Hebrew]. Jerusalem Institute for Israel Studies, Jerusalem, 1986.

————. *Greater Jerusalem—Alternative Municipal Frameworks* [in Hebrew]. Jerusalem: Jerusalem Institute for Israel Studies, 1990.

King Hussein. *My War With Israel.* Paris: Albin Michel, 1968.

Kraemer, J. L. , ed. *Jerusalem: Problems and Prospects.* New York: Praeger, 1980.

Kroyanker, D. "The Face of the City," in Prawer and Ahimer, eds. (1988).

Kupferschmidt, U. *The Supreme Muslim Council: Islam Under the British Mandate for Palestine.* Leiden: Brill, 1987.

Kutcher, A. *The New Jerusalem: Planning and Politics.* London: Thames and Hudson, 1973.

Layish, A. "Muslim Religious Jurisdiction in Israel," *Asian and African Studies* 1 (1965).

————. "The Muslim Waqf in Israel," *Asian and African Studies* 2 (1966).

————., ed. "The Arabs in Jerusalem: From the Late Ottoman Period to the Beginning of the 1990's-Religious, Social and Cultural Distinctiveness," *Hamizrah Hehadash* 34 (1992).

Lazarus-Yafeh, H. "The Sanctity of Jerusalem in Islam," in Lazarus-Yafeh, ed. *Some Religious Aspects of Islam.* Leiden: Brill, 1981.

Lehn, W., and U. Davis. *The Jewish National Fund.* London: Kegan Paul International, 1988.

Lesch, A. *Arab Politics in Palestine, 1917–1939: the Frustration of a Nationalist Movement.* London: Cornell University Press, 1979.

Little, D. "Jerusalem under the Ayyubids and Mamluks," in al-'Asali, ed. (1989).

Lorch, N. *The Edge of the Sword, Israel's War of Independence 1947–49.* New York: G. P. Putnam's Sons, 1961.

Lundsten, E. "Wall Politics: Zionist and Palestinian Strategies in Jerusalem, 1928," *Journal of Palestine Studies* 8, no. 1 (Autumn 1978).

Lustick, Ian. "Reinventing Jerusalem." *Foreign Policy,* no. 93 (Winter 1993/ 94).

Mansour, A. and E. Stock, "Arab Jerusalem after the Annexation," *New Outlook* 14, no. 1 (1971).

Markovitz, S. "The Development of Modern Jerusalem: An Evaluation of Planning Decisions and the Effectiveness of the Planning Process," Unpublished thesis, Woodrow Wilson School for Public and International Affairs, Princeton University, 1982.

Massignon, "Documents sur certains waqfs des lieux saints d'Islam." *Révue des Etudes Islamiques* (1951): 73–120.

Mattar, I. "From Palestinian to Israeli: Jerusalem, 1948–1982," *Journal of Palestine Studies* 12, no. 4 (Summer 1983).

Mattar, P. *The Mufti of Jerusalem.* New York: Columbia University Press, 1988.

Mayer, L., and J. Pinkerfield. *Some Principle Muslim Religious Buildings in Israel.* Jerusalem: Government Printer, 1950.

McCarthy, J. *The Population of Palestine: Population Statistics of the Late Ottoman Period and the Mandate.* New York: Columbia University Press, 1990.

Mendenhall, G. E. "Jerusalem from 1000–63 BC," in al-'Asali, ed. (1989).

Michelson, D. S. "Physical Development Patterns of New Neighbourhoods in Jerusalem since 1967," *Engineering and Architecture* nos. 11–12 (1977).

Natshe, Y. *al-turba al-kilaniyya* [The Kilaniyya Mausoleum]. Jerusalem: Islamic Waqf Department, 1979).

Nijm, B. K. , ed. *Toward the De-Arabization of Palestine/Israel, 1945–1977.* Dubuque, Iowa: Kendall/Hunt, n.d.

Nijm, R. *'ard tarikhi masawur 'an 'aham al-muqaddisa fi filastin w-al-'ijra'at alati tamat li-siyanat al-turath* (Fifth conference on the Holy Places, Tradition and Culture in Palestine, Cairo, 1988).

————., ed. *Kunuz al-Quds.* Amman: n.p., 1983.

Nuseibeh, S., and M. Heller. *No Trumpets, No Drums: A Two-State Settlement of the Israeli-Palestinian Conflict.* London: I. B. Tauris, 1991.

Nyrop, R. *Israel: A Country Study.* Washington, D.C.: The American University, 1979.

Offenbacher, E. "Prayer on the Temple Mount," *The Jerusalem Quarterly* no. 36 (Summer 1985).

Padon, G. "The Divided City: 1948–1967," in Eckhardt, ed. (1987).

PASSIA Annual Report, 1992. Jerusalem: Palestine Academic Society for the Study of International Affairs, 1993.

Peretz, D. *Israel and the Palestinian Arabs.* Washington D.C.: Middle East Institute, (1958).

Peters, F. E. *Jerusalem.* Princeton: Princeton University Press, 1985.

————. *Jerusalem and Mecca: The Typology of the Holy City in the Near East.* New York: New York University Press, 1986.

Plascov, A. *The Palestinian Refugees in Jordan, 1948–57.* London: Frank Cass, 1981.

Porath, Y. *The Emergence of the Palestinian Arab National Movement, 1918–1929.* London: Frank Cass, 1977.

Prawer, J., and O. Ahimeir, eds. *Twenty Years in Jerusalem, 1967–1987.*

Jerusalem: Ministry of Defence Publishing House and Jerusalem Institute for Israel Studies, 1988 (in Hebrew).

Prittie, T. *Whose Jerusalem*. London: Frederick Muller Ltd., 1981.

Reitter, Y. *Waqf in Jerusalem, 1948–1990*. Jerusalem: Jerusalem Institute for Israel Studies, 1991 (in Hebrew).

Resistance of the Western Bank of Jordan to Israeli Occupation. Beirut: Institute for Palestine Studies, 1967.

Rokach, L. *The Catholic Church and the Question of Palestine*. London: al-Saqi, 1987.

Romann, M. "Centre versus Periphery: The Development of the Jewish and Arab Sector in Unified Jerusalem since 1967," *The Economic Quarterly* 33, no. 128 [in Hebrew].

———. "The Economic Development of Jerusalem in Recent Times," in Amiran et al., eds. (1973).

———. *An Economic and Social Survey of Greater Jerusalem* [in Hebrew]. Jerusalem: Maurice Falk Institute for Economic Research in Israel, 1967.

Romann, M., and A. Weingrod. *Living Together Separately: Arabs and Jews in Contemporary Jerusalem*. Princeton: Princeton University Press, 1991.

Rossing, D. "Interfaith Relations in Israel Today," *1988 Waley-Cohen Lecture*. London: Council of Christians and Jews, 1988.

Rubinstein, D. "The Jerusalem Municipality under the Ottomans, British and Jordanians," in Kraemer, ed. (1980).

Sabella, B. "Christian emigration: A Comparison of the Jerusalem, Ramallah and Bethlehem areas." Unpublished survey for the al-Liqa Institute, Jerusalem, 1992.

Sawicki, T. "The Land Competition-Growth of Arab Settlement in the Jerusalem Region," *Israel Studies* (Spring 1988).

Schlieffer, A. "Islamic Jerusalem as Archetype of a Harmonious Urban Development," *Saqqaf* no. 172.

Schmelz, U. O. *Modern Jerusalem's Demographic Evolution*. (Jerusalem: Jerusalem Institute for Israel Studies, 1987).

Schölch, A. "Jerusalem in the 19th Century, 1831–1917," in al-'Asali, ed. (1989).

———., ed. *Palestinians Over the Green Line*. London: Zed Press, 1983.

Schweid, Y. "The Unification of Jerusalem: The Planning Aspect," *Kivunim* no. 35 (1987) [in Hebrew].

Shachar, A. "The Functional Structure of Jerusalem," in Amiran et al., eds. (1973).

Shaksky, S. *What Makes Israel Tick: How Domestic Policymakers Cope with Constraint*. Chicago: Nelson Hall, 1985.

Shalem, D. and G. Shamis. *Jerusalem*. Jerusalem: Municipality of Jerusalem, n.d.

Shapiro, S. "Planning Jerusalem: The First Generation, 1917–1968," in Amiran et al., eds. (1973).

Shehadeh, R. *The West Bank and the Rule of Law*. New York: International Jurists and Law in the Service of Man, 1980.

Shepherd, N. *The Mayor and the Citadel: Teddy Kollek and Jerusalem*. London: Weidenfeld and Nicholson, 1987.

Shilhav, Y. "Spatial Strategies of the 'Haredi' Population in Jerusalem," *Socio-Economic Planning and Science* 18, no. 6 (1984).

Shlaim, A. *The Politics of Partition: King Abdullah, the Zionists and Palestine, 1921–1951*. Oxford: Oxford University Press, 1990.

Slonim, S. "The United States and the Status of Jerusalem, 1947–1984." *Israeli Law Review* 19: 179–252.

Statistical Yearbook of Jerusalem. M. Choshen, S. Greenbaum, and N. Shahar, eds. No. 11, 1992. Jerusalem: Jerusalem Institute for Israel Studies, 1994.

Stephan, S. H. "An endowment deed of Khasski el-Sultan, dated 24th May, 1922," *Quarterly of the Department of Antiquities in Palestine* 10 (1944).

Suq al-qattanin — dirasat muqadima l-lsayid mudir al-awqaf al-'am. Jerusalem: Awqaf Administration, 1972.

Talal, Hassan bin *A Study on Jerusalem*. London: Longmans, 1979.

Talhami, G. "Between Development and Preservation: Jerusalem under Three Regimes," *American-Arab Affairs* (Spring 1986).

Thomas, R. "Demography and Settler Politics in the Old City of Jerusalem," *Khamsin* 1 (1989).

Tibawi, A. L. *The Islamic Pious Foundations in Jerusalem: Origin, History and Usurpation by Israel*. London: Iraqi Cultural Foundation, 1978.

Tivnan, E. *The Lobby: Jewish Political Power and American Foreign Policy*. New York: Simon and Schuster, 1987.

Trimingham, J. S. *The Sufi Orders in Islam*. London: n.p., 1971.

Tsimhoni, D. "The Latin Patriarchate of Jerusalem from the First Half of the 19th Century to Present Times: Institutional and Social Aspects," in Layish, ed. (1992).

Turner, M. "The Old City and its Walls," *Out of Jerusalem* 3, no. 4 (Winter 1982/83).

United Nations Resolutions on Palestine, 1947–72. Beirut: Institute for Palestine Studies, 1974.

Weigert, G. *Israel's Presence in East Jerusalem*. Jerusalem, 1973.

Westmacott, R. *Jerusalem: A New Era for a Capital City*. London: The Anglo-Israel Association, 1968.

Wilkinson, "Ancient Jerusalem: Its Water Supply and Population," *Palestine Exploration Quarterly* 106.

Wilkinson, J. "Jerusalem under Rome and Byzantium," in al-'Asali, ed. (1989).

Wilson, C. *Ordnance Survey of Jerusalem*. Her Majesty's Treasury, 1865. Facsimile edition: Ariel Publishing House, Jerusalem, 1980.

Yafeh, H. Lazarus. "The Sanctity of Jerusalem in Islam," in *Some Religious Aspects of Islam*. Leiden: Brill, 1981.

Zander, W. *Israel and the Holy Places of Christendom*. London: Weidenfield and Nicholson, 1971.

————. "Truce on the Temple Mount," *New Outlook* 19, (July/ August 1976).

Zilberman, I. "The Hebronite Migration and the Development of Suburbs in the Metropolitan Area of Jerusalem," in A. Layish, ed. (1992) (in Hebrew).

UN and Government Documents:

"European Community Declaration on the Middle East, Madrid, 27 June 1989," *Journal of Palestine Studies* 19, no. 1 (Autumn 1989).

Report of the Secretary-General under General Assembly Resolution 2254 (ES-V), UN Document S/8146 and A/6793.

UN Security Council Resolution 237, June 14, 1967.

UN General Assembly Resolution 253 (ES-V), UN Document A/6798 (1967)

UN General Assembly Resolution 2254 (ES-V), UN Document A\6798 (1967).

UNSC Resolution 478.

British Government, *Palestine Royal Commission: Report*, Command Paper No. 5479. London: H.M.S.O., 1937.

Hansard, House of Lords, UK, April 27, 1950: statement by Lord Henderson, cols. 2/31.

Committee on the Exercise of the Inalienable Rights of the Palestinian People (UNCEIRPP). *The Status of Jerusalem*. New York: United Nations, 1979.

United Nations (UN), *General Assembly Resolution 181 (II)*, 29.11.1947.

Law and Administration Ordinance (Amendment No. 11) Law, 5727–1967, Laws of the State of Israel, Vol. 21 (1966/67).

Municipalities Ordinance (Amendment No. 6) Law, 5727/1967, Laws of the State of Israel, Vol. 21, (1966/67)

Basic Law: Jerusalem, *Policy Background* (324/1.11.02) (Jerusalem: Israel Ministry of Foreign Affairs, Information Division, August 17, 1980.).

Legal and Administrative Matters (Regulation) Law (Consolidated Version), 5730–1970, *Laws of the State of Israel*, Vol. 24 (1969/70)

Absentee Property (Compensation) Law, 5733–1973, *Laws of the State of Israel*, Vol. 27 (1972/73)

Protection of the Holy Places Law, 5727, 1967

City Planning Department of the Municipality of Jerusalem and the Jerusalem Development Authority, *Jerusalem: Extending the Area of Jurisdiction: A Summary*, Jerusalem, April 1991.

Blue Book. Jerusalem: Government of Palestine, 1936 and 1937.

East Jerusalem Census of Population and Housing (1966/67) (Hebrew and

English) (Jerusalem: Central Bureau of Statistics and Jerusalem Municipality, 1968)

State of Israel, Central Bureau of Statistics, *Census of Population and Housing, 1972*, Part II, No. 10 (Jerusalem, 1979)

Jerusalem Institute for Israel Studies, *Statistical Yearbook of Jerusalem*, No. 8, 1989. Jerusalem: Jerusalem Institute for Israel Studies, 1991.

Municipality of Jerusalem, *Immigration Absorption Project*, Jerusalem, December 1991 (in Hebrew).

Jerusalem Water Undertaking (Ramallah District), *Annual Preview, 1991*, (Ramallah: Jerusalem Water Undertaking, 1991), p. 6.

Ministry of Environment, Jerusalem District, *Annual Report, 1991/1992* (hereinafter referred to as *Annual Report*), Paragraph 2.218 (in Hebrew).

Municipality of Jerusalem, Department of Information and Public Relations, *Jerusalem*, no date (probably 1989).

Municipality of Jerusalem, Information and Public Relations Department, "Water," Brochure (Hebrew) (Jerusalem, no date but probably 1989).

State Comptroller's Annual Report, No. 38, 1988, p. 374.

Ministry of Environment, *Annual Report, 1991/92* (in Hebrew).

Press Statement by Co-ordinating Committee of International Non-Governmental Organizations, "Update: Water Crisis in the Occupied Territories," February 21, 1992.

Municipality of Jerusalem, *Map of Sewage Masterplan, 1989*, Sheet No. 2 (September 1989).

Ministry of Interior, Environment Protection Services, *Fourth Annual Report: Environment in Israel*, (1976) p. 16.

Municipality of Jerusalem, *Master Plan Map, Balasha Jalon, Map*, and Ministry of Environment, *Annual Report*, Paragraph 2.2 (in Hebrew).

Legal and Administrative Matters (Regulation) Law (Consolidated Version), 1970, *Laws of the State of Israel* 24, (1969–1970).

Law of Antiquities, *Government Gazette*, August 31, 1967, p. 2159.

Census of Population and Housing, 1967, (Jerusalem: Central Bureau of Statistics, 1968), table 4, p. 10.

Committee for Moslem Religious Affairs, p. 7.

Defence (Muslim Awkaf) Regulations, 1937.

Official Gazette, Law No 26, (Amman 1966). Regulation No. 142 Article 8, iii-v, Article 9, iii, iv, vi, Article 47.

Documentation Section, *MECC Perspectives*, no.8 (July 1990)

Final communiqué of the 17th Islamic Conference of Foreign Ministers on the Question of Jerusalem (al-Quds), March 21–25, 1978, Amman, Jordan.

Index